A Workman Is Worthy of His Meat

FRANCE OVERSEAS

STUDIES IN EMPIRE AND DECOLONIZATION

SERIES EDITORS

Philip Boucher, A. J. B. Johnston,
James D. Le Sueur, and Tyler Stovall

A Workman Is Worthy of His Meat

Food and Colonialism in the Gabon Estuary

Jeremy Rich

University of Nebraska Press • Lincoln and London

© 2007 by the Board of Regents of the University of Nebraska ⁋ All rights reserved ⁋ Manufactured in the United States of America ⁋ ⊗ ⁋ Library of Congress Cataloging-in-Publication Data ⁋ Rich, Jeremy (Jeremy McMaster) A workman is worthy of his meat : food and colonialism in the Gabon Estuary / Jeremy Rich.
p. cm. — (France overseas: studies in empire and decolonization) Includes bibliographical references and index.
ISBN-13: 978-0-8032-1091-2 (hardcover : alk. paper)
ISBN-10: 0-8032-1091-4 (hardcover : alk. paper)
1. Rood supply—Gabon—Libreville.
2. Food consumption—Gabon—Libreville.
3. Gabon—Colonial influence. I. Title
HD9017.G253L57 2007
338.1'96721—dc22
2006031466

Set in Quadraat. ⁋ Designed by R. W. Boeche. ⁋

Contents

Acknowledgments   vii

Introduction   ix

Map of Gabon Estuary   xx

1. The Gabon Estuary and the Atlantic World, 1840–1960   1

2. Eating in an African Atlantic Town, 1840–1885   22

3. Newcomers, Food Supply, and the Colonial State, 1840–1914   45

4. Famine in the Gabon Estuary, 1914–1930   64

5. Town Life and Imported Food, 1840–1960   86

6. Food Supply in Libreville, 1930–1960   107

7. European Culinary Practices in Colonial Libreville   127

Conclusion   145

Appendix: Table of Libreville Population, 1863–1960   150

Notes   151

Bibliography   195

Index   213

Acknowledgments

This book may have only one author, but it owes a great deal to a range of people. First and foremost, I could never have written this study without the generosity and patience that the people of Libreville, Akok, Kango, and other towns showed me during my stays in Gabon. The kindness of Christine Angoue and the family of Marie-Noelle Eyong in hosting me and teaching me Fang were crucial in helping me along. Pila, I can never thank you enough for all the walks you led me on through Libreville to find people to interview and all the time you spent with me. Father Gérard Morel, Nicolas Metegue N'nah, Guy Rossatanga-Rignault, Brother François at Donguila, Antoine Nguema Ndong, Father Luis Moto, and many others aided me at different stages in my research. In the United States, my dissertation advisor Phyllis Martin's steady hand and straightforward opinions guided me and opened my eyes to how one should do history. Her support never wavered, and for that I owe her a debt that I can never repay. John Hanson, George Brooks, Gracia Clark, Cati Coe, Rachel Reynolds, and Paul Kaiser all provided me with commentary and advice during my years spent struggling to make this project a reality. Graduate students in history and African studies also were a vital source of support. I know this project would have taken far longer without the friendship of Scott Rosenberg, Ayman Fadel, John Aden, Geoff Coats, Heather Perry, and Liz McMachon, among others. The editorial staff at the University of Nebraska Press, especially Jim Le Sueur, also deserve praise. Heather Lundine, Linnea Fredrickson, and Sally Antrobus had the unenviable task of dealing with my erratic syntax. I thank the anonymous peer reviewers for their thoughtful commentary as well.

A special word must be given to those few pioneers in equatorial African history who have found Gabonese history a subject of endless fascination. Florence Bernault, David Gardinier, Henry Bucher, Rachel Jean-Baptiste, and Kairn Klieman have been colleagues and partners whose insights have shaped my thinking. John Cinnamon's support and advice has been one of the best assets I have had in my research. Sadly, two men who were instrumental in introducing me to African history and Gabon will never read this book. A chance subway encounter with the late François Ngolet was the unlikely beginning of a friendship that unfortunately did not last even a fraction as long as I had hoped. Above all else, the short life and career of Chris Gray has inspired me as a scholar and as a human being. His gentle humor, incisive mind, and willingness to tie his scholarship to his activism will always stay with me. He was a model of what a historian should be.

Thanks also go to the following libraries and archives that opened their doors to me: the Houghton Library, Harvard University; the Presbyterian Historical Society in Philadelphia; the Archives Nationales du Gabon in Libreville; the Holy Ghost Fathers Archives in Chevilly-Larue; the Archives Nationales in Paris and Aix-en-Provence; and the Academie des Sciences d'Outre-Mer and the Société des Missions Evangéliques in Paris. Librarian Marion Johnson helped me immensely at Indiana University, as did the library staff at Cabrini College, Colby College, and the University of Maine at Machias.

I am grateful for the friends and family who stood by me as I fumbled my way through writing on Gabon. Eric St. Pierre, David Tartaglia, Jon Levy, James Bailey, James Conlon, and Leonard Norman Primiano entertained me thoroughly over the course of a decade, and I suspect a book on food in Gabon will make for its own kind of amusement. My parents Kay and Barry, my stepmother Carol, my mother-in-law Susie Lussier, my brother-in-law Mark, and my sister Melissa know how much I owe them. Finally, my wife Chantal can rest knowing that this book is finally finished. Without her, I could not have accomplished anything.

Introduction

At first glance, the Central African nation of Gabon exemplifies France's continued hold on its former possessions. Libreville, the country's capital, is a product of colonial rule. It shows. Since independence the city has been transformed from a sleepy port of twenty thousand people in 1960 to a growing metropolis of half a million inhabitants. French soldiers and businessmen sip beers and whiskey in crowded air-conditioned bars. A flight into the city descends on a late colonial fantasy of modernization: a heap of modernist skyscrapers surrounded by dense rainforest. The conch-pink Presidential Palace, a masterpiece of early 1970s futuristic excess worthy of a science fiction epic, was designed by French architects and paid for by the flood of revenue coming from oil profits. Al-Hadj Omar Bongo Ondimba has held power since 1967, thanks in no small part to a coterie of French officials and businessmen.

Gabon is perhaps the most perfect example of neocolonialism on the entire continent. While liberation fighters and the French military waged a bitter war in Algeria, and Guinea's chief Sekou Touré espoused socialism and denounced De Gaulle, some Gabonese politicians lobbied unsuccessfully to create a national flag with a tiny tricouleur in the upper left-hand corner.[1] Gabon's first president Léon Mba assured readers of the magazine Réalités in 1960 that only strong aid from la patrie would allow his country to survive.[2] The country's national riches—uranium, gold, timber, and petroleum—kept the French government's presence firmly planted in Gabon. French conglomerate Elf-Total rapidly expanded oil production in the two decades following independence in 1960. After Mba's death in 1967, old Africa hands in the French foreign ministry aided a young officer they knew as Albert-Bernard Bongo to take the reins of the government. He has never forgotten his friends in Paris and is regularly accused of illicitly showering money upon French politicians.[3]

It is not just at the summit of political power that foreign influence holds sway. France is the lingua franca of the country. No single African language has ever served to bind together this nation of more than twenty sizable ethnic communities. Living in Libreville is expensive for locals and newcomers. According to some standards, the city ranks with Tokyo and Paris for its high cost of living.[4] Almost nothing is made in the city: electronics from East Asia, metalware from India and China, cars from France and Japan, and cloth from West Africa. Even matches are shipped in from Cameroon. One recent study estimates that over two thirds of the country's food is brought from outside Gabon.[5] The high prices and scarcity of locally produced food in Libreville bewilder residents and visitors alike. Ships and trucks deliver European imported fare and vegetables grown in Cameroon. West African immigrants berate Gabonese people for not growing enough food to feed themselves.

For some, appreciation of foreign tastes signifies wealth as well as dependence. Most sub-Saharan countries could only dream of having as many Internet kiosks, cell phones, and gleaming Mitsubishi SUVs as Gabon, which has one of the highest per capita incomes in Africa. Most of the oil money has not trickled down very far, but the profits allowed for a remaking of the city. Omar Bongo demolished numerous older buildings in favor of modernist architecture and imported luxuries. Such efforts to present Libreville as a modern city also appear in eating habits. European and wealthy African residents purchase croissants, imported sausages, and French wines in specialty downtown stores and supermarkets while manioc and plantains are scarce. The city's prosperity is likewise displayed in the older neighborhoods flanking the city center, in Glass and Louis, where Cuban, Chinese, and "authentic Gabonese" restaurants compete for expatriate and wealthy African clients.

During my first visit to Gabon in 1998 I watched affluent Libreville schoolchildren snacking on French sausage, nodding along to Parisian rap songs playing through their headphones as they struggled with their backpacks stuffed with textbooks published in France. I started to wonder how colonialism reshaped tastes and contributed to French hegemony in the country. Did cultural practices from the metropole make Gabon into a country that would not be able to stand on its own? At the beginning daily life in Libreville seemed to be perfect evidence for the critiques of Africans idealizing European culture, as in the work of Franz Fanon, Armah, and other nationalist writers.[6]

My naive ideas of European dominance in Gabon turned out to be insufferably inadequate to understanding how, what, and why Libreville people consume. From my concerns about changing everyday practices—especially in an area as vital to life as eating—emerged this study examining how Libreville residents came to eat and buy food as they do today. The histories behind their meals are testimonies to the panoply of economic and cultural links to Europe and the Gabonese interior. Townspeople created a style of living that embodied local concerns and Libreville's manifold international connections. City residents of distinction have preferred to buy rather than grow or catch their own food. This decision alternately puzzled and angered generations of urban planners determined to build a workforce willing to follow the dictates of employers and officials. The daily meals and shopping habits of urban Gabonese reflected a new sensibility that gradually spread into rural areas of Gabon. The culinary practices of Gabonese people emerged from a series of struggles and negotiations among townspeople, rural producers, European entrepreneurs, and the colonial state.

This book follows the formation of contemporary Libreville diets as part of a larger transformation of urban and rural areas of the Gabon Estuary. The region has undergone a series of major economic changes since the mid-nineteenth century. These shifts have left their mark on the physical environment of the city. Thanks to the demands of timber camp owners, piles of stray okoumé logs more than twelve feet long lie strewn along Libreville's beaches. European enterprises, besides leaving their debris on the shore, also influenced what and how townspeople ate as well as how rural people farmed, fished, and sold food. So did earlier visits by Europeans seeking slaves for the Americas, because inhabitants of the Gabon Estuary had sold captives to passing vessels on and off since the sixteenth century.

Food Supply and City Struggles

"Each alimentary custom makes up a miniscule crossroads of histories," Michel de Certeau and Luce Giard have noted, in which various levels of historical change make themselves felt in a repertoire of daily practices.[7] While changes in eating and food supply in Libreville took place in a context radically different than the French setting of de Certeau and Giard, their emphasis on the creativity of individuals knowledgeable in the science of "doing-cooking" fits well into African cities. The same maneuvering and borrowing took place in African city kitchens.[8] However, as Elias Mandala has recently and rightly declared in a provocative essay, "to become an expert on food in the world's most underdeveloped continent, one does not need to know much about food; one has to learn about such matters as the 'political economy' of its disappearance."[9] Few scholars of Africa have tried to examine foodways and food supply except in times of crisis.[10]

A calamity of consumption striking some residents of Gabon has attracted much public attention in America and Europe in the last decade, but its victims are not human. Ecologist J. Michael Fay and his sponsors in *National Geographic* have celebrated Fay as a heroic ecologist marching through "untamed" Gabon trying to stop the wholesale slaughter of animals.[11] Journalist Derek Peterson's exposé *Eating Apes* dissects the connections between the ravenous hunger of timber camp workers for meat, the insouciance of Africans to the plight of endangered species, and the complicity he feels some conservation programs have in feeding the continued slaughter of animals. His trip to Gabon included a stop at the fly-ridden stalls of the Lalala market of Libreville, where market women hawked elephant trunks and gorilla hands. Peterson advocates outside interference—to save the apes, one must be willing to criticize and change African cultural practices. His diagnosis of the disaster is not one that excuses Africans or Europeans but rather, in his words, "a Western capitalized exploitation culture that has lately careened in total collision with a traditional African hunting culture."[12]

Peterson must be lauded for his audacity, but his train wreck analogy, no matter how appealing it may be to environmentalists, does not explain how Gabonese people eat as they do today. One must look at an issue that rarely surfaces in popular discussions of animals and Gabon: colonialism. This book is an exploration of how European and African eating habits intersected and borrowed from one another. Changing food habits in Libreville epitomize a dramatic process whereby the expansion of the world economy transformed tastes in Africa in the last two centuries. From Dakar to Tonga, food tastes have been radically altered due to shifts in economic production and cultural flows.[13] Besides the introduction of new ingredients to diets, the expanded role of food as a commodity and the uneven development of wage labor have changed what and how people eat. Such statements are hardly news for scholars interested in the impact of colonialism in Africa. Jack Goody, in his overview of changing food tastes in Ghana, has briefly explored the impact of industrial mass-produced imports on eating habits.[14] Jane Guyer noted the flexibility and fluidity of food supply organization in Yaoundé; far from it being a static system, producers and the colonial state created a series of contested configurations to ensure profits for farmers and food for urban workers.[15] On a more pessimistic note, Richard Franke, among others, presents the violence and exploitation of colonial rule as the root cause of famines and malnutrition in the Third World.[16]

The story of how Libreville residents obtained food and the effects of French governance on their daily struggles to feed themselves offer insights on the colonial urban experience in Africa. This study, through the subject of food, examines a question central to recent historiography of colonial Africa: how and why did colonized people come to consume European goods and incorporate foreign consumption patterns into their own lives? This question elicits a variety of answers particularly in our present age of genetically modified foods and fast food restaurants mushrooming across the globe. One possible response is the replacement of local culinary styles by the inexorable spread of American or European imports. Half a century ago, some Europeans predicted the death of local practices in Africa under the onslaught of modernity. Novelist Doris Lessing, in a grotesque turn of parody, captures such rhetoric in a conversation between white Communists lolling in a Rhodesian bar during World War II. "I predict," one of her characters declares as he mourns the supposed demise of the local countryside, "that in fifty years all this fine country we see stretching before us . . . will be covered by semi-detached houses filled with well-clothed black workers."[17] Lessing's cocktail-swilling revolutionary does not bother to speculate on what these African laborers might eat, but one might that suspect kidneys and shepherd's pie rather than mealie meal would grace their tables.

Obviously such a future has not come to pass. In Gabon, manioc and plantains rather than French fries and beef remain common parts of meals. Instead of the elimination of local consumption practices, a messy process of appropriation and borrowing took place among African communities and fractured European groups in eating styles, dress, and drinking. While such complexity does not lend itself to simple models that extol European over supposedly backward African forms of consumption, or heroic consumers fighting Western cultural imperialism, the manifold ways Africans consumed commodities have inspired scholars in the last decade to reexamine the colonial encounter.[18] A shift in Africanist research during the last decade has produced works considering various material practices such as alcohol consumption, health and medicine, dress, and hygiene as aspects of mediated cultural contact and divisions under European administration.[19] Consumption of European clothes and the adoption of European hygiene patterns did not necessarily mean a surrender of "African" cultural practices. Instead Africans strove to remake identities and to challenge binary oppositions favored by European rulers. These works put into question narrow boundaries and rigid divisions between supposedly separate African and European cultural practices.[20]

Food has not received much attention in this genre of literature, although a few scholars have explored food consumption as a cultural practice that reveals a wide breadth of contested social meanings.[21] The attention shown by American and European cultural critics exploring gender roles, class anxieties, and ethnic identities articulated in food preparation and consumption has not been shared by Africanists.[22] An older generation of scholarship, firmly tied to underdevelopment theory, paid more attention to food supply, particularly in areas where famines repeatedly devastated rural communities. Challenging paradigms that blamed African agricultural techniques and environmental factors as the cause of food shortages, Michael Watts and Mike Davis have pointed out the important role of cash crops, capitalist development, and wage labor demands in hindering food production and the ability of workers to buy their sustenance.[23] Economist Amartya Sen's argument that rather than absolute want, the inability of communities to exchange labor or money to obtain food led to starvation among certain groups has informed researched on African famines.[24] Historians have traced the impact of wage labor and increased social stratification on food supply and how this led to famine among impoverished groups.[25] Recent work by Susanne Friedberg and Karola Elwert-Kretschmer has started to move beyond the paradigm of want in examining the rise of imported foods in West African cities.[26] Unfortunately Karen Coen Flynn and Elias Mandala's major new contributions to understanding hunger and food in Africa were published after I finished this manuscript, but their outstanding work speaks to how food consumption offers tremendous possibilities for scholars scrutinizing African societies.[27]

This study seeks to tie together issues of cultural and economic change related to food consumption. The task is not easy. Cameroonian historian Achille Mbembe has criticized proponents of "negotiated colonialism" for overemphasizing the prowess of colonial subjects in challenging oppressive policies fostered by European rulers.[28] Mbembe suggests that historians may need to review their understanding of colonial domination; rather than positing the colonial state as "weak," he contends that force and indoctrination did play a major role in shaping African societies. Ironically, this attitude fits well with earlier works on food supply that tend to focus on the imposition of capitalist demands and European political power. Rather than relegating Africans simply to the status of victims of colonial force and duplicity, though, historians might use Mbembe's intervention to reexamine negotiation more carefully.

Recent approaches that highlight the negotiation of cultural terms and older considerations of colonial poverty are together needed to grasp the causes of Libreville's dependence on foreign foods and the low productivity of Estuary agriculture. An angry Mpongwe man in the 1880s penned the title of this book, asserting that he had the right to eat the same foods and at the same prices as his American missionary employers. His ordinary struggle is part of the development of tastes that takes center stage here. The wealthy disdained agriculture out of concern for social status; the very poor increasingly could not harness the labor and land necessary to feed themselves. Performances of identity through consumption and the changing economy led to the evolution of the culinary repertoire of the city. In particular the advantages of some Libreville townspeople over rural producers in shaping policies and organizing food supply gives an example of negotiation in which cultural capital led to material benefits for an urban minority. During repeated changes in politics and the economy, townspeople managed to protect their lifestyle by ensuring their access to food.

Libreville residents used strategies to protect food entitlement for material and cultural motivations. Historian Sara Berry has illustrated the complicated nature of struggles to gain access to labor, land, and markets in various parts of colonial Africa. I concur with her that "culture, power and material resources are of equal importance, acting in mutually constructive ways to shape the course of economic and social change."²⁹ Food consumption proved to be another area in which various African rural and urban groups along with European companies and the colonial state vied for favorable terms. While officials had more force at their disposal to influence these bargains, townspeople used creative strategies to sway administrators. Food supply required many compromises. Although occasionally different members of these networks found themselves at cross purposes, participants in food supply networks negotiated to make compromises that do not fit into simple divisions of resistance and collaboration. Steven Kaplan, a historian of Parisian food supply, has made a statement that can apply to African cities as well as their European counterparts: "Far from articulating a steep hierarchy of rigorously discrete and unbridgeable strata, [the supply of bread to Paris] forged curious bonds of mutual dependence even as it reinforced cleavages within the structure."³⁰

Mbembe reminds us of the unequal terms of negotiation, in which some Africans could bargain with foreign authorities much more effectively than others could. Townspeople in Libreville proved far more capable of safeguarding their interests than did rural farmers and fishermen. Libreville residents managed to avoid farming and fishing despite radically changing economic and social conditions. However, such a victory did not always constitute a heroic example of "resistance." As the storied careers of Omar Bongo and his predecessor Léon Mba demonstrate, the skill with which some Gabonese dealt with colonial officials and private companies did not always result in challenges to European authority. Furthermore, decisions made by the colonial government and urban Africans also hampered agricultural production. While the discovery of oil in the 1950s has been blamed for Gabon's food crises and high cost of living, this study delineates a long heritage of agricultural neglect and outright incompetence by the French colonial state. The exorbitant cost of daily life in Libreville is in large part a testament to colonial policies and bargains made between a small class of urban Africans and the French government. And as the blackened carcasses of monkeys and antelope on sale in Libreville today suggest, humans are not the only victims of this heritage.

Diana Wylie rightly remarks that the richness of food as a subject of historical inquiry is problematic for historians in need of clearly defined subjects.³¹ Research possibilities may be endless, but the patience of readers is not boundless. I therefore exclude certain issues often brought up with food. Unlike in British colonies, French agricultural experts did little to construct notions of malnutrition and hunger.[32] While I decipher some social meanings broadly articulated in food consumption related to race and status, close readings of food preparation and eating as means of exploring cultural logics or constructions of gender are not on the table.[33] One must search elsewhere for African equivalents of Pierre Bourdieu's attempt to link class attitudes closely with food consumption.[34] Neither is this study a comprehensive examination of changing food patterns throughout Gabon. Although I laud efforts to construct national and regional histories of food and manners in the tradition of Ferdinand Braudel, I can make no claim of comprehensive overviews in the present work.[35] All these subjects deserve attention, but my framework does not permit it here.

Another issue worthy of more attention than I can supply is a thorough review of environmental factors that may have hindered agriculture in the Estuary region. Libreville developed as an enclave dependent for its food supply on a large region rather than its immediate surroundings. How much did ecological issues play a role in hindering food production? To my knowledge practically no work has examined ecological issues linked to food supply in the Estuary despite a wealth of ecological research in rainforest regions in the Gabonese interior. While chapter 2 gives a basic overview of climate and topography of the region, I recognize the possibility that environmental factors may have shaped the food supply question more dramatically than this work suggests.

With this litany of caveats noted, the central focus of this study is the slow evolution of changing food consumption and supply patterns in colonial Libreville. Chapter 1 is a general review of Libreville history from its beginnings as an Atlantic entrepôt through its slow growth in the colonial era. The social and environmental context of food consumption in the age of Atlantic slavery is the subject of chapter 2. Free people, from hosting European slave traders with lavish meals to worrying about what slaves might have slipped into their meals, linked eating and farming to the institution of slavery. Food production, especially agriculture, came to be seen as labor fit only for slaves and free women, and the growth of a wage economy meant that prosperous townspeople had more lucrative options than mere farming could allow.

Chapter 3 examines how Libreville culinary and consumption patterns altered as French forces invaded much of Central Africa in the age of high imperialism between 1880 and 1914. The late nineteenth century brought a new set of players to the complicated trade and agricultural networks of the Gabon Estuary.

The arrival of Fang-speaking clans and waves of foreign immigrants, rang-ing from unlucky Vietnamese convicts to Liberian manual laborers, brought new foods and new demands on Libreville's food supply. Townspeople adapt-ed to the situation in ways that furthered the development of an urban lifestyle keeping respectable people away from long hours spent cultivating, hunting, or catching food. While Fang villages managed to sate Libreville's appetite until 1914, World War I and its immediate aftermath shook Gabon to its foun-dations. Famine and shortages tore apart Estuary villages and helped fuel an urban protest movement led by Libreville residents to fight the efforts of colo-nial officials and timber companies to monopolize control over the town's food supply. Chapter 4 scrutinizes the environmental and political calamities that rural producers endured and the relative success of urban residents in guard-ing their entitlements. Townspeople demonstrated their versatility by employ-ing disparate means, from intimidating Africans with supernatural talismans to cajoling French human rights organizations, to protect their access to food from state interference.

The next three chapters address how townspeople interacted with goods, programs, and practices brought by Europeans and Americans into the Gabon Estuary. Chapter 5 explores how foreign foods made their way into Libreville stomachs. The inadequacy of the town's local sources of food made rations an important part of diets in the Gabon Estuary region and a cause of strife between Africans and Europeans struggling to define the worth of goods and labor. Bread, rice, canned goods, and beef also became part of a broad effort by missionar-ies and employers to remake Libreville society by changing the parameters of daily life. Technological and communications changes allowed foreign foods by the mid-twentieth century to become an integral part of Libreville meals.

Chapter 6 discusses urban growth and colonial policies between the Great Depression and independence. Officials might repeatedly curse the supposed laziness of Africans in the Gabon Estuary, but state interventions in local soci-ety did little to encourage agriculture or to enable farmers. State programs neglected to alleviate Libreville's position, isolated from the rest of the colony, and rarely allowed farmers from more productive parts of Gabon to ship food to Libreville. Experts on Gabon today bemoan how little Gabonese bureaucrats have done to aid farmers, to the point that one analyst has argued: "Gabon's development strategy in recent decades therefore looks in many ways like a sophisticated conspiracy against agriculture"; but French agricultural policies were rife with mismanagement.[36] As is the case today, imports proved to be an easier solution than radical methods to assist food production. Finally, the roots of the Gabonese state's tepid interest in closing the bush meat supply came in the twilight of empire, as politicians and villagers alike asserted their rights to guns and game.

Chapter 7 is an overview of European food consumption patterns in Libreville during the colonial period; the present-day segregation of town cuisine into "European" and "African" categories is a fairly recent development. Although nineteenth-century Western residents of the town adopted local eating habits and social beliefs associated with food consumption, as revealed in poison fears and rumors, political and technological advances in the colonial state and the world economy allowed Europeans to live a more segregated lifestyle. Foreign eating patterns were a barometer of racial identities and colonial power that provide a way to chart the relative strengths and weaknesses of Europeans asserting their cultural superiority over others in town.

One of my goals is to open the door to further work on food consumption as a means of reviewing the impact of colonialism on everyday life in a colonial context. It is hard to imagine a more personal or vital practice than eating, yet scholars of Africa have been slow to grasp the opportunities for looking at food as a nexus of race, gender, class, and economic transformations. Another motivation is far more mundane. From my initial stay in Libreville in 1998 through my last visit in 2004, friends and strangers alike lamented the high prices that burdened them in the city. I only hope that my work can illuminate discussion on Libreville's high cost of living, even if it offers no clear solutions.

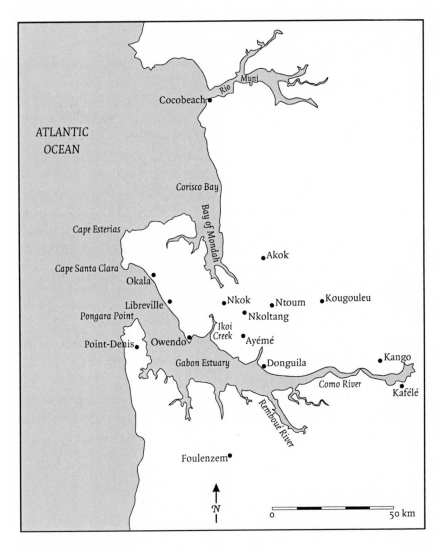

ATLANTIC
OCEAN

Cocobeach

Rio Muni

Corisco Bay

Bay of Mondah

Cape Esterias

Cape Santa Clara

Okala

Akok

Libreville

Nkok

Ntoum

Kougouleu

Pongara Point

Nkoltang

Ikoi
Creek

Point-Denis

Owendo

Ayémé

Gabon Estuary

Donguila

Kango

Como River

Kafélé

Remboué River

Foulenzem

N

0

50 km

Gabon Estuary

A Workman Is Worthy of His Meat

1. The Gabon Estuary and the Atlantic World, 1840–1960

In Libreville, the capital of the Central African nation of Gabon, the colonial past has evolved into a present indelibly marked by French rule. French soldiers still wash down their boredom with cheap liquor in local bars and garrison the city as they have since the founding of the port in 1843. Oil profits in the boom years of the 1970s paid for a towering set of modernist office and government buildings designed by French architects. High-end *supermarchés* display rows of French pâté, crispy baguettes, and much less succulent elements of French cuisine, such as the humble can of *cassoulet* stew. For hungry visitors with expansive wallets, restaurants provide French chefs well versed in the fine arts of *haute cuisine*, who serve wealthy Gabonese as well as expatriates from Europe. Rich Africans are not the only local people enjoying French tastes; so do Gabonese living in such rapidly expanding outlying neighborhoods as Ozangué, Bellevue, and Nzeng Ayong.

The ingredients of ordinary Libreville meals have a strong French flavor. Each morning well-worn trucks bear boxes of bread to thousands of small, cramped stores selling food to an exclusively African clientele. Male workers crowd the colorful open-air "cafets" staffed by West African immigrants who serve "fast food" to their customers. Senegalese fish recipes and dark sauces made from manioc leaves and okra are offered along with dishes more familiar to Westerners. Menus in black paint or chalk on the walls of these restaurants list prices for omelets, coffee and baguette combinations, spaghetti, and *frites*. African and European tastes blend together even in the choices of available condiments. Patrons can add rust-orange crushed pepper or mayonnaise, usually left exposed to the sun, to their food.

The colonial legacy also shapes contemporary eating habits in less obvious ways. West African women selling fried dough balls on the streets of Libreville became commonplace after World War I, when Togolese and Dahomean immigrants started to trickle into town. Nigerian and other West African outfits dominate local fishing today; their slow takeover of the industry began in part due to the French government's support for West African immigration into Gabon. Bags of rice, a staple of many Gabonese, entered the local culinary repertoire in the late nineteenth century, as French forces conquered Gabon and much of Southeast Asia. Even the thick blocks of prepared manioc sold at market for Africans, a staple of every meal in rural Gabon, owe a debt to colonial rule. Mpongwe people, a small ethnic community that controlled the Gabon Estuary region until French occupation in the 1840s, usually eat long and relatively thin strands of bread made from manioc tubers soaked in water and then slowly cooked into over a fire. As Libreville became an administrative center that attracted Gabonese from all over the colony, vendors started to sell other varieties of manioc: female traders now hawk thick bulky wads of the "manioc congo" popular in southern Gabon, wrapped in banana leaves, next to the tough-to-chew manioc favored by Fang people from the surrounding Gabon Estuary.

The following overview of Libreville under colonial rule provides a framework for understanding how tastes changed under the French and how access to food became an object of contention between Africans and Europeans living in the city. Influences at issue include local ecology, the rise of a Mpongwe coastal community's links to the Atlantic slave trade, the coming of French rule, and its impacts in the Gabon Estuary region: urban migration, the uneven formation of a wage economy, and the interactions among rural farmers, African townspeople, and the French colonial state. An urban community dependent on others for food was slowly developing even before colonial occupation but became much more apparent by the early twentieth century. This overview is drawn from a wide range of primary sources as well as the emerging historical literature of Gabon, especially the major contribution on Gabonese urban and gender history by Rachel Jean-Baptiste.[1]

Environment and Topography

The present site of Libreville stretches over twelve kilometers on the northern bank of the Gabon Estuary. Instead of flat lowlands found throughout other parts of the Estuary coast, hills and valleys undulate along the shore. Marshy ravines separate four hilly sections; swamps in the present site of the Batavea and Saint-Germain neighborhoods isolated the agglomeration of Mpongwe villages at Glass from other parts of the town.[2] Such rugged and uneven terrain limited the size of fields and helped lead to Libreville's present anarchic network of roads and paths.

As any Libreville resident knows, torrents of water and wind often strike. The city and its immediate surroundings receive on average more than three thousand millimeters of precipitation a year.[3] Local residents separate climate into four seasons. The rainy season begins in early September and ends normally in December. Thunderstorms and the occasional tornado, particularly at night, rumble through the Estuary region. The temperature during this season generally hovers around 27 degrees Celsius. After a brief respite of lowered precipitation in December and January, dubbed "the short dry season," rain increases dramatically from February through early May. A long dry season marked by cooler temperatures (23–25 degrees Celsius) holds sway from May until August.

Geology has also influenced food production and consumption in Libreville and the surrounding area. Most of the land touching upon the Gabon Estuary is made up of low-lying forests growing in soil with a high amount of sand and clay.[4] Such soil has supported small-scale farming in the region for over two thousand years. Historian of early Gabon Kairn Klieman has pointed out how soil within Gabon varies in fertility.[5] Roughly two hundred kilometers from Libreville, the high peaks and rich soil of Monts de Cristal furnish a much better foundation for agriculture than does the low-lying Gabon Estuary. Libreville residents today consider this area much more promising for farming than the immediate Estuary region.

A web of small rivers connects the Estuary region to Libreville. No natural passages exist on land, but the inhabitants of the region have paddled up and down these waters for centuries as their main means of transport. Small creeks such as the Tsini, Nzeme, Goungoué, and Igombiné allowed communication and trade to flourish. The Como and Mbé rivers that flow into the Estuary allowed limited access to the Monts de Cristal region. The Remboué River reaches from the Estuary southwest to the large lakes around Lambaréné and the Ogooué; it served as a major link for trade until the early twentieth century. The close proximity of the Atlantic Ocean placed the Gabon Estuary in contact with the Ogooué River and peoples along the southern coast.

Forests tower over the immediate surroundings of Libreville. As Jan Vansina has pointed out, "The expression 'rainforest' encompasses a wide range of the most complex habitats in world."[6] In the Gabon Estuary, hilly forests dominated by okoumé trees (Akoumea kleinia) occupy land away from thickets of mangroves by the shore. Estuary peoples took advantage of their surroundings by forming a rich body of ethnobotanical knowledge. Gabonese priest and botanist André Raponda Walker's extensive and weighty collection of information on local uses of plants in Gabon points to the diversity of plant life and the creativity of Estuary inhabitants in taking advantage of them.[7]

The early history of the Estuary is accessible through linguistic and archaeological sources, and it is clear that humans have lived in the area for thousands of years.[8] Archaeological research on the outskirts of Libreville has unearthed stone tools and the signs of a small series of villages well over thirty thousand years old.[9] Hunter-gatherer settlements in the Estuary traded with people in the Rio Muni region more than a hundred kilometers away.[10] Archaeologists recently unearthed evidence of sedentary agricultural settlements and the manufacture of iron in the immediate vicinity of Libreville dating from at least 200 BC.[11] Besides the material culture these peoples left behind, little is known about them.

Working with scant material, scholars are divided on the links between these sites and present-day inhabitants of the Estuary. Historian Jan Vansina, in his discussion of Bantu-speaking peoples' migration into the equatorial rainforests of Central Africa, contends that the ancestors of Mpongwe people, who comprised the major inhabitants of the Estuary in the early colonial period, arrived before 1000 BC.[12] Kairn Klieman's review of linguistic and archaeological dates suggests that by 1500 BC, the ancestors of Omyene-speaking groups like the Mpongwe had arrived on the Estuary.[13] Other scholars argue that the ancestors of Omyene speakers arrived in the Gabon Estuary only around 1400 AD.[14] No consensus is likely to develop from the controversies surrounding the chronology of Mpongwe settlement without new evidence.

While dating Mpongwe arrival in the Estuary is difficult, there is no question that their forebears belonged to a larger movement of Western Bantu speakers spreading south throughout Gabon and Congo-Brazzaville. Divided into numerous clans throughout the coast of Gabon, these groups spoke a common language called Omyene.[15] The communities include the Galwa living around Lambaréné in Central Gabon, the Orungu around the Ogooué delta, and the Nkomi of the southern Gabonese coast. Mpongwe on the Gabon Estuary appear to have traded regularly with the other groups. All of these communities acted as intermediaries between Europeans and interior African trading networks by the early nineteenth century.

After moving into the region, the forerunners of Omyene-speaking clans adjusted to their new environment, learning to take advantage of mangrove swamps and forests.[16] Bantu-speaking peoples brought into the region yams and other root crops their ancestors had raised since at least 2000 BC.[17] People also gathered numerous fruits and shellfish. They may have improved hunting and fishing techniques by learning from pygmy settlements already established in the area.[18] While pygmies had disappeared from the Estuary by the early colonial period, mutual exchange of goods and information between Bantu peoples and other forest peoples led to cultural and culinary innovations.

In many ways Mpongwe society's political and social structures reflected its heritage as part of the Western Bantu migration. Jan Vansina has described the structure of this political tradition of lineages as being divided into three categories: houses, villages, and districts.[19] Mpongwe houses were large households made up of a number of smaller families that claimed common descent.[20] They formed the main unit of political organization. Several houses that claimed common ancestry formed a clan.[21] These house alliances formed villages of up to several hundred people. Clan identities in the Gabon Estuary transcended linguistic and ethnic boundaries; for example, the Agakaza clan considers itself an ally of the Fang-speaking Essissis clan.[22]

Big men (aga) from leading houses ruled over a small number of villages.[23] The population remained thinly dispersed; European sources indicate that roughly twenty-five thousand people lived in the entire Estuary region in the 1850s.[24] While more than forty clans existed among the Mpongwe, a select few clans such as the Agakaza and Asiga dominated local politics by the nineteenth century.[25] Through trading savvy and by maintaining large numbers of wives and slaves as dependents, big men could attract enough respect to be named to political office by a council of elder men.[26] Although lineage played a major role in the choice of clan leaders, successful traders without strong claims to authority could rise to political prominence.[27] These big men were dependent on other free people for support.

Territorial mobility was a hallmark of Mpongwe society. Much like other societies in Equatorial Africa, Mpongwe people tended to identify themselves with their clans or lineages rather than with a fixed locale. Geographer Roland Pourtier has characterized notions of space in Gabonese societies as fluid and marked by ever-shifting boundaries rather than the fixed borders more familiar in a European context.[28] Historian Christopher Gray noted how villages and clans in precolonial southern Gabon moved frequently and partitioned themselves with areas of unoccupied forest.[29] With soils unable to maintain fields for long periods, villagers needed to search for new farmland.

Even so, the local ecology was far from the only explanation of mobility among the Mpongwe. Commerce and politics also dictated migration patterns. Oral traditions denote villages on the south bank of the Estuary abandoned over time.[30] Individuals and families often moved. Strife among lineages and clans led to divisions of villages and the formation of new settlements. For example, rivalries between big men of the Agakaza clan led to the formation of the villages of Louis and Glass.[31]

Trade contacts furnish another explanation of movement. With the rise of European trade in the Estuary during the late eighteenth century, the Agakaza decided to move to north bank for better access to European vessels.[32] Agakaza villages such as Anongo-Ambani, Nk'Azuwa, and Olumi had emerged on the present site of Libreville.[33] Visiting sailors referred to these towns by the names they had given local clan leaders and prominent traders: Glass, Quaben, Louis, and Kringer. By the early nineteenth century Mpongwe free merchants had long participated in the Atlantic economy that brought cultural innovation and foreign material goods to the area.

Gabon and the Atlantic World, 1500–1840

Mpongwe people traded with Atlantic newcomers and inland peoples for centuries. They profited from their ties with interior peoples from central and northern Gabon and participated in a commercial coastal circuit that reached from southern Cameroon to Angola.[34] The slave trade also slowly took root in the region. References to the Gabon Estuary emerge from Portuguese and Dutch naval accounts as early as the late sixteenth century.[35] Unlike the case of the Loango area to the south, few slaves went from Gabon to the Americas before the mid-eighteenth century.[36] Portuguese traders occasionally visited the region from their colonial settlements on the islands of São Tomé, several hundred miles off the coast. Dutch vessels soon followed in search of ivory, ebony, and other natural products.[37] Oral traditions hint at conflicts between Dutch traders and Mpongwe people in the early seventeenth century, though few reliable details are available.[38] Atlantic slave trade exports began in earnest during the mid-eighteenth century.[39]

Mpongwe people themselves rarely raided for slaves, and no strong monarchs sold off captives in the region. Like a wide range of African communities on the Atlantic coast, wealthy Mpongwe made their fortunes through their intermediary position between the interior and Europeans seeking out slaves.[40] They monopolized access to the interior, even telling stories of cannibals and savages as a way to frighten visitors. Unlucky free Mpongwe might be sold off as payment for debts or as punishment for a crime. However, Africans leaving the Estuary in chains usually came from inland regions.

The Atlantic slave trade left in its wake increased social stratification. Clan leaders and prominent traders obtained imported goods in advance from Europeans and then exchanged goods with neighbors for slaves and natural resources.[41] Mpongwe men recognized their advantages in dealings with Europeans, who could wait only a certain amount of time before risking their health. For slavers, the poor health of slaves brought in caravans from southern Gabon made delays caused by disputes costly.[42]

Slavery dominated Mpongwe villages by the early nineteenth century. Local society was sharply divided between slaves (asaka), children of slaves with limited rights (imbamba s'asaka), and a hierarchy of free people ranging from commoners to wealthy merchants and clan leaders. Some slaves came from central and southern Gabon.[43] Others were captured during fighting with Séké villages in the Estuary.[44] The new influx of dependents permitted free people to favor trade over farming. Owning slaves became a crucial sign of prestige in Mpongwe society, much as it did elsewhere.[45]

Wealth in Mpongwe society was a matter of controlling people rather than land. Through the distribution of imported goods men could obtain slaves, clients, and knowledge.[46] By these standards clan leaders were rich indeed by the 1840s. John Leighton Wilson, an American pastor who cofounded with Reverend William Walker the Protestant mission at Baraka in 1842, noted that each Mpongwe clan chief owned at least two hundred slaves.[47] Asiga clan leader

Rapontchombo (c. 1780–1876), known to Europeans as Dénis or King William, controlled roughly five hundred slaves at his death.[48] Catholic nuns noted with dismay in 1849 that one clan leader had more than eighty wives.[49] While the Sisters' inexperience may have skewed the accuracy of their estimates, Catholic priests reported twenty years later a recently deceased chief left over twenty widows behind.[50]

The changing nature of the slave trade created new profits after 1800. The British government's decision to liberate slaves from Spanish and Portuguese vessels inadvertently aided Mpongwe traders. Gabon, a much less popular stop for slave ships before the Napoleonic Wars, became a favorite precisely because of its obscurity. Few British warships regularly visited Gabon. Portuguese and Brazilian slavers could quickly travel from Gabon to the Portuguese islands of São Tomé. By the 1840s Spanish and Portuguese slave buyers settled in Mpongwe villages for months. Agakaza and Asiga clan leaders vied for the most lucrative connections with foreign merchants. The growth of slave trading would lead to the rise of French power in the 1830s.

French Occupation, 1839–1875

The Gabon Estuary fell under the sway of French political power between the late 1830s and 1875. Problems related to the slave trade and European firms sapped the grip of Mpongwe traders over local commerce. Political divisions meant that local objections to French annexation had little ability to deter European occupation. However, the waxing and waning of individual French naval officers' interest in the fledgling colony and the extremely meager support for the settlement from Paris made Gabon a "middle ground," to use the phrase of Native American historian Richard White, where French and Mpongwe people co-authored a loosely organized set of political and economic bonds. Not until the 1870s did French commandants act forcefully to limit local autonomy.

The pretext for French occupation developed in the late 1830s. Edouard Bouet-Willaumez, an ambitious French naval officer, eyed the Gabon Estuary as a possible supply point for the South Atlantic naval division assigned to stop slave traders.[51] Until Gabon became French, the only secure French port of call was in Senegal. Bouet-Willaumez also could use justice as a motive to occupy the region. Some Mpongwe pillaged shipwrecked French vessels.

French officers obtained legal rights from the famed Mpongwe trader Rapontchombo during 1839. Rapontchombo agreed to accept claims of French authority but encouraged officers to set up a base among his Agakaza clan rivals on the north side of the river. Such maneuvers speak to the negotiating power of clan chiefs in early French-Mpongwe contacts.[52] While Rapontchombo was left to conduct his affairs without interference in the 1840s, Europeans took a much sterner view toward other clan chiefs. Bouet-Willaumez and other French military men distrusted Agakaza leaders who had raided and robbed several French vessels. Some clan leaders preferred English and American traders. Agakaza *aga* (clan chiefs) such as Re-Dowé signed treaties in return for European military outfits and a wide variety of goods in 1842 and 1843.

Such treaties from the Mpongwe point of view appear to have been the continuation of older policies of commercial alliances. Much as in many other European enclaves in West Africa, Mpongwe traders granted land to foreigners in return for trade agreements.[53] The difference between local and French interpretations of these agreements became rapidly obvious. Paris officials pushed for the annexation of the entire Estuary. A French trader apparently duped R'Ogouarouwé, the most defiant critic of French rule, into signing a treaty surrendering his independence in 1844. Agakaza clan members turned to British sea captains and American missionaries to intercede against the French presence. After the refusal to fly the French flag brought on a short assault by French troops in 1845, R'Ogouarouwé and noted Agakaza big man N'Toko reluctantly agreed to accept European control.[54]

This triumph of force over diplomacy did not translate into financial rewards. French efforts to make the colony profitable stagnated. Besides making token efforts to ban the export of slaves, officials did little to interfere with local politics.[55] Several French entrepreneurs founded plantations in the Estuary during the 1840s, but poor funding and an inability to attract cheap labor led to bankruptcy.[56] Enriching themselves by selling ivory, dye woods, and rubber, Mpongwe merchants had little motivation to support French companies.

While French efforts foundered, British and German traders used the settlement as a springboard to move into the interior. By the early 1850s the Liverpool firm of Hatton and Cookson along with the German Woermann company had set up stores in Libreville.[57] French traders struggled with their foreign rivals until the First World War.[58] German and English merchants gave out credit and offered goods at much lower prices than their French counterparts.[59] Mpongwe residents in Glass favored British and German firms to the point that English remained the lingua franca of commerce there until the 1880s.[60]

Mpongwe society faced challenges from an array of angles. The arrival of European stores sounded the death knell of the old monopoly on interior trade networks. Most men became employees of the colonial government or private firms by the 1860s.[61] Big men thus lost many of the previous economic advantages that had allowed them to control large numbers of dependents through purchase or marriage.[62] By the late 1850s the last generation of independent big men except for Rapontchombo had died.[63] Chiefs lost a great deal of their former prestige.[64] In short, older strategies of obtaining wealth and power had altered in the new conditions of French Libreville.

The influence of Catholic and Protestant missionaries posed another threat to the Mpongwe social order. At first missionary efforts did not bring about radical change. After their arrival in 1842 Congregationalist pastors from the American Board of Commissioners for Foreign Missions (ABCFM) worked to spread the Gospel with relatively little success.[65] Few free people endorsed the calls of Protestant preachers to abandon polygamy, local religious beliefs, and alcohol.[66] Catholic priests of the Holy Ghost Fathers and nuns from the Sisters of the Immaculate Conception encountered similar difficulties in the 1840s.[67] Disease and opposition from heavy-drinking and sexually promiscuous Europeans hampered Catholic and Protestant efforts.

These new elements provided a small cosmopolitan town community made up of Mpongwe, West African workers, and other Gabonese, a rich repertoire of material and cultural practices to draw upon. In August 1842 newly arrived American Congregationalist pastor John Leighton Wilson made a visit to the Mpongwe village of Quaben. Walking on a path now buried under asphalt and concrete and European-styled homes in Libreville, Wilson strolled to the home of the notable trader Re-Dowé. In his spacious house Re-Dowé offered his American visitor a seat "in what he called his parlor."[68] His home featured two bed stands with mosquito nets, a table covered by a French oil cloth, a bureau, a hand organ, six "neat" European chairs, and two sofas.[69] Rather than wishing to speak of God, Re-Dowé preferred to speak with his guest on matters of trade.

Well-versed in European manners, rich Mpongwe people flaunted their taste and their wealth for others to see. These merchants had long treated Europeans as equals in commerce. Succeeding generations of Libreville townspeople continued to draw liberally from foreign influences while innovating on indigenous ideas about status and wealth. Mission education provides one example of the willingness of the Mpongwe and other African residents of Libreville to incorporate European influences. From the 1840s on, free people sent boys and girls to mission schools to learn French and English.[70] Missionaries became increasingly despondent as their school graduates often engaged in heavy drinking, took employment with irreligious traders and officials, and claimed equal legal status with Europeans. Félix Adende Rapontchombo, a Catholic convert who became head of the Asiga clan in 1876, declared himself a loyal Frenchman and evangelist while owning hundreds of slaves.[71]

Libreville communities continued to assert their autonomy. Perhaps one of the most striking examples of this independence was the failure of a plan to resettle former slaves in the colony in the late 1840s. French officers, mimicking their British rivals in Sierra Leone, decided to resettle over one hundred Africans rescued from the Spanish slave ship *Elizia* at the French fort of Gabon.[72] Fashioning a well-ordered settlement with fields and gardens, officials hoped the newcomers would provide the workers needed to unload ships and tend state fields. Rather than doing so, however, some former slaves revolted against the French authorities.[73] Most of the settlers entered into trade instead of remaining menial laborers.[74] The colony, hamstrung by miniscule budgets and dependent on remote superiors in Dakar (1843–54) and Gorée (1854–59), did not attempt to replenish the small settlement with more rescued slaves.

By the 1860s French officials maintained only a loose hold over the region, as exemplified by relationships between men and women and masters and slaves. The local government never banned domestic slavery and intervened only haphazardly in disputes between masters and bondspeople. Free Mpongwe executed slaves with impunity on the grounds that they used supernatural forces to harm others. Slaves were still buried alive with notable chiefs through the 1870s. On occasion some captives in turn menaced free people by threatening to use sorcery.[75] But although officials appeared impotent, they did develop other ways of building alliances with local people.

Many Mpongwe women, willingly or under the pressure of older male and female relatives, entered sexual relationships with state employees, traders, and even a few wayward missionaries.[76] Such practices had gone on for centuries, but the concentration of European men in the town altered these practices. Much as in other coastal regions of Atlantic Africa, individuals and families used intimate relations with foreigners as a personal or a collective strategy. Some girls evidently suffered sexual assault as family members shoved them into the arms of Europeans. Others sought out European men and used their profits to start their own businesses. Visitors celebrated these relationships as care-free *amours congolaises*. Catholic and Protestant ministers detested the decision of Mpongwe women to cohabit with European men. One American minister expressed his rage in an 1882 diary entry: "Rottenness is among Mpongwes and white men. No shame and no virtue on all this plain of ruin. They raise daughters to sell body and soul for the vilest of purposes."[77]

Libreville townspeople and foreign residents created mutually beneficial bonds through the late 1870s. French, English, and German employers hired Mpongwe men as cultural and economic brokers with other Africans. European firms scoured Gabon searching for ivory, rubber, and dye wood, and they needed Mpongwe intermediaries. French commandants slowly extending their reach from Libreville also relied on Mpongwe interpreters and office workers. One result of this evolution was the flow of foreign goods and hard currency in Libreville. By the 1870s European money was in common use. Well-heeled adult free Mpongwe men and women wore the fashions of London and Paris.[78] It is little wonder that Mpongwe people repeatedly expressed their view of them-selves as civilized people worthy of legal equality with any French citizen.

The Age of High Imperialism, 1875–1900

Unfortunately for the hopes of Libreville residents, imperial ambitions and a more rigid notion of racial difference took root in France. Libreville changed from a backwater post to become the command center, briefly, of rapid colonial expansion in Central Africa between 1875 and 1900. After the Franco-Prussian war cut Libreville off from regular communication from Paris, a new genera-tion of administrators pushed French military and political power in Gabon. Commandants between 1875 and 1885 fettered townspeople's freedom: they banned slave executions, made teaching French mandatory at mission schools, and coerced free people to trudge through the streets to cut weeds without pay. Félix Adende Rapontchombo, the last Mpongwe political leader who maintained a shred of independence, ended up a fugitive from French law throughout much of the 1890s after being charged with reenslaving runaway slaves.[79]

Domestic slavery slowly declined after a dramatic series of murders plagued the town. Between 1877 and 1879, mysterious assailants attacked free women and slaves working in fields outside Libreville, leaving at least twenty dead in the town of about three thousand.[80] Gutted corpses slashed by leopard claws, often missing vital organs, sent townspeople into a panic. Disregarding missionaries and slaves who blamed the violence on free people, French commandants executed slaves accused by slave owners of morphing into leopards. The killings ended suddenly in late 1879. Though colonial administrators backed free people over slaves in this case, they proved less willing to support domestic slavery. An illicit commerce in captives survived, but gradually former slaves gained a modicum of independence. Unfortunately the precise nature of the decline of slavery and its causes are hard to analyze given the scant documentation on this transition, especially between the late 1890s and 1918.

Libreville society was further transformed thanks to the formation of the French Congo. Pierre Savorgnan de Brazza launched a series of expeditions in the Central African interior in the 1870s and 1880s that sparked a French invasion.[81] Libreville became a supply point between France and the interior, and its harbors beckoned to foreign traders, soldiers, and craftsmen. West African soldiers, Senegalese craftsmen and seers, jewelers and cooks from Accra in Ghana, manual laborers from the Kru coast of Liberia, and Angolan and São Toméan farmers crossed paths in the town's streets.[82] Libreville also became a convenient dumping ground for opponents of French rule elsewhere. Legendary West African warlord Samoré Touré's sons lived in exile in Libreville along with Dahomean princes, the children of Muslim warlords from Chad and Ubangi-Shari, and even Vietnamese prisoners.[83] The lines binding Libreville in a web of imperial and Atlantic commercial networks brought foreign workers into the region and allowed Mpongwe people to try their luck elsewhere in Africa and Europe.

Libreville was a center of communication networks within the colony, but these lines of contact through thinly populated rainforests proved unreliable. Traders, missionaries, and colonial troops had to rely on narrow paths through dense jungle to reach areas not linked to Libreville by rivers. Only in fits and starts did the capital slowly develop ties with much of the rest of the colony. No administrators took the initiative to improve the situation by sponsoring road construction. This anarchic environment posed hurdles to easy communication between the Gabonese hinterland and Libreville.

Despite the islandlike nature of Libreville, some African arrivals did open the door for better linkages between town and country. The migration of Fang-speaking clans from northern Gabon and Cameroon altered town life. More than forty Fang clans moved in the Gabon Estuary region from the 1840s onward.

Mpongwe abandoned villages far from Libreville in part out of fear of the new-comers, as did small forest-specialist communities like the Séké (Sékiani) and Akele. Fang and Mpongwe communities ostensibly had little in common.[84] Clan feuds inspired by competition for trade, rival ambitions of big men seek-ing dependents, and women fleeing or being kidnapped for husbands led to nearly constant fighting between the 1860s and World War I. Fang people wore little more than amulets, bark cloth, and occasionally odds and ends of cloth and other European imports. French officials, imagining Fang people to be somehow more virile than the supposedly degenerate Mpongwe, hoped Fang men would furnish them with the docile workforce they wished for.[85] However, Fang clans embarked on a series of skirmishes with colonial troops over pay-ing taxes, scuffles with European traders and their Mpongwe agents, and other disputes. American missionaries found that they could not hire Fang workers as porters, since evangelizing sorties in the Estuary region invariably encoun-tered a clan with a grudge ready to brawl with these employees.[86]

Gender roles also distinguished Fang people from Mpongwe and other groups to some degree. Free Mpongwe women, by the late nineteenth century, had often established their own households and lived relatively independently of men. Low bridewealth payments meant couples could divorce relatively eas-ily.[87] Thanks to their dependents, some female Mpongwe slave owners enjoyed leisure time unimaginable to Fang women, who were expected to bear children and handle most farming tasks and were often married off at a very young age. Big men marrying many wives, a common practice among Mpongwe traders and clan chiefs prior to French occupation, became less frequent by the late nineteenth century. Possible reasons for this decline include the decisions of younger men and women to work as traders or as the mistresses of Europeans far from Libreville; the increased participation of townspeople in Catholic and Protestant congregations; and the relative independence of free Mpongwe wom-en. In contrast, towering Fang bridewealth prices often required men to work and trade for years before marriage.[88] Since divorce required wives' families to repay husbands, married men and wives' kin had a vested interest in ensur-ing stable unions. Fang men expected wives and female family members to obey. Fang women did form *mevung* power associations similar to the power-ful female *njembe* society in Mpongwe communities, but they had more diffi-culty challenging elder male authority.

Despite their differences from townspeople, Fang clans slowly entered the

Libreville community in different ways, often through building alliances with locals. Catholic and Protestant missionaries opened their doors to Fang students. Others recognized the growing market for food in town (see chapter 3). Still others landed jobs as manual laborers for Libreville employers. By the early twentieth century neighborhoods like Atong Abé and Lalala had become home to Fang households.

Indigenous communities adjusted to European and African immigrants. First they asserted their equality with French residents of the colony. When the colonial government restructured French Congo in 1910 into a federation of colonies dubbed French Equatorial Africa, lawmakers incensed Libreville townspeople by passing the hated indigènat code, which allowed administrators wide latitude to fine, jail, and punish Africans. Mission-educated Mpongwe elites dashed off letters to colonial inspectors bemoaning how men could be "jailed with a whisper at the club" from malevolent settlers to administrators and how in Gabon, "There is no liberty possible, equality even less so, and no fraternity at all."[89] Carpenter Jean-Baptiste N'dende led protests against a short-lived campaign to segregate the city on ethnic and racial lines between 1912 and World War I.[90]

Mpongwe also challenged African newcomers. Some snubbed Fang people. According to missionaries, townspeople often saw the migrants as barbaric upstarts.[91] Mpongwe women refused to travel aboard boats with Fang, and Fang men found it nearly impossible to marry women of Mpongwe descent.[92] Protestants lamented that many townspeople in the 1890s disliked American pastors' recruitment of Fang to attend services.[93] Mpongwe people jealously guarded their own unique identity, yet also remained open to making alliances with Africans and Europeans. The cruel days of war and famine from 1914 to 1930 would test their ability to negotiate with the colonial state and private companies.

Timber and Travails of Modernity, 1914–1930

The developments of the nineteenth century in Gabon crashed to a halt as war swept through Europe.[94] Commerce nosedived in the city.[95] Few ships came to the Gabon Estuary during the war.[96] The old trading economy never recovered. Fighting between German and French colonial armies in Gabon and southern Cameroon lasted until 1916, sending Fang clans scurrying away from French army recruiters seeking new soldiers and porters. Worsening the hardships, the French doubled the head tax from five to ten francs and decreed that all who could not pay this sum in hard currency had to work without pay for two weeks per year.[97]

The border war with Cameroon ended in French victory, but a host of miseries held sway in rural Gabon. As discussed in chapter 4, the war capped a half century of fighting in the Gabon Estuary. Sleeping sickness and the influenza pandemic of 1919 wiped out a tenth of the entire population. Hunger haunted most of the Gabonese interior. The war led officials to reconsider Gabon's economic potential and the ad hoc nature of local administration. Beginning in 1919, the Gabonese government followed the directives of Minister of Colonies Albert Sarraut to focus on economic development.[98] Timber exports, interrupted by the war, offered administrators a path to increased revenue and stability.

Okoumé trees furnished the raw material that private enterprises exported to buyers in Germany, Holland, and France, where European firms processed the lumber into plywood.[99] The French government supported French businessmen willing to stake a claim by offering access to the forest and by coercing men from throughout the colony to serve as manpower in coastal timber mills. Formidable companies like the Consortium des Grands Réseaux Français based on the south bank of the Gabon Estuary employed thousands of migrants. Individual entrepreneurs and firms vied for land, labor, and food needed to support their staff. The high concentration of workers in areas occupied by scattered and tiny Fang villages led to conflict and hardship.

Townspeople in Libreville also had to adjust to the new climate. Not many Mpongwe men could afford the fees officials set for *okoumé* export, but a few became rich.[100] Most others could only ride the coattails of the booming economy by working as clerks, interpreters, and accountants. Libreville people, though enjoying some prosperity, acted forcibly in the first half of the 1920s to challenge discrimination and the denial of older Atlantic notions of equal African and European partnerships. Their skill in forming alliances with Europeans continued to make its presence felt. Townspeople established a Libreville chapter of the League of the Rights of Man, and its members sent a barrage of letters and telegrams to French metropolitan members of parliament and the minister of colonies to protest the arbitrary nature of colonial government.[101] Women also battled the colonial state for reforms, as described in chapter 4. In turn, officials and Libreville men and women negotiated with one another over marriage laws and practices.[102]

Other political changes took place in the rural Estuary. Taking a page from

French West Africa, the governor of Gabon appointed Fang chiefs.[103] A host of clans lived in separate villages within a small amount of territory, but no one from one clan could govern the domain of another clan until the government intervened. The crushing burdens of the World War I era left Fang villages too weak to take up arms against colonial military might. Some chiefs manipulated bridewealth practices and their access to state funding to enrich themselves.[104] New political leaders, like the young Léon Mba, redefined chieftaincy to include European bureaucratic models and to incorporate new components like the establishment of bwiti syncretic religious movements.[105] However, other Fang villagers lost out with state reforms. State troops could more effectively quell unrest, imprison rural people, and drag men and women into forced labor details in the 1920s.

Options changed for both men and women in the timber era. Some Fang women went to Libreville to escape husbands and male family members.[106] Profits from food sales and work for Europeans may also have made bridewealth more expensive, as missionaries alleged.[107] Men could no longer obtain wives and dependents through raids on other clans, which meant that the exchange of cash as bridewealth became the only avenue to have a formal marriage. Fang men tried to restrict women's options for leaving arranged marriages as wives turned to colonial legal institutions, chiefs, and guards to widen their range of choices.[108] Anthropologist John Cinnamon has postulated a similar remaking of bridewealth payments based on the radical transformation of the economy in northeast Gabon.[109]

Timber and the war expanded the links between the Gabon Estuary and the rest of the colony, even if the colonial administration did little to build roads to further this development. Southern Gabonese communities, derisively dubbed bilop by the Fang of the Estuary, moved into timber camps along with northern Fang. They had trouble bargaining with French state and private interests since they lived far from their homes without access to local kin networks. Fang Estuary people escaped the brutal exploitation of these migrants in dangerous working conditions, slowly gravitating toward Libreville. Estuary Fang began to consider Libreville an attractive destination, and by the late 1940s they outnumbered Mpongwe communities in the city.[110]

With the Great Depression disrupting German markets in 1929 and 1930, the timber industry ground to a halt. However, the temporary collapse of the lumber industry came after two decades of dramatic events of town and rural society in the Gabon Estuary. World War I and the famine years of the 1920s had broken the independence of Fang communities in the Gabon Estuary. Libreville townspeople also suffered setbacks with the end of the old trading economy and the rise of timber. The strengthened capability of the colonial state to survey and control the movement of urban and rural people set the stage for the expansion of Libreville's size and links with the rest of Gabon in the last three decades of French occupation.

Libreville and Late Colonialism, 1930–1960

Compared to the trauma of earlier decades, Libreville seemed to be a calm, well-ordered town during the final years of French empire in Africa, even as its population rose from 6,500 in the mid-1930s to over 20,000 at independence in 1960.[111] The Depression brought some social tensions to the fore, especially with the troubled state of the timber business, but these conflicts did not bring on the fierce labor and political tensions found in larger African cities.[112] Burgeoning metropolises such as Lagos or Dakar dwarfed the Gabonese capital's tiny population, but Libreville underwent transformations as well. The lure of schools brought young people to the capital. Rural Fang communities recovered from the onslaughts they had endured, but the limited economic and political options available outside of the city made a Libreville a common destination.

More outsiders also lived in Libreville. New trading and fishing diasporas made up of West Africans made the port their home (see chapter 3). Hausa merchants from Cameroon peddled goods in the Gabon Estuary and in Libreville. Southern Gabonese workers originally toiling in the timber camps took part in Libreville's expansion. The Great Depression led timber workers without employment to move to Libreville, much to the annoyance of administrators seeking to expel them back to rural areas. Even when the timber camps flowered again in the late 1940s and 1950s, men like Gabriel Mabenga chose to live in town.[113] A member of an Nzebi clan from southern Gabon, he walked in 1959 to Kango and then Libreville after hearing "they killed people" at the timber camps.

Others made a living from trade. Female West African merchants sold cloth and odds and ends in the town's main market, while Fang women established food markets in outlying neighborhoods like Nkembo.[114] Mpongwe women claimed property rights and rented out houses to Africans and Europeans alike. Though Mpongwe and Fang men sat on "customary" African courts, some women did find recourse to the law to end marriages and to defend their rights. As in other African cities, urban life in Libreville posed challenges but also opportunities not found in rural areas.

Europeans seeking to boost their finances came to Libreville as well. Increased metropolitan state funding and the rebirth of the timber industry after World War II more than doubled the European population of Gabon. This generation of arrivals often drew from older notions of Gabonese identity that at least made a pretense of transcending racial differences. French aviator Jean-Claude Brouillet described Libreville town life as a place where white settlers in the timber trade and African townspeople were part of one harmonious community, even if some clubs and restaurants did not admit black men.[115] Despite these prejudices, African politicians like Léon Mba openly welcomed the support of white townspeople.[116] Mba's willingness to form alliances was part of the distinct Libreville urban political culture that had existed for decades.

Mba's career as a clerk with ambition—he worked as the head manager of the English John Holt store in the early 1950s before being elected mayor of Libreville in 1956—reflected the conservative nature of townspeople's aspirations. Estuary Fang and Mpongwe households, already well established in Libreville, continued to follow older paths of social advancement. Gradually, affluent Libreville people gained more political rights. After the early chaos of World War II, when governor of Gabon Georges Masson rallied to Vichy and unsuccessfully resisted an invasion of Free French forces in 1940, townspeople began to make their voices heard through forming small political parties.[117] African politicians took advantage of reforms under the Fourth Republic with the formation of a territorial assembly and limited representation in the French parliament.

The capital, not surprisingly, was the center of political intrigue in the colony. Libreville politics became a struggle between Mpongwe elites—Mba's Bloc Démocratique Gabonais (BDG) party—and the more confrontational Union Sociale et Démocratique Gabonaise (USDG) party led by Jean-Hilaire Aubame between the late 1940s and 1960.[118] Mba won the open support of the colonial administration; despite his exile to Ubangi-Shari for embezzlement from 1932 to 1946, administrators preferred the wily Fang leader to the USDG. Mba served as mayor of Libreville and vice president of Gabon from 1956 through independence in 1960. Mpongwe and French colons rallied to Mba in Libreville, in part because he presented himself as someone who rejected ethnic and racial politics.

Besides being the seat of power, Libreville offered social services and facilities that did not exist in much of the countryside.[119] Electricity and refrigeration were within the grasp of well-off Libreville residents. The town contained the highest number of schools in the entire colony. Drivers sped on paved roads, and airplanes flew to Europe, African cities, and to other parts of Gabon. Through their personal connections and their privileged access to education, town residents could also obtain social relief from the colonial government.[120]

Though Libreville enjoyed the benefits of urbanization common to other African capitals, it remained a difficult place to reach from the countryside. The government's plans to integrate the capital with the rest of the colony sputtered until the 1960s. Road construction plans in the Gabon Estuary commenced in earnest in the mid-1930s, but right up until independence travel by truck on poorly maintained roads between Libreville and rural centers still took days.[121] No road capable of year-round travel connected Libreville with the Cameroonian border until the early 1970s. Planes and boats remained the only ways to travel between the capital and Port-Gentil, the second largest city in Gabon. Tax revenue from Gabon was often used to pay for less solvent colonies in French Equatorial Africa, to the point Léon Mba and other Gabonese politicians did not support talk of creating a united independent state out of French colonies in Central Africa.[122]

Libreville was thus in some ways a typical small late colonial African city, yet it retained some unique qualities. It kept elements of its Atlantic past, from wooden plank homes typical of the late nineteenth-century construction to its anarchic organization that defied physical racial segregation. The port could not rival such giants as Lagos or even Brazzaville, but Libreville boasted a rich blend of communities from all over Gabon and other parts of the continent. Unlike most cities, Libreville still remained isolated from much of the countryside to the end of the colonial era.

A Food Supply Digestif

Within the narrative of Libreville history, food consumption and production barely appear, save in the era of adversity between 1914 and 1930. What does emerge is a set of themes familiar to African and imperial historians: the rise and fall of the Atlantic slave trade; the unsteady movement from slave exports to "legitimate" trade; European colonial occupation; urbanization and changing relationships on gender and rural-urban lines; and the rise of African political opposition to colonial policy. Only in times of crisis does food supply come into view as a serious and controversial issue. This lack of interest in how city dwellers fed themselves and acted as consumers is commonplace in African history. There is a special irony in this, since historians of Africa have gone to great lengths to examine how urban communities in cities like Libreville worked to better their own lives and to form the contours of mundane struggles against state authorities and European companies. Hardly any studies of African urban life use food consumption and supply to test out how these standard themes of colonial African histories took shape in a vital aspect of everyday life: eating. I concur wholeheartedly with Elias Mandala's recent assertion that food consumption and production, often understood by ordinary people as a cyclical and seasonal phenomenon rather than as part of linear narratives of history, poses difficulties for African historians.[123] To follow up on his provocative review of African food studies, I argue that food was not at all a tangential issue for Libreville residents and farmers in the Gabon Estuary countryside, even if historians rarely consider how central a concern food is for city dwellers.

The rest of this volume explores how food supply and consumption illuminate tensions, alliances, and the diverse consequences of changing ties between the global and the local in colonial Libreville. Whether in times of crisis or plenty, the availability, quality, and cost of food captured the attention of townspeople, just as it does in Western Europe and North America. Food exchanges and the incorporation of foreign foods and eating styles were important elements in the development of Atlantic commerce. The single issue that incited the most active protest movement in the entire history of French Libreville was state interference in the food market. The development of private industry and a money economy also shaped diets, and the unsteady integration of the city with the rest of Gabon could be tracked by how and from where people brought food to the city.

Townspeople thought of eating as a vital necessity, even though scholars of Gabon and of urban Africa generally have not spent much time addressing sustenance. Rather, the fact that food is so rarely mentioned in urban histories of Africa means that scholars have missed out on a central concern of townspeople as consumers, farmers, traders, employers, and fishermen. Against the backdrop of the preceding sketch of major events, the present study examines how urban people ate, from whom they obtained their nourishment, and how a separate Libreville set of lifestyles emerged. With the table set, so to speak, now we can move on to the first course: eating and Atlantic commerce in the age of slavery.

2. Eating in an African Atlantic Town, 1840–1885

Soon after arriving in the Gabon Estuary to set up a Protestant mission in 1842, American pastor John L. Wilson went to work. He took a canoe from Libreville to spread the Gospel at Mpongwe leader Rapontchombo's home village across the Estuary. The Asiga clan chief was a man of means. When his boat touched shore, Wilson was in for a surprise. Rapontchombo knew how to throw a dinner party. Slaves announced lunch at eleven o'clock sharp—a sight that may have reminded Wilson of his own table in America, since slaves manned the kitchen at his South Carolina family home.[1] They brought out four different meats on plates. Two bottles of French wine came to table. After the main course Rapontchombo offered Wilson cordials and cigars.[2] Male sociability crossed the lines of race and language.

The decorum surrounding this meal may have been unexpected for Wilson, but it was part and parcel of eating and commerce for a Mpongwe trader in Atlantic commerce. Centuries of passing traders had left behind forks, plates, and etiquette. Orange trees around Mpongwe villages testified to the coming of Portuguese visitors centuries before Wilson met Rapontchombo. The unfree hands that served food to Wilson visibly displayed Rapontchombo's power of to command bodies as well as tastes. Out of Wilson's sight, slaves and free women dug manioc plants from the ground, weeded gardens, and pounded manioc roots into porridge to be served at their masters' homes.

However, Wilson knew why Rapontchombo could afford such expensive fare. On the same day the minister visited a slave pen in the chief's village run by a Spanish trader, where 432 slaves sat on logs when Wilson arrived. Chains locked all adult men pairs in pairs. A group of about fifty women had been imprisoned together. The pastor walked through the unfortunate crowd without one slave saying a word. Perhaps their silence came from prudence, as the Spanish merchant had gunned down a rebel slave only days before Wilson's impromptu inspection. Soon afterward, Wilson's colleague William Walker watched as slave owners jeered at a slave child left to die exposed on the shore, and in traveling out of town he met old slaves dying of hunger.[3]

Mpongwe townspeople constructed ways of eating and ideas about consumption during the age of Atlantic slavery. These practices withstood the end of slave exports in the nineteenth century. Free people often purchased food rather than producing it. Europeans and Americans were disgusted to find Africans buying food rather than tilling the land—an odd criticism, since most foreign residents of Libreville showed little interest in performing agriculture themselves. The manner in which Mpongwe people ate expressed volumes on how rooted domestic slavery had become in their society. Where Mpongwe people saw labor-saving techniques and hospitality, missionaries and administrators saw degeneration. For a people deemed incorrigibly lazy by so many observers, Mpongwe people constructed a food supply system that, even with some serious drawbacks, remained in place until the arrival of Fang migrants in the Gabon Estuary by the 1880s.

How Mpongwe people obtained food in the nineteenth century and the ways in which slavery influenced consumption patterns can be reconstructed from a foundation of missionary reports, official correspondence, accounts by travelers, and oral traditions. Such sources offer insights into the farming, fishing, and trading practices when Europeans and Americans arrived in the region, how domestic slavery and gendered economic options affected food, and the conflicting ways in which European and Americans understood Mpongwe tastes and eating habits.

Choosing Local Foods

By the 1840s two crops furnished the starchy mainstays of Mpongwe cooking: manioc and plantains. Atlantic commerce brought manioc to the region. Originally found in various forest regions of South America, manioc is a tuber crop that flourishes in lowland tropical regions.[4] Able to grow in relatively poor soils and survive periods of variable rainfall, manioc had long been a major staple in much of Brazil. Portuguese colonists in Angola introduced the crop to provision ships bearing African slaves to the Americas.[5]

Manioc has several advantages greatly prized by Central African peoples even though it is a very labor-intensive crop to prepare and to cultivate. Since the tuber is left in the ground until it is needed, it can survive longer and is less vulnerable to theft than bananas.[6] Its initial planting can be undertaken at most times of the year and produces a full crop twelve to eighteen months later.[7] Although very perishable as a tuber once removed from the soil, it can survive in the ground for up to two years. Once the tuber is soaked for roughly a week to eliminate cyanide, it is normally left to dry in the sun, placed over a fire to bake, and then pounded into a long baton.[8] These tasks required a great deal of time and effort.

Manioc slowly spread to the Gabon Estuary. Linguistic evidence suggests that by the seventeenth century the Lunda state located several hundred kilometers from the coast had adopted manioc cultivation.[9] The introduction of manioc may have come with the region's trade ties to the kingdom of Loango, where manioc was grown by the early seventeenth century.[10] Another source may have been traders from São Tomé.[11] Mpongwe clearly associated the crop with the Portuguese; they dubbed one variety of manioc putu (meaning Portuguese).[12]

Manioc is versatile as an ingredient in dishes. It can be roasted into flour, known as farigna in Omyere (derived from Portuguese) and able to last several months.[13] Mpongwe did not prepare manioc in this fashion; they had to rely on Orungu coastal communities living on the Ogooué Delta farther south for this durable food. Besides the root, the leaves can be pounded in a mortar and served as a sauce.[14] In a fashion similar to uses of bananas and plantains, Mpongwe and other residents of the Gabon Estuary used parts of manioc as remedies against skin maladies.[15]

Of course, slavery did not determine every aspect of Mpongwe diets. Several foods introduced from other parts of the world furnished the main staples of Mpongwe households. Bananas became a major source of carbohydrates throughout Central Africa.[16] These plants, originally from Asia, had diffused in a series of long-distance interactions from northeastern Africa.[17] Some scholars estimate that bananas had arrived in Gabon by the end of the first millennium AD.[18] Bananas and plantains were fairly easy to grow even in the sandy soils of the Estuary. They do not require the burning of fields, can survive in the dry season, and can easily be planted by moving small plants.[19]

Gabonese had an array of uses for the plant. Banana leaves have long been a main form of wrapping food.[20] The versatility of the leaves is astounding. People used them to cover pots, wove them into nets, and made rope comes from the fibers.[21] Placed on cuts, leaves serve to bandage wounds. Cures for various symptoms from toothaches to dysentery could be made from parts of banana plants. Villagers prepared and consumed bananas and plantains in many ways: mashed into a purée, steamed in a pot, dried in the sun, fried in oil, or simply served raw. Most households had at least one banana tree near the house fertilized by human waste and garbage.[22]

Certain types of bananas and the ways they were prepared also held supernatural meaning for Gabon Estuary people. Families planted some kinds of bananas in a grove designed to protect villages from harm.[23] Brothers and sisters were prevented from eating particular types of plantains together, while women were warned to avoid other varieties.[24] Ties between sorcery and bananas are hardly distinctive to the Gabon Estuary.[25] Members of bwiti religious movements throughout Gabon revere some varieties of bananas as sacred plants.[26]

Besides manioc and plantains, other ingredients had long been part of local meals. Yams and taro were occasionally cultivated, but they were rare dishes. The coastal Gabonese forest is rich in wild fruits.[27] Resembling a small violet egg, the atanga fruit has a salty flavor. Roundish scarlet mvut fruit packs a mouth-watering sour core. So many different species of fruit flourish in the forest that anthropologists have rightly noted that hunter-gathering strategies in Gabon may have been more logical than coping with the problems facing local farming. Squash, beans, okra, and greens served as condiments or as the foundation for sauces mixed with palm oil.[28] Odika sauce made from crushed and grilled mango seeds accompanied some meals, while nyembwe sauce was made of palm nuts.[29]

Estuary peoples consumed a number of other foods from abroad besides manioc and plantains. Societies on the West African coast adopted European, Asian, and South American plants into their diets.[30] Lemons came from European contact or perhaps with escaped slaves from São Tomé.[31] Orange and papaya trees, apparently brought in by Portuguese or other European Atlantic visitors, also grew close to Mpongwe settlements. Cayenne pepper came from America by way of Europeans.[32]

Gabon Estuary people did not live on vegetables and fruit alone. From early times the ancestors of the Mpongwe took to the sea and rivers in search of fish. Men specialized in fishing. Like other Central African trading peoples, Mpongwe men may have entered trade through their travels in search of fish.[33] The sardine remains the centerpiece of many Mpongwe household meals. Men caught larger fish with small nets or barbed spears. Women, particularly at night, dammed up small streams, set nets, and used poisonous herbs to kill fish.[34] To this day older members of Mpongwe families admit their fondness for fish over beef or other meats.[35]

Smaller nearby communities in the Estuary also developed a notable tradition of fishing. The Benga, related by language and culture to coastal groups around the Rio Muni river over a hundred kilometers north of the Estuary, settled on Cap Esterias northwest of Libreville.[36] Deep sea fishing became one of their specialties. They were joined by the Séké—a group of fishing and forest specialists living in scattered villages in the rural Estuary region. Another dispersed group of hunting and foraging people, the Akele, made a living killing game and capturing sardines and other fish in the Estuary.

All groups also hunted game in the region, but even so, meat was not consumed as commonly as fish. French officials noted with displeasure how scarce bush meat was in Libreville. Reasons for its absence are unclear. Perhaps the decision of Mpongwe families to concern themselves with trade, fishing, and farming made hunting more of a domain for forest specialists like the Séké. Overhunting does not seem to have been a problem; elephants regularly ripped apart Estuary fields in the 1840s. Wild game did not constitute the only source of meat, but the other option was not especially tempting, at least to foreigners. Gaunt chickens strutted about Mpongwe villages. Mpongwe people did not keep other livestock, as cattle and sheep could not survive sleeping sickness and other ailments.

Did the wide range of foods provide a reasonable diet? The nutritional content of precolonial Gabonese diets is hard to gauge. Nutritional surveys conducted in northern and central Gabon during the early 1960s suggest that most people received sufficient calories and vitamins save for deficiencies in vitamin B2, but it is hard to judge how what they ate corresponds to mid-nineteenth century diets.[37] The findings of the survey indicate that malnutrition was not a serious problem. Admittedly, as Diana Wylie has shown in South Africa, European ideas surrounding nutrition are culture-bound concepts, but from the scattered information available, it appears that precolonial diets did furnish many vitamins necessary for Gabonese survival.[38]

The links Mpongwe settlements had to local and international trade networks thus set the contours for eating in the mid-nineteenth century. Villagers in the Gabon Estuary adopted a range of cooking ingredients. Mpongwe homes differed from those of other Gabonese societies not in the composition of their meals but rather in who prepared and farmed the ingredients. Like coastal peoples in West Africa but in marked contrast to peoples such as the Fang, Mpongwe villages relied on slaves for farming. Culinary practices rested on the foundation of slave labor and social stratification.

Domestic Slavery in Mpongwe Towns, 1840–1865

Atlantic slavery radically altered eating habits through the lands it touched. Imagine Louisiana cuisine without gumbo, South Carolina without rice, or English and French kitchens bereft of sugar. Historians examining the slave trade have done a much better job of exploring how foods from Africa became standard fare through much of the Americas than of looking at innovations in tastes and eating habits in African regions deeply involved in Atlantic commerce.[39] Yet the literature does uncover some elements of culinary shifts in Atlantic Africa in the slave trade era that altered what entered the mouths of local people. The sumptuous locally made French bread, Madeira wines, and European dinnerware that French visitors used during their visit to the Slave Coast port of Whydah in 1731 illustrate Atlantic African culinary innovations, but all too often these references to eating changes have not been seriously examined.[40]

One area in which African historians have begun to probe the effects of plantation slavery on foodways is agriculture. Pier Larson, a historian of Madagascar, suggests that a rise in exports of male captives to Indian Ocean island plantations led to the feminization of rice agriculture.[41] In contrast, Walter Hawthorne's work explores the masculinization of rice farming and alterations in farming techniques as consequences of heightened slave raiding on the Guinea-Bissau coast.[42] Few others have taken forays into Atlantic African culinary history. Besides its impacts on farming, Africanists have not paid much attention how servitude abetted the development of food consumption patterns. Everyday practices related to eating and the social meanings they embody and perform, as in the case of divination in Sierra Leone as discussed by anthropologist

Rosalind Shaw, furnish a partial glimpse of the ways in which slavery became embedded in daily life.[43]

It is hard to determine changes in food production before the nineteenth century, but by the 1840s domestic slavery revolved around farming. By the early nineteenth century leading clan members left domestic chores such as farming and cooking to slaves.[44] Slaves and offspring of mixed free-slave marriages grew food with free wives in outlying fields. Most slaves of free people did not live with their masters. Instead they lived in the ompindi—houses close to fields, well away from the homes of free people close to the Estuary shore. Townspeople cultivated small gardens, growing banana trees and vegetables, but the bulk of manioc and plantains were cultivated far from villages.[45] On the ompindi, much as in slave quarters on plantations in the American South, slaves lived with relatively little interference from masters.[46] Seasons dictated the tasks slaves had to perform. During the annual dry season between May and August, some free men and women joined their slaves to prepare fields for the fall rainy season; others joined their chattel during harvest time between February and April, to the point that they did not return to their homes for weeks at a stretch.[47]

Gender and social status influenced how people participated in agriculture. Some women worked alongside or supervised their slaves and dragged their daughters out with them.[48] A mature woman in the 1890s reminisced about her childhood to Protestant missionary Robert Nassau. She recalled collecting firewood with other children and carrying water to her mother and adult slaves. Her mother wore cloths around her feet to protect herself as she hacked brush away with a machete.[49] Older or less well-off female residents of Libreville were more likely to take up farming. Missionaries disliked this state of affairs. American missionary Jane Preston watched Mpongwe free and slave women troop off to the fields each morning and wrote: "Groups of poor women would pass, with heavy laden baskets upon their backs, supported by a strap passing around their forehead. They walked with a long staff to support themselves. They had been working all day on the plantations and were coming home with food. They had to cook for their husbands and sons [and could] not eat for themselves until they had finished."[50]

This dour opinion ignored the ability of some women of youth or means not to farm. Since some free women owned their own homes, could divorce their husbands, and kept much of their produce themselves, it would be a mistake to view them merely as victims.[51] Younger women, able to find African and European suitors as Europeans sought out mistresses, often stayed in town.[52] Famed explorer Richard Burton observed in 1862 that "the [Mpongwe] 'ladies' also refuse to work at the plantations, esp. when young and pretty, leaving them to the bush-folk [slaves], male and female."[53] The wealth of individual households could determine whether free women had to work. Wealthy Agakaza and Asiga clan members might own tens or even hundreds of slaves, but the ordinary household would own only a handful and so would need to provide their own labor to help their slaves.[54]

A distinctive feature of Mpongwe masculinity was the absence of men from farming. Unlike fishing—considered an acceptable activity by free men, as attested to by the fact that Mpongwe fishermen sold missionaries fish in return for brandy—tilling the soil was snubbed by free men.[55] Europeans and Americans leveled a barrage of criticism at Mpongwe male reluctance to enter fields. An American trader expressed a common view when he opined, "The men, as in all uncivilized countries, despise agriculture."[56] Culinary labor was women's work. Women gave birth, cooked, and farmed—or so their husbands hoped. "The men consider it degrading to till the soil; that is employment for women, slaves and white people," missionary Jane Preston complained after living in Libreville in the 1850s and 1860s.[57] British explorer Richard Burton, during his 1862 stay in the town, decried the refusal of Mpongwe men and well-off Mpongwe women to work in fields.[58] Young men saw farming as an affront to respectability. Catholic missionary Maurice Briault recalled in the 1890s punishing a young Mpongwe student at the Catholic school with work in the fields for having hidden some food in a workshop. The pupil begged his teacher not to send him off to work. He pleaded, "Father, anything that you want but that. I am a child of the Mpongwes and among us only slaves do that work. Father, listen to me. If a young girl of my village finds out, I will never be able to get married."[59] Instead of celebrating violence, Mpongwe men showed off their leisure time as well as their familiarity with foreign dress and taste.

Free men made sure to distance themselves from the majority of slaves and lower-class people in town. Masters and favored slaves in other regions, like Chikunda slave soldiers of southeastern Africa, shrugged off farming.[60] A Mande from a wealthy family enslaved and brought to Maryland in the 1730s later recalled his difficulty adjusting to hard field labor that he had never performed in Africa.[61] For Mpongwe men farming detracted from the leisure that dependents provided. They also had more profitable activities to attend to. Male Mpongwe spent much of their time moving into the interior to obtain slaves and valuable exports like ivory. Jean-Rémy Bessieux, the first Catholic Bishop of Libreville, noted soon after his arrival in Gabon in 1842: "It is easy to understand why a people of traders who have nothing themselves to trade are always moving."[62] Roland Pourtier has noted that Gabonese men involved in hunting, fishing, and trading required mobility, which limited their ability to maintain fields.[63]

Once they had food, Mpongwe households did not all eat in the same way. Less wealthy free Mpongwe, people of low social status, and slaves ate the same dishes as wealthy people in smaller amounts.[64] They used leaves as plates.[65] Earthenware, calabashes, and shells served as glasses. Though many people used wooden spoons and forks, hands rather than utensils appear to have remained the norm. Among Mpongwe villagers men generally ate in separate buildings from women. Food was cooked in women's quarters known in the Omyene language as kisini (derived from the English word kitchen). Thus gender identity and the sexual division of domestic labor were clearly marked in local food production, preparation, and consumption.

Higher on the social scale eating styles had a different flavor. Free Mpongwe households obtained iron kettles, knives, spoons, and other metal utensils useful for cooking.[66] According to oral traditions collected in the 1930s, a mixed payment of goods exchanged for one slave included brass basins used to prepare manioc.[67] One missionary stationed in Libreville in the 1840s recalled that the Mpongwe "take their meals at table, and use knives and forks as gracefully and naturally as any other people in the world. Some of the wealthier men spread tables that would be inviting to any one, and not infrequently have a variety of French wines to offer their guests at the same time."[68]

Free men and women relied on slaves and wives to bring them food and expected these people to prepare meals for them on occasion. Slaves in the fields brought their produce to the families of their owners, while others carried baskets of manioc along with other goods for their masters.[69] When Franco-American trader Paul Du Chaillu visited a free daughter of Mpongwe clan leader Dénis, she had slaves prepare plantains for him.[70] Women were expected to serve older men before taking their own turn to eat.[71] Meals and food production thus exemplified the power of masters over slaves and of married men over female family members.

However free people may have presented their authority over their slaves in the matter of meals, they recognized how vulnerable their dependence on slave labor made them. Between 1840 and 1870 rumors ran rampant regarding malicious slaves scheming to kill masters. Free people blamed slaves for calamities. In 1847 inhabitants of a Mpongwe village panicked after elephants trampled their crops. Some blamed wily slaves who had used arcane means to transform themselves into elephants.[72] William Walker recorded a slave servant's execution in the same year. Free people killed the victim on the grounds that he had slipped poison into drinking water.[73]

In Mpongwe culture eating was a practice that made one susceptible to harm. Members of individual clans were not allowed to eat certain foods.[74] Prohibitions were also imposed for health reasons. Pregnant women were prevented from eating particular foods—sometimes for reasons that women preparing to have children did not want to tell their husbands.[75] Some of these taboos came from rituals that individuals went through as children to obtain protection from spirits.[76] Fang people also had a list of taboos (bétchi or béki) that denoted age, gender, clan, and generational identities; only older men were allowed to eat some animals, and pubescent boys could eat só meat (a type of red antelope) only after submitting to a series of ceremonies designed to test their bravery and endurance.[77] Children who underwent healing rituals were sometimes warned to stay away from certain foods, while pregnant women were told to avoid eating snakes, turtles, and other animals to ward off birth defects.[78] Swallowing food among the Mpongwe could open the body to supernatural forces; some spiritual practitioners were said to create concoctions like the ntchwe-mbezo, which allowed women to seduce men.[79] Finally, eating was a metaphor of power and mystical harm; witches with evil inyemba spirits living in their organs could eat the souls of hapless victims.[80]

With large numbers of slaves growing and cooking much of their food, on occasion free households displayed fear of their dependents. Europeans in the nineteenth century referred to such concerns as "poison." People in the Gabon Estuary had access to botanical knowledge that included powerful toxins. As noted, poisonous herbs were used to kill fish.[81] André Raponda Walker and Roger Sillans gave a list of more than thirty toxic plants in their weighty ethnobotanical work Plantes utiles du Gabon.[82] Poison could be administered via food, by small sticks or spines smeared with deadly concoctions, through the nose, or by skin contact.[83] In the late nineteenth century Mpongwe women boasted to American missionary Robert Nassau that they controlled men by placing love medicine in their suitors' meals.[84]

Mpongwe people in the nineteenth century made no distinction between death through intangible supernatural forces and through scientifically verifiable poisons.[85] For those unfamiliar with Central Africa, perhaps imagining devious assassins placing deadly toxins in glasses as in Renaissance Italy, it must be remembered that poison cannot be separated from supernatural concerns. In Omyene the same word describes sorcerers and those using poison.[86] Death in the Gabon Estuary was seen as an unnatural event caused by the malevolence of others. William Walker remarked with characteristic cynicism: "Long ago, the Mpongwes killed Mpongwes for inyemba [sorcery]. Now it is only the slaves. A Mpongwe can bribe a slave to do it. But the Mpongwe escapes and the slave suffers in trial for inyemba."[87] Masters voiced their distrust of their slaves in the Estuary. "Poisoning is so prevalent in ordinary deaths that when a M'Pongue of a certain importance dies, poisoning by relatives or enemies is always the first thing suspected," a French officer wrote in 1856.[88]

Supernatural beliefs in Gabon on "poison" are similar to those of other Central African communities. While Europeans labeled these attitudes "witchcraft" or "magic," Africanist scholars have long acknowledged the diversity of ideas obscured by outsider generalizations.[89] In societies without a centralized political hierarchy and fraught with divisions over status, as in the forest communities of Cameroon and Gabon, witchcraft accusations thrived as no single authority could furnish protection from supernatural threats.[90] Poison accusations recorded in the nineteenth century reveal how the rise of a slave population increased the anxieties of free people.

While sources by European officers and missionaries do not permit any reliable way to understand "actual" cases of poison, they did capture the atmosphere of dread and hidden threats within coastal African communities involved in the Atlantic slave trade. Free men and women often denounced slaves for poisoning and/or supernatural means of harming others.[91] Catholic missionaries lamented how commonly slaves faced punishment for supposedly poisoning masters.[92] "Poisonings are almost always attributed to slaves," Bishop of Libreville Pierre-Marie Le Berre wrote in 1873, "with a desire of vengeance that one would naturally expect."[93] These fears articulate terrors surrounding slaves and their close proximity to masters; it is impossible to say if slaves did kill their owners through occult means, but they certainly scared free people.

Even in good times, slave labor had troubles feeding the entire population, forcing Mpongwe to purchase foodstuffs from neighboring groups. Akele, Séké, and Benga hunters and fishermen, dispersed widely but thinly from the Rio Muni delta through various parts of the Estuary, regularly sold their wares at Mpongwe towns.[94] Organized along roughly the same lines as in Mpongwe villages, Séké agricultural work and fishing impressed colonial officials.[95] After William Walker disparaged Mpongwe agriculture, he added that "the Gaboon people [Mpongwe] depend a great deal on trade and buy a part of their provisions from the Bush people [Séké]."[96] In the 1870s Séké women continued to sell manioc to Libreville residents.[97] Older informants also recalled that Benga and Akele fishermen had long traded fish in Mpongwe towns.[98]

Conflicts often cut off Mpongwe clients from neighboring suppliers. In 1843 skirmishes ensued after the death of some Séké wives living in Mpongwe villages.[99] More often, commercial alliances incited warfare. Mpongwe men often sold pawns taken to ensure trade contracts or refused to honor deals made for ivory collected by Séké hunters.[100] During times of war, famine struck. Visiting one Mpongwe town in the Gabon Estuary, an American missionary noted: "Started this morning for King George's and arrived in good season. But found the people in a state of starvation. The elephants, they say, are eating all of their plantations and the people have so many palavers with the bushmen [Séké] that they cannot buy."[101] Fighting cut off Libreville from food in 1857 to the point that missionaries had to search more than a hundred miles away for food.[102] Short-lived wars between Séké and Mpongwe continued until at least the late 1860s.[103]

The risks that free people took in depending on servile labor for food production became apparent in the 1860s. During a fierce smallpox epidemic from 1863 to 1865, fears reached a fever pitch. The disease began its rampage after a passing Portuguese ship brought it to town. Smallpox ravaged Libreville.[104] Slave communities, hit particularly hard by the disease, had great difficulty working the fields.[105] Free people and clan chiefs, convinced that their relatives were being killed by servants through sorcery, executed a series of slaves.[106] An outbreak of dysentery killed many townspeople as well.[107] Harvests consequently diminished in size. By the spring of 1865 famine scoured the town.[108] When rains came unexpectedly during the dry season between May and August of the following year, starvation set in until 1870.[109]

Such insecurity indicates that Mpongwe people could not feed themselves

adequately without buying from other groups. The point is even more stark-
ly made in Mpongwe-Orungu trade ties. Orungu communities on the Ogooué
River delta, occupying the same middleman role as the Mpongwe, had grown
wealthy from Atlantic commerce.[110] Some Orungu regularly brought prepared
foods to Libreville.[111] Their large canoes equipped with sails allowed them to
make the trip to Libreville in a day.[112] One commentator noted in 1855: "Manioc
flour is [the Mpongwe's] last resort; they buy it from the [Orungu] when there
is famine, which is to say every year."[113] Manioc flour was an Orungu specialty
that Estuary peoples do not seem to have mastered. As the flour can last for
several months, it was highly prized.

Thus by the 1840s the peoples of the Estuary had problems with food supply.
Regardless of their previous experience, Mpongwe villages on the present site
of Libreville battled food shortages in the mid-nineteenth century. Missionaries
and officials recorded several famines in the 1850s.[114] The scant descriptions
of these famines give little information on their causes. It is unclear whether
the arrival of Europeans undermined a formerly successful food supply network or if the region had long suffered from bouts of scarcity. However, the
dominance of trade in Mpongwe society at the onset of colonial rule placed the
food supply of townspeople at risk. Such difficulties suggest possible problems
within slave agriculture. Did slaves withhold food or sabotage efforts to work
on their masters' fields? Were environmental factors or structural problems
inherent in local farming practices behind the shortages? Again the dearth of
sources makes definitive answers to these questions impossible. It is evident,
however, that Mpongwe agriculture suffered from serious problems derived
in part from Atlantic commerce.

The shortages suggest that the Estuary had entered an intermediate period
in forms of poverty and hunger. Historian John Iliffe has characterized African
poverty in several categories.[115] The first, conjunctional poverty, describes how
crises such as wars brought famine to communities.[116] Structural poverty and
famines, for Iliffe, came about in societies with ample land, such as in the
Gabon Estuary, due to a lack of labor or regular periods of drought. Within
many premodern societies, structural famines caused by climatic conditions
led to cycles of plenty with hunger between harvests.[117]

The most serious form of hunger in Mpongwe villages did not come from
structural problems, however. Masters used hunger as a weapon. Slaves might
be referred to as younger relatives by free people. Briault wrote: "When you ask

the identity of an old Nzebi [slave] of the Glass plains or a somewhat mixed Pygmy of Quaben, the poor devil will tell you he is the son of Aleka, Rambé, or Rakongola [common Mpongwe names], even though in age he appears to be the father of these individuals who are in reality their masters."[118] But the idiom of kinship did not lead to generosity toward old or sick captives. Catholic and Protestant missionaries often made the grisly discovery of elderly slaves left to starve to death in wooded areas away from villages.[119] Not surprisingly, slaves fared worse than free people as they together endured the smallpox outbreak.[120]

At least on the Gabon Estuary, food production and consumption rested on the unstable foundation of domestic slavery. It does not appear to have worked well in providing food on a regular basis. Atlantic slavery and the imported goods Mpongwe traders received in return for human cargo furthered Mpongwe commerce with neighboring peoples, allowing them to purchase rather than produce their sustenance. However, this style of consumption placed Mpongwe villages at risk of starvation if they could not trade. Once masters started losing control over their slaves, this already precarious network of supply and production ran into further troubles.

Economic Options and Culinary Changes

Libreville has a decidedly ironic name. French naval officers planned to make their Gabon Estuary base into a supply center for antislaving patrols and a means of stopping exports of slaves from the region to Brazil, Cuba, and São Tomé. The fort did relatively little to restrict slave exports from leaving the region in the 1840s and 1850s. Between 1857 and 1862 a French government scheme even called for the "recruitment" (namely the purchase) of slaves from Libreville for shipment to the West Indies as "emigrants" to make up for the loss of servile labor on Martinique and Guadeloupe. The resettlement of roughly two hundred slaves taken from a Spanish slaver in 1849 may have made the area briefly a second Freetown, but a combination of poor funding and recalcitrant former captives undid the program by the mid-1850s. French commandants proved to be lax about domestic slavery in Mpongwe society.

Masters and slaves entered into a complex set of negotiations on the matters of farming and service. The European occupation had not put slavery to an end by decree, and until the 1870s masters still often killed slaves without serious risk of harm. Missionaries recorded such deaths of more than twenty slaves in the 1840s and 1850s. William Walker wrote in 1862: "[The local people] will tell me everything and make no concealment. But when the sergeant of police comes, the slave, the master and all of the people will declare that it was an accident. . . . The cleanest cut of the sharpest instrument will be testified as the laceration of a stick or stone or the horn of a vicious bullock; thus the master gains impunity and the slave is more enslaved."[121] Police rarely did much to punish free murderers of slaves. The blood of captives flowed through the late 1860s.

Even severe punishments did not end the growing autonomy of some slave communities. Masters had difficulty retaining their authority over these distant villages. Whether this was a problem that predated the French takeover is difficult to say, but by the early 1860s some slaves had become openly defiant of authority. The collapse of clan leadership around Libreville made such independence more likely. Unlike the feeble reign of his Agakaza cohorts around the town, Rapontchombo held sway over the south Estuary bank with an iron grip and without much threat of French involvement, and he still owned hundreds of captives. Catholic priests in Libreville noted in 1855 that slaves had begun to act as free as their masters.[122] Protestant ministers had their hands full with rambunctious slaves, even if they had more luck converting the servile than the free. A mob of slaves wielding axes and torches chased a bondsman to the Protestant mission accusing him of bewitching someone; they threatened to set the wooden church ablaze, but William Walker managed to chase them off.[123] Mpongwe masters employed Séké slaves who belonged to the secret and greatly feared omowétchi power association to curse and harm escaped slaves. Several years later Walker failed to stop the execution of a slave by omowétchi members; Mpongwe clan leaders, rather than heed the pastor, chose to pay off the omowétchi rather than investigate the crime.[124]

Government and missionary reports record references to famines in the late 1860s, and the chaotic relations between slaves and the free provide one likely cause for these hardships. With the anarchic status of slaves on ompindi, it is hard to imagine these slaves easily or regularly surrendering food as tribute. Without access to mission education or trade connections, slaves would have had a hard time amassing capital to pay workers or to invest in technology that might improve their productivity. Some slaves did take the initiative to sell food to mission establishments. Schoolchildren at the Baraka mission made life miserable for slave women selling manioc: some duped one unfortunate woman into dragging her basket of food into a female American missionary's bedroom. Pranksters mocked the single cloth slaves wore every day and their heavily accented Omyene.[125]

The mean-spirited trickery of the Baraka mission school indicates how free people continued to disparage farming and manual labor, particularly as missionaries inadvertently gave local people the means to obtain more lucrative kinds of income than agriculture could provide. Protestant pastors viewed their students as scornful of hard toil. Younger girls infuriated about how older children bossed them around at Baraka would say, "Am I your parent's slave? Go and call your own sister or mother to work for you!"[126] A generation later in the 1890s a Native American woman who had espoused a Mpongwe man told missionary Robert Nassau that her son should do no hard labor at school and he should be permitted "a personal slave servant to do his bidding and to wait on him in other ways as his valet!"[127] However, free people realized that learning foreign languages and styles of dress and etiquette, and for female students domestic skills, could pay off in the future.

Mpongwe free people recognized immediately the benefits of mission schools in teaching their children skills useful for finding work with Europeans.[128] Many boys and young men entered into mission schools as early as the 1840s. By learning English or French they became immediately attractive to state officials and European traders. Missionaries could not compete with the high salaries that mission graduates earned from trading companies and the colonial administration.[129] Free men became commonly employed as clerks, sailors, and interpreters. Women also used mission education as cultural capital to find work with Europeans. While for the first decades of mission activity families did not send many girls to school, by 1860 increasing numbers of girls learned how to sew and do needlework and laundry from nuns or American female missionaries.[130] In other colonial African contexts girls' education served similar purposes by introducing European gender norms and ideals, opening up opportunities besides farming for a living.[131]

Mission programs for female education held a particular irony. Looking for women who could run bourgeois European households and understood Western consumption patterns, European traders and officials sought out many of the Libreville mission graduates as mistresses.[132] Living with traders, such women were mainly occupied with maintaining a European partner's household.[133] Some mission graduates worked as laundresses for European residents as well as furnishing sexual favors.[134] Most missionaries and officials painted lurid pictures of greedy Mpongwe women enriching themselves from lustful foreigners. "As a result of her career," Canadian pastor Robert Milligan stated in his typical condescending tone, Tito "had acquired heaps of clothes, a miscellaneous assortment of jewelry from glass to gold, and an awful temper."[135] Awash in Victorian fantasies of female desire and disorder, Mpongwe women appear in some accounts to live a life of ease, far from the hoe and the soil.

In negotiating within this continuum ranging from financial benefit to brute exploitation, many women moved away from farming as their central occupation. British traveler Richard Burton remarked after his stay in Libreville in the early 1860s that the position of Mpongwe women was "comparatively high. . . . They have conquered a considerable latitude of conducting their own affairs. When poor and slaveless and naturally no longer young, they must work in the house and in the field, but this is not singular."[136]

By the 1870s some women used their close ties with European men to purchase slaves and live independently of Mpongwe men. Several of the Mpongwe concubines of British traders bought slaves from central Gabon with their lovers' aid.[137] Marie Ndar earned enough as a mistress to buy ten slaves.[138] Some women thus followed the path away from farming as a primary economic activity that was first taken by free men in Mpongwe society. However, this does not mean they left gardening behind entirely. Stereotypes of lazy townswomen dominate descriptions of Libreville, but the numbers of women engaged as wage laborers or as paramours of Europeans cannot be fixed with certitude. According to older Mpongwe residents of Libreville, their grandmothers born between about 1860 and 1890 maintained small fields but did not sell at market.[139] They were adamant in their assertion that the manioc and plantains from these fields served the women's households. In similar fashion to slaves, most free women lacked the ability and capital to control large amounts of labor for commercial farming, and affluent female residents entered commerce.

One explanation for the discrepancy between written accounts of farming and female Mpongwe oral testimonies may come from generational differences. Rachel Jean-Baptiste's discussion of marriage in nineteenth- and early twentieth-century Mpongwe communities points out the fluidity and complexity of matrimony.[140] Rather than passively accept marriages made by their families at a young age, younger women could divorce their husbands, seek out European or West African immigrants, or take lovers while their husbands were away trading. Through these options these women could avoid gardening or farming for family members. However, middle-aged and elderly women may have had more interest in farming for themselves or their families. Some Mpongwe women who had once been the partners of European men in the mid-twentieth century had either developed long-term relationships with African men or left European lovers behind.[141] Administrators refused the requests for aid from older Mpongwe women during World War II on the grounds that they still farmed for themselves.[142] It is difficult to determine if this trend of older women entering farming was common, but it would be a logical choice for women who did not have the opportunities available to younger women. Poor older women in mid-twentieth-century Libreville also had kin obligations to support elderly relatives and children.[143] Impoverished women most likely lacked the finances and the manpower to cultivate extensive fields.

Regardless of the causes of low productivity among urban food producers, missionaries thundered against the effects of wage labor on agriculture. Father Maurice Briault lampooned the port's African population: "[The Mpongwe] became scribes of all sorts, policemen, postmen, interpreters . . . [but] the Pongwe tribe did not produce a single farmer and soon was reduced to living off imports."[144] Although exaggerated, Briault's views point to the continued ability of townspeople to avoid farming by buying food from African and European sources. Mpongwe men working at an office, a trading post in the interior, or aboard ship had little time available to farm, besides having no inclination. Women juggling numerous tasks for Europeans had less space in their schedules to visit their gardens. Robert Nassau admitted as much: "In the march of Civilization, at Gabon, large numbers of the natives are non-producers of food."[145] Rather than engaging in farming to feed the diverse and growing population, Mpongwe free people with the most access to capital and labor preferred jobs in the colonial economy.

Starting in the mid-1870s, French commandants kept a tighter reign over Libreville. Commandant Clément, who directed the colony in 1875 and 1876, weakened the ability of masters to ensure the obedience of their slaves. He threatened to burn the Louis neighborhood as a punishment for slave executions.[146] Clément also obliged free people to do menial labor without pay, much to the dismay of townspeople and missionaries alike.[147] Domestic slavery began to crumble in this environment. Ironically, this was not a central aim of the French administration. Instead French authorities inadvertently made slaves more difficult to control and obtain. One move that did open possibilities for freedom to slaves was the French ban on the capital punishment of slaves in 1875. Tensions between free people worried about losing their power over their slaves sparked bloodshed in the late 1870s.

Beginning in the summer of 1877 unknown assailants murdered people working in fields on the outskirts of Mpongwe villages.[148] Women and male slaves were the main targets of the attacks. As noted in the preceding chapter, their bodies were found mutilated; often the perpetrators removed internal organs and beheaded their victims.[149] By May terror had settled on the port as more than twenty people had been killed in the town of three thousand. The Commandant of Gabon wrote: "The murders have multiplied in Gabon for several months in frightening proportions; the locals are under the rule of a veritable horror, they hardly dare move during the day. No one goes out at night; they lock themselves up and barricade themselves in their houses."[150] Masters invariably blamed slaves for the killings, even though slaves made up the bulk of the victims.[151]

The murders played havoc with the town's food supply. Most slaves and free women, fearing for their lives, did not work in their fields for the next two years.[152] Food became so scarce that Catholic missionaries faced great difficulties in feeding their employees and students.[153] The murders ended without explanation in late 1879, but they had ramifications on town agriculture for years to come. The events demonstrate the inability of masters to depend on slaves to feed themselves. For the next several years missionaries recounted shortages in fish and manioc as well as continued fears of murderers lurking in fields.[154]

Domestic slavery ran into difficulties, but it remained a part of town life even during its decline. Under the scrutiny of French officials who wished to stamp out slave trading, slaves from the interior became rare, although some Mpongwe traders surreptitiously smuggled slaves to town.[155] Some slaves stayed close to masters.[156] Idioms of kinship permitted slave owners to obscure the relationship between slaves and owners; a physician in Libreville noted: "The black owner does not like to say this terrible word [slave] and the servants he supports are well-trained on the subject. . . . Owanga, a supposed son of my gardener having committed an error, I complained to his father who refused to accept responsibility. 'You know,' he said to me, 'he's not exactly my son.'"[157] This dwindling group continued to work as servants and farmers. Slaves became incorporated into households through the vocabulary of kinship, but it seems likely that fewer captives from the interior came to replace them.

The clandestine nature of domestic slavery complicates tracking its decline. Slaves drop out of official bureaucratic correspondence after 1890, but others continued to mention slaves in their letters and diaries. Robert Nassau's copious daily entries in his journal record references to slaves, as the minister disdained the practice of masters collecting their bondsmen's pay each month.[158] One writer noted a small band of elderly slaves around Libreville as late as 1927.[159]

Catholic missionaries also developed a way in which servants might achieve their freedom. They established a village of ex-slaves, who were often purchased from free people at the mission's expense behind their Sainte Marie church. From the 1850s onward slaves provided the Sainte Marie mission with a large and fairly loyal set of laborers for its agricultural projects. To promote Christianity and to furnish needed hands for the mission, Catholic priests bought slaves from masters.[160] By setting up villages of clients the Catholic mission solved practical concerns and articulated ideological beliefs simultaneously. While the mission never became entirely self-sufficient in food, its community of former slaves did offset costs of feeding large numbers of students. Priests did not hesitate to boast of their paternalist treatment of Africans. Food played a part. In 1885 the annals of the Sainte Marie mission claimed that starving and ill slaves came to the mission and pleaded with Bishop Le Berre with phrases such as "I want to be your child" and "I want to give myself to you."[161] Such pleas of patronage remind one of other mission experiences with slaves in the late nineteenth century, when slaves in search of new masters turned to missions.[162] By accepting mission authority ex-slaves had to follow Catholic teaching to stay in the settlement.[163] Even in the 1890s the mission could still obtain new residents. One priest noted early in the decade that most free families still held ten to fifty slaves back in the ompindis.[164]

Catholic missionaries may have emancipated some slaves, but the process by which slaves became incorporated into free town society remains largely obscure. Some followed older traditions of moving from being slaves to owning their own people, as a French officer noted in 1873: "At Libreville, something that strikes one with sadness is to see former slaves themselves own slaves and who have taken on [Mpongwe] customs we pretend to punish to the point that it is very difficult to distinguish them from the real [Mpongwe]."[165] Some contemporary residents of Libreville argue that certain families claiming to be

Mpongwe were in fact descended from slave ancestors. The details are sketchy, but one point is clear: neither oral sources nor written records indicate a sizable amount of slaves in Libreville by the First World War.

Changing notions of wealth and status in town may also explain why domestic slavery lost its attractiveness for free people. Older ideas about wealth in people can be summed up in a comment made by a priest in the early 1880s: "Wealth is considered to be having large fields of manioc. To have that, one must have women and slaves, since only they work."[166] Big men thus displayed their wealth through their control over dependents, whether free wives or slaves. However, knowledge of foreign tastes and access to foreign goods also denoted affluence. Mpongwe men and women adopted expensive suits and dresses imported from Europe, chatted with English tourists about British art galleries, and portrayed themselves as civilized people meriting equal treatment with Europeans.[167] Fields became less crucial to defining wealth.

The gradual emancipation of slaves placed older forms of food supply in jeopardy. The end of the slave trade cut off a small number of free people from agricultural labor and dependents.[168] Free households had to find other sources of agriculture manpower. With free people disdainful of food production as a means of making a living, other sources had to be developed to satisfy the needs of the diverse population of Libreville. The next three chapters examine different solutions developed to alleviate the weaknesses of Mpongwe and Libreville food supply. Gabonese people from outside the Mpongwe community along with migrants from other parts of Africa entered the food trade. Imported foods from Asia and Europe made up for the agricultural deficiencies of the town. Finally, the colonial government made often feeble and poorly organized efforts to encourage food production in the Gabon Estuary. Through this varied collection of resources the town managed to survive, albeit with crises such as the famines of 1918–26 and at the cost of high food prices. Agriculture and cooking expressed the desires and fears of free Mpongwe people in Libreville— but also the challenge their formation as a community posed for productivity and self-sufficiency.

Food production and consumption in the Gabon Estuary went through many changes before the establishment of French rule. Although a lack of sources stymies efforts to understand the complexities of food consumption developments, archaeological and linguistic sources show a slow evolution of eating habits and agricultural patterns. Western Bantu-speaking migrants brought with them the cultivation of new foods such as bananas and taro. In many ways their styles of farming and eating were similar to those of other groups in Equatorial Africa.

Mpongwe eating styles and food supply owed a great debt to the Atlantic slave trade. Atlantic commerce brought shifts in local culinary styles. New crops from Asia and South America altered diets and farming. The rise of Gabon as a source of captives for the Atlantic market in the eighteenth century changed the meanings articulated in food consumption. Increased participation by Mpongwe people in the slave trade augmented numbers of captives in the Estuary. Eventually unfree farmers comprised the bulk of agricultural labor, while free people entered into trade as a primary activity. The advances in goods Mpongwe people received from Europeans allowed them to purchase their own slaves who farmed for them.

Atlantic slavery brought a host of innovations in its wake. Free men's sense of masculinity became tied to leisure, and they relegated to women and chattel the tasks considered menial. Mpongwe households, through their direct connections with European traders and their goods, used their commercial position to buy food. They also appropriated certain European cooking techniques and presentation. Eating, along with numerous other adaptations of European culture, became part of a "civilized" identity at odds with the supposed backwardness of surrounding groups.

The formation of this Mpongwe trading society led to a range of negotiations between different elements of society. Since masters worried that slaves might take advantage of their role in domestic labor to harm their owners, certain limits existed on demands they could place on their dependents. On a more tangible level, the purchase of food made commercial disputes a threat to households' ability to feed themselves. Yet commerce provided more wealth and more prestige than farming, and urban families involved in entrepreneurial ventures or employment with Europeans could expect to obtain the goods and money needed to purchase food rather than maintaining fields. Some families might obligate older women to farm, but the fluctuating economy of Libreville offered options for women to stay off fields by trading for themselves or by relying on West African and European partners.

Colonial rule and the rise of European commerce in the Gabon Estuary added to the instability of Mpongwe food supply. The first seven decades of

French rule undermined the foundations of Atlantic slavery, but in a haphaz-
ard and uneven manner. Slaves managed to gain a measure of independence.
Some continued to farm, but their ability to sate the needs of the town left much
to be desired, given the ubiquity of food shortages in Libreville from the 1850s
through the 1870s. Masters did not turn to agriculture themselves to make up
for the loss of slave labor—instead they chose to focus their efforts on obtaining foods from other Africans and Europeans. Slave labor and Atlantic commerce thus helped to create a food supply system that fostered consumption
over production and favored trading enterprises over agriculture.

3. Newcomers, Food Supply, and the Colonial State, 1840–1914

Between 1840 and 1914 Libreville changed from being a tiny colonial outpost to become the administrative headquarters of French imperial ambitions in Central Africa. Visitors considered it a sleepy haven in a colony rife with violence. English tourist and collector Mary Kingsley rhapsodized on the friendly and quaint manners of Africans in town.[1] Africans from all over Gabon and beyond made the port their home. One missionary remarked: "All the colors and languages meet in Libreville. Whites, blacks, [and men of] yellow, coffee or milky tint come there. French, German, English, Chinese, Mpongwé, Pahouin [Fang], Boulou, Akele all can be heard."[2] Libreville's links with the global economy expanded as the town became a seat of colonial ambitions. The town's population, and consequently its culinary practices, diversified.

The ways townspeople obtained food underwent a series of transformations. Domestic slavery declined. The Atlantic slave markets closed forever. Townspeople left independent commerce behind to serve the needs of companies seeking rubber and timber. The sight of Fang-speaking women carrying baskets of manioc in Libreville, a rarity before the 1870s, became part of daily life. Fang people came to dominate the town's food supply. The presence of European companies and a more intrusive French government led to innovations in eating.

European missionaries, traders, and officials struggled to develop stable sources of sustenance for themselves and their African clients—workers, former slaves, mistresses, and students. The colonial government never managed to improve agricultural production and neglected to develop roads and infrastructure to assist African farmers. Catholic missionaries proved more capable tillers of the soil, yet even their fields did not allow them to escape the scourge of shortages and high prices. They too turned to Africans outside the Mpongwe community. Older inhabitants of the Estuary region like the Séké and incoming Fang clans allowed the city to obtain food.

Even so, problems continued to trouble the town. Competition over international exports and French political ambitions engendered a chaotic series of conflicts that embroiled the entire Gabon Estuary region. The ferocious conflicts endemic to the Estuary hampered food production and transport. Other controversies came from the complex relationship between Mpongwe townspeople with Fang clans and West Africans. Mpongwe people stubbornly defended their privileges as the original inhabitants of Libreville against European and African rivals. On occasion they worked to defend their rights as consumers against state interference and African producers.

Yet Mpongwe people also counted on others to furnish them with their daily sustenance and rewarded foreigners with land and mutually beneficial partnerships. Port residents adapted older concerns of taste and status as their diets and their sources for food altered over time. Foreigners and Fang people coming from the interior posed a new set of challenges, but Mpongwe townspeople managed to defend their ways of consumption by taking advantage of their position as intermediaries between Africans and Europeans. By making alliances with Fang people bearing food and asserting their right to imported foods at a fair price, Mpongwe women and men ensured their ability to eat without having to spend much time farming themselves. Just like their European neighbors, Mpongwe people bought their food and shirked agriculture. Purchasing in the anarchic era of early colonial occupation came at a high cost, though, as conflicts continued to sweep through the Libreville hinterland and obstructed regular food supply in town.

European Food Supply Difficulties, 1840–1914

Food supply furnished a logistical nightmare for French officers in Gabon for most of the nineteenth century. Dependent on a supply chain that relied on regular visits from ships coming from Senegal and France far to the north, the colony's staff suffered hardship. The long voyage on slow-moving ships from France and Senegal damaged many foodstuffs en route. Officials in Paris did not care much for the stomachs of the French garrison of Gabon, either. Reading this 1847 description of provisions at Libreville is best avoided by those with weak stomachs: "The flour is bad, the biscuit is poorly cooked and cannot be conserved; the vegetables are horrible beyond description, and the wine goes bad after three or four months. All of this, Commandant, is not due to the climate but rather the terrible nature of these foodstuffs."[3] The rations offered little comfort to men already scoured by illness and heavy drinking.[4] The paltry funding from Paris increased the misery of Africans and Europeans stationed in Gabon. The acting commandant of the fort observed that he lacked both provisions and goods such as tobacco or soap, with which workers might barter for food.[5]

Poverty led to crime. Some state employees stole food from government warehouses.[6] Such chicanery regarding food supplies continued to trouble Libreville for decades. In the late 1870s one officer committed suicide after he had been caught embezzling money intended for buying food and paying cooks.[7] Europeans on the Gabon Estuary encountered hunger and adversity for the first three decades of the colony.

Given the grave situation, it is no wonder that French officers immediately tried to grow their own food. By 1845 the post had begun growing rice and European vegetables near the fort.[8] These plans struck an unforeseen impediment. Mpongwe people had no intention of working fields for Europeans.[9] A colonial government so miserly that even its own employees did not regularly receive their salaries could offer few inducements to attract menial laborers. Mpongwe men served French officers only as interpreters or pilots. Such a scarcity of manpower placed French administrators in a troublesome quandary: how could they find the labor to ameliorate food shortages?

One possible source emerged in 1848. French officers, mimicking their British rivals in Sierra Leone, decided to resettle at the French fort of Gabon over one hundred Africans rescued from the Spanish slave ship *Elizia*.[10] Administrators hoped the newcomers would provide the workers needed to unload ships and tend state fields. The plans did not succeed. Early on, some members of the settlement did till the soil willingly for the government.[11] However, most former slaves moved into trade or artisan crafts.[12] The colony, hamstrung by miniscule budgets and dependent on remote superiors in Dakar (1843–54) and Gorée (1854–59), did not attempt to replenish the small settlement with more rescued slaves.

West Africans furnished French officials with a more reliable source of labor. African troops from Senegal worked at manual labor as well as military tasks.[13] The Senegalese contingent in Gabon worked in the fields and in construction, much to the dismay of some French officers, who discovered that the soldiers could use a shovel but had no idea how to fire a gun.[14] Private and public employers preferred Kru workers to Senegalese troops for the fields. Male workers from the Kru coast of Liberia, used on European ships and in the British colony of Freetown in Sierra Leone, also arrived in numbers from 1847 onward.[15] Agreeing to stay in Libreville for one or two years in return for payment in goods, Kru workers unloaded ships, paddled boats, and performed numerous other menial jobs.[16] By the 1860s several hundred Kru workers lived in town.[17]

Europeans hired Kru workers to grow food for several reasons. Since rice was their staple crop and was previously unknown in Gabon, missionaries and officers relied on Kru expertise to grow it.[18] Unlike slaves and free people from the Estuary, Krumen depended almost entirely on the goodwill of their employers. Even so their high value and their salary demands made them a very expensive option.[19] State officials and British traders did not help matters by breaking contracts, beating workers, and skipping payments.[20] At times in the early years of the colony the situation became so grim that Kru workers robbed Mpongwe pirogues of plantains and fish so that they might eat.[21] Finally some Krumen rejected farming altogether.[22]

When West African labor did not fulfill the hopes of the administration, the government tried to take matters into its own hands. The colonial government fared poorly. State fields, though initially a source of food for the colony in the late 1840s and early 1850s, soon became reduced to a small experimental garden where various cash crops and tiny amounts of European vegetables were raised.[23] The government decided to encourage agriculture and promote the use of livestock by organizing a colorful fair each Bastille Day. A collection of French and African judges handed out prizes for gardening, cooking, and arts and crafts. Though the fairs might have helped in a small way to create legitimacy for French rule among Libreville residents, they did not inspire radical changes in food supply. Only one French settler attempted to sell manioc in the mid-1880s, and apparently he abandoned the job after several years.[24]

One bright spot for the colonial settlement was the presence of Séké traders. They continued to follow patterns of exchange set with Mpongwe villages by selling poultry and manioc to Europeans on occasion as well. The French fort suffered from tremendous food supply problems, so the Séké village of Nkembo (now a Fang-dominated neighborhood in the city) was a godsend for the hungry garrison of the fort, just as Séké female vendors aided the Catholic mission three decades later.[25] These deals allowed the Séké to maneuver around the old monopoly of direct contact with Europeans that Mpongwe had so jealously held. Textiles, brandy, and particularly tobacco furnished the main forms of currency.[26] An American pastor stationed several miles from Libreville reported: "[Africans] refuse articles which cost double the price for tobacco and at times will even bring their choice food (the Dika) in hopes of purchasing their favorite weed."[27] Thus African food producers took advantage of their position, but the small and scattered Séké community could not fully sate demand.

Missionaries encountered the same troubles as the government—high prices and instability in food supply—but Catholics and Protestants split on whether missions should grow food themselves. Protestant ministers initially planted breadfruit trees and sponsored farming but gave up on the practice by the 1860s.[28] Americans did not set up large fields, believing that manual labor detracted from their main goal of attracting converts.[29] Catholic missionaries had a radically different opinion.[30] Bishop of Libreville Jean-Rémy Bessieux became an outspoken zealot on the moral virtues of agriculture. Bessieux spelled out his motives in 1860: "This agriculture obtains for us a triple advantage: by it, we obtain the food for the children, we give an example for the people of the country, and we furnish ourselves a means of support in the future."[31] His fervor inspired a strong link between the Catholic presence and agriculture. Efforts rapidly included fruit trees, sugar cane, rice, cocoa and cotton. By the early 1860s the mission also grew plantains and manioc to feed its workers and students.[32]

Catholics missionaries played their trump cards—their influence and the education they offered—to fashion a workforce of students and former slaves. Catholic schoolchildren, much to the chagrin of their relatives, worked in mission fields regardless of their background.[33] Several American pastors in Libreville grumbled that their "Papist" rivals' fields made Catholic schools more appealing to Mpongwe families than the Protestant mission, which required relatives to pay for food.[34] Besides serving to feed students and mission employees, farming became a conscious method by missionaries to engrave notions of order and discipline on Africans.[35] Attempts to change agricultural practices also involved challenges to local gender hierarchies, ecological knowledge, and other elements of everyday life.[36]

However, missionaries in the Gabon Estuary never convinced free townspeople to continue farming. Unlike in South Africa, no class of Christian Africans using European farming techniques ever appeared in the Estuary.[37] Townspeople accepted the fact that their children would toil in mission fields so that they could gain skills useful in the trading economy. Slaves, in need of patronage, also agreed to labor in missionary agriculture. But such measures had limits. They did not inspire many free people to grow large amounts of food for sale. Nor did breadfruit and other imported crops cultivated by missionaries become a major part of local diets.

Evidence for this lack of success can be viewed in the rampant food shortages of the 1870s. Even before the terror of the latter part of the decade, missionaries and officials struggled to purchase enough food for their staff and dependents. The Franco-Prussian war left the colony bereft of supplies between 1870 and 1873.[38] Orungu fishermen switched from selling smoked fish in Libreville to resuming the clandestine slave trade to São Tomé once they recognized that no French patrol boats were coming.[39] The student population dropped by half in 1872 when priests could no longer nourish all their pupils; two years later, during the summer dry season, the entire school was closed when a supply ship arrived several weeks late.[40] "We believe ourselves to be in the poorest country in the world as far as food is concerned," mission head Father Pierre-Marie Le Berre wrote to his French superior.[41] Drought compounded these difficulties in the short dry season of 1876.[42] Finally, the wave of murders in the late 1870s left free people and slaves too frightened to visit their fields.

The next decade did not begin much better, but the arrival of Fang immigrants would radically alter the food supply system between 1880 and 1885. Pierre Savorgnan de Brazza's expeditions into the interior sucked away food from the rest of the town, whether while stationed in Libreville or on the move elsewhere in Central Gabon.[43] Periodic shortages continued on occasion later in the decade, especially during the traditionally hard times of the short and long dry seasons.[44] Yet the encroachment of Fang villagers from northern Gabon assuaged these hardships. Fang men had traded ivory and other goods in town since the 1850s, and by 1880 they had started living with their families within a few miles of Libreville itself.[45]

The first half of the 1880s was a crucial time for the town's food supply. French commandants viewed the Fang as the saviors of the colony. One administrator gushed: "The [Mpongwe] have become so lazy that if the [Fang], who are the future of the colony as they are energetic and hardworking, did not bring plantains and manioc, the [Mpongwe] would have nothing to eat."[46] Officers and missionaries alike praised the rush of canoes carrying Fang women loaded with food.[47] The miniscule sales of food by Mpongwe to the Catholic mission ceased as Fang women took over the market.[48] Catholic missionaries expressed their joy about the situation by comparing the dearth of food in the 1870s with the relative plenty that came with Fang vendors by the end of the 1880s.[49]

Neither the government nor missionaries could resolve the troubled state of affairs in the town's endless woes over food. West African workers were too expensive and often had too much else to do for their employers to be spared to grow crops. Séké and Orungu fishermen might contribute at times but not enough to make up for the deficiencies of Mpongwe food supply. Students and slaves assisted in but could not achieve the Catholic mission's aim to be self-sufficient. It would be up to Fang clans to better the situation. However, bloodshed among Fang would lead to setbacks. The same 1882 government report lauding Fang immigrants also noted a vicious brawl between several of them that ended in one man's death.[50] It would take a world war to end these disputes and break Fang clans' military resistance to the colonial administration.

The Coming of the Fang

European observers heralded the coming of Fang clans to the Estuary as the end of the Mpongwe. Renowned among explorers such as Burton and Du Chaillu as fierce warriors, groups of Fang men belonging to over forty clans forced Akele and Séké villagers to flee to Libreville and the Ogooué River during the 1860s and 1870s. Officials hoped that the Fang would supplant Mpongwe people and work as menial laborers. The coming of the Fang greatly changed the organization and dynamics of food supply to town.

Scholars have shed much ink on Fang migrations from Cameroon into Gabon; I will not attempt to retrace disputes regarding the origins of Fang people.[51] Linguistic and fragmentary oral sources suggest that Fang speakers came into Gabon from northern Cameroon. During the early nineteenth century, as best it can be determined, a series of raids—either between Fang clans or from outsiders entitled *uban* in later traditions—drove many to migrate into northern

Gabon.[52] From there some Fang groups pushed toward the coast, in part to enter into commerce directly with Europeans.

However, contrary to European views, conflicts between these groups did not come from ancient ethnic hatreds. Commercial disputes lay at the heart of the antagonism between Estuary communities, and fighting proved to be a useful form of negotiation. Mpongwe traders, serving European firms interested in buying rubber, ivory, and lumber, alienated their Fang contacts by taking women from villages as wives or as lovers and by cheating clients out of agreed payments in imported goods.[53] Mpongwe and European merchants faced duplicity on the part of Fang men willing to take hostages or rob traders for goods. Violence often erupted over commerce. Mpongwe traders used their close ties to Europeans to convince French officers to raze Fang villages in retaliation.

Fang groups entering the Estuary differed substantially from Mpongwe peoples. No institution of clan head existed in an organized fashion among villagers. Instead, clan members formed settlements of roughly one hundred people claiming membership in the same descent group or clan. No centralized leaders commanded more than several villages. Adult men met in houses classified as spaces reserved for men and discussed conflicts. Slavery did not exist in Fang society, although prisoners of war acted as marginal clients of households.

Food production reflected gendered divisions in Fang society. Other than clearing and burning fields in the dry season, men specialized in hunting and fishing. After some time, male Fang villagers living close to the Atlantic Ocean or Gabon Estuary mastered fishing with harpoons and small nets to catch sardines.[54] They hunted with muskets obtained from trade or with crossbows and spears, dug traps and obscured them with leaves, and fabricated snares to capture game. According to missionaries living in the Estuary, few men worked in fields during most of the year. "It makes my heart ache to see these poor [Fang] women, some of them quite old, going by with the heaviest burdens on their backs and the men sitting in the palaver house. 'Real men' don't work, they say. This is what women are made for," American pastor Sadie Boppell wrote near Kango at the mouth of the Como River.[55] Although missionaries tended to present women as passive victims, it is clear that work in the fields was largely seen as women's work.

Fang food production relied primarily on farming, similar to that of Mpongwe households. Estuary Fang women planted crops of manioc, taro, various types of plantains, squash, yams, and more rarely sweet potatoes and corn.[56] Most of these crops generally bore edible fruit a year after planting. Fields required heavy weeding and vigilance against wild animals such as wild pigs or elephants. Such labor demands left women out for long periods in their fields, although certain tasks, like the planting of squash seeds, were taken up by multiple households working together.[57] In many cases women built small houses (mfini) at the fields on land chosen by their husbands.[58] They generally left for their fields roughly at dawn and returned in the mid-afternoon.[59] Besides farming women also prepared manioc and fished in streams, much like their Mpongwe counterparts. A common technique was to dam a stream, place various poisonous herbs in the water, and then collect the fish killed by these potent toxins in a round net.[60]

Fang settlements moved a fair amount in the late nineteenth century. Some French observers believed Fang clans would move for frivolous and irrational reasons, but on close inspection frequent movement made sense for social, economic, and ecological reasons. First, farmers recognized the inability of Estuary soils to maintain good yields for a significant length time. Fang people evaluated land fertility by creating categories of land use: angoma (virgin forest), ekorge (new fields), esen (abandoned fields that could support esen trees, a sign that they could possibly support agriculture again), and mbur (old cultivated land where some hardwood trees had returned as forest growth slowly recovered). It took about twenty years for old fields to return to esen—which were not always attractive to Fang clans looking for more promising terrain— so farmers were obliged to search out new land.[61] Fang men seeking better trade connections and control over commercial networks also chose to shift locations quickly, as did their counterparts in southern Gabon.[62]

Several factors converged to attract Fang clans to move closer to Libreville. French commandants repeatedly invited their chiefs to come to town.[63] While government plans never coalesced into a coherent program, the central position of Libreville as home to two competing missions enticed many Estuary villagers. Fang clan leaders from the 1860s on sent boys to study at Sainte Marie and Baraka.[64] Protestant and Catholic rivals from Libreville regularly ministered to Fang villages throughout the Estuary and recruited children for their schools. Mission students learned to read French and acquired knowledge of trades such as shoemaking and carpentry.[65] As missionaries gained more adherents in the Estuary, some Fang came to Libreville for major religious holidays. Zimbé Michel spoke in 2000 of Fang villagers arriving in canoes from the Estuary south bank to celebrate Easter in town.[66]

Fang people came to work as well as pray. By the 1890s Robert Nassau hired Fang men to do odd jobs such as cutting grass and carrying lumber to build houses.[67] When the colonial administration imposed a new head tax after 1900, some men elected to work in Libreville, where they could more readily obtain salaries in money.[68] Besides working from necessity Fang men also could indulge in shopping for goods unavailable elsewhere in the region. "Touching a few dollars at the end of the day and quickly buying some nice outfits like those of the whites is a dream of the Fang," a Catholic missionary remarked in 1906.[69] The newcomers thus encroached on Mpongwe dominance in Libreville, yet Fang farms allowed townspeople to continue to purchase food rather than grow it themselves.

Profits from fish and manioc sales drew Fang people to town. As forest products such as rubber and ivory became exhausted, villagers from the north and south Estuary banks turned to the food market as a source of income.[70] Fang women bearing on their backs heavy baskets full of manioc and plantains became a standard sight in town.[71] Those living close by walked to Libreville.[72] Others from the Mondah Bay region to the north and from the Como River and the Estuary south bank used pirogues to reach the port.[73] An American missionary living in Libreville in the late 1890s wrote: "The Fang thus easily sell all the food they can raise. In the morning looking out from the mission house, one can see the bay covered with white sails like a flock of sea-gulls—the sails of the Fang canoes bringing food to the market."[74] After the establishment of a head tax in money in 1902, many Fang preferred to sell food in Libreville to obtain hard currency to pay the fees imposed by the government.[75] To the consternation of Father Maurice Briault in 1900, Fang selling fish and atanga fruit in Libreville threw down on the ground the priest's offer of tobacco leaves and demanded cash; farther from town he fared little better—villagers asked for plates and kettles instead of the goods he offered to trade.[76] Benga, Mpongwe, Akele, and Séké men managed to keep hold of ocean fisheries, but produce was almost entirely a Fang affair by the turn of the century.[77]

Since women were engaged in farming it might be expected that they considered the profits of their harvests to be their own.[78] Other than presenting Fang women as beasts of burden, written sources yield practically nothing on women's economic strategies. Oral sources, while agreeing with mission accounts, probably reflect gender tensions today as much as they reveal information on food sales in the past. Informants, particularly men, stated that Fang women gave up their profits to husbands.[79] Research on contemporary African market women and their manifold methods of protecting their profits from husbands suggests that some women may have guarded their market income.[80] Much as elsewhere in Central Africa, though, it is clear that conflicts and insecurity acted in ways to enforce the power of male relatives and husbands over women. Until the eve of World War I near-continual skirmishes between Fang clans and with colonial authorities impeded both farming and delivery of produce to Libreville.

The bewildering number of feuds and short-lived wars between Estuary Fang clans between the 1870s and 1914 escapes measurement. Raiding parties from other villages struck over marriage palavers and access to trade.[81] As earlier mentioned, American Protestants could not hire Fang porters for their ministry tours of the Estuary since they would invariably belong to a clan at war with rival villages en route.[82] Colonial intrusions and internal African conflicts undermined food production in Fang villages. Besides the constant battles between male clan leaders, French authority abetted the spread of violence. From the 1890s until World War I state attempts to extract labor and taxes incited revolts.[83] Even though the demand for tax payment in money may have promoted food sales in town, the destruction brought on by the colonial military may have damaged the ability of farmers to grow food. Guards often burned villages and molested village women in similar fashion to French colonial military operations elsewhere in Gabon.[84]

Women working in fields or traveling to sell food were easy targets for attacks from rival clans. Although some women may willingly have left husbands with raiders to skip complicated bridewealth exchanges and the opposition of family members, others were taken by force.[85] Missionaries, horrified by polygamy and violence against women, recorded many examples of assaults against women in clan warfare. In 1880 warriors from rival villages stole several women from Donguila fields while they picked plantains. A bridewealth dispute had set off the fighting.[86] Living near Kango on the Como River, Protestant pastor Albert Bennett observed: "Owing to a bitter feud it is often impossible for the women to work in the gardens or fish in the river. The consequence [is] a great scarcity of food. In Foulabifong, where I resided, a woman palaver lasted over 10 months and the three adjoining towns were in a state of famine. . . . During these feuds, many women are shot while walking the path."[87] Raiders even abducted women from villages within ten kilometers of Libreville.[88]

Women did come to town to sell food but relied on family members to defend their safety. Armed men guarded women going to market.[89] Although some women may have maneuvered to guard their profits from sales in town, combat put female vendors and farmers at risk, and men watching over women could more closely observe how they made money at market. The threat of raids and feuds made travel in the Estuary difficult even for short distances. It is little wonder that villagers encountered adversity in their attempts to sell in Libreville. Mpongwe people had successfully made bonds with Fang groups, but internal disputes over gender and status along with opposition from the colonial government impeded farming. The colonial government and townspeople tried to find new groups of farmers to supplement unsteady and irregular Fang suppliers. West African workers and Vietnamese convicts provided new sources of labor as well as new foods.

West African and Vietnamese Contributions to Libreville Cuisine

Besides the arrival of Fang clans in the Gabon Estuary, another amendment to town life came with French expansion in the 1880s. Columns of African troops commanded by French officers marched into the interior of Gabon and engaged in a series of guerilla wars that lasted through World War I. The "Scramble for Africa" made its presence felt in Libreville. From 1886 to 1904 Libreville was the headquarters of the French empire in Central Africa. Officials proved more concerned with military campaigns and collecting taxes than with promoting agriculture or seriously reforming food supply in Libreville. Overcoming its dismal financial record and making the colony of Gabon pay took top priority. The colonial administration did spare the town one ill that came with the new colonial program; the concessionary companies that so brutally exploited much of the Gabonese countryside did not receive any territory in the Gabon Estuary region. The new colonial order drew artisans, clerks, soldiers, and other skilled workers along with prisoners to Gabon.

The government engineered a tragic migration of foreigners into Libreville. In 1886 French officials, including former explorer Pierre Savorgnan de Brazza, devised a scheme in which Vietnamese convicts would be exiled to Libreville.[90] They hoped the program would solve the problem of African town hostility to manual labor and poor government wages. French Congo administrators won over the governor of Cochin-China to their plan. French forces had battled a revolt by Vietnamese officials rallying around the young king Ham Nghi in central Vietnam. The French administration in Vietnam decided to ship off to Gabon some captured rebels, and nearly five hundred male and female Vietnamese prisoners arrived in Libreville in 1887.[91] The exiles, often unable to speak any French, drained swampland in the neighborhood of Batavea.[92] Such hard labor proved fatal. Over half the prisoners sent to Libreville in 1887 died within three months from malaria; a French priest assigned to help care for them wrote, "When the Annamites were deported to Libreville, they dropped like flies."[93]

Those who managed to survive proved themselves valuable to French administrators. A council of settlers and officers decided to give the Vietnamese land as "it is not impossible that they might provide a lesson to follow by drawing a profit from their produce for European consumption."[94] Their gardens prompted unanimous admiration from missionaries, travelers, and officials.[95] During the French invasion of Dahomey in 1891 the produce of Vietnamese prisoners in Libreville fed colonial troops.[96] Mary Kingsley commended their efforts: "They cultivate in a tidy, carefully minute way, so entirely different from the slummacky African methods of doing things."[97] Impressed with their prisoners' work, officials lobbied the Ministry of Colonies in vain for more prisoners.[98]

Even if some Mpongwe considered the prisoners merely as slaves, Vietnamese cooking and farming influenced both Africans and Europeans.[99] Gabonese appropriated the use of Asian types of bananas and vegetables from the prisoners.[100] The hilly neighborhood of Derrière l'Hôpital, once covered with Vietnamese gardens, became a center for vegetable cultivation among later generations of Gabonese residents of Libreville.[101] Their influence did not encourage the Vietnamese to stay. By 1909 only six remained in Gabon as the rest had died or returned home.[102]

The administration directly intervened on other occasions on food supply. African entrepreneurs did not usually receive benefits from these programs, as the case of bread illustrates. From the dawn of the colony officials tried with little success to ensure that their staff received bread in Gabon. Since the tropical climate damaged flour and dissuaded bakers from settling in the colony, Europeans began to depend on African labor to produce bread.[103] In the kitchens of Sainte Marie Gabonese converts worked as apprentices and baked for the Libreville market.[104] Some Ga men from the Gold Coast bought flour from American ships for bread in 1886, but state officials refused to issue them licenses.[105] Two years later another African resident of Libreville asked for the right to make bread for the colony. In desperation officials reluctantly agreed to support him, but the venture ended quickly as a Portuguese retailer became the sole source of bread by 1892.[106] Slowly bread baked in establishments run by Europeans appeared on African menus.

Other state policies unrelated to food supply also affected African diets, especially the recruitment of foreign African labor. The colonial government and private traders encouraged skilled male workers from West Africa to work in Libreville. Besides Kru laborers, high wages brought men from the Gold Coast, Senegal, Dahomey, and Loango. Each group developed its specialties. Vili from Loango often worked as tailors or domestic servants; Senegalese men took jobs as carpenters and masons.[107] Men from Sierra Leone and the Gold Coast worked as traders for English companies, tailors, jewelers, and even as photographers.[108] Finally, runaway slaves from São Tomé and Angolan sailors set up fields in various parts of the city.[109]

The cosmopolitan nature of this immigrant community made itself felt in several areas. Most skilled workers arrived without slaves, wives, or relatives and generally relied on others to produce and cook food for them. Their work schedules and their lack of land rights precluded agricultural labor. Blaise Daigne, later the first Senegalese deputy in the French parliament, stayed and ate his meals at a boarding house in Libreville in 1898 while working as a clerk.[110] Most firms continued to hand out hard tack, salted fish, and beef to their workers.[111] Senegalese soldiers and workers bartered their alcohol rations in the market for food.[112] In search of domestic labor in similar fashion to Europeans, some men hired domestic servants while others married Mpongwe women.[113]

Their presence, besides creating increased demand for food, brought about changes in eating habits that generally escaped the attention of Europeans. One Mende trader from Sierra Leone grew rice outside the town.[114] Trained by Protestant missionaries in their homeland, some Gold Coast men baked bread in Libreville in the 1880s.[115] Miss Kate, also from Ghana, had "a restaurant that was for a long time the only hotel in the region. By her industry, by her title of foreigner, by her knowledge, Miss Kate found between the black and white world a good situation."[116] The quality of Kate's pastries earned her a state commendation in 1891.[117]

The government thus instigated policies that indirectly benefited the town. When officials passed certain decisions that impinged on townspeople's ability to obtain food and trade freely, they faced opposition. Not surprisingly, urban residents guarded their prerogatives as consumers to trade freely for food-stuffs without restrictions or obstacles from the colonial government. Libreville townspeople used creative methods to challenge state impositions in the late nineteenth and early twentieth century that succeeded in limiting the author-ity of administrators.

Resistance to Colonial Food Supply Policies

Colonial officials tried to control food sales. In 1888 officials passed a decree that prohibited the sale of foodstuffs outside the state market from 6:00 AM to 6:00 PM in town or within its immediate surroundings.[118] Europeans and Africans alike ignored the order. For example, missionaries hired African fish-ermen to deliver directly to them, and Fang vendors hawked manioc and chick-ens at Sainte Marie.[119] With the 1910 reorganization of the colonial administra-tion that turned French Congo into the federation of French Equatorial Africa, administrators placed more pressure on vendors to obey market regulations. The government passed a new indigènat legal code that gave officials wide pow-ers to arrest or fine Africans.[120] Guards under the command of administra-tors who wished to enforced the new legal code fined Libreville vendors for selling food outside the market.[121] This decision, along with a plan to compel African residents to grow food, aroused anger. The bishop of Libreville wrote soon afterward: "There is a general uproar against the police. Neither whites nor blacks have any security. One is robbed with impunity. . . . The natives are forced to work for various companies and food is robbed all along the beach. This is the work of the police commissioner, an old drunkard with a purple nose nicknamed the 'lighthouse of Ovendo.'"[122] A Mpongwe woman complained to colonial inspectors about the aggressive and bullying tactics guards inflicted upon her and other women.[123] Such resistance illustrates Libreville residents' deep commitment to free exchange of food.

Missionaries and administrators recognized the willingness and skill towns-people often showed in challenging legal restrictions to their right to purchase food and control land. Mpongwe fishermen launched a boycott in 1870 after a grievance with the Catholic mission over prices.[124] Later on, to promote European commercial agriculture, authorities granted a French settler a large tract of ter-ritory in Louis in the late 1880s. However, the governor of Gabon warned the Frenchman that he would not evict Mpongwe on the concession since "they will become obsessed with sending complaints to the Administration."[125] Educated women used colonial courts to protect their property rights to their fields. They obtained land titles, demanded reimbursement when runaway cattle from visiting ships damaged their crops, and received state money for land taken from them for Vietnamese cultivation.[126] This tradition of legal wrangling over land and food distribution policies continued for many years.

The most dramatic rebuff to state controls came in 1899. In April the colonial administration in French Congo decided to place a high surcharge on a variety of imported goods, such as salt, alcohol, and tobacco. European traders tripled their prices on these goods immediately afterward.[127] Once announced, this decision incited great discord among the Mpongwe community. Imported alcohol played a major role in daily social life, marriage, and funeral rituals as well as being a means of exchange, particularly with Fang villagers.[128] Thus the decree weakened the buying power of African residents of Libreville.

Mpongwe clan chiefs, long derided by missionaries and French officials as pompous and impotent figures, rejected the arbitrary order. On May 8, 1899, they announced that they had a placed an *omowétchi* beneath the bridge at M'Pyra connecting Glass to the center of Libreville. This item, still greatly feared among the Mpongwe community to this day, remains shrouded in mystery, and my informants had little to divulge on this topic. Several informants warned me of its secrecy and danger.[129] Associated with a Séké male power association of the same name, it is described in fragmentary references as a thing, a spirit, and a male power association (often at the same time).[130] In previous conflicts involving European traders and slaves, Mpongwe clan leaders had announced its use as a means of killing opponents. R. B. N. Walker, a British trader and explorer whose son André became a major scholar and the first Gabonese Catholic priest, had the *omowétchi* set on him by Mpongwe clan chiefs after he and his brother killed a Mpongwe employee in 1869.[131]

Chiefs thus turned to supernatural means to assert their authority over a variety of groups outside their control. They declared that the "fetish" would kill anyone who entered a European store or sold food and would slay any Mpongwe woman who had sexual relations with a European.[132] Out of terror Fang villagers refused to sell to Europeans, and as a result the Catholic mission had to close its schools.[133] Through the *omowétchi* the chiefs intimidated Fang vendors. Furthermore, the prohibition against Euro-African relationships reinforced the sagging influence of male family members over women, and chiefs acted to protect their consumption patterns from colonial state interference.

French tourist and government accounts of the boycott offer contrasting views. Baron Edouard de Mandat-Grancey, an aristocratic dandy who visited Libreville several days after the end of the boycott, mocked the event as grist for an opera buff.[134] Despite its supposed frivolity, the aristocrat also noted that the boycott caused great concern among officials. He declared that the boycott had been abandoned after Félix Adende Rapontchombo, the most respected clan leader among the Mpongwe, was brought in chains to Libreville as the instigator.[135] The commissioner general of French Congo declared that Rapontchombo had negotiated a settlement with the government and neglected any mention of food in his report.[136]

French missionary sources suggest a much different resolution. Infuriated by the Mpongwe chiefs since the mission could no longer feed its students, the priests at Sainte Marie closed the doors of the schools. On May 14 several chiefs went to the mission to discuss the boycott with Bishop Adam of Libreville. The bishop declared that henceforth only Fang children would be admitted into the Catholic mission.[137] Although the chiefs promptly declared they would allow an exception for the mission to buy food, the bishop refused to relent on his ban.[138] Two days later chiefs agreed to end the protest despite enduring a tongue-lashing from Bishop Adam, who violently attacked polygamy and their willingness to allow female family members to become concubines of Europeans.[139] The next day missionaries at Sainte Marie received food again, while government officials decided to lower the surcharge.[140]

These documents reveal a tense debate over the status of the Mpongwe in Libreville. The policy of feeding students had helped allow Catholic missionaries to influence the town's moral economy greatly. Clan chiefs acceded to Bishop Adam's imperatives because of practical concerns as well as moral doubts. By cutting off students from school, Adam offered a threat to their social advancement. Clan chiefs, though willing to oppose state taxation policies, did not want to imperil their children's access to education and material benefits. They also reveal a concern among some Mpongwe men regarding the unwillingness of Mpongwe women to follow older gender conventions. French officials made fun of these crises of masculinity. A pornographic review of Libreville life from the late 1880s scorned Mpongwe men as hypocrites, renting out their wives before marching to the governors' office to ask for a ban on Euro-African sexual unions.[141]

The protest reveals a host of tensions regarding food distribution and sale.

Ironically, the group of town residents least involved in any aspect of food production managed to outmaneuver government officials, farmers, and women over how food should be distributed. Fang villagers from the Estuary found themselves at the mercy of urban consumers. European traders also ran into trouble with their attempts to profit from high tariffs on imported goods. Mpongwe clan chiefs had discovered a way of augmenting their greatly diminished political power. Furthermore, the boycott served as a means of voicing different African and European concerns over Mpongwe women. The food boycott illustrates how debates over access to food and prices could involve a host of other social conflicts in colonial Libreville.

Between 1880 and 1914 Mpongwe people recast changes in everyday life in their favor even with the arrival of new settlers and new colonial political institutions. Through their command of local idioms of supernatural power and European bureaucracy, Libreville residents protected their rights as consumers against colonial impositions. They drew from foreign settlers' repertoires of culinary and agricultural knowledge to diversify their tastes. While their numbers might have diminished and their independence had been severely curtailed, townspeople managed to guard their privileged position as consumers.

Some scholars have suggested that social and economic changes sweeping through Libreville and the Gabon Estuary between 1840 and 1914—advancement of Fang clans into the surrounding region, the decline of domestic slavery, shifts in local gender roles, and a more firmly established colonial regime—marked the end of Mpongwe independence in the face of new African and European challengers. While the political autonomy of townspeople may have diminished and events altered the ways townspeople obtained and consumed food, Libreville residents demonstrated their ability to adjust to new conditions. Rather than increase their involvement with agricultural work, free people engaged in wage labor and made bargains with Fang villagers that ensured they could continue to consume food without giving up access to wage labor. Changes within local society did modify the evolution toward the commodification of food sales.

Like other Libreville residents, European commandants and missionaries struggled to develop stable supplies of food. Besides the shortcomings of slave agriculture, these foreigners struck other obstacles: poor funding, occasional rows with Libreville residents, and the leopard man murders of the 1870s. Fang migration bailed out European employers just as it did Mpongwe townspeople—they were saved from having to engage in food production themselves. For the French colonial government, the willingness of Fang vendors to risk attack by bringing food to market also liberated them from seriously encouraging agriculture.

Just as townspeople and foreigners negotiated with Fang migrants to ensure their ability to buy meals, Libreville residents shaped the impact of colonial policies on their lives. Officials had little luck convincing local people to farm; rather than forcing Africans to grow food, they turned to Vietnamese prisoners. The 1899 boycott demonstrates the skill of some local people in recasting state laws viewed as unduly intrusive on daily life. Africans in Libreville succeeded in guarding their autonomy and asserting their demands on food supply. However, such consumption habits would put Libreville residents at dire risk if Fang villages faced oblivion, as the events from 1914 to 1930 would prove.

4. Famine in the Gabon Estuary, 1914–1930

Gabonese rural dwellers and townspeople alike became enmeshed in the global catastrophe of World War I. German and French armies staffed by African soldiers squared off in much of northern Gabon in the first two years of hostilities. Besides the toll of combat, the population of the Gabon Estuary grappled with other losses in the wake of war: the collapse of international trade, the need for raw materials and manpower to support French needs in Europe, and the rarity of foreign supplies in the colony. The colonial administration, teetering from minuscule budgets and a deficiency of manpower, took a series of severe measures designed to break the independence of Fang and Mpongwe communities alike in the Estuary. Neither the pretensions of Mpongwe autonomy nor the freedom of Fang clan settlements survived intact during the war.

The following decade signaled the explosion of the timber industry in the Estuary. Officials heaved a collective sigh of relief. Finally French Equatorial Africa had a profitable colony. The *okoumé* tree, common in Estuary forests, sparked a rush of entrepreneurs into the colony. Administrators and private recruiters dragged thousands of Gabonese men to toil in the harsh confines of timber camps. European capital and industry triumphed. The colonial government also finally had the resources and the will to remake the region radically. Their heightened power over Africans proved instrumental in creating a famine, much as French efforts to promote obligatory agricultural projects in West African colonies weighed heavy on rural people.[1] Officials could not agree on why the famine had taken hold or how to solve the problem.

The war also inspired new social and political movements in the Estuary. Fang clan leaders could no longer take up arms against state forces with any hope of victory. Léon Mba and other state-appointed chiefs negotiated with the French government in ways that heightened their own authority at the expense of the liberty of ordinary rural people. The 1920s put Libreville intelligentsia in better communication with leftists in France. The League of the Rights of Man (LRM) became a vehicle for townspeople to deliver their calls for reform. Food supply and distribution were two issues that united town and country in indignation against the colonial state.

The shortages in the Gabon Estuary demonstrate the problems of entitlement and of Libreville's position as an enclave dependent on far-reaching supply networks for food. Economist Amartya Sen has claimed that famines are crises of exchange rather than a primary consequence of environmental fluctuation. For a number of reasons, he argues, some groups' ability to claim food declines to the point that they starve.[2] While accepting Sen's general discussion, other scholars have argued that environmental factors also played a part in constraining the amounts of food.[3] The case of the Estuary famines illustrates Sen's point, taken in conjunction with ecological factors.

In comparison to the astounding toll that other catastrophic famines left in the twentieth century, the food crises of the Gabon Estuary between 1914 and 1930 are but a few drops in a deluge of catastrophes. Food shortages in the Soviet Ukraine and Communist China killed millions, and many thousands died from the famines that struck the West African Sahel in the 1970s and Ethiopia and Darfur in the following decade.[4] Population figures for the Estuary region outside Libreville do not have even a pretense of reliability before the late 1920s, and the French government in Gabon did not record famine deaths in an organized way. Perhaps no more than between five and ten thousand Gabonese may have died in the Estuary. The population of the Kango district of the Estuary, a region hit hard by starvation, dropped from fifteen thousand to eleven thousand in the 1920s, although the unreliable nature of census documentation and the pull of timber camps and Libreville may account for some of the decline.[5] During the absolute dearth that gripped the Estuary in 1925 and 1926, a doctor stationed at the giant Consortium timber camp estimated that five men died from malnutrition a day.[6] But given the low numbers of people and widely scattered settlements in the region, the famine may have killed almost a quarter of the entire population. Accurate estimates are impossible, but even if in terms of sheer numbers starvation in the Estuary did not reach the level of death in more widespread famines in other parts of the world, this certainly does not provide comfort to the Gabonese who survived this tragedy, nor does it excuse the appalling lack of concern for African lives shown by administrators and private companies.

The dearth that urban and rural people faced around Libreville came from radical economic changes combined with heavy rains and droughts that undermined food production and limited access to sustenance.[7] Fang farmers endured disaster thanks to disease, the horrendous impact of World War I, and the uncontrolled expansion of timber exports and migrant labor. Similar tragedies ensued in other parts of Gabon during the same period.[8] Unlike in rural areas, where Africans generally had little influence on policy, town residents manipulated their position as privileged intermediaries to assert their goals of free exchange of food. The ability of townspeople to demand aid and change regarding food distribution illustrates the growing disparity between rural communities and Libreville. Urban people negotiated with the state for food supply; many timber camp workers and farmers simply died from hunger. Poverty had fundamentally changed from a shortage of food to a lack of access to labor, government aid, and money in the Estuary.

World War I and Food Supply to Libreville, 1914–1917

World War I created a host of miseries throughout Gabon.[9] The collapse of the Atlantic export economy and wartime troubles brought food shortages to a number of ports on the West African coast.[10] War between the colonies of French Gabon and German Cameroon (Kamerun) had immediate negative repercussions on the Estuary economy. Though the Germans were driven out of northern Gabon by early 1915, the war effort disrupted Fang settlements in the Estuary. First, the forcible recruitment of soldiers and porters for the French army took many men out of their villages.[11] Bishop of Libreville Louis Martrou wrote in January 1916: "Our [Fang] people hide—they say, 'Why fight? We're not angry!'"[12] To worsen matters, the government doubled individual taxes.[13]

Ironically, the defeat of German troops in Cameroon led to calamity. In early 1916 more than three thousand African troops who had fought in the German colony arrived in town. Bishop Martrou noted: "We have been invaded by the South Cameroon troops. Results—famine since the garrison wasn't ready for such a large number—the manioc is being used up and being sold at excessive prices."[14] Fang fishermen and farmers did not waste the opportunity for profit. By July many Europeans and African residents of Libreville complained about the exorbitant amounts demanded by Fang suppliers.[15]

Troops in the town stretched the limited resources of the region. Since the beginning of the conflict, Governor Guyon of Gabon had promulgated a series of decrees giving the military the right to requisition food.[16] African guards bought incoming fish themselves and resold it at higher prices.[17] Some soldiers stole food from visiting fishermen.[18] Even with the incentive of large profits, local production could not keep up with demand. Missionary Julien Macé wrote to a friend in November 1916 that he had not been able to buy manioc to feed his schoolchildren.[19]

The administrators tended to blame the lack of adequate food supply on a cornerstone of colonial policy: the lazy "native." However, Africans appear in the archival record to have not been idle. Fang farmers tried to sell food in Libreville, but obstacles stood in their way. African guards extorted payments from farmers before permitting them to continue toward the capital.[20] Villagers lacking pirogues had to rent boats, and village chiefs en route would sometimes extort bribes to let them pass.[21] Unable to pay taxes by working in their own villages, men went to find employment in Libreville and other parts of the coast.[22]

Another scourge spreading in the war's wake was the resurgence of wild animals. Just as warfare disrupted controls over wild animals in early colonial Tanzania and Darfur, the conflict impeded hunting in Gabon.[23] It is impossible to determine animal density in the Estuary before World War I, but several incidents show how the conflict sapped the ability of Fang people to protect their fields. Laws restricting firearms, high prices for powder due to the collapse of European trade, and the absence of men from villages allowed elephants and wild pigs to lay waste to manioc and banana fields.[24] Five herds of elephants ran amok in the Estuary during early 1918. The herds gobbled manioc fields and trampled gardens underfoot. Without the money to buy ammunition, villagers could do little but flee; some resorted to robbing other settlements for food. Their inability to farm left them unable to pay the annual head tax. People moved to Libreville rather than waste their time planting crops that would only be destroyed by pachyderms.[25] Georges Guibet, head of the Estuary region, tried to sway Governor Thomann in April 1919 to hand out guns and powder to villagers.[26] Governor Thomann took umbrage at the idea of handing out weapons.[27] These issues led to food shortages through much of the region.

In 1917 the increasingly despondent Bishop Martrou wrote: "The great misery of Gabon is the famine that holds sway throughout the colony."[28] Though the Ogooué River region appears to have endured greater hardships, Libreville was not spared. A blight struck manioc plants in the Estuary.[29] Protestant missionary Henry Perrier had to close the mission school at Libreville in late May since he could not find manioc or bananas.[30] Administrator Charles Bobichon, in an attempt to control food supply better, passed an ordinance in mid-1917 fixing prices and banning the sale of all food outside markets, yet food supply did not improve.[31]

Governor Thomann in his 1917 annual report blamed the famine on a combination of causes: blights, poor weather, the high expense of gunpowder, but most important, the lack of productivity of his subjects.[32] The war, forced recruitment, and tax hikes did not receive much mention despite their critical role in the spread of food shortages. Instead the governor argued that European-style agriculture could triple manioc production and solve the crisis. Africans had other ideas. Libreville townspeople worked through numerous channels to undermine state food distribution policies based on force.

Food Scarcity and Social Conflict, 1918–1919

Louis Martrou, bishop of Libreville since 1913 and an old hand in Gabon, had a front row seat to the horrors of starvation in the Estuary at the end of the war. Apocalyptic images loomed in the bishop's letters to his superiors in 1918 and 1919: "Our [Gabonese] farmers at the Colonial Congress ought to say: 'Our administration—unprepared, arbitrary, and without any practical foresight—will have killed off the colony in 20 years,'" read a typical jeremiad.[33] For a missionary the fumbling efforts of colonial officials in Gabon must have appeared as the fruit of an incompetent and perverse government. Martrou had even more reason to be dour as the war drew to a close.

The year 1918 marked a nadir in the decline of local food production. The effects of limited exports, onerous demands on the local population, and the near-disappearance of imports brought the food supply system to an all-time low. Supplies of imported goods continued to dwindle while prices rose. By May no local foods reached the Libreville market.[34] In desperation townspeople began eating unripe papayas.[35] Georges Guibet, the administrator in charge of the Estuary and Libreville, responded with coercion, commanding Fang villagers to bring regular supplies of manioc to Libreville or else face severe punishment by state guards.[36] Fears of punishment and military recruitment made many Fang flee Europeans and guards alike.[37]

Woes battered the Gabon Estuary for the next two years. A severe drought, followed by the arrival of Spanish influenza in late 1918, scourged Fang villages.[38] Missionaries estimated that 10 percent of the entire population in the Kango region of the Estuary died of influenza.[39] The rains proved unusually light in the spring.[40] Governor Marchand, estimating that the 2,800 African residents of Libreville ate 700 plantains per day, noted that only 40 bunches of plantains arrived during the entire month of February 1919.[41] Unable to find food, Gabonese marched daily to the Catholic mission for food.[42] Although food began to arrive in larger amounts after September 1919, prices continued to skyrocket.[43]

Government reports throughout the period frequently discussed the hardship of food shortages, but individual officers could not agree on a remedy.[44] Guibet tried new strategies that tacitly recognized the harmful effects of government policies. He postponed tax collection to allow villagers to concentrate on farming and asked the governor to ease restrictions on gun laws so that farmers could protect their fields.[45] Taken to task repeatedly by Governor Thomann, Guibet declared that he had warned his superiors of the threat of famine, but his ideas had been rejected.[46] Despite clear signs to the contrary, Thomann's conviction about the idleness of villagers remained undimmed. In his rebuff to Guibet, he wrote: "[The Africans'] laziness is the only reason they lack food."[47]

Administrators at the local level also worked at cross purposes on how the state should involve itself in food production, as illustrated in squabbles arising over food production in the Kango subdivision roughly a hundred kilometers from Libreville. Refugees fleeing forced labor and military recruitment from the north had entered the Kango region, further overwhelming the scant resources of the battered villagers.[48] From the summer of 1918 through April 1919 a settler named Vecten penned a blizzard of letters to Guibet. Vecten had convinced Louis Tastevin, a low-level official, to command Fang villagers to bring food for his ill-treated and often starving plantation workers.[49] The crafty plantation owner then loaded his boat with food to sell for marked-up prices in Libreville, annoying other settlers and administrators with his blatant profiteering.[50]

Townspeople, frustrated with the situation, asked the government repeatedly
to lower prices and aid food production. By late 1919 some Africans in the town
had decided to take matters into their own hands. Mpongwe clan chiefs and
a rising group of educated intellectuals attempted to lower food prices. Their
disparate protests included refusing to buy from English stores and writing
telegrams to French human rights organizations. This boycott underlines the
social tensions caused by food scarcity and the colonial government's inability to control them.

The Libreville Boycott of 1920

The boycott of January 1920 reveals a host of divisions within African communities in Libreville regarding food scarcity. The protest pitted Mpongwe townspeople against visiting Fang villagers and European traders. In turn, administrators
at different rungs of the colonial hierarchy did not agree on solutions to the crisis. The boycott displays the state's inability to control the behavior of urban consumers and rural food suppliers. Traditions of political power forged in the cauldron of Atlantic slavery could still be put to use against the dictates of French
authorities. They could work side by side with European models of lobbying.

Two years of famine had burdened the inhabitants of Libreville by the end of
1919. In early December Fang fishermen refused to come to Libreville for several days after the administration tried to put a tax on the sale of fish.[51] Town
residents grew desperate for action. During the course of the war clan chiefs
and mission-educated townspeople had already protested against high taxes
and called for the establishment of a Mpongwe monarchy and the expulsion
of foreign Africans.[52] Jean-Baptiste N'dende, a former mission apprentice and
state employee, established a branch of the French human rights organization
League of the Rights of Man (LRM).

N'dende and some clan chiefs, such as Loembe Morris from the outlying
village of Nomba, threatened a boycott of European stores and Fang fishermen as a means of lowering prices. They took the successful 1899 boycott as
their model. To intimidate European firms Mpongwe male notables demanded that English store managers lower their prices. British traders, apparently unimpressed by the warnings, augmented prices for soap, cloth, and
other commonly purchased merchandise.[53] These firms had also used their

boats to buy manioc and plantains in the countryside to resell for double the price in the capital.[54] Store managers furthermore snubbed Mpongwe leaders who wanted personal discounts.[55] Although some town representatives met with newly arrived Governor Marchand, the French administration did not try to defuse the explosive situation.[56] Officials threatened to fine European stores, but such decisions did not appease the boycott movement.[57]

By early January 1920 townspeople became aware of the possibility of a boycott and built up reserves of food.[58] Just as in 1899, Mpongwe notables placed the omowétchi talisman underneath the M'Pyra bridge separating Glass from Libreville on 12 January.[59] They forbade any African, regardless of ethnicity, to sell food in the local market or to enter a European store. Head administrator of Libreville Georges Guibet noted: "The Omouetchi is one of the most feared fetish practices of the natives, even among educated Mpongwes. As a result all the blacks whether they are Libreville residents or the Pahouins who live in Libreville . . . were faced with the impossibility on pain of death of entering the trading houses."[60]

The bold move paid immediate dividends. Fang farmers arriving in Libreville refused to disobey the Mpongwe chiefs. A British tourist found his Sierra Leone domestic servants unwilling to enter any stores without his presence.[61] The boycott thus succeeded in voicing the concerns and strength of urban consumers.

Officials could not find a clear solution to the dispute. Though Guibet could not openly support the protesters, he concurred with their sentiments.[62] Marchand gave Guibet orders to end the boycott the following day.[63] He could not. The markets and the trading houses remained bereft of customers for three weeks.[64] Europeans declined to drop prices.[65] Rather than the government, the Mpongwe chiefs and Fang farmers negotiated to close the boycott.

The notables' resolve to continue the boycott dissolved after several weeks. On 28 January they met to discuss the effects of the protest.[66] Clan chief Loembe Morris, who had served the colonial administration on occasion since the mid-1880s, wanted to end the boycott, while N'dende and several others wanted the struggle to continue. Morris won out. The protest ended, but N'dende sent a telegram to the Paris office of the LRM demanding Guibet's removal. Fang residents of Libreville may also have weakened the resolve of the protestors. Several years after the conflict, self-styled Fang chief of Libreville Vincent Ndongo boasted of brokering a deal with Guibet and European traders so that Fang arriving from the interior could sell food.[67] Since Ndongo appears to have been fairly corrupt and unscrupulous, it is difficult to determine how honest he was regarding his role in the event. Whatever was negotiated, the Mpongwe chiefs removed the *omowétchi* by mid-February.[68] Though sorcery shut down the city's market, the boycott does not appear to have been successful as regards lowering prices. The movement did embarrass the administration to the point that Guibet was immediately transferred to Chad. Former Libreville administrator Charles Bobichon wrote to a friend that Guibet had received no support from Governor Marchand in the affair.[69] Though only partially successful, the boycott does show how townspeople tried to control food supply.

The incident also reveals much about the strategies of Libreville men in the early twentieth century. Mpongwe clan chiefs worked with mission-educated intellectuals to develop a plan of action and drew on Séké ritual specialists, much as previous generations had done. Idioms of power, linked directly to the heritage of slavery, continued to function in Libreville. The telegrams to French human rights organizations and the invocation of supernatural forces involved carefully crafted appeals to local and international audiences. Gabonese protesters had mastered the rhetoric of human rights, a staple of French republicanism at home, to pressure the colonial administration. The role of Ndongo may suggest how Estuary Fang chiefs might have begun to take an active role in shaping Libreville affairs. Struggles over access to and supply of food among Mpongwe townspeople, Fang villagers, and the colonial administration would continue throughout most of the 1920s. In most of these battles, townspeople won out.

The Famine of 1921–1922

Another round of shortages ravaged Libreville in late 1921 and early 1922. The causes include a refrain of problems all too familiar in the Estuary: poor environmental conditions, harsh government policies, and competition over limited resources. Several new elements entered the picture as well. The slow prewar growth of the timber industry accelerated dramatically after 1920.[70] The French government with the support of major railroad corporations set up a company, the Consortium des Grands Réseaux Français, popularly known as the Consortium, in 1920. The Consortium originally aimed only to provide lumber to rebuild French railways, but it soon became the largest exporter of *okoumé* in the entire colony of Gabon.[71] African and European entrepreneurs rushed to obtain concessions from the French government in the early 1920s.

How would the meager resources of the Estuary feed thousands of male workers? Officials did not account for the consequences on food supply that the stampede for timber would have. By a decree passed by the governor-general of French Equatorial Africa, administrators had orders to force Africans to increase food production and to imprison or fine those who disobeyed officials' commands.[72] In the Estuary administrators appointed chiefs in Fang villages and set up communal fields to supply food to Libreville.[73] Since no central chiefs had existed among the fractured Fang clans, policymakers hoped this new institution would furnish discipline and order to food production and settlement patterns. Such plans did not always impede protests. For example, some Fang villagers displeased with the lowering of sardine prices boycotted European consumers in February 1921.[74]

Timber hindered food supply to Libreville. The town could not compete with African agents hired by the Consortium to purchase food for their workers. These agents offered more for sardines and other foods than the official standard, since local foods were much cheaper than importing rice or dried fish.[75] Bishop Martrou lamented in April: "One immediate result of this establishment is a food shortage in Libreville. Nothing comes, no manioc or bananas from the Como."[76] The food situation improved slightly in 1920, yet famine returned with a vengeance by the summer of 1921.[77] When the rainy season began a month early, gardens were devastated.[78]

Unwilling to raise prices to attract village farmers, administrators turned to coercion. The government closed down markets in Glass and in the outlying Fang village of Sibang to ensure that more food would come to the central market.[79] Ozimo Trumann, a clerk working for the administration, requested that these markets be reopened.[80] He joined other African residents in Libreville in demands to reopen the Sibang market and criticized government attempts to feed prisoners and state employees before private citizens.[81]

Fang villagers became less willing to come to Libreville. The closing of the Sibang market was extremely inconvenient for them. When the market closed, their plantains spoiled as it took several days to unload a canoe and bring its contents to market.[82] Administrator Tastevin ordered his guards to requisition villages for manioc and to stop all pirogues carrying food.[83] A Protestant missionary wrote: "There is nothing in the native markets. The Fang do not dare bring [food] directly for fear the Administration will take everything going to the market."[84] Without Estuary suppliers, chronic shortages struck with fury. From early

November through January 1922 African policemen found the corpses of famine victims strewn about in abandoned trading houses and huts around the city.[85]

After calling together officials and timber camp owners, Governor Marchand decided to reorganize food supply. He first ordered that the timber camps furnish part of their workers' rations with food grown at their concessions.[86] Second, he created markets at Libreville and in Estuary villages. Through this order the governor tried to control competition between timber camps and city residents. Marchand also threatened to cut off labor recruitment to timber camps that did not grow food.[87] Finally, all food brought to Libreville by Africans was henceforth taken directly to the administration. The governor-general accepted these orders initially as emergency measures.[88]

State officials and leading Europeans met to discuss reforms of food supply policy several times a month from December 1921 onward. As usual, African townspeople had no representatives in attendance. The group's main goals were to sate the needs of the timber camps and Europeans in the city. They called for strict controls over village food production.[89] When individual timber camp owners complained that villagers preferred to sell their food in Libreville, officials promised to force Africans to bring them manioc and plantains. Administrator Moesch, head of Libreville and the Estuary in late 1921, received the full support of Governor Marchand and his successor Cadier. The latter was quite satisfied with the new arrangements.[90] After the law took effect no new deaths from starvation in the city were reported, and enough food arrived to feed hospital patients and state workers.[91]

While administrators gloated about their successes, Libreville and Estuary residents groaned. Africans and missionaries objected to the policy on the grounds that the administration had taken control over food supply. The supplies requisitioned by officials first served the needs of state-run institutions such as the prison before going to the regular market.[92] Food was thus rationed out twice a week.[93] Missionaries at Donguila complained that guards took all available food from Estuary villages.[94] Market regulations angered many townspeople. Just as in the boycott, educated townspeople again battled state authorities through political lobbying to protect their endangered lifestyle and diets.

African Protests and Colonial Food Supply Policy

Mpongwe intellectuals again pulled together to protest state policies on food, and this time townswomen took to the forefront of protests as well. In February

1922 educated women joined in the tumult and sparked reactions that exposed numerous tensions over gender and race as well as over food when a group of roughly fifty Mpongwe women marched on the colonial government headquarters protesting state policies on food production. They first entered the governor's offices and then confronted administrator Moesch, head of the Estuary. Moesch ordered African policemen to disperse the crowd and imprisoned several women for several weeks.[95] Women demanded to have the right to buy food without restrictions or fines. "We do not know, Governor, the fault we are guilty of for letting us die of hunger. The prisoners have right to food and we believe . . . we ought to have the same right," they wrote.[96] Their treatment raised a scandal throughout the town, as these women presented themselves as respectable mothers wronged by a callous government.

Not all townspeople supported the women; gender tensions around female autonomy and agriculture made their presence felt. Several Mpongwe chiefs even demanded the right to beat their wives to make them work in the fields.[97] This tension derived from the fact that the majority of the protesters were mistresses of Europeans living in the colony. Critics of the administration even went so far as to state: "For ages, settlers and officials have taken for concubines native women who become accustomed to a life of idleness and obtain a certain comfortable way of life."[98] Moesch scorned their complaints since "they were rather luxuriously dressed and made up" in European clothes.[99]

While mutual concern over women's independence resulted in alliances between certain African men and European administrators, other Mpongwe residents of Libreville took up their pens to resist state authorities. An anonymous group of women wrote to the governor-general requesting the liberation of the jailed women.[100] Members of the LRM wrote letters to two French deputies along with Senator Berenger of Guadeloupe. They complained about the imprisonment of African women, restrictions on food purchase in Libreville, and the lenient treatment of several Europeans accused of killing Africans in the Estuary.[101] Yet again, Mpongwe in Libreville had manipulated the colonial chain of command to their advantage.

After receiving the letters the minister of colonies in Paris ordered an inquiry. Moesch and newly installed governor Cadier, asked to explain the protests, replied that the women warranted reprimand.[102] Their superiors did not share their position. Governor-General of French Equatorial Africa Antonetti, after an investigation, annulled the order of 10 December 1921 and criticized the treatment of the protesters.[103] Since the Mpongwe often wrote "exaggerated attacks" against administration policies, Antonetti first ignored their complaints but later found that Africans and Europeans alike were "insulted" by the imprisonment of these women.[104] Both Cadier and Moesch received censure as a result.

Perhaps emboldened by their victory, the LRM also acted to defend the interests of other Libreville and Estuary residents by again raising questions of human rights and republican ideals. Another protest, mounted on behalf of Mpongwe trader Charles Mouheha, sheds light on food supply to Libreville. In June 1922 N'dende wrote a letter claiming that Mouheha had been fined for "selling food to Africans" and wrote: "This fine burdens Mouheha and you to have to understand how the strictest laws . . . enforced under Governor Marchand . . . impede the existence and commerce of natives."[105] Mouheha, originally given a trading license in January, was penalized by Moesch for selling manioc at prices three or four times higher than the official price. Not allowed to trade in food, Mouheha turned to the LRM for aid. Although the end result of this protest is unknown, African townspeople again moved around colonial bureaucratic channels to protect free trade.

Other Africans used letters to challenge state policies or European planters. However, their letters generally concerned individual cases rather than general attacks on colonial food regulation. Some residents of Obello, a small Fang town on the south bank of the Estuary, received orders from administrator Charbonnier to move to the larger town of Mavoul in late 1921. Unwilling to leave, two men sent a letter to the "Great Governor of Gabon" in broken French.[106] After stating their willingness to sell manioc and fish in Libreville and their willingness to enlarge their fields, they demanded that they be given the right to stay. If their request was not accepted, the men offered this threat: "Great Governor, we are told you have given orders to make big fields. One does that in the village of natives, but we don't know if it is the truth that we must abandon them and leave them at the mercy of the animals. Charbonnier made us abandon our fields. If it is like that, our village will come to Libreville to work for the whites."

Given officials' fears of rapid urbanization and "vagabonds" living in the city without fields, their warning was a means to get leverage with the administration. Although they eventually backed off, the ringleaders of the protest demonstrated the effectiveness of the LRM in presenting food supply as a human rights issue.

The written word offered an alternative of circumventing European private and public policies and practices. Writing formed one strategy employed by townspeople. Much as in previous years, gender tensions and alliances between Fang and Mpongwe intellectuals influenced public manifestations of discontent by Libreville residents. Just as their determination brought about the end of harsh controls over food sales by the state, their activities would continue to disrupt the small world of Gabonese politics throughout the decade of the 1920s. While rural people began to have their voices heard, urban residents continued to dominate negotiations of food supply.

Riot, Recovery, and Rain, 1922–1925

After the governor-general ended tight controls, more food came into Libreville on a regular basis. Manioc and bananas began to reappear at markets. Farmers in the Kango and Médègué subdivisions sold food in the city.[107] Though other parts of the Estuary expanded production of crops, some products remained scarce, among them fresh fish.[108] Despite the improvements, the timber trade continued to hinder the steady supply of food. First, European and African camp owners still paid better prices than could be had in the Libreville market. On the Estuary south bank, where most of the large timber camps were located, fish and other staples sold for twice the town market price.[109] Though required by law to supply workers with food grown around the camps, timber entrepreneurs did not stop buying food elsewhere or recruiting Africans to bring them supplies.

Heavy rains in the summer and fall of 1924 washed away complacency. Bishop Martrou wrote in September: "Year of calamity—There was no dry season in Gabon this year from June until September. We had as much rain in these months as in May. From this, our gardens produced nothing. No fishing possible on lakes and reserves are non-existent. . . . The natives were not able to burn their fields and plant corn or bananas or manioc. Beware of the famine next year! One wonders if the end of the world has not come!"[110]

The heavy rains impeded fishing for sardines and exposed manioc roots.[111] Though missionaries recognized the seriousness of the threat of food scarcity looming over the region, administrators remained oddly confident. Governor Bernard pronounced the food crisis finally over.[112] In 1925 the head of the Estuary region reported that his jurisdiction had enough food to last until September, even though his own subordinates warned that manioc had disappeared in many areas.[113] To make matters worse, the government decided to make Estuary men work off their taxes through unpaid labor in Libreville during the spring.[114] Considering that many men had already left their villages to work in the camps, the result was that very few men stayed in villages to help wives or female family members work in the fields or to fish.

Food vanished from both the city and the timber camps by June. Much as in 1921, Estuary villages had to supply set amounts of manioc and plantains by official decree.[115] Guards stuffed jails in the Estuary countryside with prisoners. The Kango subdivision chief fined and imprisoned more than sixty men for "persistent negligence in weekly supply of bananas and food to Kango post market," for selling food outside the capital, for not supplying timber camps with food, and for fleeing food convoys headed for Libreville.[116] Some men were locked up for several years for stealing a few chickens.[117] After refusing to follow the orders of a French agriculture expert, Estuary men and women stayed in jail for weeks.[118]

Such draconian measures proved particularly wearisome given the utter dearth of food in the region. "Right now we have at Libreville and in the Haut Ogooué the worst famine I have ever seen in 19 years in Gabon," the head of the Catholic mission wrote.[119] No manioc came to Libreville from July to November 1925.[120] Starvation swept through Estuary villages. Much like Estuary farmers without state connections, timber camp workers died thanks to their inability to obtain food from their employers.[121] The famine would continue its grip over the town until the summer of 1926.[122]

The government's program was fixated on rote stereotypes of African incompetence. Governor Bernard, in a report sent to the governor-general in December, attacked his Gabonese subjects. "The Fang, among the . . . most backward peoples in the world, are lazy and apathetic to excess. There is no divergence from this opinion among all that have lived with them," he declared before attacking their supposedly backward forms of agriculture.[123] His recommendations to alleviate the situation did not display much creativity. They consisted of prohibiting food sales without authorization from officials, forcing the timber camps to grow food, and corporal punishment. Governor-General Antonetti shared Bernard's sentiments.[124]

Few townspeople died; their relative affluence allowed them to take a different approach to the problem of food scarcity. Mpongwe residents rallied again around Jean-Baptiste N'dende. At the height of the famine in July 1925, N'dende sent a letter to Governor Bernard demanding that Estuary head Pechayrand be removed from office, just as Guibet had been in 1920.[125] N'dende contended that Pechayrand had supported corrupt African chiefs, had arbitrarily imprisoned Africans, and had botched the food supply question. The head of the LRM in France sent a telegram to the governor-general criticizing Pechayrand.[126] Laurence Antchouey, founder of the short-lived newspaper L'Echo Gabonais and a member of the LRM, also wrote a protest to Senegalese deputy Blaise Daigne.[127]

Pechayrand responded that a handful of educated Mpongwe had misrepresented the truth regarding his policies. He boasted that his ration cards and the famine had been a "hard lesson" for Libreville residents but that they had spurred Africans to expand fields.[128] Given that Pechayarand was the his brother-in-law of Governor of Gabon Bernard, who had himself previously been responsible for the Estuary region, Bernard backed his subordinate.[129] The governor-general did not concur.[130] Pechayrand was removed from office. Though the change of office did not radically alter food supply policy, it showed once again that educated African townspeople could exploit their contacts to challenge local colonial administrators.

The defeat of Pechayrand may have also come from the impatience of officials in Paris. The Gabonese administration had a terrible reputation in high colonial circles. The position of governor had changed hands eleven times between 1917 and 1924.[131] Inspectors in 1924 berated Governor Bernard and his subordinates as wasteful and unfit to govern the colony.[132] The governor-general noted in his review of the inspection: "One could very well say Gabon had not been governed for twenty years and I wonder whether Bernard is able to bring this disastrous situation under control."[133] In light of such unpopularity, it is little wonder that Bernard sacrificed his son-in-law.

Despite Pechayrand's downfall, coercive policies continued to strike Estuary farmers. In the summer of 1926 administrator Tastevin—the very same so despised by missionaries—took the place of the unlamented Pechayrand. Tastevin's reputation for harsh decrees against Africans proved justified, as he ordered Estuary villagers to supply food to Libreville through village chiefs. If they did not, he threatened to impose six-thousand-franc fines on villages.[134] Unlike in 1925, however, food did not vanish from markets.

No major famines struck the Estuary region after 1926, but periodic food shortages caused adversity in town. In late 1927 the new bishop of Libreville, Louis Tardy, noted: "Thanks to God, the crisis appears over. Native foods are still rare and remain at a high price especially where timber commerce is intense. However, the undertaking of our work has become just about normal."[135] Although high prices continued to vex Africans and Europeans alike, the climate did not furnish the catalyst for disaster as in 1925.[136] Timber camps still paid higher prices than urban consumers.[137] Food remained scarce around Donguila in 1928 due to competition from timber camps and state guards.[138] A drought hit the Estuary in the early part of 1929.[139] Despite such complaints and troubles, writers did not report any catastrophes comparable to those earlier in the decade. Part of the amelioration of food supply came from the timber firms. Owners and managers agreed to allow the families of workers to live at the camps to grow food and also handed out more imports.[140] Officials warned that the colonial regime would restrict the arrival of migrant workers unless timber camps adequately furnished food.[141]

Such arrangements no longer elicited action from Libreville residents. After 1926 townspeople stopped voicing complaints on food supply and softened their public disagreement with the administration. Once they ensured that the government would not interfere with their access to food, Libreville residents may have lost their greatest motivation to take on officials. Furthermore, the entrance of Jean-Rémy Issembé and other Mpongwe men into the timber trade made attacks on colonial food policies a possible threat to their own commercial interests.[142] While rural people continued to suffer from forced labor and authoritarian commandants, Libreville residents found themselves in a privileged position.

Fang Society in the Hunger Years

How did the famine alter farming and society in Estuary Fang communities? Written records emphasize the agency of townspeople and colonial officials. Few Fang could write, and even those who did had little ability to refuse the commands of state authorities. However, oral traditions combined with fleeting references to villagers furnish some perspectives on how rural food producers coped with hunger. Population movement, the establishment of canton and village chiefdoms that reigned over people without regard for clan, and a sense of impotence appear time and again in oral interviews I conducted with older Fang Estuary residents in 2000 and 2004. Few of the survivors of the 1920s famines still lived, and their children recalled a reluctance of older people to tell them about those days of adversity. Though many of my informants had heard of the calamity, I heard only a few detailed oral accounts of the 1925 famine either in Libreville or elsewhere in the Estuary.

A central theme in stories of the famine was the disintegration of mutual obligations. Roughly twenty years after the horrors of the great famine era had come to an end, an older relative spoke with a young man named Ndoutoume Nkobe Justin about the hardships of the past.[143] The old man warned Ndoutoume: "There are two things to fear in life: war and famine. You don't think of your family, your mother, or your children. You look out only for yourself." At the height of starvation, thieves made noises of wild animals designed to scare people away from their fields. Once the farmers had fled, the robbers made off with the manioc. Another man recalled a story told to him by his stepfather. During the famine, the stepfather had visited some relatives searching for food and passed through villages where rotten corpses lay strewn about. No one was left to bury the dead. Once he managed to reach his wife's village, he eyed a young boy eating a yam. The boy tossed him a scrap once he had finished, and the old man danced for joy as he eagerly chewed on the tiny bit of food. "Afterwards, he felt shame at what he had done," his stepson recalled.[144] Boys could take on the provider roles of men, while adults acted like children.

In the topsy-turvy world of the famine, the power of elders was undone and family members neglected to support one another. Fang communities take great pride in holding elaborate funeral and mourning ceremonies, but starvation victims passed away without any fanfare. Other oral traditions of the famine often mentioned desperate people dropping dead after failing to find food.[145] Informants agreed that many died, particularly around Kango and along the Como.[146] At least one informant's testimony suggests that food scarcity also led to divisions within Fang villages. Afraid of having food stolen from their family fields, an old woman recalled that her father set up scattered fields deep in the forest and refused to share food with others.[147] One man asserted that his parents told him all they had had to eat were taros (a food not nearly as popular as manioc or plantains) brought from far away from the upper Como.[148] Some families turned to eating bush fruits normally avoided as poisonous, while others became clients of missionaries to obtain rice.[149]

The state's ability to watch over African communities in the Estuary also meant more efficiency in extracting labor and wealth. Households had to surrender food to soldiers. Forced labor details that could last up to several months awaited those who could not pay taxes in money. Villages set up communal fields, nicknamed "the fields of the commandant," to appease the demands of the government. Some men starved to death after their travail ended. Guards, often from other parts of Gabon or from other French colonies, enforced the commands of administrators. Fang men told stories of how these soldiers violated gender and generation conventions with impunity—ordering younger brothers to hit their elders or even raping Fang women with their husbands bound underneath their beds.[150] Though these narratives may not be historically accurate, they convey the sense of impotence men felt after having celebrated a lifestyle of fighting and raiding before 1914. It is little wonder that new religious traditions like bwiti made headway during these decades of disappointment.

Though most rural people were in a pitiable condition, a few individuals favored by the colonial administration enhanced their power. At the tail end of the famine in mid-1926, Tastevin accused Fang canton chiefs Abogho Nze and Eyeghe Ndong of corruption and abuses of power. These charges included keeping most of the profits earned from selling sweet potatoes harvested by different villages and from handing out government hoes. Fang witnesses testified that Nze paid them only half of what they should have earned from potato sales based on the official prices.[151] On an issue dear to men determined to control female labor, villagers testified that Nze and Abogho charged fees for settling marriage disputes of women.[152] The governor-general chided Tastevin for weakening the prestige of chiefs.[153] By undermining chiefs, Tastevin undermined the state's ability to control food production. Thus higher ranking members of the colonial administration recognized that their food supply demands required aid from African intermediaries.

Chiefs also appear as powerful figures in stories told by missionaries and local people. Félicien Endame Ndong, chief of the Fang of the Kango region, became a powerbroker distributing food in the 1920s. Endame Ndong had a flamboyant touch. Porters held him aloft in a hammock when he inspected villages in the fashion of colonial officials, and he would judge a dispute only if all interested parties bowed before him and kissed his cane.[154] Endame Ndong's control over dependents and ties to the state allowed him the labor necessary to grow cash crops next to manioc and plantain fields.[155] Finally, a new generation of big men, notably Léon Mba, could make food shipments to the government evidence for his ability to serve the government. The food shortages and social turbulence of the era made the state-appointed chiefs' largesse hard to resist.

Well-placed men seem also to have profited from the food trade to town and to the timber camps. The instability of the era seems to have constrained the ability of Fang women to follow successfully the example of female market entrepreneurs elsewhere. The bloated power of chiefs, difficulties with transportation, and direct negotiations between European and African men for regular contracts put women at a disadvantage in guarding profits from selling food. Bridewealth prices rose, as food sales and timber camp work led to higher profits.[156] The Great Depression would allow the region to recover from the excesses of the 1920s, but the legacy of male influence over transport and supply continued well afterward. Famine might have broken Fang autonomy, but enterprising men adapted to the situation while the Gabon Estuary as a whole dealt with deprivation.

When asked why the famine occurred, some informants gave a telling response: it was God's punishment against the Fang for their sins.[157] This is hardly unique; Sudanese battling drought and hunger gave the same response decades later.[158] Such an answer does little to illuminate the causes of the famine, but this statement suggests one form of cultural fallout from the famine years. This time of deprivation spelled the end of Fang independence from French authority in the Estuary, and so Fang communities had to account for the disaster. Cultural historian Wolfgang Schivelbusch, writing of the myriad impacts of military defeat in France, Germany, and the American South, notes that one aspect of what he terms the "culture of defeat" is that losers seek to borrow ideas from their conquerors, but that "learning from the victor involves not just simple adoption or imitation but a complex, multivalent process of assimilation and cultural adaption."[159] The famine made for a similar existential challenge to Fang communities. It is little wonder that the numbers of catechists and converts to Christianity began to expand dramatically in the Estuary region in the late 1920s and 1930s, even if most Fang men continued to aspire to marry multiple wives and guarded indigenous religious practices. Villages visited by missionaries for decades before World War I became willing to join Catholic and Protestant churches only after 1920. The famine not only eliminated missionaries' concerns for security with the end of clan warfare, allowing them to visit settlements without fear of attack; it also inspired some Fang people to incorporate missionary teachings into daily life.

The 1920s set in motion a radical series of changes that transformed rural life in the Gabon Estuary. Missionaries had greater ease in finding converts seeking material as well as spiritual aid. Colonial officials could curtail the autonomy of village communities. Older generational hierarchies crumbled, and some well-placed younger men rose to prominence as a result. French business interests and the colonial state helped prepare the way for the famine years, and their ability to penetrate and survey Fang villagers was greatly aided by the catastrophes that came in the wake of the food crisis.

The food shortages that repeatedly devastated the Estuary region and Libreville were the result of a combination of climatic changes, negative consequences of the war, government impositions on local labor, and the expansion of timber companies' activity. The war disrupted village agriculture and fishing, cut off the town from French supply lines, and doubled its population. The colonial administration, by placing heavy impositions on the labor of the local Estuary population, provided obstacles for agricultural production. Its attempts to oversee all aspects of food production often created more problems than they solved. The development of large timber firms in the Estuary after 1920 radically changed the food supply situation by creating a rival market for regions that had previously sold only to Libreville. The flu epidemic, droughts, and the heavy rains of 1924 thus undermined a food supply system that even in good seasons barely met local needs.

Through these adversities townspeople retained their determination to maintain free trade of food and their lack of involvement in agriculture. They sought to use the colonial state to support their interests, often at the expense of other groups. Boycotts, marches, and written protests illustrated the role of food supply as a crucial issue in their everyday lives. In turn, the colonial administration was rife with discord over how the famines should be handled. Libreville residents exploited these divisions for their own advantage. While farmers bore the brunt of hardship, townspeople had yet again defended their lifestyle and their claims on food. Famines thus heralded the final establishment of industrial enterprises in the Estuary and the acceleration of poverty linked to low wages. Rural Gabonese were at a severe disadvantage in coping with the transformations of food supply and political power between 1914 to 1926, and their weakness was reflected in their limited options in surviving starvation and social disruption.

Many of the same factors that led to other prolonged famines drove the starvation that plagued Libreville and its hinterland. Authoritarian policies designed to maximize control over production and labor at the expense of rural communities during wartime led to hunger in Algeria, India, and Vietnam during World War II. As in so many other places, wars and sudden, radical economic changes weakened food production and access to entitlements to the point that environmental difficulties spelled disaster. Much as in the Great Leap Forward, the hunger of rapid economic development drove administrators to promote plans that disregarded basic human concerns. Though the French government did not consciously use relief as a means of social control, as would Ethiopian and Sudanese leaders in later decades, administrators did favor townspeople in ways that elicited professions of loyalty to France. Libreville residents juxtaposed the lofty fictions of republican imperial France against the dreary realties of callous exploitation. The Gabonese famines certainly did not kill as many people as other major food crises in the twentieth century, but the root causes of starvation in Gabon were all too depressingly similar.

5. Town Life and Imported Food, 1840–1960

James Patten, an African employee of the Libreville Protestant mission, wrote to the Presbyterian Board of Foreign Missions in 1888 a fiery condemnation of how the missionaries treated their staff. He believed American ministers defrauded men and women like Mpongwe pastor Ntoko Truman by not paying them enough: "Although [Truman] is in sickness . . . under his life time no chop [food] was given to that poor old man . . . he was done evil in the sight of the Lord . . . he ought to get chop and some allowance."[1] Patten's rage centered on the lack of rations as part of workers' salaries and that the missionaries, in his scornful words, charged double market value for goods from their own store. In the past, "Carpenter always get there chop 7 lbs. Rice biscuits 7 lbs. Beef 7 lbs. 7 lbs. Tobacco 1 bar soap sea salt pipe 2 bottles kerrozine [sic] one tin sugar 2 bunch plantain for a weak [sic] . . . according to there work and value."[2] Imported food became part and parcel of an exchange system where goods embodied reciprocity and respect for African workers.

Six decades later another set of Libreville residents expressed discontent about food imported into Gabon in the midst of World War II. Aware that his colony would be cut off from metropolitan supply lines, Governor of Gabon Masson in 1940 created a system of ration cards for buying milk, sugar, and flour; only French citizens could eat food deemed "European."[3] Ration restrictions irked

Libreville families. Once Masson decided to back Vichy rather than the Free French, ration laws become much stricter, and the subsequent Gaullist victory did not alter the regulations. Bread became available only to Europeans and Africans with French citizenship.[4] Since métis people usually received French citizenship by 1940, rations led to animosity.[5] "Only mixed race people had bread," elderly Libreville resident Adolphe Revignet recalled of his youth in the 1940s.[6] Some Africans turned to métis friends to obtain bread and canned goods.[7] These privileges angered educated Africans, who considered themselves worthy of French citizenship.[8]

Importing food, and having the money and connections necessary to obtain it, were major issues, especially in a town as rife with shortages as Libreville. Imported ingredients and culinary styles became means of denoting social and cultural distinctions in the town. The incorporation of foreign tastes and the willingness of workers to demand rations made food a venue for raising complaints about employers and the colonial state. Some townspeople, especially West African laborers or mixed-race townspeople, acted to guard their entitlements to rice, meat, canned goods, and bread. The adoption of European foods also signified the mundane ways in which Libreville society participated in global innovations in consumption patterns. The colonial government, private companies, and missionaries introduced new foods and eating practices to Gabonese people through work and school. Some Americans and Europeans believed changes in how and what one ate were part of the evolution from "primitive" to "civilized" culture. Other foreigners were far more concerned with cutting costs than with grandiose plans for remaking African society. In either case, inhabitants of Libreville did not simply abandon older foodways but selectively added and ignored foods and eating styles introduced from outside Gabon.

Imported Foods in Nineteenth-Century Libreville

As we have seen, the port of Libreville became a meeting place of different eating styles. French sailors, Catholic priests, and American pastors brought their tastes to the town. Barrels of flour, salted pork and fish, and small amounts of canned goods came to the Gabon Estuary from Europe.[9] As early as 1849 flour, rice, and beans filled government warehouses.[10] European foods did not keep well in Gabon. Imported cattle from Angola and West Africa rapidly fell victim to sleeping sickness.[11] One observer recalled in 1850 seeing warehouse walls so riddled with holes that dogs made off with most of the colony's supplies.[12]

Despite such poor conditions some European foods entered the culinary repertoire of townspeople. Just as educated Mpongwe people followed the latest European styles of fashion, they consumed imported foods. These first served as trade goods in a similar fashion to cloth, brandy, and other objects. Missionaries and officials often traded biscuits throughout the Gabon Estuary.[13] In 1869 an American trader in Libreville offered a two-hundred-pound barrel of salted pork along with nails and wooden boards to Benga traders for rubber.[14] British and German pots and pans appeared in bridewealth payments by the 1860s.[15]

Employment and education had a culinary component that made its way into everyday life as well. The colonial government passed out rations to Catholic missionaries and their Gabonese staff.[16] Salted fish from Angola and the North Atlantic became more common. Hard bread and beans long consumed on European vessels became another part of meals.[17] Catholic and Protestant pastors fed students and workers a hodgepodge of imported and local dishes: manioc, beans, salted cod, and biscuits.[18] Finally, European traders doled out foods with largesse. English tourist Mary Kingsley lauded English traders for giving ample rations and providing well-made houses to African employees.[19] Mpongwe men at the Protestant mission concurred with Kingsley. One remarked in 1880 that British firms gave African agents beef, rice, biscuits, preserved meat in tins, coffee, sugar and "all that is fit to them."[20]

Food consumption for missionaries and officials offered one way to influence African behavior. Foreign Christians in colonial Africa saw dress, drinking, and marriage as parts of everyday African lives in need of reform.[21] In some regions food became another arena of mediation between mission concerns and local beliefs. Nancy Rose Hunt has argued that the control of eating practices served as an object lesson on European domestic order and hygiene for supposedly backward Africans.[22] She has called such beliefs part of a "knife-and-fork" doctrine that pitted the supposed cannibalism of Africans against missionary domestic education.[23] Mission educators in Libreville also taught students how to eat with forks, knives, and plates.[24]

Rather than focus on silverware alone, missionaries in Libreville consciously put in place a timed schedule of meals that contrasted greatly to local notions of time. Through the use of church bells mission students learned to eat at fixed times.[25] American pastors proved particularly zealous in enforcing schedules. When Robert Nassau found workers eating at work outside set times, he threw their food away and smashed their plates.[26] Nassau also fined and struck Africans for cooking their own food in the mission kitchen.[27] Through such acts of discipline, Europeans hoped to instill values of orderly work habits in their students and laborers.

Mission education influenced the tastes of their students, but social concerns also played a role. Such concerns were part and parcel of eating in many parts of the world outside Europe in the late nineteenth century.[28] Some people accepted imported food as part of a "civilized" lifestyle that denoted high status. Foreign food and nonalcoholic beverages also became a tangible sign of gentility. Mission-educated Africans by the turn of the century threw lavish parties where guests snacked on lemonade and cake; Mpongwe mistresses of European men developed a taste for desserts and pastries.[29]

Beef also became a luxury item. Few foreigners, let alone Africans, could get their hands on it.[30] "Veal is so rare in the colony that one loses quickly a taste for it; butter and milk would be unknown if the importation of European conserves did not bring it," one French doctor observed.[31] Scarcity led to some bad behavior on the part of local residents. One French naval quartermaster around 1890 charged with guarding the state-owned cattle herd illicitly sold beef to a Portuguese retailer until an African employee at the store informed on the officer.[32] In 1898, on a day when beef was in short supply at market, a female Protestant mission employee sent a domestic servant to pick up two kilos of meat; her American minister and supervisor, incensed that the woman's employee had beat his own servant to the store, commanded she give up her meat so it could instead grace his table.[33] Eating beef was a sign of well-being in other ways. Mpongwe chiefs like Félix Adende Rapontchombo imported and raised small cattle herds between the 1870s and World War I, even though cattle had difficulty living in the Estuary.[34] The cost of restocking a herd of cattle in the unfriendly confines of Libreville showed off the riches of a big man even more than a taste for high-priced meat purchased from a butcher.

Discussions of food often included concerns about the relative autonomy of town women. Imported meals became associated with Mpongwe female indolence. Some Mpongwe men blamed their inabilities in finding a marriage partner on mission education. Younger men grumbled to Catholic missionaries in 1904, "How do you want me, my Father, to marry a Christian girl? She only wants to eat bread . . . She doesn't know how to plant manioc."[35] Such talk reveals one aspect of male anxieties in town, but it was not entirely accurate. A woman raised at the Protestant mission had trouble gardening after she was forced to live on her own, but Catholic schoolgirls did in fact work in mission fields.[36] A French priest wrote that Mpongwe women preferred to buy food, even at the risk of famine, with wages earned by husbands or lovers.[37] European missionaries and male urban residents thus criticized women by arguing that their independence sapped their ability to cook and grow food for families.

Food was not just a matter of presenting one's own sense of "civilization" or a battleground over the proper role of wives, though—it also was a matter of survival. Given the shortcomings of Libreville's food supply and that food prices were high, it is little wonder residents added salted pork, bread, and other products to their diets. As early as the 1870s a British trader stated: "At present the natives of Gaboon and of many places to the southward of that place do not produce sufficient food for their own consumption, and are to a greater or lesser extent dependent on the importation of rice, biscuit, &c."[38] Foreign food was pricey. Robert Nassau, a minister who knew the Gulf of Guinea coast well from southern Cameroon to the Ogooué River, asserted in 1894 that Libreville had the highest prices for local and imported food in the region. Local scarcity and high customs fees made the cost of living hard on missionaries.[39] Others echoed his sentiments.[40] Cut off from an extensive and reliable food supply chain, townspeople became consumers instead of producers. Their privileged access to wage labor and commercial contacts allowed them to buy or acquire food—but this same position made food a source of friction between employers and their African staff.

African workers demanded that they deserved to be fed in similar fashion to Europeans. Rather than simply wishing to imitate Europeans out of a sense of insecurity, Mpongwe townspeople and West African contract laborers wanted equal treatment and salaries. Many of them drew from their own views of "civilization" in their calls for access to foreign foods. Such discussions brought out contradictions in the European colonial project of transforming everyday life. Rather than successfully imposing their views of order on Africans, employers found themselves involved in labor disputes with workers who took foreign food as a sign of their value and education.

Rations, Salaries, and Labor, 1870–1914

Ration issues angered two African communities in particular in Libreville before World War I: laypeople associated with the American mission at Baraka and migrant laborers from the Kru coast of Liberia. Gabonese pastors, artisans, and teachers felt that their American colleagues thought of them as slothful and corrupt because they did not always succeed in producing all the food needed to support themselves. Their protests drew from a sense of respectability that American missionaries brusquely violated with impunity. Kru stevedores and sailors were illiterate, and so had to forgo petitions. Even so, Kru people ultimately were better than the Gabonese of Baraka mission at bargaining for better rations by hinting they would boycott the colony altogether unless they received the foods they usually ate at home.

American missionaries became the butt of criticism from their African staff over rations. Joseph Reading, stationed at Baraka in the 1880s, evokes in rich detail how workers were fed: "At eleven o'clock a single stroke of the bell calls each group of workman or colored mission family to come and get the provisions for the day. There is no regular supply of native [provisions], and the mission must feed everyone in its employ except the mission family itself, which must buy its own food or go without!"[41]

Food distribution was itself an education for African students and workers. The bell marked the audible arrival of a Western model of measured time, and the weekly exchange also signified the paternal role of American ministers as bosses feeding their staff. This notion of reciprocity and mutual obligation did not sit well with the Americans of Baraka, even though they made rations part of the amount of goods paid as wages each month.

American pastors mocked the eating habits of their Mpongwe clients. They felt that their charges, tempted by the material trappings of Western clothes and objects, had fallen victim to the supposed vices of civilization. Mpongwe workers' demands for aid and better rations only demonstrated their decadence. "Hunger will urge most people to work but women here sit beside the street and cry 'Njanla,' hunger, when they see one passing," Walker wrote in 1881, "but they will not work or remit rum and tobacco for food."[42] Robert Nassau, who resided in Gabon almost forty years, voiced in his diary a common opinion about his flock. "As if the mission was to feed and clothe and bury all these idle people," he wrote after being asked to aid with a funeral in 1895.[43] A few female missionaries enjoyed coming to the aid of hungry and often elderly and infirm members of the congregation, but these appear to have been exceptional cases.[44] To Americans, Mpongwe converts and workers needed discipline rather than material aid.

Laborers complained of unfair treatment over rations by condescending missionaries. An early and explosive example of discontent at the Libreville mission is cited in an 1873 letter by African-American ship pilot William Miller. Declaring there was no way to cook aboard ship and that the pots about the vessel were "not good to cook Swill in," Miller bemoaned the fact that he had been given only a poor supply of rice for a three-week voyage.[45] Disgusted by his treatment since he had to eat food given out as part of his salary, Miller decided to quit his job. He denounced this practice and lauded rations distributed on English ships: "I will tell you—one pound of beef, one and a quarter pound of pork a day which makes two and a quarter pounds of meat per day . . . [On an English ship] we have a Different bean codfish plumb pudding and Rice a day. The six pounds of beef 4 lbs. pork 5. lbs. bread and 19 of rice has had to last me almost four weeks. I will stand no more fooling." The precise list of food and measurements marked a sense of self-worth; Miller believed himself worthy of better than the paltry amounts the mission provided. In his conclusion Miller blasted Bushnell for treating him like "a bush nigger" by assuming he would put up with such treatment.

Some skilled African workers shared Miller's attitudes, but food became a contentious issue for two other reasons. Besides the fact that local food was hard to purchase at times, late nineteenth-century Libreville was a place where hard currency and barter coexisted. There was no clear break between exchange in goods and the use of money; rather, a bewildering amount of variations could appear in economic transactions between initial colonization and World War I. Catholic missionaries bought slaves and paid workers in a mix of French francs and assorted goods.[46] Senegalese artisans and soldiers in 1890 received cash, rice, tobacco, and some items that would not often be on the shopping list of a practicing Muslim—namely brandy and salted bacon. Some Senegalese did have an inordinate taste for liquor, but others needed brandy and pork in order to buy fresh fish, palm oil, and bananas from vendors apparently not interested in money.[47] Tobacco remained a standard medium of exchange in the rural Gabon Estuary even after World War I; British traveler Frederick Migeod in 1920 stocked up on tobacco leaves after being told they were a necessity in rural areas.[48]

African traders and workers thus had to calculate the value of goods and money for exchange to determine what would be the optimal mixture of payment. What makes the dietary showdown at Baraka intriguing is that one has an opportunity to see how skilled Libreville workers compared payments in goods with payments in money. Africans wanted money. Missionaries who were extolling wage labor over slavery wanted to compensate their staff in goods alone. Debates over rations thus became a conflict over labor and the slow rise of French currency in the town economy.

Ntoko Truman recognized the discrepancy in food prices between the trading houses and their employers. The first Mpongwe pastor, Truman voiced his criticism of American missionaries' racist attitudes. In very colorful language, he disapproved of the lack of respect he received from missionaries in 1880: "The Scriptures say the workman is worthy of his meat. The Gaboon mission say no food to be given people who work in the Mission ever since I joined with the mission here, next August will be 10 years and many times I have complained to the Mission about my ration but they all say no. I must buy my food myself."[49]

Since the Americans refused to tell Africans how much the food they gave out as salary was actually worth in money, Truman asked that he receive his pay entirely in cash. Missionaries found Truman's requests appalling and considered his assertion of his needs as proof of Mpongwe vanity. In July 1880 an American woman at Baraka mocked Truman for having the gall to ask that servants cook his food, just as they did for white Americans.[50] William Walker, head of the mission, denigrated the Mpongwe in the very same summer. At Baraka, he reported, "food is easy here & laziness flourishes here like the growth of weeds & just as troublesome."[51]

Truman, receiving no response from his immediate superiors, wrote to the head of the Presbyterian mission board in New York City demanding that the situation be changed. In his polemic he included many specific details regarding rations and salaries.[52] Americans forced Gabonese to buy their supplies and food from the mission storeroom for prices far higher than elsewhere in Libreville. For example, one pastor stated to Truman two bars of soap were equal to a "dollar" of goods or money when any customer could buy five bars of soap for a "dollar" at a store. When the African minister complained, Americans told him how Mpongwe people just wanted to eat and sleep without working or suggested that he sell his own house to pay for food and necessities. Exasperated, Truman replied, "How can I sell the house when I live in it? It is the same as telling a man to sell his suit of clothes that he has on." Again, rations are presented as an expression of the value of workers; traders understood this far better than did Protestant clergy. Truman's remarks also show the actions of skilled workers aware of their position as consumers in need of money and rations to feed them.

Truman had no luck winning over his bosses. Pastor Joseph Reading refused to pay Truman in money on the grounds that it was commonly used in Libreville.[53] Truman struck back the following year by writing two angry missives to America, again decrying the high mission store prices. "Mr. Walker says what use for a black man to drink coffee and Tea," the Mpongwe pastor wrote, "I thought he came to enlighten the place."[54] His discussion illustrates a central issue in the battle over rations. Protestant missionaries had come to Gabon ostensibly to "civilize" Africans through introducing evangelical Christianity and American etiquette. Even though African workers did adopt Western models of consumption to the point of buying their food, missionaries still criticized educated Africans for their supposed weakness for the material trappings of Europe. Far from being unaware of this contradiction, Truman referred to it repeatedly.

> By suffering so year after year that young man goes away to the factories to ask for work. He gets his salary and the factory feed him too. That is the reason the young man go away from the mission. If you have a dog and you give that dog enough to eat so there is no room in his stomach to hold anything, that dog would not go. . . . Why, it is because there is no room in his stomach to hold anything. So it is about the mission and young men here in Gabon.[55]

Thus Truman asserted that Americans alienated potential converts and workers by refusing to respect them as equals in conduct and in salary. Changing food tastes meant assimilation to Western, Christian mores; therefore Mpongwe men should have the same right to consume in a "civilized" manner as any American. He also asserted a counternarrative to the perpetual complaints of American Presbyterians that Christianity never could flourish among the worldly Mpongwe because of their weakness of character—instead, Truman illustrated how missionaries should not expect educated townspeople to be treated like naïve and lazy children.

American missionaries remained firm in their refusals throughout the 1880s. Up until his death in 1894 Truman never relented in his requests for higher salaries and free rations.[56] Other Africans shared his views. James Patton, another Mpongwe employed by the mission, expressed his fury over treatment in a diatribe against missionaries in 1888. He attacked missionaries' presumptions of their moral superiority over European traders: The missionaries "are nothing but a trader they do more than what the merchant trying to do. . . . See lots of money and goods you are sending to the Gaboon mission what are they doing with it. . . . the workmen in the yard cannot get their rashon [sic] rights."[57]

Such outbursts present access to European imported foods as a sign of respect. A new form of poverty, familiar to the poor teeming in European cities, had come to Libreville.

In the end, as a result of these complaints, Americans at Baraka changed their position slightly regarding rations. They requested authorization to pay workers only in money and to eliminate rations entirely in 1889.[58] When Africans complained about the food question, missionaries trotted out their stock of clichés about the incurably lazy Mpongwe. Baraka head William Gault grew annoyed with his assistant Ovendo Lewis's requests for food. "He demanded somewhat [more] when he found out how much his usual supply of rations cost him. But I told him that he was a man, and that I was tired of giving out food," Gault stated in 1890.[59] Rations thus became tied to missionary notions of masculinity and self-sufficiency as well as labor.

This lack of cultural understanding helps explain the decision of the Presbyterians to move elsewhere. By the late 1890s American missionaries had swung their attention away from the thorny Libreville mission field for southern Cameroon. Libreville had disappointed them. Due to the strong opposition of the French government to teaching in English, their schools were run by visiting French and Swiss teachers.[60] Furthermore, their inability to combat the influence of European traders or Euro-African sexual relationships made them consider Libreville a spiritual wasteland.[61] "I most emphatically object to [being stationed] at Gaboon [Libreville]. . . . I couldn't name a spot in America that has more Gospel privileges and less Gospel fruit than Gaboon," one American missionary wrote in 1892.[62] Presbyterian missionaries slowly moved out of Gabon and left the Baraka mission post vacant from the turn of the century onward. The Baraka mission was officially ceded to French Protestant missionaries in 1913, but Americans had largely abandoned the mission a decade earlier. Thus their attempts to monitor and control African workers rigidly ceased altogether.

One reason not brought up by irate missionaries for their lack of success was the ration problem. From Nassau's obsession with the eating habits of day laborers to skirmishes with African pastors and artisans, the American contingent's neglect of reciprocity made negotiations over rations with townspeople extremely divisive. Free townspeople who believed they deserved food at reasonable cost as a method of valuing their toil and to offset high food prices protested against the American Protestants. William Walker, Robert Nassau, and others viewed Mpongwe disenchantment as proof of their degeneration and character flaws. From the complaints registered, free people asserted that the Americans were ungenerous and thus unattractive as patrons. Catholic missionaries, by contrast, could better fulfill the expectations of patronage by offering food from their own fields.

Mission workers were not the only group in Libreville to make rations a serious issue for labor disputes. Kru workers in Gabon often protested regarding their rations. They could not write voluminous letters or contact people outside of Gabon. Also, their demands differed somewhat from those of the African employees of the Protestant mission. Their methods of articulating their discontent ended up ultimately being more successful than those of workers at Baraka. Employers greatly valued their Kru staff and were willing to make compromises about rations to keep them satisfied.

From the scattered source materials available, it is evident that the composition of rations mattered most to Kru workers. Kru laborers had selective tastes; they abhorred plantains and manioc and received brandy, rice, salt, tobacco leaves, and salted fish or pork each day.[63] Certain other foods prompted Kru anger. Around 1900 one Kruman told a Protestant missionary, "Milk be fit only for piccaninny, I no be picaninny."[64] Instead they wished to eat foods similar to those of their homeland. Furthermore, they lacked fields and family members to sustain them. Thus rations played a critical role in their everyday lives.

English writers Richard Burton and Winwood Reade, in their excursions to Libreville in 1862 and 1863, hired Kru workers to handle domestic chores and portage.[65] Both men admired the work ethic of Krumen. While indulging in supposedly scientific expeditions centered on hunting, Burton and Reade dragged Kru workers from southern Gabon to Equatorial Guinea. Reade noted that his Kru workers did not enjoy long travels and preferred to have regular food supplies.[66] When Reade asked his Kru workers to travel with him to Corisco, a small island roughly on hundred miles away from Libreville, he received a rude response. One of his workers told him, "We no catch good chop [food] there. S'pose Kruman no chop fine, he no fit work there—for true."[67]

This incident offers several points of interest regarding rations. Just as William Miller used food as a means of separating himself from Krumen, these workers sought to distinguish themselves from other Africans through "chop." Second, rations as well as wages were criteria for accepting work. Richard Burton ran into similar battles over rations.[68] Twenty years later a French officer encountered similar skirmishes over rations with his Kru workers. "Over a minor question of food, did not my men want to assault me in broad daylight in Libreville?"[69] For migrant contract laborers the issue was not a trifling luxury. Kru workers were willing to fight to ensure that they received their due in rice and brandy.

Commandants of Gabon, unable to attract Mpongwe workers to their service for menial labor, knew well that they needed to treat Kru workers with care. Without the migrants, the administration suffered greatly from a severe lack of manpower. Determined to curry favor with skilled Kru workers, the French administration paid heed to Krumen complaints about their rations and treatment. In the mid-1870s a small cohort of American, British, and German traders often tortured their Kru workers.[70] Many times the men did not receive wages or much food; one American trader did not feed his workers for months.[71] Some came down with beriberi.[72] In response Europeans would often be jailed and expelled from the colony. Commandants did not extend such protection to other laborers in town.

When the local administration tried to save money by feeding Krumen manioc, the situation became difficult. A French naval captain assigned to recruit Kru workers in 1882 wrote to his superiors: "I was asked to promise that the Krumen be given rations of bread or rice instead of manioc. [They] complained about the food. 'In the factories,' they said, 'we get rice and if the French government gives manioc, they will not get anymore Krumen anywhere on the coast.'"[73]

The captain added, given the fierce amount of opposition to manioc, that the commandant of Gabon should follow this request. Krumen workers threatened the French government just as they had threatened European traders.[74] French officials thus generally ordered that rice be paid to their Kru staff.[75]

Krumen workers succeeded in pressuring their European employers to serve them rations that they actually wanted to eat. They used food consumption as a way of maintaining a separate identity from that of other Africans in Libreville. Their strategies were more successful than written appeals. Whereas mission workers could be replaced and remained in Libreville, Kru workers had more leverage.

European food supply policies differed greatly among various employers.

Foreign firms needed a stable workforce and thus were willing to pay more to keep workers satisfied. Colonial officials were willing to respect the rations of their workers. Protestant missionaries, on the other hand, tried to dictate food consumption patterns as part of the goal of creating hardworking Christian autonomous communities. Unlike missionaries determined to control the behavior of their workers, traders do not appear to have put restrictions on the eating habits of their labor force. Thus their ration distribution brought on less controversy.

Hard currency alone, rather than mixed payments including goods and food, became the main form of wages for work in Libreville. It is hard to determine exactly when this transition occurred. When the entire colony of French Congo faced financial ruin in the late 1890s the head of the colony suppressed rations for many African office workers and unskilled laborers employed by the government.[76] It is harder to determine when private companies abandoned rations in town. As late as 1930 French business owners argued that the government should not mandate rations for their African staff in Libreville.[77] By the 1940s only timber camps still provided workers with food.

Foreign foods continued to be a source of contention in the twentieth century. During the famine years of the 1920s colonial officials brought in tons of rice to feed workers and townspeople. Advances in shipping meant more rice, beef, and other foodstuffs came into the port. Generations of children educated by missionaries become accustomed to eating beans, beef, and other European dishes. Furthermore, townspeople of means created new ways of receiving canned goods, flour, sugar, and other items by forming cooperatives. Even foreign cooking became a part of Libreville life, as young men worked as kitchen assistants. European officials and administrators complained, but imports proved much more reliable than the surrounding countryside in delivering food—and less costly than dubious state programs designed to further agriculture. When circumstances led administrators to limit access to foreign foods, townspeople took to the streets to uphold their entitlements.

The Advance of Foreign Food, 1920–1960

Townspeople in Gabon's capital made foreign foods a key part of diets by the late decades of colonial rule. Libreville's vulnerability to disruption of the indigenous food market, its connection to the French empire, and wage labor all made imported foods an attractive option. Especially for the affluent, standard meals included dishes from Europe. However, such mainstays as salted fish and rice had their drawbacks, especially in times of war. Officials promoted foreign foods as a solution for the local food crisis rather than encouraging agriculture or building roads that could connect Libreville to the rest of the country. In the end imports were preferred by the government and by towns-people to intensive agricultural development.

As described in chapter 4, famine swept through the Gabon Estuary repeatedly between 1914 and 1925. One reason for the crisis came with the sudden decline of foreign imports. Few ships came to the once-busy harbor. Metropolitan needs made potatoes, onions, and a host of other foodstuffs very difficult to bring to Libreville.[78] Wartime troubles and the collapse of the Atlantic export economy brought food shortages to a number of ports on the West African coast, so Libreville was just one of many towns experiencing a dearth.[79] French and African troops returning from victory in southern Cameroon in 1916 also swallowed up most of the local food available, leading missionaries to serve rice.[80]

French companies, missionaries, and authorities decided to make import-ed rice a de facto panacea for the town's food supply problems. When French timber companies started to bring thousands of workers into the thinly-popu-lated Estuary countryside, they resorted to rice. To offset the famine crisis the colonial administration purchased tons of rice and corn from the Ivory Coast, the Belgian Congo, and Indochina.[81] During 1925 and 1926 alone, the colony of Gabon's rice imports went from 600,000 to over four million kilograms.[82] Father Julien Macé wrote to a colleague in France responsible for supplying Gabon: "I have more than 300 Fang stomachs to feed. Do you think two tons of rice will go far?"[83] They neglected to recognize that man cannot live on rice alone. Beriberi cases had occasionally been diagnosed among troops stationed in Libreville before 1914, but the illness became a scourge when rice became the cornerstone of workers' and soldiers' diets.[84]

Timber camp workers in the Estuary succumbed to beriberi, especially before companies encouraged family members to live with their employees on the camps in the late 1920s. Several doctors declared that the poor quality and monotonous use of rice led to poor health among workers; out of 1,200 work-ers at one camp, 155 suffered from beriberi by November 1921.[85] As mentioned, when famine reached unprecedented levels in the fall of 1925, five men a day died at the giant Consortium timber concession on the Estuary south bank. The firm's doctor believed that 40 percent of the 1,500-man workforce had either beriberi or dysentery caused by the monotonous use of rice.[86] Some workers in desperation raided villages as far as twenty kilometers away for food. On occasion, workers drove villagers away from their own fields.[87]

Beriberi also plagued soldiers stationed at the Baraka military camp in Libreville. With no other foods but rice handed out, beriberi began to strike some African soldiers as early as 1918.[88] Gabonese military men did not resign themselves to starvation. On the morning of 17 February 1923, French officers tossed twenty-seven Gabonese soldiers at the Baraka military camp in Libreville into jail when they refused to eat their ration. The soldiers, making up one fifth of the troops stationed in the town, declared that their rice when shelled equaled only half the amount they had been promised and was covered with mold.[89] When a white officer tried to give them more food that evening, the prisoners grabbed plates, pots, and spades and tried to storm out of the camp. Despite attempts by loyal African soldiers to restrain the enraged and hungry troops, some escaped and fled toward the center of the capital. A French officer gave the order to aim an unloaded machine gun at the mutineers. The sight of the weapon "had the desired moral effect" and "brought calm immediately," according to the garrison commander.[90] On investigation many of the rebels were discovered to have been involved in another riot over food supply in 1921. Lieutenant Governor of Gabon Cadier wrote to his superiors in Brazzaville on the incident expressing anxiety. "It is said the natives want to kill the whites," Cadier warned.[91]

Rice led to tragedy for some in the era of crisis, but access to outside food supplies was of vital importance for townspeople. Former students might look back in disgust at the piles of salted fish they ate at mission schools, as Gabonese politician Jean-Hilaire Aubame did in 1959.[92] However, few townspeople were reported to have died from starvation. Townspeople of means could afford to buy food or could turn to others for aid. The hinterland around Libreville might have exhausted food supplies, but townspeople did not have to worry that the town's warehouses and stores might be bereft of all sustenance after World War I ended and regular shipping resumed.

Some townspeople used their favored position with the administration unscrupulously to acquire food. Ouapa, a personal servant, asked his employer for a franc to buy some rice in February 1922. The Frenchman told him to clean the house. According to Ouapa, his employer then refused to pay up. Hungry, he took matters into his own hands, albeit with a false signature, by manipulating standard shopping practices. Retail stores in Libreville accepted written agreements from Europeans and Africans in lieu of cash before World War II. The wily servant thus forged his employer's signature on a note to buy a bag of rice.[93] The temptation to take advantage of government connections may also have inspired other clerks and servants to acquire food for themselves or for sale, but only Ouapa's case survives in the archives.

Privileged access to foreign food continued in Libreville after the local food supply networks had stabilized in the late 1920s, although the ability of households at different rungs of the social ladder to buy food varied significantly. For Mpongwe families, European and African foodways blended together, as attested by older people who grew up from the 1920s through World War II. Some Mpongwe joined a cooperative that included African and European veterans and state employees. Simone Saint-Dénis recalled that her father served wine and bread with most meals.[94] Older men and women recalled eating canned foods, rice, and bread on a regular basis as children.[95] Saint-Dénis and other children with fathers who had previously served in the French military had access to European rations unavailable to other Africans.[96] Military service and mission education also shaped meals and cooking in wealthy households. As a child, Luc-Marc Ivanga lived with his uncle, the noted politician François de Paul Vane. His uncle's fervent Catholicism made its way to breakfast. Children at the Vane home rose at the sound of the morning Angelus prayer and followed European table manners.[97] Their meals articulated a part of what informants called "our particular civilization."[98]

Much as their ancestors had in the late nineteenth century, well-off families of mainly Mpongwe descent had eating habits that distinguished them from other Africans, and it cost them. A 1962 survey indicates that Mpongwe households paid the highest amount for food in Libreville.[99] Their consumption of dairy products, wine, and canned goods greatly raised their costs. Elevated salaries allowed these households in large part to continue their "civilized" tradition of eating habits. Men often worked as accountants, interpreters, and commercial agents. Their high salaries allowed them to buy expensive imports much more easily than could most other Libreville residents. European men continued to take Mpongwe women as mistresses. These men generally expected their lovers to serve them European meals. Thus the distinctive eating habits of Mpongwe came from many sources.

Less well-to-do residents also ate foreign foods. Fang residents in Libreville who had once belonged to the army incorporated canned foods as well. The quality of such goods at times left much to be desired, but processed foods nevertheless continued to make inroads. Fang workers in Libreville cracked open cans of corned beef for lunch in the 1930s, and even rural stores sold rice in the following decade.[100] Rural farmers exchanged manioc, fish, and plantains with timber camps for rice, canned foods, and soap.[101]

The colonial government occasionally aided or impaired the ability of some townspeople to buy processed food. Mixed-race students came under more state surveillance during the Popular Front era of the 1930s. Colonial administrators decided to defend the interests of mixed-race Africans in Libreville, even when Mpongwe people did not treat métis as outcasts. At schools, children identified as mixed-race ate bread, beef, and other typical French fare rather than the sardines and manioc passed out to other children. Some Mpongwe who lacked official recognition disliked their "African" diet. In December 1999 a seventy-six-year-old mixed-race woman descended from Mpongwe clan leaders boasted in an interview, "We ate meals worthy of the children of the king."[102] Her mother, grandmother, and aunts served typical dishes such as palm nut sauce and fish along with European foods. When served the typical school menu of sardines and manioc in the 1930s, she found the food revolting. Her grandmother on occasion brought her canned sausage that she could eat as a substitute. Food designated as "African" by missionaries did not satisfy her appetite.

During World War II what was at first a policy that made an impact only at schools became a source of contention for the entire town. The colonial government decided to set up a strict ration policy along the lines of that during World War I. The liberalization of French citizenship laws modified the ways African subjects could purchase foods labeled as being primarily for European consumption: flour, sugar, milk, and other foods. Until the 1930s it was extremely difficult for any African to attain French citizenship in Libreville, as practically no French fathers would legally recognize their children with Gabonese mothers. A 1936 law allowed all mixed-race individuals the right to become French citizens regardless of the identity of their parents. Citizenship meant equality not only in law but also at the store. Older Libreville residents recalled that bread had become one food that only mixed-race Africans could easily obtain. Some remembered how friends and family members would get métis to purchase baguettes for them. Citizenship thus provided entitlement.

Tensions developed over citizenship and the foods that came with it. Shortages of imported foods during World War II compounded these concerns, as postal censors noted when they perused letters by townspeople.[103] What constituted citizenship led to debate between some Africans and administrators. Perhaps to alleviate tensions over racial privilege, Governor-General Eboué altered ration law to allow educated Africans to obtain small amounts of flour, milk, and canned goods. Within a month of Eboué's decision, state office employee Paul Nguema urged the governor of Gabon to give him a European ration card since he was an educated African and a state employee.[104] Governor of Gabon Assier de Pompignan warned Eboué not to accept Nguema's request, because others would clamor for similar rights.[105] By trying to win over educated Africans through liberal ration laws, Eboué opened the door to a new series of disputes.

Africans from the Gold Coast and other English colonies also tried to gain European ration cards. Some had become British citizens and expected to receive the same ration cards as Europeans. In September 1944 local Libreville administrators refused to give them European status. Contacting the British consul in Libreville, these West Africans submitted their demands for ration cards to the governor-general in Brazzaville.[106] Since no French equivalent existed to the British legal category of "British citizen, African by birth," local French officials struggled to place British West Africans in their ration classifications.[107] These battles over access to rations again assert how debates about citizenship could be voiced over food.

When the war ended and the timber business recovered, shortages of canned goods and other imported foodstuffs ended. However, the business of selling and importing canned goods, flour, rice, and other dishes rested in foreign hands. Townspeople tried briefly to continue to improve their ability to buy foreign foods by forming cooperatives in the late 1940s. Educated Africans with political aspirations, including Léon Mba and future Parti Démocratique Gabonais fixture Georges Damas, formed cooperatives instead of battling colonial authorities to reduce prices.[108] These organizations flickered into oblivion when African officials embezzled funds for cars and personal expenses.[109] Few leaders, even when not tempted by Mammon, showed much economic insight. Four cooperatives built their stores next to one another in Glass; and their prices for rice and canned goods were 10 to 25 percent higher than at market or in European stores.[110] The cooperative movement lost steam by the early 1950s, leaving European and Lebanese retailers in command of food imports.

One example of how local demand necessitated imports can be discerned in the advance of bread. The colonial government, Catholic missionaries, and a few enterprising West Africans, as we have seen, set up bakeries in the late nineteenth century.[111] Baguettes had become a common side dish in daily Libreville meals after World War I. One Catholic priest noted in 1935, "Everywhere there is bread, a thing [once] unknown to the Blacks."[112] René Pélisson's bakery furnished the town with most of its bread from the late 1920s to the mid-1960s. Pélisson's store became a popular stopping point in the mornings for shoppers. People had to line up at Pélisson's store in the morning in the center of town or else they often could not obtain any bread for the day.[113] Not surprisingly, domestic servants of Europeans had the right to have a separate line and thus received bread ahead of regular African clients.[114] The bakery long remained a meeting place due to its monopoly and dependability. During the coup attempt of 1964, the wife of U.S. Ambassador Arthur Darlington noted: "All businesses may be closed, I thought, but there is one that will be open no matter what: Pélisson, the baker."[115] Bread's popularity required flour from outside the country. By the 1950s bread was as much a part of Libreville life as manioc.

After World War II officials admitted that Libreville was becoming very dependent on imports. A series of reports from 1948 fingered lazy African townspeople as the culprits who made the city so reliant on foreign goods. An inspector thundered: "[Libreville residents] have lost the taste for work and at all times agriculture is seen as degrading to them."[116] Yet he also recommended that potatoes and other foods be shipped in from France.[117] Other inspectors noted how European stores cashed in on the city's growing population after 1940 by selling more canned food.[118] Over half the rice, dried fish, and canned tuna reaching Gabon came to Libreville; even if much of this went to timber camps, it still indicates how food shipments were a key factor in what Libreville people ate.[119] Foreign dishes requiring imported ingredients had become a substantial part of local diets.

Advances in transport and technology furthered the spread and availability of imports. Refrigerated boats could bring in French vegetables directly from France, for example.[120] French-run industrial fishing outfits based in Pointe-Noire supplemented the lackluster results of local fishing in the 1950s.[121] Planes delivered cattle and meat directly from Chad.[122] Imports could arrive far more quickly from Paris, Senegal, or elsewhere to Libreville than could food from much of Gabon itself. It is hardly a mystery that imports had become a major feature of Libreville diets as a result.

The final decades of French rule consolidated the demand and supply of foreign foods into Libreville. The general shortcomings of local food supply, as revealed in the cataclysmic shortages of World War I and the 1920s, led European companies to treat rice and other imports as a vital stopgap measure as well as a reliable alternative to depending on local farming. The development of wage labor positions for men and women brought an end to rations, but education and contact with Europeans continued to bring an influx to food into town. Advances in international shipping outpaced the intermittent and half-hearted efforts of the state government to connect the Gabonese capital with other parts of the colony. Finally, the addition of canned food, rice, and bread became one part of a range of practices that townspeople selectively drew from and blended together to form an urban community where sharp distinctions between "African" and "European" cultures proved impossible to make. Personal choices to protect access to "European" foods went together with structural constraints created by European employers and the disinterest that colonial officials showed in promoting local food supply.

As of 2000, some experts estimate that more than 80 percent of food eaten in Gabon comes from outside the country. Such grim statistics have not yet placed the country, especially Libreville, in danger of famine. This dependence may finally be put in jeopardy by the decline of oil production and revenue, but Libreville's hunger for foreign foods existed before a drop of petroleum left the country. Well before the rush of oil profits into the Gabonese economy, foreign ingredients entered Libreville culinary practices. Processed foods offered a partial solution to offset the deficiencies of local food supply. European employers might dislike the need to introduce foreign foods, but in the end it was easier to order shipments of beans and flour than to ameliorate farming and fishing in Gabon. For missionaries seeking to remake local society in ways designed to make farmers out of townspeople, their use of imports unknowingly reinforced the determination of the Libreville African community to act as consumers, buying rather than producing their daily sustenance. European religious and political authorities might have wanted to remake local society, but abetting the formation of an urban settlement dependent on foreign imports was not part of the plan.

The entrance of European dishes into Libreville diets shows how the incremental growth of wage labor, improved communication, and the incorporation of imported merchandise into African social practices could have consequences that colonial officials and other Europeans had no intention of fostering. Townspeople acted in ways to promote imports. Some African residents of Libreville, taking advantage of their ability to work for Europeans, viewed foreign foods as valuable because they were part of salaries. Food became a means of forming patron-client ties and a tangible sign of worth that skilled Kru and Mpongwe workers demanded for themselves. Schools and employers also fostered the adoption of foreign tastes and eating habits. The money economy, furnishing material benefits far greater than mere farming could do, also made buying processed food appealing.

Mpongwe households borrowed wholesale from French culinary repertoires in their deliberate attempt to create an urban lifestyle that drew from European and indigenous sources. Eating cheese, beef, or rice became one way to distinguish a Libreville resident from Gabonese villagers. However, local concerns about status combined with practical worries about the availability of food. It would be easy enough to see wine and bread at a Libreville dinner table as a sign of French hegemony in Gabon. This facile reading would be a serious mistake. Libreville residents chose foreign foods in part thanks to the elevated prices and unstable supply of manioc, fish, and other "African" dishes. Unlike people in rural Gabon, inhabitants of Libreville by the early twentieth century could count on regular supplies of foreign foods, thanks to their ability to demand entitlements from Europeans. Foreign foods were more a victory for pragmatism than any desire by Libreville people to abandon older cultural practices.

The uneven integration of Libreville into local and international flows of communication can also be traced by the proliferation of imports. The town continued to be better connected to Atlantic and imperial lines of trade than to the rest of the colony. Its isolation from most of Gabon was painfully obvious when one could obtain food from Chad or Senegal faster than from Gabonese towns like Tchibanga and Oyem, even in the 1950s. This has remained true until today. Because of transport problems farmers in Medouneu, Fougamou, and much of Gabon still cannot count on selling food in the capital. Meanwhile planes and boats allow stores to stock canned sardines from Morocco, tomato paste from Ghana, and French cheese. Internal communication difficulties are thus one colonial legacy that Gabon has yet to overcome.

6. Food Supply in Libreville, 1930–1960

Between 1930 and 1960 Libreville evolved from a small port town to an expanding urban center. Through a slow process rife with complications the enclave developed ties with various parts of Gabon previously cut off from the town's food market. New immigrant communities in the growing urban population improved and diversified the city's food supply. Foreign foods found a home in local kitchens and restaurants. Rural men and women took advantage of the new political and economic setting by selling food to town in ways unthinkable before the 1920s. By the Second World War state officials attempted to promote agriculture in a dialogue with African producers that did not always rely on force. Finally, advances in transport augmented food supplies from France and West and Central Africa.

In this context townspeople and rural producers continued to act to protect their interests. Libreville residents became even more divorced from production than in the past. On the rare occasions when officials or rural people endangered their right to buy food freely, some residents rose up in protest, as during the 1920s. At the same time migrants from interior regions of Gabon farmed around the city itself. Not all townspeople escaped hunger, though. By the 1930s hunger was linked to insufficient access to wages and land.

While the situation progressed for the better in the short term, the city's present food supply problems began to take shape between 1930 and independence. The expanded interaction between rural Estuary villages and town led more families to settle in the colonial capital. Government policies often articulated a profound distrust of Africans. Administrators preferred short-lived and myopic interventions rather than addressing the ominous rise of the town population and the decline of opportunity in villages. Although the government made some tentative efforts to build roads, the capital still was cut off from areas known for their agricultural productivity. This foundation of mismanaged schemes set the tone for later Gabonese development programs after independence.

Change and Population Growth

Libreville's population was expanding in size, and the upswing brought benefits to the town's food supply. A trickle of farmers from throughout the colony moved to the capital. A small minority of West African fishermen brought new technology and business innovations that improved fish supplies. While the colonial government did not encourage urban growth, few officials complained about newcomers willing to sate the population's growing appetite. On the other hand, major problems with the rural economy encouraged migration to Libreville.

The stock market crash of 1929 and the diminished fortunes of timber inspired a sizable number of former timber camp workers to live in the capital. Smaller timber camps went bankrupt.[1] Larger firms that survived let workers go as a result of the crisis; the decline of manpower led to lowered profits for Fang villages that supplied timber camps with food.[2] Many timber workers from central and southern Gabon, accompanied by family members, built homes along the length of the Estuary and began to farm for themselves.[3] Visitors to the Estuary today find many villages populated by those of southern Gabonese descent.

Even after the timber industry recovered, some migrants decided to go to Libreville. Edouard Soumouma left the Consortium timber business in the early 1950s once he discovered that he could double his monthly salary of eight hundred CFA francs in Libreville without grueling twelve- or sixteen-hour shifts.[4] Nzebi migrant Mabenga Gabriel left in 1959 for the capital after hearing that "too many people were killed" at the Consortium and elsewhere.[5] Older Fang informants recalled moving to town as students or with relatives.[6] Graduates of mission schools outside Libreville preferred to use their job skills in Libreville than at home.[7] Nze Ollome Evariste moved to the capital right before the Second World War thanks to Catholic priests recruiting catechists and students in Medouneu.[8] Still others, like Nkoghe Bekale Joseph, came to work as domestic servants or manual laborers.[9]

Fang villagers from the Estuary moved to the capital. Unlike other parts of Gabon, where the colonial regime resettled rural people in villages, Estuary Fang people moved to Libreville without coercion.[10] Estuary settlements offered younger people little economic or educational opportunity. Guy Lasserre noted in 1958 the endemic poverty and poor purchasing power of Estuary villages.[11] Without many options to enhance agricultural production, villagers slowly drifted to the city rather than eke out a meager living. The Kango and Chinchoua subdivision populations dropped from more than nine thousand people to five thousand in the 1940s.[12] An inability to find enough cash for taxes and gunpowder led farmers to quit their fields. Elephants—"a veritable plague" on the south bank, according to one Frenchman in 1943—tore up plantations and inspired people to relocate closer to the capital.[13] Medouneu villagers left their homes for Libreville by the hundreds in the early 1950s.[14] During the Second World War the French government required villages to gather latex; artificially low prices and coercion led some to abandon their homes for a new urban life.[15] Neighborhoods such as Lalala and Nkembo in Libreville gave men a sanctuary from colonial authorities.[16] Young people did not follow their older relatives' career choices to farm. By the 1970s Estuary villages had seen a dramatic loss of younger people.[17]

Women as well as men constructed homes and new lives in Libreville. Some, like Esa Meyo Alice, accompanied their mission-educated Fang husbands from remote Estuary settlements.[18] Bella Eyeghe Marie-Therese, later of Donguila, became a Libreville resident in the late 1950s; her uncles sheltered her as she went to school.[19] Some women fled to cities to escape marriages in rural areas. Ahinto Biye confessed to court officials in 1937 that she hid on the outskirts of Libreville to escape her husband.[20] Officials jailed Bilogho, a young woman from northern Gabon, for abandoning her family and spouse to prostitute herself in the capital.[21]

The gender bias in food sales began to change. Food cultivation was an important means of survival for women.[22] Some, especially in Mpongwe families and those related to salaried male workers regardless of ethnicity, farmed solely for their large families.[23] Other women traded food for money as the famine years and interclan fighting came to an end. Longtime Atong Abé resident N'no Ndong Charles helped his aunt grow manioc for sale near Libreville at the Mont-Bouet market in the 1930s.[24] A Fang woman, Mba Nkoghe Valerie, founded the Nkembo market during the Second World War by vending outside her house.[25] Unfortunately, details are scarce on female traders; no records of food markets from the colonial periods survive, and few of my informants sold food at market.

Households grew food on the sites of contemporary neighborhoods such as Nzeng Ayong, Ozangué, and Mindoube. Informants laughed as they pointed out land now covered by tin-roofed shacks and said, "Before independence, that was the bush!" or "My mother had fields there."[26] Estuary Fang and Nzebi families living in Atong Abé and Mont-Bouet, two predominantly Fang neighborhoods in the 1930s, had fields on land presently occupied by the Cité de 12 Mars.[27] Competition over land caused some discord. A few flare-ups arose between Estuary Fang newcomers and established Mpongwe families in the 1930s and 1940s. State-appointed neighborhood chiefs encountered ferocious opposition when they tried collecting taxes from people not of the same ethnic background.[28] Officials ignored several petitions to expel from traditionally Mpongwe neighborhoods "foreign" Africans from the Gabonese interior and Estuary villages.[29] Families with broad claims on territory had no luck eliciting state support.[30]

The bonds that food supply created between Mpongwe families and Fang farmers appeared in these debates. Louis Berre, the self-styled heir to Re-Dowé as "king" of Louis, dismissed Georges Ndongo from his post as chief of the Fang of Louis in late 1945.[31] Ndongo spread tales that Berre had hired assassins to kill Fang women at their fields and wrote that the Louis chief had chosen another Fang man as his subordinate because the candidate bribed Berre with fish.[32] As a result of this dispute, as well as the beating of a Fang man who unwisely chose to relieve himself on a Mpongwe family's land, this festering strife boiled over into a serious dispute.[33] Fang women retaliated by refusing to sell food to customers who could not speak their language.[34] "If you couldn't say ma zo na [Fang: I say that], they wouldn't sell you anything," Libreville resident Pierre Bissang recalled.[35] Mpongwe clerks working in European stores would not sell to Fang customers, and the Libreville commissioner of police jailed some Fang market vendors.[36] The troubles subsided after several weeks. Though they might dislike one another, Estuary Fang and Mpongwe families needed one another as clients and patrons.

Another group of newcomers improved food supply. Several hundred fishermen and skilled workers from the Gold Coast, Togo, and Dahomey came to Libreville. Small numbers of artisans and jewelers from Accra and the Fante region of southern Ghana had been present in Libreville since the 1860s, but West African fishermen settled in the town in earnest only in the early 1930s. Michael Ocloo (1897–1971), a Gold Coast native, set up a small fishing business with some relatives in 1931.[37] West Africans, dubbed "Popos" by local people, used large boats and European-style nets to catch tuna and other big fish as opposed to sardines.[38] Soon afterward other Gold Coast and Dahomey fishermen arrived with their wives; the government happily supported West African entrepreneurs to recruit fishermen in their homelands.[39] By the late 1950s several fishing firms employed well over one hundred foreign workers in Libreville.[40]

Nigerians entered the fish trade in earnest in the early 1950s. They first settled in the Cocobeach region after immigrating from Guinea and Cameroon. Like other West Africans, they used motorboats to catch several tons of fish.[41] The Cocobeach administrator praised their efforts, noting that this small group sold more fish than the rest of the Mondah Bay region's inhabitants. Some Mpongwe families in Glass invited Nigerian fishermen to settle in their village by 1955.[42] Fang, Myene, and Séké fishing ventures rapidly declined in the face of better organized immigrant ventures. By the 1970s Nigerian immigrants controlled Estuary markets; today some rural Estuary communities are entirely dependent on Nigerians for fish.[43]

With so many immigrants, the population of Libreville expanded. The number of people officially recognized as Libreville residents rose from 2,803 to 6,771 between 1921 and 1938.[44] After the Second World War the city quadrupled in size and the number of African residents rose over to 30,000 people by 1960.[45] The town, though a major center for education and the colonial administration, did not have a voracious need for labor, which helps explain Libreville's small size compared to other African cities.

Such increases had a positive short-term effect on food supply. Libreville after the 1920s yields evidence for Esther Boserup's thesis that, contrary to Malthusian pessimism regarding population growth, increased population led to a diversification and expansion of food supply.[46] Food shortages no longer appeared in colonial reports. Other than periodic outbreaks of beriberi in Estuary timber camps during the Great Depression, officials in the Estuary asserted that Fang villages had no difficulty supplying the city and timber firms with

manioc, plantains, and other foods.[47] Administrators congratulated one another
for bettering conditions.[48] Despite such optimism, obstacles continued to limit
the ability of farmers to reach Libreville regularly. Famine no longer menaced
the region, but townspeople still faced high prices and depended on a small and
widely scattered rural population.[49] Government interventions in rural society
designed to aid food production did not greatly improve the situation.

State Impositions, Rural People, and Food Supply

Administrators in the last three decades of French rule had far more latitude in
commanding Gabon Estuary villagers than their predecessors. Almost twenty
years of dearth had radically altered social conditions and had limited the ability
of hinterland communities to challenge the French state actively. Furthermore,
the timber industry poured funds into the general budget. This elevated position did not translate into effective or even coherent policies designed to further
food production. Instead, a series of government programs related to agriculture and authority sputtered between the Great Depression and the late 1950s.
They embodied mixed attitudes toward Estuary people. Geographer Thomas
Bassett has described three mentalities at work in state dealings with peasants
in the Ivory Coast, which all appear in late colonial Libreville and the surrounding Estuary: a compulsory development discourse that assumed only force could
make lazy Africans work, a rational choice model that assumed peasants would
respond to economic benefits in a free market, and a paternalistic approach
that used compulsory labor and free market incentives.[50] These points describe
the mixed and ad hoc approaches in Gabon.

Coercion had not worked well in the 1920s, but mere failure did not stop officials from relying on force. Chiefs continued to follow orders to collect food and
set up communal fields. The decision to appoint chiefs who governed territory
rather than individual clans was a radical change that administrators hoped
would curb the chaotic infighting among Fang groups, allow for better surveillance of scattered settlements, and promote better food supply. Chiefs continued to operate as agricultural entrepreneurs thanks to state patronage. Canton
chiefs like Léon Mba supervised food sales for Libreville in the early 1930s.[51]
Few men could compete with chiefs in family size. Two canton chiefs had six
and thirteen wives respectively in 1932.[52] Ada Nkoghe Veronique's father, the
village chief of Nzamaligue between Ntoum and Donguila, had seven wives.[53]
In 1948 a census of households in the Libreville subdivision reported that 63

percent of the households were monogamous and only 11 percent of men had more than two wives.[54] This labor provided chiefs with surplus manioc and plantains that could be sold in town or to timber camps.

Interestingly, Estuary Fang chiefs never could compare to the agricultural enterprises of Béti chiefs in southern Cameroon. Béti big men married tens or even hundreds of women in the 1920s and 1930s; these spouses then worked on cash crop and food crop plantains that fed the new colonial capital of Yaoundé.[55] Even Félicien Endame Ndong, Kango Fang chief and a noted food supplier and powerbroker in the 1920s, could hardly claim to be the equal of his northern counterparts, though Béti and Fang spoke dialects of the same language and shared a common cultural heritage. What could account for this radical divergence? The chaos of the 1920s, the low population of the Gabon Estuary, and the lack of land routes in Gabon account for the differences between the two regions. Cameroon to this day has a much stronger agricultural sector than Gabon.

The temptation to squeeze labor out of the Estuary was hard to resist during World War II. Demand for food went down with the downturn of the timber business after the fall of France; even when companies tried to hang onto workers so as to resume production, chiefs reported in 1941 that they had more food to sell than the market could handle.[56] Rubber for the war effort undid this early period of plenty. Villagers had to collect wild rubber at artificially low prices by the summer of 1943; production went up to almost twenty thousand kilograms in 1944, but the risk of famine climbed too.[57] Forced labor details (corvées) also dragged men and women out of agriculture for weeks or perhaps even months, and to make matters worse, road construction in unpopulated areas meant workers could not get fish, meat, or sometimes even manioc.[58] Some rural village chiefs claimed that they could not gather enough men to collect any taxes because so many men had fled to Libreville to evade their forced labor obligations.[59]

The dry season, always a time of struggle, brought food shortages in the summer of 1944. Beginning in July postal censors started finding repeated references to hardship.[60] Three Gabonese clerks excused themselves for being late to their offices in the following month on the grounds that their families had no food to eat and they had had to go to market.[61] A letter intercepted by postal officials in the fall expressed bitterness: "Eating has become really difficult. . . . There is a famine and the leaders do not want to take note of it. . . . Rumor has it that there is a possibility of even the price of fish going up again. You must be joking!"[62] High prices and nearly empty markets continued through early 1945.[63] Authorities commanded villagers to deliver more than ten thousand manioc batons a week to Libreville in February.[64] Catholic priests also became frustrated when their suppliers of manioc and sardines had produce requisitioned by the police.[65]

At the same time the war did bring some collaboration between state officials and producers. Gold Coast immigrant Michel Ocloo convinced administrators to raise fish prices, and on occasion administrators worked with Fang and Mpongwe notables to set prices.[66] State-owned trucks hauled manioc and other foods from Ntoum and other settlements far from Libreville, but gasoline shortages put a damper on these operations.[67] Other state policies, such as road construction, brought results slightly more favorable to ordinary farmers, but they never went far enough to improve the supply woes of the city significantly.

A major problem for the government and farmers in the late colonial period was connecting the capital to the rest of the colony.[68] The town depended on a relatively small and thinly populated region for food because no routes linked the capital to farmers elsewhere. Throughout the colonial period observers castigated the administration for the poor state of roads in Gabon.[69] Before 1930 only two paved roads existed, linking Libreville to the outlying villages of Sibang and Owendo. Africans and Europeans alike bewailed Libreville's isolation from other parts of Gabon.[70] Woleu Ntem cultivators, known for their densely populated villages and cocoa production, shipped their produce through Cameroon. It took two weeks for trucks to struggle on poor roads from Woleu Ntem to Libreville during the Second World War.[71] Farmers in the Ngounié and Nyanga provinces of southern Gabon had no way of reaching the capital during the entire colonial period.

The situation improved slightly after the mid-1930s as the central government in Brazzaville demanded reforms.[72] Officials commenced an ambitious road-building program linking Lambaréné on the Ogooué River with Libreville.[73] The construction project depended on men dragged out of villages by guards.[74] These efforts continued during the war with projects aimed at linking Kango with the Woleu Ntem province to the north and Lambaréné to the south.[75] After the Second World War colonial officials earmarked money for continued road construction to end Libreville's isolation. However, these projects did not bring about radical improvements in roads. Local administrators often used funds allocated to transport for other programs.[76] One of the reasons for the government's inertia lay in the dominance of timber entrepreneurs. European companies supported only projects that tied their camps with the Gabon Estuary. Guy Lasserre noted in 1958 that as long as the timber firms did not support the construction of better routes, much of the Estuary region had little hope of gaining land access to town markets.[77]

Despite their vehement dislike of forced labor employed to maintain and construct routes, Estuary villagers recognized the benefits of roads. Food suppliers could bring food to the capital from Kango and other villages in a single day by truck, whereas a trip on foot or by canoe had lasted several grueling days. However, farmers could not afford to buy cars. Timber companies and European retailers used Ford trucks by the late 1920s, but the high price of motorized vehicles vastly exceeded the meager incomes of all but a handful of townspeople.[78] Fang village chiefs asked the administration to purchase a truck so that villages far from the city could send produce to the Libreville market during Second World War.[79] In a large meeting of Fang educated men dubbed the "Congrès Pahouin" in 1947, the group's platform included requests for trucks and roads so that northern Gabonese farmers might reach Libreville.[80] Administrators heeded these requests, but their responses often failed to bring lasting benefits to rural people and urban consumers. Just as roads attracted limited interest among government policymakers, agricultural development plans foundered.

State Development and Urban-Rural Food Trade

A milestone in Libreville food supply came in 1937. For the first time the French government in Gabon formed an agency designed to promote rural interests. The Société de Prévoyance Indigène (SIP) created in each department of Gabon began with altruistic notions of aiding farmers.[81] The SIP fell far short in its efforts to ameliorate town food supply. One word describes most of the agency's activities: incompetence. The history of the SIP demonstrates how poorly conceived programs paved the way for unsuccessful development projects after independence. Other plans to back agriculture in and around Libreville reveal similar woes.

The early days of the SIP gave a hint of the troubles to come. Funding posed the first major obstacle for the association. The governor-general offered little aid and prohibited the agency from cutting timber for revenue. Thus the Estuary SIP required over twenty thousand people in the Estuary to pay "subscription fees" of three francs each to keep the agency afloat.[82] Colonial inspectors repeatedly attacked subdivision chiefs for squandering revenue allotted for the fledgling organization.[83] During the war metropolitan funding for the SIP ended, and the situation did not turn for the better after 1945. A drop in aid from Brazzaville due to budget problems in 1952 brought the agency's work to a halt for several years.[84] African representatives in the territorial assembly formed in the late 1940s took the agency to task for waste and asked repeatedly for the elimination of the organization.[85] Rather than pay for a new truck for the Estuary SIP, councilman Ange Obame preferred to do without the agency entirely.[86]

Colonial reports provide evidence to support the allegations of African politicians. Some of the SIP programs, such as raising rabbits and introducing new strains of coffee, did not catch on with villagers.[87] An inspector discovered in 1949 that the SIP chief in Kango had neglected practically every project planned in the previous year.[88] Programs varied greatly. More ambitious officials, such as the District of Libreville SIP director in the late 1940s, managed to supply the town market with ten tons of manioc per month.[89] This effort was remarkable given the fact that the SIP had no warehouse to store food and relied on a single battered truck that broke down on a regular basis.[90]

Some of the SIP's best moments (and some of its worst) came from its role in transport. Farmers supported the agency when it permitted better access to market. During the war military vehicles moved foodstuffs from Sibang and Ntoum to Libreville.[91] Improved communication to points north of Libreville allowed villagers to sell larger amounts of food; one official estimated in 1944 that over half of the manioc consumed in Libreville came from Akok.[92] Some villagers recalled trucks arriving early in the morning at Sibang in the 1950s to transport vendors and food to market.[93]

Despite these successes, SIP schemes often ended in failure, as the disappointment of Medouneu illustrates. Agency members decided to use the fertile fields of Medouneu to grow potatoes and onions in 1939. This mountainous district, roughly two hundred kilometers from Libreville, was among the most difficult areas in Gabon to reach from Libreville due to the lack of roads. Medouneu tempted SIP leaders in Libreville for several reasons. Its high elevation, relatively cool climate, rich soils, and extended dry season make it promising for agriculture. Today the area is known for pineapples, sugar cane, potatoes, and a variety of other food crops. Roughly three thousand people lived within several hours of the village of Medouneu.[94] Administrators lamented that residents had no economic opportunities for wage labor and had trouble paying taxes. Before the war government officials and missionaries rarely visited the scattered Fang villages in the region.[95] Farmers found markets in neighboring Spanish Guinea far easier to reach than Libreville, since on foot they had to travel a month on rugged paths from Medouneu to Libreville and back.[96] The high cost and time constraints made any Libreville-Medouneu venture unprofitable. SIP policymakers thus hoped to solve both rural and urban problems with their scheme.

In late 1939 after the onset of the war, the administrator in charge of the Medouneu subdivision sent several convoys of potatoes to Mitzic in Woleu Ntem using African porters.[97] After a small potato harvest, officials requested and received more seeds for planting.[98] The project stagnated at first but slowly gained support from Africans. The high cost of porters able to bring the potatoes from Medouneu to Libreville cut deeply into potential profits.[99] Skirmishes between Pétainist and Gaullist forces disrupted the colony in 1940, but the potato campaign resumed in 1941 as the war had cut the colony off from metropolitan suppliers.[100] After 1942 some Fang men took an active role in organizing this commerce. Planting potatoes required fields separated from manioc and plantains, and planters guarded these crops with care.[101] Retired Libreville resident Nzue Essone Benoit recounted how his father set up convoys from Medouneu to Libreville.[102] Nzue's father ran a store in Medouneu that sold matches, soap, and various imported goods: he thus had the connections to organize caravans of porters.

Enterprising men struggled with transport. The caravans relied on villagers en route to feed them as they hiked rough trails and to furnish aid when porters broke legs on difficult jungle paths.[103] Medouneu subdivision chief Loubet worried that the high number of porters needed to bring the produce to Libreville would drain the region of so many workers that fields would not be properly tended.[104] Furthermore, the porters marched to Libreville without any supervision or set schedule; thus in many cases officials lost track of caravans en route to the city. Estuary administrator Roland Mercat overruled Loubet's suggestion to end the caravans.[105]

Few written sources indicate opposition to potato cultivation. Much as in the case of road construction, villagers seemed willing to supply the market if they received proper payment and aid from officials. Some Medouneu men wrote a letter to the Estuary administrator on the situation.[106] Stating that porters wasted time "having fun" en route to the capital and that men needed to stay home to watch over their rebellious wives, the authors asked that state trucks pick up the produce. Besides denoting male anxieties about migration, as well as the shadowy roles of women in farming, this document also presents the caravan organizers' hopes of earning profits from potatoes.

Their aspirations ran aground on the chaotic realities of colonial rule. Officials had difficulty assessing both production and urban demand. The Estuary administrator developed a plan to have porters march for several days to the northern town of Oyem, where the government would provide trucks to move the potatoes to Libreville. Unfortunately the Estuary SIP had sold off its lone vehicle.[107] Muddy and ramshackle roads prevented companies from obtaining the potatoes later in the year, as did shortages of cars and gasoline.[108] Private truckers demanded two francs per kilo from farmers to haul potatoes to Libreville, and porters traveling on foot did not necessarily hand over the profits of sales in town.[109]

The poor planning of convoys became painfully obvious. Hundreds of porters continued to leave Medouneu for Libreville, and much of their harvest decayed due to tropical humidity since they took two weeks to arrive.[110] Too much of a good thing led to bad results. In February 1944, the Medouneu subdivision chief sent a caravan of more than a thousand people carrying fifteen tons of potatoes to Libreville.[111] Considering that the Woleu Ntem SIP had sent four tons of potatoes at the same time, the colonial capital was awash in unwanted starch.[112] No one had realized that few African townspeople cared for potatoes, and administrators found no takers for the Medouneu produce.[113] The Estuary SIP had previously agreed to buy all the potatoes. It spent its entire 1944 budget on the unexpected giant harvest, which ended up rotting away in Libreville warehouses.[114] The program continued to the end of 1946 with some support from European consumers, but officials finally abandoned it as a costly debacle.[115]

A host of instances of shortsighted decisions and uneven funding appear in other agricultural projects. In southern Gabon around the town of Tchibanga, SIP experts promoted rice as a cash crop. The region produced over nine hundred tons by 1955, but the cost of airlifting the harvest to Libreville and Port-Gentil made local rice more expensive than imports from Southeast Asia.[116] Besides coordination difficulties, another problem that marred government programs was colonial skepticism regarding Gabonese people. Officials consulted a small number of chiefs and male townspeople but rarely trusted the advice of colonial subjects.

Africans had little luck finding financial aid from the government. Officials denied the vast majority of requests for loans for hiring workers and buying capital equipment in the early 1940s.[117] Typically, officials rejected loans for the reasons given by an agricultural official against a 1941 application: "We are not obliged to support natives . . . simply because they pretend to move a few shovels' worth of dirt."[118] Rather than encourage farmers to hire workers, French officials continued to believe that small households could increase yields through greater productivity without technical improvements, better prices, or assistance with transport. Gender and education inequities shaped aid packages as well. In the surviving records, no female applicants for aid appear at all.

African politicians hungry for votes were more generous than the SIP. Léon Mba, once exiled as a threat to colonial order, became a favorite of the colonial administration in the mid-1950s as leader of the moderate Bloc Démocratique Gabonais (BDG) party. He sponsored food production ventures with an eye to shoring up his popularity. During his initial term in office he promised to give out gun authorization permits to farmers. As late as 1950 colonial officials limited permits for modern rifles to five per thousand Estuary residents.[119] Many Africans demanded the right to obtain modern firearms to protect their fields from elephants, and in 1957 Léon Mba presented himself as their defender in this: "In my opinion, one should consider the interest that the majority of farmers in the interior provinces have [to obtain] the possession of a firearm that is the best means of supplying meat to their families and especially to protect fields from the depredations of wild animals. . . . Thus, one should protect less the animals than men and their fields."[120]

The Gabonese government gave out sixty gun permits in 1958; Estuary officials noted how wild animal populations diminished afterward.[121] Unfortunately the lack of statistics on bush meat makes it impossible to note with any precision how much this increase in firearms reduced the local animal population.

Mba used agricultural and food supply interests to strengthen his BDG party, even if his plans did not accomplish much. Fishermen received state aid thanks to their handwritten requests to Mba in 1959 and 1960.[122] After Mba became vice president in 1957 supporters urged their leader to give out firearms to Estuary south bank villages to weaken opposition party support in the region.[123] In turn, Mba refused to cede gun permits to supporters of his rival Jean-Hilaire Aubame.[124] Other reforms, such as moving the Mont-Bouet market away from his family home, served his own needs rather than those of urban consumers.[125]

Despite limited efforts to build industrial chicken farms and doling out hoes and seeds to urban gardeners, Mba's administration neglected food crop farming in the Estuary for Libreville.[126]

Food supply continues to be a subject that attracts much discussion but little concrete action by the Gabonese government today. Roland Pourtier and Douglas Yates have both dissected the failure of the Gabonese government from the 1960s onward to turn revenue from oil and mineral wealth into lasting improvements for farmers.[127] Economist Sven Wunder opines that Gabon is a happy example of how oil production can prevent deforestation but argues state disinterest in agriculture explains much about the miserable state of food production.[128] Misappropriation of state funds designated for farming clearly did not originate after independence, as the case of the SIP makes clear. Many Gabonese suspect that money allocated to agricultural projects is diverted by greedy members of the government bureaucracy. Roads to the Medouneu region from Libreville still have the reputation of being among the worst in the country. Some blame politics, since opposition parties have garnered favor in and around Medouneu since the 1960s. Agricultural research remains limited.

State officials rarely acted to support Estuary farmers or to encourage food production in the last thirty years of colonial rule. Political independence brought little change to the tepid interest of state officials in food supply. Without adequate funding and clear goals, late colonial development projects foundered in similar fashion to later programs under Mba and Omar Bongo. Based on this standing policy of neglect, it is little wonder that foreigners such as African producers in Cameroon came to dominate the local food market. Imports, as some officials already admitted in the late 1940s, allowed the government to ignore local farmers.[129] Favorable developments in Estuary food production and the end of severe shortages permitted administrators to avoid confronting structural supply problems.

Social Status and the Changing Face of Hunger

Townspeople, unable to alter the effects of government policies on rural areas, continued to struggle for access to food in ways that reflected their disparate class and ethnic backgrounds. The need for wages to buy food became an everyday reality. Poor people for the first time turned directly to the colonial regime for relief. The ability of some Africans in the colonial capital to negotiate successfully with the government laid bare the growing differences between rich and poor in town.

The world war brought on a series of protests. None was as heated as during the 1920s, in part because the colonial administration took complaints more seriously. On some occasions women marched in the footsteps of their fore-runners in the 1920s. Officials decided in 1943 to close the market of Glass, a favorite shopping center for Mpongwe women searching for fish.[130] This irked older women who wanted to buy fish, since they had to walk more than ten kilometers to the Sibang dock on the outskirts of town. The neighborhood's residents did not stand idle. In a letter intercepted by colonial censors, clan leader Prince Félix Adende, a relative of the famed Asiga chief of the same name, described the affair to a friend:

> Revolution, my dear. . . . The Glass women went to protest twice . . . at the Mayor's Office. This made a sensation. . . . All the [clan] chiefs were summoned by the Mayor. That morning, the chiefs refused to present themselves [to the governor's office]. At 2 PM, we went there anyway. . . . I suffered alone with Governor Servel, who spoke of the deportation of my brother Léon Mba, and the Mpongwes having written against him in 1937. . . . Finally we reached the point of our discussion. Our market was reopened, and you should have seen the parade of our women returning to Glass.[131]

To celebrate their victory Glass women held an *ivanga* dance the next day associated with the *njembe* power association.[132] Older forms of political action worked hand in hand with formal negotiations with colonial administrators.

Townspeople again made letter writing a centerpiece of challenges to food policy. A trader from Dahomey accused administrators of favoritism for obtaining fresh fish first rather than permitting free trade.[133] Officials denied his allegations.[134] Pierre-Marie Akenda, appointed as a "native delegate" by the governor of Gabon, declared the administration guilty of organizing violent searches for vagabonds and decried the administration for allowing family members of French citizens to collect rations.[135] One frustrated man complained that the government allowed "uncultured" people from the interior to slap around market customers and steal fish.[136]

The government did not ignore these protests but instead investigated complaints. Beyond such major gaffes as the Medouneu potato program, administrators in the 1940s did manage to alleviate some concerns by allowing educated Africans a limited say in shaping food policies. The antagonism of townspeople and the French government in the 1920s did not return save in isolated moments. Such liberal attitudes appear to have been successful in appeasing educated people. After 1945 townspeople abandoned open protests on the food issue, yet some less fortunate residents went hungry.

Despite its small size, Libreville had a sizable group of impoverished residents without enough labor or money to escape want. Data on incomes, particularly for those most deprived, are rare, but court records and relief demands offer glimpses of the world of the poor. Established families with enough land and labor had fields to support themselves even without high salaries from wage labor. Little competition over fields existed before 1960, but smaller households and single individuals did not fare well as they lacked the money or the hands to farm with ease.

Homeless people ran into major troubles obtaining access to food. The colonial administration, fearful of the rise of a transient "floating population," discouraged homelessness by forcing Africans without a fixed residence to return to their original villages.[137] This placed single men from the Gabonese interior in difficult straits if they became unemployed. Several former timber camp workers or young migrants looking for work in Libreville depended on friends or relatives from their home region.[138] Some vagabonds took desperate measures; police arrested a poor Fang man without a home for robbing a chicken coop in 1937.[139] Prisoners from elsewhere released from the Libreville jail also had trouble finding food.[140] Just as mentally ill transients in Libreville pilfer stores to survive today, a psychologically troubled man in 1937 tried stealing chickens to sate his hunger.[141] With few kin or friends to aid them, these men lacked the means to obtain much food of any sort.

Physically handicapped and elderly town residents made up a part of Libreville's poor. Laurence Retigat, a World War I veteran living in Libreville in the late 1930s, suffered from Parkinson's disease. Since he could not work or farm, he relied on his elderly mother to eat.[142] Other blind or handicapped people turned to sons or cousins for meals.[143] Blind veteran Gabriel Antchoué lived off the charity of his neighbors.[144] Some elderly people, even if illnesses did not prevent them from working or farming, still endured hardship. Vili men who had moved from Congo-Brazzaville in the 1880s and 1890s suffered in their old age. An aged Vili gardener in 1949 earned eight hundred CFA a month, barely enough to buy sardines and manioc on a regular basis.[145] Widowed elderly women relying on small gardens could feed themselves, but starvation loomed if their health gave out. An official in 1944 asked his superior to reject an elderly African widow's demand for aid. "We find here at Libreville hundreds of people in the same situation, so I ask that you do not accept this request," he noted.[146]

Younger women with many children encountered adversity. Oussaka Marthe, working as a maid for Europeans, requested aid from the colonial government as she had trouble supporting her six children.[147] Women married to unemployed men tried to elicit state aid to make up for lost income.[148] Pauline Assengone, a thirty-four-year-old widow with four young children, found that her single manioc field did not furnish enough revenue or food to live on.[149] Lalala neighborhood leader Essono, having lost his parents at an early age, recalled his struggle to eat in Libreville in the late 1940s after the aunt who had taken him in died.[150] Again the lack of kin support spelled trouble. Regardless of the total amount of food in town, this motley group of destitute people encountered hunger.

Unemployed and insolvent people had several options. Just as now, affluent households might choose to hand out manioc or plantains to their neighbors.[151] If this option failed, some turned to the state after the mid-1930s. General de Gaulle created a fifty-thousand-franc fund to aid the needy of French Equatorial Africa in 1941; poorer Libreville residents, taking advantage of their European education often unavailable elsewhere in the colony, petitioned the governor of the colony with more than sixty requests for aid.[152] Governor-General Félix Eboué refused to give out much money out of a fear that welfare might replace "traditional" forms of family support with state largesse.[153] In this case some people with a good knowledge of French bureaucratic forms staved off want. Such opportunities rarely fell into the hands of the largely illiterate rural Estuary population.

As disadvantaged groups fought hunger by appealing for the government to intervene, wealthy families acted on some occasions to guard their privileged culinary tastes. The old ration system had long vanished by the 1930s. Most families grew some of the food they consumed at home. Several informants recall a small number of African restaurants in the 1950s, but eateries did not become common until after independence.[154] Even so, the elite of Libreville took pride in buying rather than producing food and acted to protect these habits.

Much like their ancestors in the late nineteenth century, well-off families of mainly Mpongwe descent had eating habits that distinguished them from other Africans. Thanks to their high level of education men often worked as accountants, interpreters, and commercial agents. Their high salaries allowed them to buy expensive imports much more easily than most other Libreville residents could do. European men continued to take Mpongwe women as mistresses and generally expected their lovers to serve them European meals. Thus the distinctive eating habits of Mpongwe came from many sources.

First, as noted repeatedly by informants, these households did not sell food or farm a great deal. Although some older women did farm, they produced far less than Fang or Nzebi women living in town. According to a 1962 food consumption survey, Mpongwe families produced little other than fruit from trees on their property.[155] Apart from such fruit, the small number of women who continued to grow manioc and plantains diminished over time. Fishing was the only exception; a small number of Mpongwe men hauled in sardines for sale until the 1960s.[156]

Mpongwe women generally purchased their food at market. The specific organization of food shopping depended on the household. Children of mixed heritage on occasion lived with their European fathers. In these homes male domestic servants often purchased food and women rarely farmed.[157] Although women in their twenties living with Europeans could expect financial support for food and clothing, they invariably moved into wage labor once their paramours left Gabon. While women escaped many agricultural duties, they were still expected to feed their families. In a typical Mpongwe household with large numbers of kin relations living in the same compound, wives or unmarried women fed the entire household. By 1960 high-ranking Gabonese officials hired African male domestic servants to feed them.[158]

Affluent diets of the town elite required high salaries. Most Mpongwe men worked as office workers in trading firms, as state officials, and as independent entrepreneurs. They began their careers as low-level clerks and advanced from there. These positions offered income dramatically higher than other groups could earn. Mpongwe clerk Benoit Anghiley made 750 FF a month in 1930, at a time when manual laborers received between 200 and 400 FF a month.[159] With the introduction of the CFA currency in 1945, inflation became a major problem. However, the discrepancy between the pay of clerks and manual workers remained very high. In the mid-1950s bank employees earned 25,000 CFA/month compared to laborers' average wages of 4,000 CFA.[160] Informants remember African timber entrepreneurs such as Jean-Rémy Issembé and Joseph Deemin as the first "millionaires" of Libreville and testified to their riches by recalling their cars and large houses.[161] European foods and later refrigerators too expensive for many families were within easy reach of these men.

According to a 1962 survey Mpongwe households paid the highest amount for food in Libreville.[162] Their consumption of diary products, wine, and canned goods greatly raised their costs. However, elevated salaries allowed these households in large part to continue their "civilized" tradition of European eating habits. Others did not have this luxury. Documenting household budgets of single and married male workers in 1954, Guy Lasserre discovered that his informants paid 49 to 90 percent of their monthly salaries on food.[163] Gabonese priest Jean-Baptiste Adiwa complained in 1946 of high prices and insufficient amounts of fish and bush meat.[164] Several African officials and townspeople criticized high prices at market in 1954.[165] After the government apparently intervened to keep prices stables, some rural producers tried a short-lived effort to organize a boycott.[166]

Between the extremes of poverty and plenty, many non-Mpongwe town residents still grew a substantial amount of food. Although much diversity existed among families, most households relied on women to grow food, according to a 1962 survey. Family members brought in up to half the manioc eaten by families.[167] Given the high expense of living in Libreville, low salaries made life hard for those without access to land and with low incomes. A Vili cook from southern Gabon who lost his fields paid half his salary to feed the seven people who lived with him in 1955.[168] His plight points to growing conflict over land close to Libreville. Households settled in Libreville for a number of years had access to fields by virtue of previous land rights. New arrivals could settle far away from Libreville's center to gain access to fields but paid the cost of being cut off from employment in the center of town.

Most of my informants outside the Mpongwe elite fell into this middle category in the late colonial period. Women grew manioc for their families with occasional trips to market to sell or to buy certain foods.[169] Some of N'no Ndong Charles's male neighbors worked as clerks while his wife went to her fields in the late 1940s.[170] Single men turned to relatives to supply them with manioc and fish.[171] Few families were entirely self-sufficient, but access to land and labor appears to have been much better in the 1950s than in the aftermath of independence. As floods of migrants came to Libreville after 1960, the fields of once outlying neighborhoods became the sites of homes for newcomers. Poorer people without cars or close proximity to fertile land had little choice but to buy food.

By the late 1950s the foundation of Libreville's present food consumption patterns was set. Families and individuals faced hunger because they lacked the resources to buy their daily sustenance, not because of a general dearth of food. The food crisis had come to an end. Rural farmers might not receive much aid from the government, but townspeople could generally count on at least a chance for support. This contrast between rural and urban entitlements would set the tone for postcolonial food supply. Estuary settlements could rarely count on steady aid for farming and transport in the late colonial and post-independence periods. Instead of viewing themselves as opposed to the state authorities, Mpongwe and other townspeople had become a somewhat restless but loyal community. However, this new sense of agreement did not ultimately solve the city's growing need for food.

After 1930 the famines and chaos linked to early colonial rule finally dissipated. Increased numbers of producers, the expanded role of imports, the slow increase of road building, and less stringent state controls over food distribution ameliorated food supply issues. Despite such progress, structural problems lurked in the political and social fabric of town life that undermined the ability of Estuary suppliers to sate urban consumers. State officials did relatively little to aid farmers. Fishermen and cultivators drifted to Libreville from the surrounding countryside as opportunities for economic and social advancement declined. By the late 1950s urban migration from various parts of the colony increased dramatically, while the population of the Estuary region outside Libreville declined.

As wages became more crucial for purchasing food, wealthy and poor people largely abandoned food production. Prosperous Mpongwe households bought their food at market to continue their lifestyle of conspicuous consumption and guard their "civilized" identity. Indigent people begged for aid as they lost access to land and labor. Prices remained fairly high. On occasion wealthy townspeople protected their ability to purchase food freely through lobbying campaigns and marches similar to older protest movements. However, these manifestations failed to provoke radical changes in state policy. Thus the stage was set for foreign imports and distributors to take charge of the city's food supply.

7. European Culinary Practices in Colonial Libreville

Libreville today is a city full of eating opportunities. Vietnamese, self-proclaimed "African," and French restaurants vie for wealthy patrons with meals that cost well over 20,000 CFA (nearly 50 U.S. dollars)—more than an average week's salary for the majority of city residents. The marble-floored Meriden Re-Ndama hotel boasts French professional chefs, obnoxiously loud air-conditioners, and buffets that only foreigners and the summit of the Gabonese elite can afford. Louis and Glass neighborhood bistros seeking out a foreign clientele lack the excessive panache of the hotels, but they too can leave one's wallet much lighter at the end of a meal. Indian, Cuban, and other ethnic cuisines favored in Europe cost almost as much as in the swanky hotels. In contrast, West African and Gabonese men eat at the rickety counters of the plethora of fast food restaurants known as "cafets." Foreigners from Europe or America rarely frequent these eateries, although they offer dishes that cost less than a tenth the price of an entrée elsewhere.

Across the city European-style supermarkets such as Superglass or M'Bolo sell imported French vegetables for more than ten times the price of produce from Cameroon or Gabon itself. While commentators lament the rise of *mondialisation* in Paris, French residents of Gabon pay for these reminders of the metropole. Americans must content themselves with one shop dubbed the

"American Store," offering discount brand ketchup, dusty boxes of macaroni and cheese, and soda at exorbitant prices. Few Gabonese can afford to buy such luxuries. Instead they go to market stalls run by West African women. Lebanese, Mauritanian, Chinese, Senegalese, and Moroccan retailers sell canned goods in cramped stores sprinkled in every neighborhood. Although no formal segregation existed in Libreville, a wide chasm divides African and European shopping and eating.

Such a separation was not an invariable outcome of colonialism. One way to trace changes in the tenuous relationships between foreigners and indigenous people in Libreville is to examine how people prepared and ate their food. I follow Sidney Mintz's contention that handling of food is not only a biological activity but one that embodies social meanings, especially those of solidarity and difference.[1] Lisa McNee has rightly noted that "food culture is the nexus for the creation of cultural identities, as well as local knowledges, and thus plays a role in the affirmation of proprietary claims to knowledge."[2] In the mid-nineteenth century Europeans and local Mpongwe people blended eating habits together. Through eating local foods and relying on African styles of preparation, Europeans appropriated elements of Mpongwe cultural practices and knowledge. This mixture reflected the considerable influence of townspeople in organizing the lived worlds they shared with foreigners. To trade and survive on the Gabon Estuary, newcomers had to accept indigenous culinary repertoires.

Over the course of the early twentieth century, African and European culinary traditions diverged. This evolution of foodways illustrates how the conjunction of changing technology, understanding of race, and economic shifts impacted the relationship between Africans and Europeans in Libreville. As scholars have insisted elsewhere, racial discourses of difference and hybridity were extremely malleable in the colonial world, rather than unchanging boundaries distinguishing Africans from Europeans.[3] Eating became one place where Europeans often struggled to limit the potential threat of African influences. Unfortunately, few historians of colonial encounters have paid attention to the ways in which food consumption might serve as a barometer of changing conceptions of race and of performed racial and cultural identities.[4]

In Libreville much of the present division between culinary styles appeared after 1914. Unlike in colonial Vietnam, where French settlers avoided drawing from local foods as much as they possibly could, Europeans in Libreville pushed local foods out of their repasts only after World War I.[5] Changing attitudes toward race and hygiene brought about a stricter separation of meals and tastes. New forms of dining eliminated African influences, while technological advances allowed Europeans access to beef, vegetables, and fruit. Urban Gabonese lost much of their previous ability to shape the contours of European everyday life once French state and private interests weakened the autonomy of local people. Until the turn of the twentieth century African landlords could use as a bargaining tool their hospitality in feeding and housing visiting European strangers. Europeans in Libreville were in peril of hunger and had to contend with the threat of poison. Changing supply routes and attitudes toward Africans undid this arrangement. The divergence of tastes reveals growing rifts between Europeans and Africans in the late colonial period; colons preferred to keep African influences off their tables.

Domestic Labor and European Eating

Throughout the nineteenth century European residents of Libreville had to cope with culinary practices far removed from foodways in France. One French sailor expressed his dismay with eating in Libreville in April 1850. Mikiel, a French naval employee, berated his superiors at the French fort of Libreville for reducing him to making his meals in an abandoned shed. He harangued African guards sent by the quartermaster to put out his cooking fire. Enraged, Mikiel was reported to have menaced one unlucky soldier with a kettle. "Do not come near me or I will throw this boiling pot of water at your body. Tell your captain that when he gets me a cook or serves me himself, I will obey his orders," he snarled.[6]

Others in the tiny garrison shared Mikiel's frustration with food preparation and diet. Before the advent of steam, supply ships from Senegal and France took months to arrive. Naval officials ran into numerous problems feeding West African troops and French personnel. Barrels and boxes regularly arrived damaged by humidity or full of worms.[7] Warehouses for the next twenty years did not advance much beyond the poor state of affairs in the 1840s.[8] Though the French administration became more firmly established in Libreville after the 1870s, enlarging its fields and receiving imported food of better quality, problems with transport and conservation of foodstuffs persisted.[9]

Europeans had no choice but to adapt elements of local cuisine and the social meanings enacted and embodied in eating and cooking. Traders and administrators still had to rely on the good graces of the Mpongwe hosts, just as other visitors needed to curry favor with African coastal landlords in the heyday of the slave trade.[10] Food preparation helped to define master-servant relations for local and foreign inhabitants of Libreville. Mikiel's anger about sweating over an open fire reflected a common sense among visiting Frenchmen that they should not have to prepare meals. When French sailors and traders began to settle in Libreville, they almost invariably hired local men to cook for them.

Cooking in the mid-nineteenth century was truly a space on the "middle ground," where African and European concerns and demands overlapped without either being able to dominate the other. Africans could shape what French residents ate, and Europeans consumed their food in the same ways that free Mpongwe families did. Culinary practices opened up job opportunities for African men seeking to enter Atlantic commerce. Winwood Reade, eating at the Hatton and Cookson British trading post in Libreville, hired a Mpongwe man who had been a cook on English ships. The man had relied on his expertise in cooking for sailors to travel on the coast of Gabon and Equatorial Guinea.[11] French and British traders expected to be served by Africans. Reade noted that traders taking their dinner at Hatton and Cookson each had an African servant stand at their beck and call.[12] Many of these employees were slaves of African masters. André Nordick, a French officer stationed in Libreville, wrote: "At this time [1873], a slave was a domestic servant that received no wages and could be had if his former master was paid a few coins."[13] Some English traders beat their cooks in a manner as brutal as Mpongwe masters' treatment of their slaves.[14] Cheap domestic labor allowed European traders to live in similar fashion to Mpongwe clan leaders.

Few French in Libreville praised the efforts of male domestic servants, and they employed comments on cuisine as a way of keeping Africans in their place. One French commandant pitied his European subordinates whose African servants made them "sad and unhealthy meals."[15] A member of the Brazza expedition in 1885 groaned of his misfortune. "What of the Gabonese who do work? 8 out of 10 call themselves cooks. But what horrible kitchen help! There are very few who can satisfy the most rudimentary needs of an employer. . . . As the supervisor of the mess, I found myself cooking our food," he wrote.[16] Maurice Briault derided his cook for boiling sardines in his coffee.[17] As a means of maintaining strict racial and cultural divisions, Europeans mocked Africans for wearing Western clothes "incorrectly."[18] Taste in food became another area where foreigners might forge cultural boundaries. Humor helped to establish boundaries that presented Europeans as common members of a superior culture regardless of class and national distinctions.

Among whites the few European and American women living in Libreville influenced white cooking. Although female missionaries such as Phoebe Ogden and Mère Louise of the Sisters of the Immaculate Conception lived in the Gabon Estuary for decades, many believed white women could not survive the tropical climate.[19] Only missionary women and several female entrepreneurs served food, which put their culinary skills in great demand. Some American missionary women in Libreville found themselves bound by prevailing gender hierarchies in the kitchen.[20] One American Protestant woman wrote of her dismay at being expected to feed people at all hours.[21] Soeur Saint-Charles, a popular nun who lived in Libreville for nearly a half century, began her career as a cook for her community.[22] The handful of European women in Libreville outside missions had more alternatives to reap profits from their culinary skills. Madame Fischer, the Swiss widow of a French trader, ran a small restaurant in the early 1860s. Burton claimed she saved more than sixty-five thousand francs in her seven-year stay in Libreville.[23] From approximately 1875 through 1900 the widow of a French trader named Pecqueur ran an eatery much as Fischer had done. A partner of a French retail merchant, Pecqueur helped to supply the colony with imported foods from France.[24]

Europeans in Libreville did not shy away from African meals. Foreign residents adopted local foods into their diets and ate on regular occasions with some Africans of high social status. In 1894 missionary Robert Nassau reported that all Europeans ate plantains in Libreville.[25] Catholic and Protestant missionaries dined with Mpongwe clan chiefs such as Rapontchombo and his son Félix.[26] On evangelizing missions along the Estuary, pastors and priests ate manioc in villages. More worldly men did not eschew *nyembwe* or Gabonese guests; French officers consumed food and rum at parties with African women in the 1880s.[27] Some, to the consternation of their superiors, inebriated themselves at weddings of their African employees, where food was undoubtedly served.[28] Frenchmen with Mpongwe mistresses became close to their lovers' families, and some social calls to African relatives included meals.[29]

As they shared repasts with Mpongwe townspeople, Europeans accepted common beliefs surrounding food. Poison and sorcery, long associated among Mpongwe people with food preparation, became a concern. Explorer Paul Du

Chaillu brought his own pots on his travels out of his worry about the sup-posed penchant of Africans for human meat.[30] Few others worried about tasting human flesh, but they were not immune to other fears. Europeans fretted about ingesting danger just as Mpongwe masters wondered if some dangerous con-coction might have been added to their meals. Anxieties about dependence on Africans also reinforced the power of landlords over Europeans. Besides dem-onstrating the close ties between white and black residents, poison opened up spaces for political and legal negotiation.

Poison and Colonial Negotiations

Europeans who ate like local people had to contend with indigenous anxieties surrounding food consumption. Close social ties that crossed over racial bound-aries in Libreville opened the way for rumors and fears to gain credence among Europeans. From the 1860s missionaries and officials noted accusations of poi-soning. American pastors believed an African cook had placed lethal toxins in the meals of Captain Lawlin, the American trader who gave John Wilson the idea to set up a mission in the Gabon Estuary.[31] A Kru worker supposedly tried to poi-son a French officer in the following year.[32] The boundaries between European "science" and African "superstition" became porous as missionaries and offi-cials borrowed and remade stories about poison.[33] Fears of racial and cultural mixing became a common theme within these tales—a theme that some, such as the njembe women and others, manipulated to their advantage.

European medicine in the late nineteenth century had difficulty discerning the exact causes of illness among Libreville residents, let alone whether illness derived from poison. Often missionaries and officers died during their first two years in Gabon.[34] The transmission and causes of malaria, the most common scourge of European residents, were not clearly understood until late in the century.[35] With high morbidity rates for Europeans and Africans in Libreville, investigations into the "true" cause of death often furnished no convincing answers. Seeing an African immigrant wracked by spasms in 1891, Nassau mused in his diary about the cause: "Epilepsy? Poison? Worms?"[36] Despite com-mon fears regarding poison, no commandant appears to have authorized autop-sies before the early twentieth century.

Townspeople heard countless stories involving poison. Missionaries, who became de facto experts on toxins through their command of local languages, thought poison ran rampant through the port. Robert Milligan, stationed at

Libreville in the 1890s, commented in a typical passage on the subject: "Africa abounds with deadly poisons, and African wives frequently contract an unpleasant habit of using them in the cooking pot."[37] Catholic missionaries retold similar tales of vengeance.[38] They also found Africans willing to describe having bewitched Europeans. Mpongwe women boasted to American pastors that they put love charms in their lovers' dishes.[39]

Europeans gave credence to these rumors. Although European observers tried to separate "poison" from "superstition," they recognized that local populations had many toxins at their disposal.[40] In the 1870s several French scientists collected samples of poison used by Fang hunters in the Gabon Estuary.[41] Robert Nassau summed up the problem by stating: "There are native poisons. This much I have to admit... but is rare [that] the proof of guilt is clear.... What I call a 'poison' is to them only another material form of a fetish power."[42] The ambiguity of poison leveled the playing field between foreigners and indigenous people—the French might have troops, but no commandant could silence the threat of toxins.

In light of the endless struggle by Europeans to set markers between themselves and Africans, poison stories served to articulate qualms over racial fears about the physical and social proximity to townspeople. Paul Barret, a doctor in Libreville in the late 1870s, remarked: "Poison, which can be placed traitorously and kills without attracting attention, is the means of revenge that [is] most common [in Libreville]. Everyone fears his neighbor and has this fear right before his eyes. And come an accident, the defiance extends and terrorizes Europeans themselves."[43]

It is little wonder that poison worries flourished in a region where educated African townspeople challenged European hierarchies of race and gender. As the njembe incident described later in this chapter indicates, unease about poison sometimes explicitly articulated fears surrounding sexual relationships that crossed racial frontiers. A British tourist noted in 1920: "There died a very old Mpongwe woman who was not above suspicion [for poison] during her lifetime. Up to the last, she had preserved her good looks and had lived with many Europeans."[44] Just as sorcery fears among Africans denoted anxieties over status and slaves, European concerns about the overturning of gender and race conventions appeared in discussions of poison.

Some Africans employed these beliefs to frighten Europeans and gain leverage in quarrels. Around 1877 two German traders working for the Woermann company in Libreville decided to investigate the activities of the secret power association *njembe*, open only to Mpongwe women.[45] Their "native wives" and African friends refused to provide any information. Undaunted by this wall of silence, they managed one night to stumble upon a meeting of *njembe* women. When discovered, they fled back to their trading post after the women tried to seize them.

> Njembe did not dare assault them, French policemen being within call; but next day word was sent by the society denouncing them both, laying a curse on them and plainly saying that they should die. If the threat had been by other means of death, these gentlemen would have laughed; but the women did not hesitate to add that they would poison the men in their food. This would have been entirely possible, even without collusion among the several men and boys who ranged from steward to cook and waiters as their household servants.

One of the Germans, the head manager of Woermann in Gabon, offered to pay a fine to the women through the auspices of his mistress. As she was a member of *njembe* herself, he soon settled the dispute by giving a payment to the organization.

However, the women had no mercy for the other clerk. As his health deteriorated, *njembe* members claimed they were killing him. His colleague agreed to pay a very large fine. The organization, "having demonstrated its power, standing victorious before the community," claimed to have spared the man's life. No legal proceedings were apparently raised during the affair. Nassau's account does not furnish a shred of scientific evidence for the supposed poison. Yet the interdependence of Europeans and Africans in Libreville meant *njembe* could vanquish one of the most influential trading houses in Gabon.

Mpongwe men resorted to similar tactics in a dispute in 1883. A French trader visiting the Libreville office of Hatton and Cookson shot twice in a fit of drunken rage a domestic servant of the store manager.[46] Mr. Carlill, the manager, barely rescued the Frenchmen from an angry mob. The commandant of Gabon recounted the incident to the minister of colonies: "The natives of Glass had a fetish (this is to say a reunion of chiefs and notables to discuss the affair) and the result was they warned Mr. Carlill that if the wounded black died, Carlill himself or his representative Mr. St. John would be killed by poison or other means."[47]

The commandant sent six African guards and a white corporal to guard the store. Unable to guarantee his safety, the administration placed the Frenchman aboard a ship docked in the Estuary. The British firm agreed to pay fines to Mpongwe in the town; European authorities thus paid heed to poison threats.[48] Carlill skipped town for Liverpool but never arrived in England. He died of fever on the voyage home. The doctors may have blamed malaria for his demise, yet some Hatton and Cookson traders believed such deaths were no mere accidents. Behind every fever might be a fiendish poison.[49]

Officials and European visitors also accepted beliefs that foreign Africans such as Vili from the Loango region in Congo-Brazzaville were masters of poison. Working as domestic servants and cooks in town, Vili men faced accusations from Mpongwe residents of Libreville. Some told English explorer Mary Kingsley in 1895 that Loango servants were "'too much likely to be devils to be good too much' and are undoubtedly given to poisoning which is an unpleasant habit in a house servant."[50] In August 1905 via an autopsy, French authorities found a Loango cook guilty of poisoning another African.[51] Ten years later another cook was executed for attempting to poison a French official.[52] Senegalese marabouts, arriving with West African soldiers stationed in Gabon, also had a reputation for using poison.[53]

With autopsies being a rare occurrence, Europeans depended on the same rumors and hearsay that Africans used in reviewing poison cases. French officials arrested a man after a Vili cook named Tati claimed the suspect had "made medicine" against him around 1906.[54] After Tati's death the suspect admitted that he had bewitched the victim but refused to explain how he had killed Tati. With such ambiguous evidence officials could not determine the difference between sorcery and "real" poison. The case of Andrew Ferguson shows how such ambiguity allowed Europeans as well as Africans a means of evading colonial authority.

French authorities charged British trader Andrew Ferguson with murdering his Loango cook at a trading post in the Gabon Estuary in late 1921.[55] Ferguson, after a heavy drinking bout, shot his cook Guillaume Mafoungou and attempted to set his expiring body on fire. When Africans reported the crime to French authorities Ferguson declared that Mafoungou was a known practitioner of the occult and had put poison in his tea. Several African witnesses claimed Ferguson had been told that Guillaume was a "sorcerer," but none could give any evidence that the cook had actually committed any crime. The medical examiner, in turn, could not state with certainty the cause of Ferguson's illness or confirm the use of toxins. A French official, called to the stand, declared that local villagers commonly used poisons but could not shed any light on the case. The Ferguson case demonstrates the pervasiveness and obscurity of poison fears. In the end Ferguson's attempt to use his poison defense to exonerate himself failed; he was jailed and exiled from Gabon.

Peter Geschiere, in his groundbreaking ethnography of witchcraft and politics in southern Cameroon, brings up issues that directly pertain to poison in colonial Libreville. "[Witchcraft beliefs] are representations that heavily emphasize human action but that, at the same time, hide the actors and their acts from view," he noted.[56] Poison worked to explain a variety of events to Africans and Europeans. Geschiere also asserts that witchcraft plays on a shifting balance between secrecy and public performance: its power derives from the mysteries surrounding its workings and from public knowledge regarding their results.[57] The same can be said for poison. Europeans, far from denying the power of sorcery, expressed an awareness of their own vulnerability through poison tales. The common social worlds that Africans and Europeans formed through everyday practices such as eating habits made Europeans active participants in sorcery and poison discussions.[58] The introduction of local eating practices in daily life resulted in the selective spread of unwanted poison rumors. Such ties radically diminished after 1914, when changes eroded cross-racial social bonds that were replaced by increasingly fixed racial differences.

Separate Tables

The First World War had radically altered the economic playing field open to Africans in the Gabon Estuary. Timber camps largely controlled by Frenchmen replaced African independent cutters and brought an end to older trades in rubber and ivory. New competition squeezed out local merchants. Europeans and West African petty merchants took over trade in most imported goods. Hausa traders, some arriving from the north as early as 1910, clearly controlled trade in clothes and many manufactured goods by the late 1920s.[59] By the 1940s lists of permits at market reveal names common in Dahomey, Togo, and northern Cameroon, with no Fang or Myene participants.[60] Furthermore, import-export stores such as Compagnie Française de l'Afrique Occidentale, Hatton and Cookson, and smaller businesses run by Frenchmen and a smattering of Lebanese greatly outnumbered local entrepreneurs in the consumer goods market by 1930.[61] Few local people had the money to pay for licenses to trade.[62] Prince Félix, a leading descendent of Félix Adende Rapontchombo, criticized the need to pay over twenty thousand CFA francs for an import-export permit in 1948.[63] In this new economic climate, most city Africans lost out.

Racial lines became more deeply drawn between black and white after 1914, even if Libreville never lost entirely its older traditions of hospitality between Africans and Europeans. First, administrative policies that favored the acceptance of educated Africans fell into disfavor. French officials feared the agitation of educated urban elites and abandoned earlier notions of assimilation.[64] Increasingly concerned with hygiene, urban planners used racist arguments that associated Africans with filth and disease to call for racially divided cities.[65] Europeans thus went to greater lengths to separate themselves from others. Libreville was unique in one respect of race relations. Unrestrained development and local land claims had precluded any systematic policy of segregation. Although officials never implemented any formal plan to separate the city into European and African sections, more scrutiny was placed on relationships that crossed racial dividers. For example, the Euro-African relationships that had brought the town so much notoriety before the First World War became less publicly acceptable. Some authors claimed to French audiences that such affairs had become rare and were no longer respectable, even though any visitor to Libreville could see that this supposed decline had never taken place.[66]

Attitudes toward gender had changed as officials in Paris called for white women to domesticate the colonial empire.[67] Much as in Brazzaville, more women moved to Libreville after 1918.[68] Between 1920 and 1940 the three hundred Europeans in Gabon's capital included roughly seventy-five women.[69] By the 1950s geographer Guy Lasserre cited marriage as a major reason for the improved health of Europeans in the city.[70] However, it would be a serious error to believe that Euro-African unions declined as white women entered town life. French timber entrepreneurs continued to celebrate their unions with townswomen, even though French women had also made a home in the Gabonese capital.

These trends left their mark on eating habits and domestic labor. African men no longer ate as often with whites. In a letter to Senator Boisneuf, a member of League of the Rights of Man asserted that he was the only person of color allowed into European restaurants.[71] Another critic of colonial policies in the early 1920s attacked the rise of social distance between blacks and whites. The anonymous writer remarked: "In 1885, the two elements were friendly to

each other. The white worker and the black worker walked together, drank and
ate together at the same table. Was it not the time of the real 'entente cordia-
le?' Now, in our time . . . our Frenchmen apply against the blacks the inhumane
lynch law enforced in America."[72]

While perhaps idealizing race relations in the late nineteenth century, the
statement does accurately note a sea change in European eating habits and social
behavior in Libreville. By the 1940s no Gabonese men could sit in a European
eating establishment.[73] Given the longstanding favoritism of French officials
toward African women, it was much easier for female Libreville residents to eat
where they pleased. Gabonese mistresses sat in the same clubs as their French
lovers in the timber business.[74] However, even with women, race influenced culinary habits. Mistresses of several European men in autobiographical novels of
colonial Gabon ate dessert with their lovers but took their meals in their own
homes.[75] Considering that Europeans had no restrictions placed on their purchase of food during the era of famines, it would not be surprising if educated
Africans saw food distribution policies as a visible sign of white supremacy.

Unlike their predecessors, Europeans in Libreville after the First World War
had the option of avoiding African foods if they so wished. Advances in transport from the 1920s allowed European staples to arrive faster than in the past.
Regular visits by steamers ensured the supply of cheese, flour, canned goods,
and vegetables. No matter how much famine scoured the Gabonese countryside, Europeans could avoid starvation themselves, even well away from the
capital. A Frenchman fondly recalling his days as a trader in central Gabon
in the mid-1920s waxed nostalgic about his meals, a medley of hunting victo-
ries, local fruits, and iron-flavored sardines, cassoulets, and sausages.[76] Whether
the colonial hunger for canned foods was one factor in the slow acceptance of
canned goods in metropolitan France is a question that has not yet been considered.[77] There was no mystery about how colonial power and food came together
in the Estuary, though. At timber camps where malnutrition killed off scores
of Gabonese workers, European managers selected from choice cuts of lamb,
beef, and chicken.[78]

French mastery over hunger was matched by their control over animals.
Europeans could afford to purchase permits for guns without the hurdles the
vast majority of Gabonese faced, and so hunting big game brought meat to
the table. Perhaps the Europeans of Libreville ate even more bush meat than
Africans, considering that more than sixty elderly residents in Libreville report-

ed a paucity of wild animals sold at market before independence. The town's isolation from the rest of the colony, the government's firm limits on African gun ownership before the 1950s, and the ready market for meat at timber camps outside Libreville meant hunters had a better market closer to wild animals. Besides testing their virility, French hunters could also take on the role of benevolent fathers. Some French expatriates boasted that they fed their workers by hunting.[79]

Retail companies ordered foods primarily for Europeans, and red meat was one of the more choice supplies that they delivered. Boats and planes delivered cattle mainly for European consumption in Libreville.[80] Beef remained expensive but became a more common item on European menus. While many older African residents recalled the site of the butcher shop now occupied by the Lalala market, practically none could afford beef. Officials in the 1940s grumbled that high prices for cattle limited the African market for steak.[81]

The ingredients of meals consumed by Europeans changed over time, but anxieties did not. The hostility to manual labor shared by many townspeople of high social rank continued regardless of race. Practically no European residents save Catholic missionaries cultivated food. Before 1945 only a handful of Europeans took up commercial fishing. Police regarded these small operators with disdain. When a French former government employee asked for aid to grow vegetables and to fish, colonial administrators refused to allow him to stay in the colony.[82] Instead of supporting his efforts, the chief of the Estuary region noted: "His financial position is always precarious. This European, installed miserably at Nomba, lives off the sale of his garden produce and fishing."[83] When several European residents of Libreville struggled to recruit workers for their fishing company, the administration refused to intercede on their behalf.[84] A Hungarian sailor led a fruitless four-year quest to gain government support for his fishing venture. Police reports described him as a "poor wreck" who "lived like an African."[85] Much like wealthy Mpongwe families who scorned agriculture, among whites the maintenance of respectable European identity precluded small-scale farming or fishing for a living.

Separate foodways continued to develop within the French settler population after 1945, as the European population of Libreville rose dramatically. By the mid-1950s some 1,500 Europeans lived in the rapidly expanding town of almost 20,000 people.[86] The vast majority of these newcomers came from France. With enough money to purchase refrigerators and hire large numbers of African domestic servants, Europeans could eat like households in France.[87] Pâté, frozen meat, and fruits and vegetables from South Africa and France poured into the city. French administrators recommended importing European vegetables rather than trying to grow them in Gabon.[88] "Appreciating a refreshing papaya, savoring an avocado in vinaigrette as an appetizer or very rarely asking the cook to prepare a chicken in *nyembwe* sauce in palm oil are the only tropical fantasies of European menus," Guy Lasserre noted.[89] Much as today, this cuisine left its mark in expatriate wallets. Over half of European expenses in the city went to food and drink in 1959.[90]

Food and meals became closely linked to a style of settler life in which Gabonese featured only as servants. Two hotels, La Résidence and Hôtel Central, served as restaurants and gourmet stores in the 1950s. White-jacketed and gloved waiters served English journalist Russell Warren Howe a thirty-course dinner when he ate with the English consul.[91] The local official daily bulletin, *Agence France Press*, advertised Bréton and Basque meals for 750 CFA.[92] The average monthly salary of African domestic servants and laborers in Libreville, by contrast, was between 3,000 and 6,000 CFA.[93] Hotels sold expensive sausages and various wines and cheeses from France. Besides the public display of wealth through lavish meals, French society revolved around a series of private dinners and parties. As in many other colonial locales, such occasions served to unite Europeans in Libreville through leisure.[94]

The French outside the safe confines of the city could not often taste the good life in the late colonial era. They still had to eat what Africans provided. Some French settlers, especially missionaries and self-styled eccentrics, consumed local foods. Missionary Marcel Lefebvre, the future doyen of traditionalist Catholicism, ran the St. Jean seminary in Libreville in the 1930s. A Fang student laughed as he watched Lefebvre chew some manioc; the priest replied that his pupil would not last long in school.[95] French timber apparatchik turned big game hunter Georges Trial asserted his nonconformity by requiring that his European guests eat *nyembwe* at dinner.[96] Trial, obsessed with proving he had the heart of a true "primitive," adored a fine meal of *nyembwe* and claimed that *n'tchivo* fish was as tasty as cooked bass. Culinary practices provided one element of lifestyles Europeans constructed to claim fluency in African as well as European ways.

Others exhibited the same paranoia about food that European residents had shown before World War I. A French plantation manager in Kango worried that a spiteful Mpongwe woman had slipped cat whiskers into the dinner of a French acquaintance after he abandoned his plans to marry her. The sharp ends of the whiskers had supposedly destroyed his intestines.[97] Other European poison tales demonized hired help as well as African lovers. A settler penned a novel in the 1930s involving a fiendish Gabonese man, a former circus clown corrupted by a stay in Paris, who on his return to Libreville toadied up to a heroic timber camp manager. The duplicitous veteran of the circus became the unwary man's cook and then bought a potion from a sorcerer designed to kill his employer. The Frenchman barely survived ingesting a soup full of venom at his remote concession.[98] Male African auxiliaries could be as two-faced in the settler imaginary as bitter mistresses. Even though talk of venom still colored local gossip, expatriates in Libreville itself could find them entertaining without having to take them seriously, as the following experiences of the wife of the first American ambassador to Gabon indicate.

Madame Darlington's Account of High Dining

The formation of separate European and African styles of eating by the time of independence is made clear in the writing of Alice Darlington, the wife of the first American ambassador in Gabon. She recorded her domestic experiences as an active participant in high dining in the early 1960s. She found daily shopping a tedious chore. "Everything we ate, with the exception of avocados, pineapples and bananas, was imported from France, Chad or Cameroon," she grumbled.[99] As a privileged but novice member of a small expatriate community, Darlington had to learn the unwritten codes of eating and shopping in Libreville at the end of colonial rule. Describing her multiple roles as a popular guest and a manager of a small staff of servants, her autobiography exposes many of the town's culinary conventions left out of the archival record.

First she had to learn to buy food. "Altogether shopping was a most frustrating experience," she noted.[100] While most French households left shopping to servants, Darlington took her basket to market, but her lack of "inside connections" limited her choices. Until she discovered that French families reserved advance orders of imported food, Madame Darlington had to sort through scraps of vegetables once European retailers opened their doors.[101] Good fish required cultural capital. Before her husband made a private arrangement with a French fishing company, she bemoaned waiting in line with several hundred Gabonese women.[102] The limited qualities of many common staples pestered her shopping days. Sugar, rice, and potatoes vanished from the town for weeks. Storekeepers at the four main European retailers dispensed with politeness and, in Darlington's words, "a ruder lot I never saw."[103]

Shopping woes notwithstanding, Madame Darlington became a familiar sight on the Libreville social circuit. Only a few Gabonese ministers offered lavish parties. French residents hosted a barrage of dinners and cocktail hours with few Africans present.[104] Even at events hosted by President Léon Mba's wife Pauline, French and Gabonese guests tended to fraternize along racial lines.[105] Besides the survival of a separate white identity among Libreville residents, the lack of educated Gabonese women meant that few who were not from Libreville were accustomed to socializing with whites or to European eating habits. Pauline lamented to Darlington her lack of experience with European table manners. "But you always have known how to use a knife and fork. You had parents to teach you when you were young. Here, at my age, I have to learn how to do this," she said.[106] Mpongwe households accustomed to sending their children to France did not share Mba's predicament.[107]

Darlington's own efforts to enter the social scene had mixed results. Like most white employers, she found many "troubles" thanks to the unfamiliarity of her domestic servants with dining conventions. She claimed her cook and servants, mainly Téké from eastern Gabon, fumbled through meals.[108] Their mishaps furnished European residents a chance to display their supposed cultural superiority over Africans in the city. After one servant overcooked a beef dish, a guest reassured Darlington that these events took place everywhere in Africa.[109] These stories worked to underline distinctions between herself and her staff, just as French residents had separated themselves from their hired help in the past.

Conversations about poison persisted in this period, even for someone as privileged as Darlington. One cook accused Darlington's female Mpongwe secretary of bewitching others in the household; another warned his employer that a cook had cast a "fetish" on her to prevent her from firing him.[110] Unlike Europeans in the nineteenth century, however, Darlington found these stories amusing rather than possible sources of alarm. By the time of her stay in Libreville the power of officials and expatriates to shape everyday life had eliminated older arenas of negotiation and conflict associated with food. Technology had removed the leverage of earlier generations of Mpongwe people as the main suppliers of food to Europeans. With the establishment of French settler cuisine, what could have been the source of real fear in the late nineteenth century had become merely a colorful anecdote.

Darlington's experiences give no indication of the survival of older culinary practices that had flourished in the late nineteenth century. Other commentators noted the relative remoteness of Europeans from the surrounding African population during the dusk of colonialism in Libreville.[111] While independence brought numbers of mission-educated Africans into positions of power, and formal segregation vanished, few Africans in Libreville could or can afford to import French champagne or hire domestic servants. Oil profits allow a few Africans to partake in the expensive meals available to wealthy expatriates, but the vast majority of city dwellers remain excluded from European styles of eating.

While the strict racial segregation that divided European and African dining habits no longer exists in Libreville, many of the elements of separation and social distance continue to appear. Few African families can afford to dine at Le Bacchus or other gourmet restaurants in Louis and Glass. International chains of hotels with expensive bars and restaurants, such as Novotel, cater to wealthy foreign businessmen and rich Gabonese officials. All the amenities of French cuisine can be purchased at various stores. However, mutual borrowing between cuisines is rare save among certain groups of expatriates, such as American Peace Corps volunteers and missionaries.

These shifts in food habits over more than a century demonstrate the slow rise of French authority in Libreville. For decades Europeans depended on local sources of food and domestic labor. They thus had to adopt and appropriate many elements of local cooking. These early relationships fit into reciprocal agreements that George Brooks has called "landlord-stranger" relationships between visiting European traders and coastal African communities.[112] Through furnishing labor and sustenance, Mpongwe townspeople, much like their counterparts elsewhere in West Africa, found ways to negotiate with colonial authorities. Even in the age of high imperialism, Europeans and Americans grew to accept indigenous beliefs about mystical harm through the idiom of poison.

Changing racial standards and the transformation of the colonial economy altered these arrangements. The firm establishment of a colonial administration over Libreville and the entire Estuary region undermined Mpongwe autonomy. An evolution of racial attitudes among French residents made the mutual cultural borrowings between African and Europeans less acceptable. Through eliminating African meals and refusing to eat with local people, Europeans articulated a firm line between themselves and colonized subjects. The experience of Libreville illustrates how improvements in technology and transport helped to foster segregation. Food still delineates inequalities in urban Gabon today.

Conclusion

The ballooning population of Libreville has not helped the town's longstand-ing difficulties with food supply. In 1960 Libreville's population barely exceeded 30,000 people out of over 470,000 for the entire country.[1] Ten years later well over 100,000 inhabitants populated the rapidly expanding city. A flood of rural migrants continues to enter the city.[2] Most farmland used in the colonial peri-od around Libreville disappeared as settlers formed new neighborhoods. An increase in land claims restricted the ability of poor people to grow manioc in unoccupied terrain. Grandiose buildings erected in the 1970s, such as Omar Bongo's Cité de la Démocratie, wiped out fields in Nkembo, Atong Abé, Mont-Bouet, and other neighborhoods.[3] With the burden of paying for daily trans-port to fields and a reduction in unclaimed land available near the city, urban poor people lost the option of cultivating the bulk of their own food.

The exploitation of coastal petroleum reserves after 1956 supplanted tim-ber as the country's main industry, and the resulting economic shifts have not aided rural farmers or the city's food difficulties. Revenue from multinational oil companies such as Shell and Elf flowed into the coffers of the Gabonese gov-ernment. Lucrative state jobs and educational advancement are easier to obtain in Libreville than in the benighted rural Estuary region, which has been almost entirely neglected by the Bongo regime. Even Akok, home of Léon Mba's wife

Pauline, suffers from poor access to health care and schools. Rather than invest-ing money in agricultural projects, officials chose to support gigantic develop-ment projects, such as the creation of the Trans-Gabonais railroad connecting Franceville in southern Gabon with Libreville.[4] State attempts to form com-mercial plantain plantations and rice crop fields foundered on logistical and funding problems.[5] Scholars such as David Gardinier blame oil and its perni-cious effects for the high food prices.[6]

Given the host of changes that followed independence, a radical alteration in Libreville food supply and diets is not surprising. With a swelling urban population and the economic decline of rural areas after 1960, the immediate hinterland of the capital could not cope with the upsurge of demand. The mea-ger resources and numbers of rural Estuary farmers could not hope to sate the growing city's appetite, and foreign merchants and farmers have become the main suppliers of the city's food. Road construction furnished Libreville with one solution for soaring food prices. The construction of a reliable road link-ing the northern Gabonese province of Woleu Ntem with Libreville in the ear-ly 1970s permitted farmers and truck drivers from southern Cameroon to take over the city's market for manioc, plantains, and other crops that had been grown locally in the past. A disregard for road maintenance has left farmers from Medouneu and much of southern Gabon unable to reach the city mar-ket.[7] West Africans, Lebanese, Chinese, Mauritanians, and Moroccans moved to Libreville after 1970 and now control the flow of industrially processed foods into the capital, while many Gabonese farmers remain unable to sell in the cap-ital because of the terrible state of the roads.

For the moment the markets of Gabon's capital have escaped food shortages. In the mid-1970s inflation and scarcity troubled the city, but improved ties to Cameroon have stayed further spells of hardship.[8] Libreville has become addict-ed to food imports. High prices are a constant theme of discontent heard in the kitchens and bars of the city.[9] The few scholars interested in this radical change have pointed to the region's ecology and to oil as two causes for this unfortunate state of affairs without considering the economic, social, and political transfor-mation of the Gabon Estuary in the colonial period. A 1981 U.S. Department of Agriculture survey summed up a common view. This report asserted: "Rising incomes and changing tastes and preferences associated with urban life have given impetus to a seemingly voracious urban demand for non-traditional food whose domestic production is marginal or non-existent."[10] No background on past troubles with food supply and the role of state projects appears, save for a rosy discussion of "efficient" colonial agricultural programs that deteriorated after independence.[11] This interpretation relies on a series of unflattering stereotypes particularly popular among Europeans in Gabon: lazy Africans, unwilling to farm, mesmerized by the lure of foreign goods, and unable to manage revenue from natural resources efficiently, become dependent on foreigners rather than working to produce their own sustenance.

Such a straw man may seem far too flimsy to require a thorough and prolonged thrashing. Unfortunately, my conversations with Europeans and Americans during my stay in Gabon suggest otherwise. I have questioned this viewpoint by noting the varying impact of wage labor, state policies, and social unrest in colonial Libreville and the Estuary. The formation of a relatively affluent town community, determined to distinguish itself from rural people out of a concern for status that took root in the era of the Atlantic slave trade, resulted in a group who recognized the attractions of wage labor and eschewed farming. Although painfully obvious to anyone familiar with the country's history, the dramatic upheaval associated with European commercial expansion and military occupation curtailed the development of rural farming through the first ninety years of French rule.

Oil and political independence alone did not bring about high prices and food supply problems. Political scientist Douglas Yates, in scrutinizing the ways oil has radically shaped Gabon, has examined its impact on productivity. He argues that "Gabon has confused allocation with development. . . . By spending what were effectively unearned incomes from its oil the state promoted an institutionalized largesse which has brought it twice to the brink of ruin."[12] Such attitudes on the part of the urban elite who dominate Gabonese politics did not come solely from riches derived from natural resources, nor is the situation a recent phenomenon. Oil has acted to create wealth without leading to investment in infrastructure. Bargains made by Mpongwe leaders and mission-educated Africans with authoritarian European officials favored patronage over entrepreneurial activity.

Libreville is a particularly striking example of a city suffering from problems in food supply since 1960. It is not alone. The residents of Dar Es Salaam in Tanzania battled shortages in basic foodstuffs created by import dependence, ill-planned forced resettlement in villages, and bureaucratic interference in farming and marketing.[13] Urbanization has taxed the ability of cities to obtain required amounts of food. The ecology of the surrounding region and the thorny difficulty of transport make for serious problems; other cities, such as Brazzaville, have struggled at times with similar troubles.[14] In Southeast Asia and the Pacific the popularity of Western foods and the expansion of capitalist wage labor has brought on rising consumption of imports.[15] The low population density of the Gabon Estuary created challenges at times more serious than in the thickly settled countryside around Lagos, Duala, and Abdijan. Even so, urban colonial politics and social changes influenced later problems in other cities.

The history of food supply to Libreville raises issues common to other parts of colonial Africa. The slow move from a slave export economy to "legitimate" trade undoubtedly had an impact on the mundane lives of people throughout much of West and Central Africa. The survival and malleability of attitudes formed at the height of the Atlantic slave-trading era deserve more treatment from scholars. Though the impacts of the odious commerce on everyday life in coastal societies may never be fully understood, changes in farming and eating practices caused by Atlantic commerce did not stop with the introduction of new crops and implements. The ability of urban groups who previously profited from slavery to grapple with early colonial rule is striking.

Libreville's troubles with food also offer an opportunity to consider the effects of Atlantic commerce and colonial rule on African consumption patterns. Historians of Atlantic trade have highlighted the role that African consumer desire had in setting the terms of negotiation for slaves.[16] Jeremy Prestholdt has recently examined the complex role that East African consumption patterns had on commerce from New England to Bombay, and his study points to the importance of local agency in influencing trade and production in regions commonly deemed as "core," to use the terminology of world-systems theory.[17] Libreville's food problems indicate both the role of African communities in determining how and what they would consume and the constraints placed on individual agency by colonial rule. Townspeople could choose to abandon farming, but the famine years indicate how the government and private interests could dictate consumption patterns. Had Libreville residents or timber camp employees not accepted rations, they could not have survived. Unlike cloth, guns, alcohol, or other goods already discussed by historians interested in consumption, food is one product that people must have, and if consumers lack the leverage and the resources to obtain sustenance, then they have to accept the choices of those who have control over food supply. At the same time the unwillingness of Gabon Estuary residents and officials in the late colonial and postcolonial eras to support agriculture shows how the unfettered choices of Africans can lead, paradoxically, to increased dependence on imports.

Though social historians have explored the use of foreign goods in the performance of urban identities in colonial Africa, the vital role imported food played in colonial cities remains a largely untold story. Mpongwe workers and leaders declared repeatedly that food supply was an issue tied to labor rights, gender roles, and the extent of colonial influence over tastes and markets. Like changing fashions in dress, food on occasion acted as a lightning rod for debates over status and the impact of colonial rule on local communities. Despite European claims, however, Libreville residents did not turn into Western-style consumers overnight. These narratives do not lend themselves to facile statements on the boons and disadvantages of ties with the world economy. It is hard to state as yet to what extent food debates in Libreville had counterparts elsewhere. Much more research needs to be done on shifts in urban African food consumption to see how the case of Libreville fits into a comparative context.

The ubiquitous concept of negotiation in colonial African history works well in examining colonial food supply. A tangled series of past decisions has shaped what is offered on Libreville tables, the manner in which food is eaten, and why people choose to consume what they eat today. The skill of townspeople in defending their tastes has been a central topic here. On the one hand, Libreville residents affirmed their claims to food without producing more themselves; their efforts might appear to be effective acts of resistance against the colonial state and timber companies. On the other hand, the silence of politicians and townspeople in the last decades of colonial rule show a willingness to cooperate with government authorities. Government officials learned to placate urban elites. Save during the 1920s, few urban residents showed much concern for rural farmers. The ability of wealthy townspeople to purchase food relatively easily in the late colonial period may have had the unintended consequence of continued neglect of agriculture and fishing on the part of private companies and the government after independence. Just as French officials derided lazy townspeople and promoted imports, Gabonese policymakers seem to have arrived at similar conclusions. Estuary agriculture continues to languish as a result.

Appendix

Libreville Population, 1863–1960

Year	Approximate population
1863	2,000
1884	3,500
1894	3,500
1912	3,000
1916	4,077
1921	2,730
1927	2,880
1930	3,455
1935	5,444
1940	7,350
1947	16,944
1949	11,000
1950	11,432
1953	18,230
1958	21,565
1960	31,000

Sources: "Le Gabon," Revue maritime et coloniale 9 (1863): 52; Payeur-Didelot, Trente mois au conti-nent mystérieux (Paris: Berger-Levrault, 1899), 117–18; "Sainte Marie de Libreville," BCSE 17 (1892–1894): 364; Gérard Morel and Maria Rohrer, Sur la route de la sainteté: Mère Cécilia (Paris: Editions du Bosquet, 1994), 51; Rapports Annuels, Colonie du Gabon, 1913, 1916, 1921, ANSOM 4(I)D10, 4(I)D14, 4(I)D19; Rapport Politique, Circonscription de l'Estuaire, 4th semester 1927, ANSOM 4(I)D33; Lt. Gov. Gabon to GGFEA, May 1930, ANG Carton 1608, Correspondance en-tre le GGAEF et le Lieutenant Gouverneur du Gabon 1930; Rapport Politique, Dept. Estuaire, 3rd trimestre 1935, ANSOM 4(I)D41; Inspecteur Aff. Admin. Bartoli for Gov. Gabon Masson to GGFEA (Affaires Politiques), 31 May 1939, ANG Carton 318, Correspondance Diverse 1939–1942; Gov. Gabon Masson to GGFEA, 10 August 1940, ANSOM 4(I)D48; Rapport Annuel, Colonie du Gabon, 1947, ANSOM 4(I) D54; Chef Reg. Estuaire Biscons-Ritay, Rapport Annuel, Région de l'Estuaire, 1949, ANG Carton 44, Rapport Politique Annuel Territoire du Gabon 1949, 1954; Sec. Gen. Lanata to GGFEA (Affaires Politiques), 27 August 1951, ANG Carton 967, Correspondance Générale Correspondances Diverses 1951; Gov. Gabon Digo to GGAEF (Affaires Politiques), 26 January 1953, ANG Carton 992, Correspondance Générale Correspondance Diverse 1953; Rap-ports Annuel, Service de l'Agriculture, 1958 and 1960, ANG Carton 762, Ministère de l'Agricul-ture Service de l'Agriculture Rapports Annuels 1958, 1960.

Notes

Abbreviations

ABCFM Papers	American Board of Commissioners for Foreign Missions, Houghton Library, Harvard University, Cambridge, Massachusetts
ACSE	Archives de la Congrégation des Pères du Saint-Esprit, Chevilly-Larue, France
AN FM	Archives Nationales, Fonds Ministriels
AN FM SG	Archives Nationales, Fonds Ministriels, Séries Géographiques, Aix-en-Provence, France
ANG	Archives Nationales du Gabon, Libreville, Gabon
ANSOM	Archives Nationales, Section Outre-Mer, Aix-en-Provence, France
BCSE	Bulletin de la Congrégation des Pères du Saint-Esprit
CGFC	Commissioner General of French Congo
DEFAP	Archives of the Société des Missions Évangeliques
GGFEA	Governor General, French Equatorial Africa
JOAEF	Journal Officiel de l'Afrique l'Afrique Équatoriale Française
PCUSA	Presbyterian Church of the U.S.A., Board of Foreign Missions, Africa Letters, Gaboon and Corsico Missions, Presbyterian Historical Society, Philadelphia, Pennsylvania (consulted on microfilm from Stanford University)
RNP	Robert Nassau Papers, Archives Nationales du Gabon, Libreville
SME	Société des Missions Évangeliques
WWP	William Walker Papers, State Historical Society of Wisconsin, Madison, Wisconsin

Introduction

1. Interview, Luc-Marc Ivanga, Montaigne-Sainte, Libreville, 27 November 1999.

2. "Le débat dont depend le destin de l'Afrique," Réalités 173 (June 1960): 42.

3. Péan, Affaires africaines; Verschave, Noir silence.

4. According to research conducted by staff members of the Economist magazine, Libreville ranks eleventh in international cost of living for cities in 1999. The BDP, an opposition party, has placed these statistics on its website. See www.bdpgabon.org/articles/catagories/economie/eco162.shtml.

5. Statistics on food imports in Gabon sold in Libreville are difficult to come by. Besides my personal observations made during thirteen months in Libreville and the Gabon Estuary between January 1998 and November 2000, other studies of the postcolonial food supply situation point to the high level of imports and the poor productivity of agriculture. See Nsa-Ngogo, "Les conditions de vie," 344–64; Wunder, Oil Wealth, 99.

6. Fanon, Peaux noires; Armah, The Beautyful Ones.

7. De Certeau, Giard, and Mayol, The Practice of Everyday Life, 171–73.

8. For a brief overview of townspeople incorporating European and local cooking styles, see Bonzo, Kitson, and Wardrop, "Talking Food."

9. Mandala, "Beyond the 'Crisis,'" 288.

10. Chastanet, Fauvelle-Aymar, and Juhé-Beaulaton, *Cuisine et société en Afrique*; Mandala, *End of Chidyerano*.

11. *National Geographic* covered and sponsored Michael Fay's trip in 2000 and 2001 and further exploits—including a meeting with President Omar Bongo Ondimba. See Quammen, "The Green Abyss," and "Saving Africa's Eden" and Fay, "In the Land of Surfing Hippos."

12. Petersen, *Eating Apes*, 204.

13. There are exceptions to this general rule of neglect of food and colonialism. For Oceania, see Pollock, "The Early Development of Housekeeping and Imports in Fiji." Historians of Latin America have been much more attentive on this score. For varying examples of research on European foods, identity and supply in colonial contexts in Latin America, see Super, *Food, Conquest, and Colonization in Sixteenth-Century America*; Pilcher, *¡Que vivan los tamales! Food and the Making of Mexican Identity*; Bauer, *Goods, Power, History: Latin America's Material Culture*, 63–69, 154–56.

14. Goody, *Cooking, Cuisine and Class*, 179–80.

15. Guyer, "Feeding Yaoundé," 143–45.

16. Franke, "The Effects of Colonialism and Neocolonialism on the Gastronomic Patterns of the Third World." For other discussions of famine that find colonial rulers culpable in the French empire, see Ngo Vinh Long, *Before the Revolution: The Vietnamese Peasants under the French*, 121–36; Chastanet, "Les crises de subsistances dans les villages soninke du cercle de Bakel, de 1858 à 1945"; Gado, *Une histoire des famines*; Marshall Van Nguyen, "Issues of Poverty and Poor Relief in Colonial Northern Vietnam."

17. Lessing, *The Golden Notebook*, 369.

18. A good critique of such models can be found in Diawara, "Toward a Regional Imaginary in Africa," 116–23.

19. On alcohol see Crush and Ambler, *Liquor and Labor in Southern Africa*; Akyeampong, *Drink, Power, and Cultural Change*. On health and medicine see Vaughan, *Curing Their Ills*; Janzen and Feierman, *The Social Basis of Health and Healing in Africa*; White, "'They Could Make Their Victims Dull'"; Hunt, *Colonial Lexicon*. On clothing see Martin, *Leisure and Society in Colonial Brazzaville*, 154–72; Hendrickson, *Clothing and Difference*; Fair, *Pastimes and Politics*; Sharkey, *Living with Colonialism*, 47–50; Allman, *Fashioning Africa*. And on hygiene see Burke, *Lifebuoy Men, Lux Women*.

20. One of the most succinct overviews of this change can be found in Nancy Rose Hunt's "Introduction," in Hunt, Liu, and Quataert, *Gendered Colonialism in African History*, 4–6.

21. For several exceptions, see Weiss, *Making and Unmaking*; Hansen, "The Cook, His Wife, the Madam, and Their Dinner."

22. Readings of food consumption practices have a long pedigree among anthropologists and historians in North America and Western Europe. The following works provide a brief introduction. Carole Counihan has edited several anthologies that yield a variety of theoretical approaches to food. See Counihan and Van Esterik, *Food and Culture*; Counihan and Kaplan, *Food and Gender*; Counihan, *The Anthropology of Food and Body*.

23. Watts, *Silent Violence*; Davis, *Late Victorian Holocausts*.

24. Sen, *Poverty and Famines*, 1.

25. Vaughan, *The Story of an African Famine*; McCann, *From Poverty to Famine in Northeast Ethiopia*; Iliffe, *The African Poor*, 155–61, 250–59.

26. Elwert-Kretschmer, "Culinary Innovation"; Friedberg, "French Beans for the Masses."

27. Flynn, *Food, Culture, and Survival*; Mandala, *End of Chidyerano*.

28. Mbembe, *On the Postcolony*, 5–6.

29. Berry, *No Condition Is Permanent*, 13.

30. Kaplan, *The Bakers of Paris*, 10.

31. Wylie, *Starving*, xiii.

32. For those interested in this topic, see Vaughan and Moore, *Cutting Down Trees*; Wylie, *Starving*; Brantley, *Feeding Families*.

33. On this subject in African societies, see Weiss's brilliant analysis of Haya social understandings expressed through food consumption, in Weiss, *Making and Unmaking*; see also Feldman-Savelsberg, *Plundered Kitchens, Empty Wombs*, 51, 71–98, 123–29, 181–82. The present work does not approach food consumption in the structuralist tradition of Claude Lévi-Strauss and Mary Douglas; see Lévi-Strauss, *The Raw and the Cooked*; Douglas, "The Deciphering of a Meal."

34. Bourdieu, *Distinction*, 176–202.

35. Braudel, "Food and Drink," in *Civilization and Capitalism*, 183–265. Other examples of this genre include Chang, *Food in Chinese Culture*; Smith and Christian, *Bread and Salt*; Anderson, *The Food of China*.

36. Wunder, *Oil Wealth*, 123.

1. The Gabon Estuary and the Atlantic World, 1840–1960

1. Jean-Baptiste, "Une Ville Libre?"

2. A more technical description can be found in Lasserre, *Libreville*, 10–13.

3. Information on the Gabonese climate can be found in Lasserre, *Libreville*, 84–86; Fehr, *La climatologie du Gabon*; Richard, *Le Gabon*, 90–99; Clist, *Gabon*, 23–24.

4. Richard, *Le Gabon*, 46–48, 63.

5. Klieman, *"The Pygmies Were Our Compass": Bantu and Batwa in the History of West Central Africa*, 38.

6. Vansina, *Paths in the Rainforest*, 39.

7. Raponda Walker and Sillans, *Plantes utiles*.

8. Bernard Clist's recent thesis has become the definitive work on the prehistory of the Estuary. See Clist, "Des premiers villages aux premiers européens autour de l'estuaire du Gabon."

9. Clist, *Gabon*, 93–94.

10. Clist, *Gabon*, 119–21, 127–29.

11. Clist, *Gabon*, 141–52; Vansina, *Paths*, 58–59.

12. Vansina, *Paths*, 50.

13. Klieman, *Pygmies*, 53–56.

14. Bucher, "Mpongwe Origins"; Ratanga-Atoz, "Les peuples du Gabon occidental pendant la première période coloniale," 49–66.

15. Debate exists over the exact nature of ethnic identity among Omyene speakers. French ethnologist François Gaulme contends that Mpongwe, Galwa, and other speakers did not claim a communal identity until the twentieth century. Gabonese historian François Anges Ratanga-Atoz contends that this identity predates European contact. See Gaulme, *Le Pays du Cama*, 66–67; Ratanga-Atoz, *Peuples*, 66–75.

16. Clist, *Gabon*, 164–68, 200–201.

17. For an overview of food production developments in Iron Age Central Africa, see Birmingham, "Society and Economy before AD 1400," 8–14; Klieman, *Pygmies*, 96–99.

18. Clist, *Gabon*, 210.

19. Vansina, *Paths*, 73–83.

20. Vansina, *Paths*, 74–77.

21. Bucher, "The Mpongwe," 28–32.

22. Interviews, Simone Saint-Dénis, Plaine Niger, Libreville, 11 December 1999; Pierre-Celestin Evoung Ndong, Plaine-Niger, Libreville, 5 September 2000. Madame Saint Dénis, a Mpongwe woman and Agakaza clan member, lives next to Monsieur Evoung Ndong, who is a Fang member of the Essisis clan. Both noted their clan ties as a reason for their willingness to live alongside each other.

23. Bucher, "The Mpongwe," 29–32; Ratanga-Atoz, *Peuples*, 199–203.

24. Bucher, "The Mpongwe," 39–43; Patterson, "The Vanishing Mpongwe," 222–26.

25. Raponda Walker, *Notes d'histoire du Gabon*, 80–82; Bucher, "The Mpongwe," 122–30; Ratanga-Atoz, *Peuples*, 207.

26. Bucher, "The Mpongwe," 32–36; Ratanga-Atoz, *Peuples*, 204–8.

27. Patterson, *Coast*, 29–67; Bucher, "The Mpongwe," 149–75.

28. Pourtier, *Le Gabon: Espace-histoire-société*, vol. 1, 146–54.

29. Gray, "Territoriality, Ethnicity and Colonial Rule," 94–114, 125–29.

30. André Raponda Walker's survey of place names in the Gabon Estuary denotes the sites of many former Mpongwe settlements abandoned during the nineteenth century. See Raponda Walker, *Notes*, 250–86.

31. Raponda Walker, *Notes*, 51–52.

32. Bucher, "The Mpongwe," 122–30.

33. Raponda Walker, *Notes*, 250–54, 266–69.

34. As noted by MacGaffey, *Kongo Political Culture*, 217.

35. Patterson, *Coast*, 6–16.

36. For a discussion of trade and political events on the Loango coast, see Martin, *External Trade of the Loango Coast*.

37. Patterson, *Coast*, 15–16.

38. Patterson, *Coast*, 11.

39. Estimates taken from slave ship records suggest that five hundred slaves a year were taken from Gabon in the eighteenth century. See Picard-Tortorici and François, *La traite des esclaves*, 38, 61.

40. Patterson, *Coast*, 26–47.

41. Patterson, *Coast*, 60–66; Bucher, "The Mpongwe," 23–28, 137–40.

42. Patterson, *Coast*, 62–64. Such tactics were common on the Angolan coast a century earlier. See Miller, *Way of Death*, 392–401.

43. De Bellay, "Le Gabon 1861–1864,", 286; Le Berre, "De l'esclavage au Gabon," 757; Interrogoires de M'Pounga, Ogoula, and Odeumasso, 15 May 1878, Gabon-Congo VIII-4, in Archives Nationales, Fonds Ministriels, Séries Géographiques, Aix-en-Provence, France (hereafter cited as AN FM SG); Briault, *Une soeur missionnaire*, 62; Raponda Walker, *Souvenirs d'un nonagénaire*, 17–18.

44. William Walker to Rufus Anderson, 22 June 1863, ABC 15.1, Western Africa, vol. 4, West Africa 1860–1871, American Board of Commissioners for Foreign Missions, Houghton Library, Harvard University, Cambridge, Massachusetts (hereafter cited as ABCFM Papers; all on microfilm); William Walker to Commandant du Gabon, 26 June 1869, box 1, Correspondence 1864–1870, William Walker Papers, State Historical Society of Wisconsin, Madison, Wisconsin (hereafter cited as WWP); M'Bokolo, *Noirs et blancs*, 92.

45. For other examples, see Martin, *External Trade of the Loango Coast*, 28–29, 166–68; MacGaffey, *Religion and Society in Central Africa*, 25–36; Harms, *River of Wealth*, 24–39, 85–86, 103, 148–53, 181–86.

46. "Wealth in people," first coined by Suzanne Miers and Igor Kopytoff, has been endorsed as a concept particularly apt for Equatorial Africa. Recently, Jane Guyer has called for a more complex view of the interaction between exchange of currencies, the acquisition of clients of dependents and access to various forms of knowledge. See Vansina, *Paths*, 251; Guyer, "Wealth in People and Self-Realization"; Guyer, "Wealth in People, Wealth in Things"; Guyer and Belinga, "Wealth in People as Wealth in Knowledge."

47. John L. Wilson, "Some General Remarks . . .," 1842, ABC 15.1, Western Africa, vol. 2, West Africa 1838–1844, microfilm reel 150, ABCFM Papers.

48. M'Bokolo, *Noirs et blancs*, 22–23.

49. Letter of Mére Louise Reynauld, 26 December 1849, cited by Sister Marie Sidonie Oyembo Vandji, *Les Soeurs de l'Immaculée Conception de Castres*, 40.

50. Stoffel to Oeuvre de la Sainte Enfance, 15 February 1869, boîte 2II.4a, Vicariat des Deux Guinées Divers 1843–1869, Archives de la Congrégation des Pères du Saint-Esprit, Chevilly-Larue, France (hereafter cited as ACSE, with box number and file title).

51. Patterson, *Coast*, 90–107.

52. For a full account of these events as an example of local resistance, see Bucher, "The Village of Glass and Western Intrusion."

53. For other examples in West Africa, see Brooks, *Landlords and Strangers*, 188–93.

54. Bucher, "Village of Glass."

55. Mpongwe traders continued to sell slaves illicitly to Orungu merchants still free to trade with European merchants until the late 1850s. See M'Bokolo, *Noirs et blancs*, 90–98.

56. A. Le Cour to Ministre de la Marine et des Colonies, 8 December 1845, ACSE boîte 2II.4a, Vicariat des Deux Guinées Divers 1843–1869; Bucher, "The Mpongwe," 231–38; M'Bokolo, *Noirs et blancs*, 98–103.

57. Albert Bushnell to Rufus Anderson, 23 December 1851, ABC 15.1, Western Africa, vol. 2, West Africa 1847–1859, microfilm reel 151, ABCFM Papers; Patterson, *Coast*, 121–22; Chamberlin, "Competition," 88–89; M'Bokolo, *Noirs et blancs*, 115–16; Pedlar, *The Lion and the Unicorn*, 79–81.

58. M'Bokolo, *Noirs et blancs*, 178–87.

59. "Rapport sur le Gabon," 1 September 1854, SG Sénégal IV-40, Archives Nationales, Section Outre-Mer, Aix-en-Provence, France (hereafter cited as ANSOM, with file numbers).

60. Commandant du Gabon to Ministre des Colonies, 10 October 1883, ANSOM 2BII.

61. Patterson, *Coast*, 122–24; Chamberlin, "Competition," 87–94.

62. M'Bokolo, *Noirs et blancs*, 141–44.

63. "Note sur les chefs du Gabon," n.d. (1856), ANSOM 2B2; Bucher, "The Mpongwe," 297–303, 313–16, 326–34; M'Bokolo, *Noirs et blancs*, 138–47.

64. Patterson, *Coast*, 128–29.

65. Patterson, *Coast*, 115–16. The best summary of early American missionary efforts in Libreville is Gardinier, "American Board and Presbyterian Board Missions." Also see Gardinier, "Schools of the American Protestant Mission," and "The American Presbyterian Mission in Gabon."

66. MacGaffey, *Kongo Political Culture*.

67. For the initial project and first years of Catholic mission activity in Libreville, see Morel, *Naissance de l'église catholique*, and Gardinier, "Beginning of French Catholic Evangelization."

68. John Wilson, "Visit to King Qua Ben's Town," 2 July 1842, ABC 15.1, Western Africa, vol. 2, West Africa 1838–1844, microfilm reel 150, ABCFM Papers.

69. Wilson, "Visit to King Qua Ben's Town."

70. Gardinier, "Schools of the American Protestant Mission."

71. Rich, "King or Knave?" Félix Adende Rapontchombo (1844–1911) was the grandfather of Félix Adende, a Mpongwe neighborhood chief during the 1930s and 1940s. This last individual is identified as Prince Félix Adende.

72. For a more detailed discussion of the trouble-filled origins of Libreville, see Kankoila-Nendy, "Les Libérés"; Bucher, "Liberty and Labor."

73. M'Bokolo, Noirs et blancs, 129–32.

74. Lasserre, Libreville, 66–68; Deschamps, Quinze ans, 311–13, 316–18.

75. For a broader discussion see Rich, "Leopard Men."

76. I deal with these relationships more extensively in Rich, "'Une Babylone Noire'" 149–70. Rachel Jean-Baptiste explores nineteenth-century Mpongwe women's strategies in marriage. See Jean-Baptiste, "Une Ville Libre?" 53–63.

77. William Walker Diary, 9 March 1881 entry, WWP, box 3.

78. Rich, "Civilized Attire."

79. Ratanga-Atoz, "Les résistances Gabonaises à l'imperialisme," 161–203; Rich, "King or Knave?"

80. Rich, "Leopard Men."

81. For a general overview of French occupation of Gabon, see Coquéry-Vidrovitch, Brazza et la prise de possession du Gabon; Coquéry-Vidrovitch, Le Congo au temps des grandes compagnies concessionaires; Austen and Headrick, "Equatorial Africa under Colonial Rule"; Metegue N'nah, "Histoire de la formation du peuple Gabonais." On occupation in northeastern Gabon, see Cinnamon, "Long March of the Fang." For southern Gabon, see Gray, Colonial Rule and Crisis.

82. For a discussion focused on Senegalese and Vietnamese migrants in late nineteenth-century Libreville, see Rich, "Where Every Language Is Heard." Surprisingly, given the large numbers of African foreigners in Libreville and Gabon, little research has been done on these immigrant communities at any period in Gabonese history.

83. On Dahomey exiles, see Commissioner General of French Congo (CGFC) to Governor of Dahomey, 20 October 1895, ANSOM 2B103. For Rabih's family, see CGFC to Bishop of Libreville Adam, 3 February 1901, ANSOM 2B104. On Samori Touré, see CGFC to Governor General of French West Africa, 8 February 1902, ANSOM 2B107. Vietnamese prisoners are discussed in chapter 3.

84. For published work on Fang society in the late nineteenth and early twentieth centuries, see Chamberlin, "Migration of the Fang"; Fernandez, Bwiti; Swiderski, La religion bouiti.

85. Fernandez, Bwiti, 49–73.

86. Robert Nassau Diary, 3 February 1898 entry, Robert Nassau Papers, Archives Nationales du Gabon, Libreville (hereafter cited as RNP).

87. Interview, Simone Saint-Dénis, Plaine Niger, 11 December 1999.

88. On Estuary bridewealth in the 1880s, see Adolphus Good Papers, box 1, folder 2, Diary 1882–1884, 10 March 1883 entry, Presbyterian Historical Society, Philadelphia. For bridewealth information from the turn of the century from the Estuary, see Milligan, The Fetish Folk of West Africa, 132–33. For a general overview of Fang marriages and gender tensions in the nineteenth century, see Jean-Baptiste, "Une Ville Libre?" 68–78.

89. Eleven male Mpongwe clerks and traders (Tambani, Kidney, Renamy, Bouma, and others)

to Inspector General Frézouls, 7 December 1910, AN FM Affaires Politiques Mission Frezouls 1910–1911, Dossier 3123, Administration General des Circonscriptions du Gabon.

90. For a general treatment of N'dende and Mpongwe protest movements from 1910 through 1930, see Ballard, "Development of Political Parties," 109–23.

91. Le Berre, "Lettre du 12 Août 1881," 414.

92. Robert Nassau Diary, 4 August 1896 entry, RNP; Milligan, Fetish Folk, 30–31.

93. "Autobiography," 1444–45, RNP.

94. For a general overview of the impact of World War I on Gabon, see Loungou Mouele, "Le Gabon de 1910 à 1925"; Dubois, "Le prix d'une guerre."

95. Lt. Gov. du Gabon to Chef Circ. Estuaire, 21 August 1914, carton 853, Maire de Libreville 1914–1917, Archives Nationales du Gabon, Libreville, Gabon (hereafter cited as ANG, with box number and title); Lt. Gov. Gabon Guyon to Governor General of French Equatorial Africa (GGFEA), "Enquete sur le commerce Austro-Allemande de l'avant-guerre au Gabon," 1 July 1916, AN FM Affaires Politiques carton 116, Dossier 1.

96. Valdi, Le Gabon: L'homme contre la forêt, 69–70.

97. Loungou Mouele, "Le Gabon de 1910 à 1925," 320.

98. On Sarraut's mise en valeur policies in colonial Africa, see Conklin, Mission to Civilize.

99. On the timber industry and famines in Gabon in the 1920s, see Sautter, De l'Atlantique au fleuve Congo, 2:761–74, 852–64; Nzoghe, "Les problèmes du travail"; de Dravo, "L'Exploitation forestière du Gabon"; Cinnamon, "Long March of the Fang," 325–58; Gray and Ngolet, "Lambaréné, Okoumé, and the Transformation of Labor"; Gray, Colonial Rule and Crisis, 170–94.

100. Bernault, Démocraties, 62, 96.

101. Ballard, "Development of Political Parties," 109–23.

102. Jean-Baptiste, "Une Ville Libre?" 81–120.

103. Lt. Gov. Gabon Marchand to Chef Circ. Estuaire, 27 November 1919, ANG carton 929, Affaires Civiles 1919–1938.

104. Complaints about chiefs abounded in the 1920s and 1930s. See "Jugement du tribunal indigène de la circonscription de l'Estuaire," 2 October 1926, ANSOM 5D61, Dossier Abogho Nze; "La population "indigène" to GGFEA, 8 August 1936, ANSOM 4(1)D44.

105. On the origins of Fang versions of bwiti, see Fernandez, Bwiti; Swiderski, La religion bouiti; Mary, Le défi du syncrétisme.

106. For escape strategies using missions or turning to prostitution to make a living, see ANG Registres, Registre 104, Deuxième Tribunal Indigène de la Commune de Libreville, Affaire Nkoé, 3 March 1938; and Registre 82, Premier Tribunal Indigène de la Commune de Libreville, Affaire Bologho, 21 July 1938.

107. Edouard Panchaud to Directeur, Société de Missions Évangeliques (SME), 4 November 1928, SME Correspondance Gabon, fiche 2642, Archives of the Société de Missions Évangeliques (hereafter cited as DEFAP, with fiche number); Father Joseph Soul, "Compte Rendu St. Paul de Donguila, 17–23 December 1928, ACSE boîte 4J1.6b Divers Gabon 1920–1949, Visites.

108. Jean-Baptiste, "Une Ville Libre?" 121–71.

109. Cinnamon, "Long March of the Fang."

110. Chef de Région de l'Estuaire Biscons-Ritay, Rapport Annuel, Région de l'Estuaire, 1949, 13, ANG carton 44, Rapport Politique Annuel Territoire du Gabon 1949, 1954.

111. Rapport Politique Dept. Estuaire, 2eme trimestre 1938, ANSOM 4(1)D46; ANG carton 762, Ministère de l'Agriculture, Service de l'Agriculture, Rapports Annuels 1958, 1960, Rapport Annuel 1958, 8.

112. For a more detailed review of social and economic struggles in the Depression, see Jean-Baptiste, "Une Ville Libre?" 125–38.

113. Interview, Gabriel Mabenga, Diba-Diba, Libreville, 25 February 2000.

114. Interview, Jean Kiala, Joseph Mebeke, Nkembo, Libreville, 11 October 2000.

115. Brouillet, L'avion du blanc, 44–56, passim.

116. On Mba in the 1940s and 1950s, see Bernault, Démocraties, 215–234.

117. Bernault, Démocraties, 94–100.

118. Bernault, Démocraties, passim.

119. The best source on the city during the 1950s is still Lasserre, Libreville.

120. Rich, "'I hope that the government does not forget my extraordinary services.'"

121. Meunier, "Le réseau des routes au Gabon"; Thompson and Adloff, Emerging States, 361–63.

122. Thompson and Adloff, Emerging States, 352.

123. Mandala, "Beyond the 'Crisis.'"

2. Eating in an African Atlantic Town, 1840–1885

1. On John L. Wilson, see Bucher, "John Leighton Wilson."

2. John L. Wilson, "Excursion to King William's Town," 8 July 1842, ABC 15.1, Western Africa, vol. 2, West Africa 1838–1844, ABCFM Papers.

3. William Walker Diary, 27 and 30 December 1842 entries, WWP, box 1.

4. For general botanical and agricultural information of manioc, see Onwueme, Tropical Tuber Crops, 109–28, 145–52; Karasch, "Manioc."

5. Jones, Manioc in Africa, 62–64.

6. Von Oppen, "Cassava," 75.

7. Jones, Manioc in Africa, 20–23; Onwueme, Tropical Tuber Crops, 118–36.

8. A good description of Fang methods of manioc preparation in the late nineteenth century can be found in Bennett, "Ethnographic Notes on the Fang," 82–83.

9. Von Oppen, "Cassava," 48–49.

10. Historian K. David Patterson contends that the Mpongwe may have traded on a regular basis with Loango merchants. Such proximity may have brought manioc cultivation in its wake. See Patterson, Coast, 20–23. Dance traditions among Mpongwe and other groups, such as the ivanga dance, replicate royal titles from the Loango state. See Ambouroué-Avaro, Un peuple Gabonais, 107–14. On manioc in Loango, see Martin, External Trade of the Loango Coast, 13.

11. Raponda Walker and Sillans, Plantes utiles, 461.

12. Raponda Walker and Sillans, Plantes utiles, 461; Ratanga-Atoz, Peuples, 219.

13. Jones, Manioc in Africa, 105–8; Ratanga-Atoz, Peuples, 220–21.

14. Ratanga-Atoz, Peuples, 219.

15. Raponda Walker and Sillans, Plantes utiles, 171.

16. For an introduction to the diffusion of bananas, see Purseglove, Tropical Crops.

17. On the spread of bananas in Central Africa, see Vansina, Paths, 61–65; Schoenbrun, A Green Place, 79–83.

18. Vansina, Paths, 87.

19. For general information on Central African plantain cultivation, see Perrault, "Banana-Manioc Farming," 6–28, 116–42.

20. Nassau, "West African Native Foods."

21. Raponda Walker and Sillans, Plantes utiles, 303–4.

22. Ratanga-Atoz, Peuples, 216–18.

23. Raponda Walker and Sillans, Plantes utiles, 305.

24. Raponda Walker, "Le bananier plantain au Gabon," 11, 15.

25. Weiss, Making and Unmaking, 70–92.

26. Raponda Walker and Sillans, Plantes utiles, 306.

27. For an overview of fruits and gathering in equatorial African rainforest, see Hladik, Bahuchet, and Garine, Food and Nutrition.

28. Raponda Walker and Sillans, Plantes utiles, 49–50, 140, 257–58, 273, 406.

29. British traveler Mary Kingsley wrote of her enthusiasm for odika after her 1895 sojourn in Libreville. Kingsley, Travels in West Africa, 210–11.

30. Alpern, "European Introduction of Crops"; Wright, The World and a Very Small Place, 89–91.

31. Raponda Walker and Sillans, Plantes utiles, 380–81; Alpern, "European Introduction of Crops," 14–19.

32. Alpern, "European Introduction of Crops," 27–28.

33. Harms, River of Wealth, passim.

34. Bucher, "The Mpongwe," 154–55. Such practices are common among other peoples in Gabon. For a parallel in Southern Gabon, see Dupré, Un ordre et sa destruction, 68–69.

35. Interviews, Simone Saint-Dénis, Plaine Niger, Libreville, 8 and 11 December 1999; Madame X., Louis, Libreville, 21 December 1999; Charlotte Izouré, Cheferesse de Glass, Libreville, 1 September 2000.

36. Mombey, "Les Benga: Peuple du Gabon."

37. Bensaid, Économie et nutrition, 254–58.

38. Wylie, Starving, 39–55; Bensaid, Économie et nutrition, 9–14.

39. For a short and hardly exhaustive list of works, see Mintz and Price, An Anthropological Approach to the Afro-American Past: A Caribbean Perspective; Taylor, Eating, Drinking, and Visiting in the South; Mintz, Sweetness and Power: The Place of Sugar in Modern History; Carney, Black Rice.

40. Harms, The Diligent, 206–7.

41. Larson, History and Memory in the Age of Enslavement, 124–31.

42. Hawthorne, Planting Rice and Harvesting Slaves.

43. Shaw, Memories of the Slave Trade.

44. The following information is drawn from several sources. See Bucher, "The Mpongwe," 147–52; Wilson, Western Africa, 242–43, 273; Du Chaillu, Explorations and Adventures, 46–47; Ratanga-Atoz, Peuples, 210–24.

45. Ivanga, "Contribution à l'histoire des Mpongwe," 62.

46. Wilson, "Mr. Wilson's Description of the Gaboon," 233; John L. Wilson, "Some General Remarks," 1844, ABC 15.1, Western Africa, vol. 2, West Africa 1838–1844, ABCFM Papers; William Walker, "Mpongwe Customs or Laws," n.d. (c. 1855), WWP, box 1.

47. William Walker to Prudential Committee of the ABCFM, 28 December 1843, ABC 15.1, Western Africa, vol. 2, West Africa 1838–1844; Hubert Herrick to Rufus Anderson, 26 August 1854, ABC 15.1, Western Africa, vol. 2, West Africa 1847–1859, pt. 1, both in ABCFM Papers; Bucher, "The Mpongwe," 147–52.

48. William Walker to Rufus Anderson, 28 December 1843, ABC 15.1, Western Africa, vol. 2, West Africa 1838–1844, ABCFM Papers; M'Bokolo, Noirs et blancs, 20–22, 92, 119.

49. Nassau, Tales out of School, 64.

50. Preston, Gaboon Stories, 29.

51. Burton, Two Trips to Gorilla Land, 1:80; Nassau, Fetichism in West Africa, 4–5.

52. On Euro-African interracial sexual unions in Libreville, see Rich, "'Une Babylone Noire.'"

53. Burton, Two Trips to Gorilla Land, 1:73.

54. Le Berre, "De l'esclavage au Gabon," 757–59.

55. Guennegan to Oeuvre de la Sainte Enfance, 2 February 1861, ACSE boîte 211.4a, Vicariat des Deux Guinées Divers 1843–1869.

56. U.S. Commercial Agent (illegible) to Secretary of State, 9 March 1867, United States Consulate, Dispatches from American Consuls in Gaboon, 1856–1888, National Archives microfilm, no. 1466.

57. Preston, Gaboon Stories, 47.

58. Burton, Two Trips to Gorilla Land, 1:73.

59. Briault, Récits, 63–64.

60. Isaacman and Isaacman, Slavery and Beyond, 16–17.

61. Alford, A Prince among Slaves, 45.

62. Faugère, "Biographie Manuscrite de Monseigneur Jean-Rémy Bessieux," n.d. (c. 1892), 226, ACSE boîte 21.1b.

63. Pourtier, Le Gabon, 1:223–25.

64. This seems similar to the reconstruction of precolonial Zulu diets. Wylie, Starving, 45.

65. Ratanga-Atoz, Peuples, 195–97.

66. In a list of goods exchanged for slaves and natural resources between 1820 and 1850, European items useful for cooking appear repeatedly. See Bucher, "The Mpongwe," 168–70.

67. Saint-Blancat, "Coutume Mpongwe" (unpublished mimeograph, 1939), 3, ANG Library.

68. Wilson, Western Africa, 262.

69. Preston, Gaboon Stories, 9; Lejeune, "L'esclavage au Gabon," 333.

70. Du Chaillu, Explorations and Adventures, 163–64.

71. Preston, Gaboon Stories, 29.

72. William Walker Dairy, 9–10 November 1847 entry, WWP, box 1.

73. William Walker Diary, 20 September 1847 entry, WWP, box 1.

74. Interview, Madame Rabeno, Nombakele, Libreville, 3 February 2000. Mme. Rabeno is a specialist in Mpongwe healing practices.

75. Interview, Madame Rabeno, 3 February 2000.

76. Nassau, Fetichism in West Africa, 78–79.

77. On Fang supernatural beliefs and food, see Aubame, Les Béti du Gabon et d'ailleurs, 2:81–93.

78. For example, one informant was told never to eat manioc after an illness as a boy. Interview, Felicien Ndong Ona, Melen, 28 October 2000.

79. Raponda Walker and Sillans, Rites et croyances, 89–90.

80. Raponda Walker and Sillans, Rites et croyances, 82–83.

81. Polaillon and Carville, Étude physiologique sur les effets toxiques.

82. Raponda Walker and Sillans, Plantes utiles, passim.

83. Raponda Walker and Sillans, Rites et croyances, 44–45; Marquis de Compiègne, L'Afrique équatoriale, 188; Fleuriot de Langle, "Croisières à la côte d'Afrique," 264–65.

84. Nassau, Fetichism in West Africa, 184–85.

85. Walker, "Mpongwe Laws."

86. Bucher, "The Mpongwe," 61.

87. Walker, "Mpongwe Laws."

88. Lestrille, "Note sur le comptoir du Gabon," 445.

89. Blier, "Truth and Seeing," 143–51; MacGaffey, Kongo Political Culture, 3–14.

90. Geschiere, The Modernity of Witchcraft, 61–68.

91. Many missionaries, tourists, and other residents of Libreville made passing references to poison and witchcraft accusations toward slaves in the mid-nineteenth century. Albert Bushnell to Rufus Anderson, 7 February 1845, ABC 15.4, Southern and Western Africa, vol. 4, West Africa 1844–1846, ABCFM Papers; Marchandeau to Archbishop, 8 January 1859, ACSE boîte 4J1.2b, Correspondance 1853–1869.

92. Delorme, extract from letter of 27 August 1872, Bulletin de la Congrégation des Pères du Saint-Esprit 9 (1872–1874): 192 (hereafter cited as BCSE); Lejeune, "L'esclavage au Gabon," 331–33.

93. Le Berre, "De l'esclavage au Gabon," 759.

94. For general information on Séké communities, see Obouyou, "Les Séké de l'Estuaire"; Ratanga-Atoz, Peuples, 126–28. On food sales, see Bucher, "The Mpongwe," 23–25.

95. Commandant of Gabon Vignon to Commander of the West African Coastal Naval Division, 17 August 1851, Senegal IV-40, AN FM SG.

96. William Walker to Rufus Anderson, 28 December 1843, ABC 15.1, Western Africa, vol. 2, West Africa 1838–1844, ABCFM Papers. Catholic missionaries also reported on this trade. See Lossedat to Warlop, 6 January 1847, ACSE boîte 4J1.2a, Correspondance Deux Guinées 1846–1852.

97. "Résidence de St. Marie du Gabon," BCSE 10 (1876–77): 156.

98. Interviews, Jean Kiala, Nkembo, Libreville, 11 October 2000; Pierre Bissang, Gros Bosquet, Libreville, 16 October 2000.

99. William Walker Diary, 13 February 1843 entry, WWP, box 2.

100. William Walker Diary, 30 December 1842 entry, WWP, box 2; William Walker to Rufus Anderson, 31 December 1847, ABC 15.1, Western Africa, vol. 2, West Africa 1847–1859, ABCFM Papers; William Walker to Rufus Anderson, 22 June 1863, ABC 15.1, Western Africa, vol. 4, West Africa 1860–1871, ABCFM Papers; "Letter," Missionary Herald 59 (1863): 295.

101. William Walker Diary, 9 November 1847 entry, WWP, box 2.

102. Peureux to Le Berre, 16 August 1857, ACSE boîte 4J1.2b, Correspondance 1853–1899.

103. Faugère, "Biographie Manuscrite de Monseigneur Jean-Rémy Bessieux," n.d. (c. 1892), 293–94, ACSE boîte 21.1b

104. "Journal de Communauté," May 1863 and Pierre-Marie Le Berre to Archbishop, 23 May 1864, ACSE boîte 4J1.3a, Lettres 1861–1864; Tornezy, "Les travaux de la mission Sainte-Marie," 161–62.

105. "Communauté de Sainte-Marie du Gabon," BCSE 5 (1864): 347; Albert Bushnell to Rufus Anderson, 3 November 1864, ABC 15.1, Western Africa, vol. 4, West Africa 1860–1871, ABCFM Papers.

106. William Walker Diary, 14 and 27 March, 3 April, 25 June, and 1–2 December 1865 entries, WWP, box 2; Albert Bushnell to Rufus Anderson, 24 March 1865, ABC 15.1, Western Africa, vol. 4, West Africa 1860–1871,; Commandant of Gabon to Commander of the South Atlantic Naval Squadron, 26 March 1865, ANSOM 2B18.

107. Briault, Une soeur missionnaire, 85.

108. Pierre-Marie Le Berre to Archbishop, 23 February 1865, ACSE boîte 4J1.3a, Lettres 1865–68; Albert Bushnell to Rufus Anderson, 1 March 1865, ABC 15.1, Western Africa, vol. 4, West Africa 1860–1871, ABCFM Papers; Pierre-Marie Le Berre to Archbishop, 22 April and 26 May 1865, ACSE boîte 4J1.3a, Lettres 1865–68.

109. Pierre-Marie Le Berre to Archbishop, 6 September 1866, 22 December 1867, ACSE boîte

4J1.3a, Lettres 1865–68; Father Neu, "Notes sur le Gabon," c. 1883, Cahier 15, 260–61, ACSE boîte 4J2.19a Travaux Divers.

110. Patterson, *Coast*, 68–89; Ratanga-Atoz, *Peuples*, 96–100.

111. Raponda Walker, *Souvenirs d'un nonagénaire*, 49.

112. Ratanga-Atoz, *Peuples*, 90.

113. Ricard, "Notes sur le Gabon," 254.

114. Ordonnateur to Commandant of Gabon, 30 May 1852, ANSOM 2B1; Pierre-Marie La Berre to Boulanger, 14 June 1853, ACSE boîte 4J1.2b, Correspondance 1853–1899; Tornezy, "Les travaux de la mission Sainte-Marie," 153.

115. Iliffe, *The African Poor*, 4–5.

116. Iliffe, *The African Poor*, 5–6.

117. Wylie, *Starving*, 28–29.

118. Briault, *Zéro*, 129.

119. Le Berre, "Situation du Vicariat des Deux Guinées"; Samuel Gillespie to Lawrie, 16 August 1872, Board of Foreign Missions, Presbyterian Church of the U.S.A., African Letters 1837–1903, Gaboon and Corsico Missions, Presbyterian Historical Society, Philadelphia (consulted on microfilm from Stanford University and hereafter cited as PCUSA with reel numbers); Le Berre, "De l'escalavage au Gabon," 759.

120. Albert Bushnell to Rufus Anderson, 3 November 1864, ABC 15.1, Western Africa, vol. 4, West Africa 1860–1871, ABCFM Papers.

121. William Walker to Rufus Anderson, 18 April 1862, ABC 15.1, Western Africa, vol. 4, West Africa 1860–1871, ABCFM Papers.

122. Father Peureux to Archbishop, 15 December 1855, ACSE boîte 4J1.2b Correspondance 1853–1899.

123. William Walker to Rufus Anderson, 22 September 1864, ABC 15.1, Western Africa, vol. 4, West Africa 1860–1871, ABCFM Papers.

124. William Walker to Commandant of Gabon, 26 June 1869, Correspondence 1864–1870, WWP, box 1.

125. Nassau, *Tales out of School*, 96–98.

126. Nassau, *Tales out of School*, 27–28.

127. Nassau, *My Ogowe*, 240–41.

128. Gardinier, "Schools of the American Protestant Mission," 168–70, 176–83.

129. "Report of the Gaboon Mission for the Year 1852," ABC 15.1, Western Africa, vol. 3, West Africa 1847–1859, pt. 1, ABCFM Papers; H. W. Bacheler to John Lawrie, 28 February 1882, PCUSA microfilm reel 15; Patterson, *Coast*, 118–20.

130. Preston, *Gaboon Stories*, 21–23; Nassau, *Corisco Days*, 149; Nassau, *Tales out of School*, 62–63; Le Berre, "Situation du Vicariat des Deux Guinées," 111; "Aperçu de l'oeuvre des Soeurs de l' Immaculée Conception à Libreville," 1898, Archives of the Sisters of the Immaculate Conception, Libreville; Oyembo Vandji, *Les Soeurs*, 94–97; Martin, *Leisure and Society*, 23–24.

131. For a sample of other studies on this theme, see Gaitskell, "Housewives, Maids or Mothers"; Hansen, *African Encounters with Domesticity*.

132. Rich, "'Une Babylone Noire.'"

133. Compiègne, *L'Afrique équatoriale*, 190; Nassau, *My Ogowe*, 177.

134. William Walker to Rufus Anderson, 1 April 1850, ABC 15.1, Western Africa, vol. 2, West Africa 1847–1859, pt. 1, ABCFM Papers; Robert Nassau Diary, 14 January 1891, 7 October 1893 entries, RNP; Soeur Marie-Germaine, *Le Christ au Gabon*, 126–27.

135. Milligan, *The Jungle Folk*, 250–51.

136. Burton, *Two Trips to Gorilla Land*, 1:80.

137. Journal de la Mission 1875, 3 August 1875 entry, ACSE boîte 211.3b, Dossier Personnel Monseigneur Le Berre, Journaux de Libreville 1861–1891; Klaine to Le Berre, 6 August 1875, ACSE boîte 4J1.3a, Lettres 1873–1876.

138. Journal de la Mission entries, 12 December 1874, 6 December 1875, 31 January 1876, 8 December 1880, 13 January 1881, ACSE boîte 211.3b, Dossier Personnel Monseigneur Le Berre, Journaux de Libreville 1861–1891; Soeur Marie Germaine, *Le Christ au Gabon*, 132–33.

139. Interviews, Simone Saint-Denis, Plaine-Niger, Libreville, 8, 11, and 15 December 1999; Rahindi Ivenendgani, Glass, Libreville, 15 December 1999; Antoinette Folquet, Plaine Niger, Libreville, 15 December 1999; Agathe Iwengha, Plaine Niger, Libreville, 31 January 2000; Madame X, Louis, Libreville, 23 December 1999; Henriette Izouré, Glass, Libreville, 1 September 2000.

140. Jean-Baptiste, "Une Ville Libre?" 57–64, 95–106.

141. Interviews, Simone Saint-Denis, 5 December 1999; Madame X, 20 December 1999; Annette Folqué, 21 December 1999.

142. Angèle Agnoure to Chef Dept. Estuaire, 9 November 1944, ANG carton 474, Secours 1944–1946.

143. Rich, "'I hope that the government does not forget my extraordinary services.'"

144. Briault, *Une soeur missionnaire*, 60.

145. Robert Nassau to Rev. Gillespie, 23 March 1894, PCUSA microfilm reel 21.

146. Commandant of Gabon to Minister of Colonies, 4 August 1875, ANSOM 2B28.

147. Commandant of Gabon to Commander of the South Atlantic Naval Squadron, 1 October 1875, 12 and 19 February 1876, ANSOM 2B28; Pierre-Marie Le Berre to Archbishop, 16 January and 28 February 1876, ACSE boîte 4J1.3a, Lettres 1873–1876; Delorme, "Observations sur le Gabon," 1876, Gabon-Congo XIII-3, AN FM SG; Metegue N'nah, "Le Gabon," 315.

148. I treat the murders more extensively in Rich, "Leopard Men."

149. Médecin Principal du Gabon Delpench to Commandant de la Division Navale de l'Atlantique Sud, 10 May 1878, Gabon-Congo VIII-4, AN FM SG.

150. Commandant of Gabon to Commandant de la Division Navale de l'Atlantique Sud, 18 May 1878, ANSOM 2B7.

151. Rich, "Leopard Men."

152. "Communauté de Sainte Marie du Gabon," BCSE 11 (1879): 421–27; Pierre-Marie Le Berre to Archbishop, 11 August 1879, ACSE boîte 4J1.3b, Lettres 1877–1880; "Communauté de Sainte Marie du Gabon," BCSE 12 (1882): 578; Gachon to Le Berre, 15 May 1882, ACSE boîte 211.5, Deux Guinées Diverses 1870–1891, folder 1881–1883.

153. "Notes sur Mgr Pierre-Marie Le Berre et la Mission Catholique du Gabon," Gachon or Alexandre Monnier, n.d. (1892), 53, ACSE boîte 211.3b, Dossier Personnel Monseigneur Le Berre.

154. Some references can be found in the following: William Walker Diary, 30 July and 25 August 1880, 21 September 1881, 14 October 1882 entries, WWP, box 3; Stoffel to Monseigneur Le Berre, 18 July 1881, ACSE boîte 4J1.3b, Correspondance Gabon 1877–1892, Lettres 1881–1884; "Rapport de l'Ordonnateur sur la marché des divers services du Gabon," 20 July 1882, Gabon-Congo VII-7, AN FM SG.

155. Payeur-Didelot, *Trente mois au continent mystérieux*, 130–31; Milligan, *Fetish Folk*, 32–35; Briault, *Zéro*, 125–29.

156. Milligan, *Fetish Folk*, 144–45.

157. Barret, L'Afrique occidentale, 1:157.

158. Nassau, Fetichism in West Africa, 145.

159. "Promenades des missionnaires," Chronique de l'institut des frères de l'instruction chrétienne de Saint-Gabriel 87 (1927): 138–40.

160. Pierre-Marie Le Berre to Archbishop, 21 September 1862, ACSE boîte 4J1.3a, Lettres 1861–1865; Journal de la Mission 1870, 7 September 1870 entry, ACSE boîte 2I1.3b, Dossier personnel Monseigneur Le Berre, Journaux de Libreville 1861–1891; "Communauté de Sainte-Marie du Gabon," BCSE 9 (1872–1874): 476; Pierre-Marie Le Berre to Archbishop, 6 July 1878, ACSE, boîte 4J1.3b, Letters 1877–1892, Lettres 1877–1880; Raponda Walker, Notes, 262.

161. "Communauté de Sainte Marie du Gabon," BCSE 13 (1885): 783.

162. Wright, Strategies of Slaves and Women; Glassman, Feasts and Riot.

163. "Communauté de Sainte Marie du Gabon," BCSE 9 (1872–1873): 476–77.

164. Lejeune, "L'esclavage au Gabon," 330–68.

165. "Rapport," Captaine Aymes, April 1872, Gabon-Congo III-1, AN FM SG.

166. Father Neu, "Notes sur le Gabon" c. 1883, Cahier 14, 236, ACSE boîte 4J2.19a, Travaux Divers.

167. I deal with this subject at greater length in Rich, "Civilized Attire."

168. The Mpongwe shared a common problem with the Bobangui trading people on the Congo River as the end of the slave trade decreased access to unfree labor for agriculture. On slavery among the Bobangi, see Harms, River of Wealth, 150–54, 184–85, 230.

3. Newcomers, Food Supply, and the Colonial State, 1840–1914

1. Kingsley Travels in West Africa, 104–22.

2. "Saint Pierre de Libreville," BCSE 23 (1903–1906): 20.

3. Le Lieur, Capt Elan, 6 October 1847, Archives de la Marine, Paris, BB4, Dossier 650.

4. For typical reports on spoiled food, see Commandant of Gabon Brisset to Commandant of Gorée, 28 March 1848; Chargé de Service Administratif to Commandant of Gorée, 25 April 1848; and Commandant of Gabon to Commandant of Gorée, 9 October 1848, all in ANSOM GGAOF 6G-5. As for the poor moral and physical state of the fort's staff in the 1840s and 1850s, see M'Bokolo, Noirs et blancs, 82–88.

5. Commandant of Gabon Brisset to Governor of Senegal, 7 March 1847; Commandant of Gabon Brisset to Governor of Gorée, 7 March 1847, both in ANSOM GGAOF 6G-4.

6. Commandant of Gabon to Commandant of Gorée, 15 October 1858, ANSOM 2B2; M'Bokolo, Noirs et blancs, 87–88.

7. Father Neu, "Notes sur le Gabon," c. 1883, Cahier 13, 226, ACSE boîte 4J2.19a Travaux Divers.

8. Commandant of Gabon Brisset to Commandant of Gorée, 1 March and June 1845, ANSOM GGAOF 6G-2; Mekanene-Nze, "L'evolution de l'agriculture coloniale," 21–22.

9. Captaine of Caraibe Pigeaud to Commander of Naval Forces of the Western African Coast, 7 September 1846, and Commander of Naval Forces of the Western African Coast Montagnies de la Rocque to Minister of the Navy, 26 October 1846, Archives de la Marine, BB4, Services Génerales, Dossier 639.

10. Fuller discussion of the origins of Libreville is in Kankoila-Nendy, "Les Libérés"; Bucher, "Liberty and Labor."

11. Kankoila-Nendy, "Les Libérés," 130–31, 147, 155–57.

12. Lasserre, *Libreville*, 66–68; Deschamps, *Quinze ans*, 311–13, 316–18.

13. William Walker Diary, 1 August 1847 entry, WWP, box 2; M'Bokolo, *Noirs et blancs*, 86.

14. Commandant of Gorée to Commandant of Gabon, 8 May 1850; Commandant of Gabon to Chef de la Division Navale d'Atlantique Sud, 31 November 1857; Commandant of Gabon to Commandant of Gorée, 13 February 1858, all in ANSOM 2B1.

15. Behrens, *Les Kroumen de la côte occidentale*, 60–62, 71, 79–80; M'Bokolo, *Noirs et blancs*, 86.

16. For a general discussion of Kru tasks see Behrens, *Les Kroumen de la côte occidentale*, 29–48.

17. Albert Bushnell to N. G. Clark, 22 November 1867, ABC 15.1, Western Africa, vol. 4, West Africa 1860–1871, microfilm A 467 reel 153, ABCFM Papers.

18. For Kru workers in Gabon in the 1840s and 1850s, see William Walker Diary, 28 January, 11 July, 4 August and 20 December 1847 entries, WWP; Preston, *Gaboon Stories*, 141.

19. François Ricard to Minister of Colonies, n.d. (1855), ACSE boîte 2I1.4b, Madame Tourznay.

20. Commandant of Gabon to Minister of Colonies, 21 August 1859, ANSOM 2B21. British traders in the 1870s, according to French administrators, were notorious for torturing Kru workers and withholding their wages. See Commandant of Gabon to Minister of Colonies, 8 May, 1 June and 23 September 1876, ANSOM 2B28.

21. Louet, "Établissements," 7, Gorée et Dépencies IV-2, AN FM SG.

22. "Extrait du rapport du mer de M. le Captaine du *Loiret*," 15 December 1874, Gabon-Congo XIV-1, AN FM SG.

23. Deschamps, *Quinze ans*, 322; Pierre-Marie Le Berre, "Rapport sur les cultures du Gabon," 16 November 1863, ACSE boîte 211.4a, Vicariat des Deux Guinées Divers 1843–1869; Raponda Walker, *Notes*, 256.

24. Procès-Verbal du Conseil d'Administration, 5 April 1887; Procès-Verbal du Conseil d'Administration, "Marché de gré au gré Wiedenbach," 1887; Procès-Verbal du Conseil d'Administration, 5 May 1887, all in Gabon-Congo VII-11, AN FM SG.

25. Commandant of Fort d'Aumale Brisset, 1 October 1844, Senegal IV-38, AN FM SG;Commandant of Gabon Brisset to Commandant of Gorée, 15 November 1844, ANSOM AOF 6G-1. RP Jean-Rémy Bessieux to Aragon, 18 October 1845, ACSE boîte 211.4a, Vicariat des Deux Guinées Divers 1843–1869; "Résidence de St. Marie du Gabon," BCSE 10 (1876–77): 156; Kankoila-Nendy, "Les Libérés," 173.

26. E. J. Pierce to Rufus Anderson, 16 February 1856 and 30 September 1857, ABC 15.1, Western Africa, vol. 2, West Africa 1847–1859, pt. 1, ABCFM Papers; Pierre-Marie Le Berre to Ignace Schwindenhammer, 23 July 1859, ACSE boîte 4J1.2b, Correspondance 1853–1899; Faugère, "Biographie Manuscrite de Monseigneur Jean-Rémy Bessieux," n.d. (c. 1892), 243, ACSE boîte 21.1b; Rocques, *Le pionnier du Gabon*, 74.

27. E. J. Pierce to Rufus Anderson, 16 July 1855, ABC 15.1, Western Africa, vol. 2, West Africa 1847–1859, pt. 1, ABCFM Papers.

28. Maurice Briault, "Quelques chapitres sur la vie de Monseigneur Bessieux," n.d., 60, ACSE boîte 211.1, Vicariat des Deux Guinées; Le Berre to Liebermann, 4 January 1847, ACSE boîte 4J1.2a, Correspondance Deux Guinées 1846–1852; Du Chaillu, *Explorations and Adventures*, 25.

29. Gardinier, "Schools of the American Protestant Mission," 174–75.

30. Tornezy, "Les travaux de la mission Sainte-Marie."

31. Faugère, "Biographie Manuscrite de Monseigneur Jean-Rémy Bessieux," n.d. (c. 1892), 263, ACSE boîte 21.1b.

32. Pierre-Marie Le Berre, "Rapport de la Communauté du Gabon 1860–1861," 11 August

1861, ACSE boîte 211.4a, Vicariat des Deux Guinées Divers 1843–1869; Duparquet to Basillec, 6 January 1863, ACSE boîte 4J1.3a, Lettres 1861–1864.

33. "Communauté de Sainte-Marie du Gabon," BCSE 6 (1867–68): 231; Marquis de Compiègne, "Les Missions Catholiques dans le Gabon," BCSE 9 (1872–74): 760; Briault, *Récits*, 63–64; Raponda Walker, *Souvenirs d'un nonagénaire*, 27.

34. Albert Bushnell to Rufus Anderson, 20 November 1858, ABC 15.1, Western Africa, vol. 2, West Africa 1847–1859, pt. 1, ABCFM Papers; William Gault to John Gillespie, 16 July 1887, PCUSA microfilm reel 18.

35. Comaroff and Comaroff, *Revolution and Revelation*, 2:119–51.

36. Comaroff and Comaroff, *Revolution and Revelation*, 2:119–39; McCann, *Green Land, Brown Land*, 158–66.

37. Scholars have covered at length this evolution and only a brief sample of works on this subject is given here. Bundy, *The Rise and Fall of the South African Peasantry*; Comaroff and Comaroff, *Revolution and Revelation*, 2:140–65.

38. Pierre-Marie Le Berre to Archbishop, 10 and 20 December 1870; Welty to Le Berre, 11 November 1872; Welty to Archbishop, 14 February 1873, all in ACSE boîte 4J1.3a, Lettres 1869–1872 and 1873–1876

39. Pierre-Marie Le Berre to Archbishop, 25 September 1871, ACSE boîte 4J1.3a, Lettres 1869–1872; Father Neu, "Notes sur le Gabon," c. 1883, Cahier 15, 267, ACSE boîte 4J2.19a, Travaux Divers.

40. Welty to Propagation de la foi, 8 September 1872, ACSE boîte 211.5, Deux Guinées Diverses 1870–1891; Pierre-Marie Le Berre to Archbishop, 3 March 1874, ACSE boîte 4J1.3a, Lettres 1873–1876; Journal de la Mission 1874, June 1874 entry, ACSE boîte 211.3b, Dossier Personnel Monseigneur Le Berre, Journaux de Libreville 1861–1891.

41. Father Pierre-Marie Le Berre to Archbishop, 3 March 1874, ACSE boîte 4J1.3a, Lettres 1873–1876.

42. Journal de la Mission 1876, December 1876 entry, ACSE boîte 211.3b, Dossier Personnel Monseigneur Le Berre, Journaux de Libreville 1861–1891.

43. Father Stoffel to Archbishop, 20 October 1884, ACSE boîte 4J1.3b, Letters 1877–1892, Lettres 1881–1884.

44. William Walker to Alfred Walker, 22 April 1880, Correspondence 1879–1883, WWP, box 1; Lydia Jones to Executive Committee of the Gaboon and Corisco missions, 1884, PCUSA microfilm reel 16; Journal 1886, December 1886 entry, ACSE Boîte 211.3b, Dossier Personnel Monseigneur Le Berre, Journaux de Libreville 1861–1891.

45. Commandant of Gabon to Minister of Colonies, "Rapport du 23 aout à 23 octobre 1880," ANSOM 2B9.

46. Commandant of Gabon to Minister of Colonies, 14 September 1882, ANSOM 2B11.

47. Buléon, *Sous le ciel d'Afrique*, 41.

48. Gabon Journal de la Paroisse de Sainte-Marie de Libreville 1870–1907, 25 April 1885 entry, ACSE microfilm T2 B3.

49. Father Gachon or Father Monnier, "Notes sur Mgr Pierre-Marie Le Berre et la Mission Catholique du Gabon," n.d. (c. 1892), ACSE boîte 211.3b, Dossier Personnel Monseigneur Le Berre, Journaux de Libreville 1861–1891.

50. Commandant of Gabon to Minister of Colonies, 14 September 1882, ANSOM 2B11.

51. General information on Fang migration, social organization and gender roles can be found in Fernandez, *Bwiti*, 75–98, 126–68; Chamberlin, "Competition," passim; Cinnamon,

"Long March of the Fang"; Assomou, "Le mariage et la dot chez les Fang du Gabon"; Ratanga-Atoz, *Peuples*, 157–89.

52. Cinnamon, "Long March of the Fang," 228–36.

53. Missionary and official records from the late nineteenth century are bursting with references to various trade disputes. Christopher Chamberlin found 102 separate trade palavers between Mpongwe and Fang people. See Chamberlin, "Competition," 95–102.

54. Interview, Pierre-Celestin Evoung Ndong, Plaine-Niger, Libreville, 5 September 2000.

55. Sadie Boppell to Miss Hawley, 28 September 1898, PCUSA microfilm reel 25. Other missionaries recounted similar anecdotes. See Milligan, *Fetish Folk*, 224–25.

56. The following is a synthesis taken from various oral interviews conducted in Libreville, Donguila, Akok, Kangom and other Estuary villagers between September 1999 and November 2000. Also see Aubame, *Les Béti du Gabon et d'ailleurs*, 1:236–39.

57. Aubame, *Les Béti du Gabon et d'ailleurs*, 1:236–39.

58. This, like many other cultural traits of the Estuary Fang clans, may have been a late nineteenth-century innovation based on Mpongwe farming techniques. One Fang informant told a Protestant missionary at Kango in 1898, "Our fathers did not have *mfini*." Bennett, "Ethnographic Notes on the Fang," 83.

59. Interview, Marie-Thérèse Bella Eyene, Donguila, 23 March 2000.

60. Aubame, *Les Béti du Gabon et d'ailleurs*, 1:233–36; interviews, Joseph Ntoutoume Medoua, Ntoum, 23 September 2000; Pierre-Marie Abone Ndong, Ntoum, 23 September 2000.

61. Aubame, *Les Béti du Gabon et d'ailleurs*, 1:207–8.

62. Gray, *Colonial Rule and Crisis*.

63. Lt. Gov. of Gabon to Capt. *Basilic*, 14 June 1890, ANSOM 2B58; Raponda Walker, *Notes*, 263.

64. Gardinier, "Schools of the American Protestant Mission," 168–84.

65. Interview, Joseph-Bernard Mba Okoue, Chef de Quartier, Atong Abé, Libreville, 26 January 2000.

66. Interview, Michel Zimbé, Lalala Feu Rouge, Libreville, 5 January 2000.

67. Robert Nassau Diary, 4, 14, 17, and 18 December 1894 entries, RNP.

68. Bishop Adam to Sécrétaire des Missions d'Afrique, 29 April 1903, ACSE boîte 4J1.4b, Correspondance Gabon 1891–1920, Lettres 1901–1910.

69. "Communauté de Sainte-Marie de Libreville," BCSE 24 (1905–7), 164.

70. Chamberlin, "Competition," 110.

71. Mandat-Grancey, *Au Congo*, 49.

72. Fourneau Cahier, March 1890 entry, ANSOM 4Y4.

73. Milligan, *Fetish Folk*, 245.

74. Milligan, *Fetish Folk*, 128.

75. Gabon Journal de la Paroisse de Saint-Paul de Donguila 1887–1919, 17 October 1905 entry, ACSE microfilm T2 B11; Rapport Politique, Commune de Libreville, February 1914, ANSOM 4(1)D11.

76. Dossier Personnel Maurice Briault, Cahier 1900, 4 January 1900 entry, ACSE boîte 2D.2b.

77. Barret, *L'Afrique occidentale*, 1:214; "Notes de Route d'Alfred Fourneau," 28 March 1890, 8, ACSE boîte 2D60.5a, Fonds Pouchet, Paroisses de Libreville, Libreville Documents; Chef de la Circonscription de Libreville to Lt. Gov. of Gabon, 4 April 1910, ANG carton 64, Colonie du Gabon Rapports Politiques 1904–1913; Briault, *Zéro*, 40.

78. Claire Robertson has noted how female traders in Kenya enriched themselves in food trade to the aggravation of British administrators and African older men. Robertson, *Trouble Showed the Way*, 91–100, 130–45.

79. Interviews, Seraphine Mba and Barthelemy Nguema Ndong, Donguila, 16 March 2000; Pierre-Marie Abone Ndong, Ntoum, 20 September 2000; Felicien Ndong Ona, Melen, 28 October 2000.

80. For several examples, see Guyer, "Dynamic Approaches to Domestic Budgeting"; Schroeder, "'Gone to Their Second Husbands.'"

81. A small and hardly exhaustive sample of accounts of clan fighting includes RP Delorme to Le Berre, 5 February 1879, ACSE boîte 4J1.3b, Letters 1877–1892, Lettres 1877–1880; "Résidence du St. Paul de Dongila," BCSE 13 (1883): 621; "Communauté de Sainte Marie de Libreville," BCSE 23 (1904): 17; "Communauté de Sainte Marie de Libreville," BCSE 24 (1907): 162; "Rapport d'ensemble sur la situation de la Colonie du Gabon et les évènements de la guerre en 1914 et 1915," AN FM Affaires Politiques 116.

82. Arthur Marling to Gillespie, January 1883, PCUSA microfilm reel 16; Robert Nassau Diary, 3 February 1898 entry, RNP.

83. Gabon Journal de la Paroisse de Saint-Paul de Donguila 1887-1919, entries for 11 January 1905, 3 August 1909, and Journal de Vicariat Apostolique des Deux-Guinées, 4 August 1909 entry, all in ACSE ACSE microfilm T2 B1; "Mission du Gabon, Communauté de Sainte-Marie de Libreville," BCSE 24 (1905–7): 164; Brunschwig, "Expeditions punitives au Gabon."

84. Gabon Journal de la Paroisse de Saint-Paul de Donguila 1887-1919, entries for 10 April 1905 and 25 November 1911, ACSE microfilm T2 B11.

85. On women's agency in eloping with men, see Aubame, Les Béti du Gabon et d'ailleurs, 2:205–11; Mvé, Gabon entre tradition et post-modernité, 70.

86. RP Delorme, "Rapport du St. Paul de Donguila," 16 January 1880, ACSE boîte 211.5, Deux Guinées Diverses 1870–89.

87. Bennett, "Ethnographic Notes on the Fang," 93.

88. Monsignor Adam to Gerrer, 16 March 1897, ACSE boîte 4J1.4b, Correspondance Gabon 1891–1920, Lettres 1893–1900.

89. "Notes de Route d'Alfred Fourneau," 28 March 1890, 13, ACSE boîte 2D60.5a, Fonds Pouchet, Paroisses de Libreville, Libreville Documents.

90. For a lengthier discussion of this episode, see Rich, "Where Every Language Is Heard."

91. On central Vietnam and the Can Vuong rebellion in the 1880s, and French expansion into central and northern Vietnam in the 1880s, see David Marr, Vietnamese Anticolonialism (Berkeley: University of California, 1971), 44–76; Charles Fourniau, Annam-Tonkin (1885–1896): Lettrés et paysans vietnamiens face à la conquête coloniale (Paris: Harmattan, 1989), 141–59, 163–73, 185–207; Nguyen Thê Anh, Monarchie et fait colonial au Viêt-Nam (1875–1925): Le crépuscule d'un ordre traditionnel (Paris: Harmattan, 1992), 111–34, 165–66; Pierre Brocheux and Daniel Hémery, Indochine: La colonization ambigüe, 1858–1960 (Paris: Découverte, 2001), 51–60.

92. CGFC to Minister of Colonies, 16 August 1899, ANSOM 2B40.

93. Communauté du Saint-Pierre de Libreville," BCSE 15 (1887–89): 483; Milligan, Fetish Folk, 25; Chavannes, Le Congo français, 187; Bridel to Mère X, 18 August 1911, ACSE boîte 4J1.4b, Correspondance Gabon 1891–1920, Lettres 1910–1920.

94. Procès-Verbal du Conseil d'Administration, 22 May 1890, Gabon-Congo VII-11, AN FM SG.

95. Lt. Gov. of Gabon to Minister of Colonies, 20 September 1894, ANSOM 2B102; Robert Nassau Diary, 5 September 1896 entry, RNP.

96. Blim, "Congo," 267.

97. Kingsley, Travels in West Africa, 120.

98. "Rapport Politique du Gabon," 15 January–15 February 1891, ANSOM 2B57;

Commissionaire Général of Congo Français de Brazza to Lt. Gov. of Cochinchine, 13 December 1894, ANSOM 2B102. It is unclear where the idea to import Vietnamese prisoners came from or why French officials decided to withdraw their support from the venture.

99. Briault, Récits, 64.

100. Ratanga-Atoz, Peuples, 218.

101. Raponda Walker, Notes, 265.

102. Conseil d'Administration de la Colonie du Gabon 1909, Séance du 3 June 1909, ANSOM 9D4.

103. Administrators testified on many occasions to the deleterious effects of heavy rains and poor conservation on flour supplies. A list of references includes Commandant of Gabon to Minister of Colonies, 23 October 1880, ANSOM 2B9; Lt. Gov. of Gabon to Minister of Colonies, 7 December 1886, ANSOM 2B15; Chef de Service Admininistratif, Colonie du Gabon-Congo, 15 July 1890, Gabon-Congo VII-8, AN FM SG. As for illnesses among bakers, see Lt. Gov. of Gabon to Minister of Colonies, 7 December 1886.

104. "Communauté de Sainte Marie du Gabon," BCSE 16 (1892), 367; Augustin Berger, "La Jubilé du Frère Sidoine Stoeckler," Echo des Missions, March 1937, ACSE boîte 4J1.6b, Divers Gabon 1920–1949, Missionnaires, Prêtres et Soeurs Indigènes.

105. Procès-Verbal du Conseil d'Administration, 3 July 1886 and 8 August 1888, Gabon-Congo VII-11, AN FM SG.

106. Procès-Verbal du Conseil d'Administration, 8 August 1888, 1 March 1889 and 26 November 1892, Gabon-Congo VII-11, AN FM SG.

107. For Senegalese soldiers and carpenters, see Rich, "Where Every Language Is Heard."

108. For some references to Gold Coast and Sierra Leone workers and traders, see Albert Bushnell to Dr. Lowrie, 27 January 1872, PCUSA microfilm reel 13; Commandant of Gabon to Minister of Colonies, 15 October 1885, ANSOM 2B15; Robert Nassau Diary, 25 April 1894 entry, RNP.

109. Unlike other African contract workers, they did maintain large gardens on the contemporary sites of Batavea, Lalala, and Cocotiers. Though this community is rarely mentioned in contemporary documents, see Briault, Une soeur missionnaire, 105, and Zéro, 62.

110. CGFC to Minister of Colonies, 6 September 1898, ANSOM 2B117.

111. Commandant of Gabon Pradier, "Arrêté Local Portant Modification et Unification dans les Diverses Rations d'Indigènes du Gabon," 5 July 1886, Bulletin Officiel Administratif du Gabon-Congo, 1886.

112. Lt. Gov. of Gabon, "Reponse aux observations et une demande d'explications fait au sujet du ravitaillement des magasins de la Marine au Gabon jusqu'à 1 septembre 1890," 18 July 1889, ANSOM 2B17; Blim, "Congo," 258.

113. Nassau, Fetichism in West Africa, 84–85; Diop, Eliwa Zi N'Gaba, 112.

114. Migeod, Across Equatorial Africa, 15.

115. Procès-Verbal du Conseil d'Administration, 3 July 1886 and 8 August 1888, Gabon-Congo VII-11, AN FM SG.

116. Briault, Une soeur missionnaire, 179–80.

117. "Concours Agricole du 13 juillet 1891," unmarked page from Bulletin Officiel Administratif du Gabon-Congo, 20 July 1891, ACSE boîte 211.5, folder 1891.

118. CGFC, Arrêté of 19 March 1904, ANG carton 221, Affaire concernant la mercuriale des prix dans les marchés du Territoire du Gabon 1918–1947. I could not obtain an original copy of the 1888 decree; however, the 1904 decree repeated the same terms evidently first set in November 1888.

119. Robert Nassau Diary, 1 March 1895, 10 June 1896, and 29–30 July 1896 entries, RNP; Gabon Journal de la Paroisse de Sainte-Marie de Libreville 1870–1907, 10 May 1899 entry, ACSE microfilm T2 B3; Silas Johnson Papers, Diary 1906–1910, 9 April 1907 entry, Presbyterian Historical Society, Philadelphia; Raponda Walker, Souvenirs d'un nonagénaire, 29.

120. Austen and Headrick, "Equatorial Africa under Colonial Rule," 42.

121. Rapport de Service de la Circonscription de Libreville, 29 May 1911, AN FM Affaires Politiques Mission Frezouls 1910–1911, Dossier 3123, Inspecteur Général Frézouls, Administration General des Circonscriptions du Gabon; Lt. Gov. of Gabon to Chef de la Circonscription de l'Estuaire-Como, 17 June 1912, ANG carton 745, Correspondance Générale Territoire du Gabon 1912.

122. Journal de la Vicariat Apostolique des Deux-Guinées, 3 July 1910 entry, ACSE microfilm T2 BI.

123. Angelique Bouye Dinga to Inspecteur Frezouls, 24 November 1910, AN FM Affaires Politiques Mission Frezouls 1910–1911, Dossier 3123.

124. Pierre-Marie Le Berre to Archbishop, 17 May 1870, ACSE boîte 4J1.3a, Lettres 1869–1872; "Sainte-Marie du Gabon," BCSE 8 (1870–72): 586–88.

125. Procès-Verbal du Conseil d'Administration, 28 March 1892, Gabon-Congo VII-11, AN FM SG.

126. Procès-Verbal du Conseil d'Administration, 23 June and 30 September 1890, 22 January 1891, all in Gabon-Congo VII-11, AN FM SG.

127. Monsignor Adam to Secrétaire Générale Grisard, 15 May 1899, ACSE boîte 4J1.4b; Mandat-Grancey, Au Congo, 32.

128. Though the important place of imported alcohol in Mpongwe social life cannot be fully discussed here, it resembles in many ways that discussed by Emmanuel Akyeampong in his social history of alcohol in Ghana. See Akyeampong, Drink, Power and Cultural Change. For examples of the use of imported alcohol in local practices, see Barret, L'Afrique occidentale, 171, 175; Milligan, Fetish Folk, 42–47; Patterson, Coast, 55; Butcher, "Mpongwe People," 151.

129. Interview, Madame Rabeno, 3 February 2000; personal communication, Pierre Mavoungou, October 2000.

130. Missionary references are generally ambiguous. Undoubtedly the secrecy surrounding this talisman and its ability to escape clear definition are part of its power. See Peureux, "Notice sur la fétichisme au Gabon" n.d. (c. 1859), ACSE boîte 211.4a, Vicariat des Deux Guinées Divers 1843–1869; William Walker to Commandant of Gabon, 26 June 1869, Correspondence 1864–1870, WWP, box 1.

131. William Walker Diary, 19 and 21 May 1869 entries, WWP, box 3; Commander of Naval Forces on the Western African Coast to Minister of Colonies, 22 July 1869, Gabon-Congo I-7, AN FM SG.

132. CGFC Lemaire to Minister of Colonies, 8 December 1900, Roi Félix Dossier, Gabon-Congo IV-16, AN FM SG; Ratanga-Atoz, "Résistances," 205–6.

133. Gabon Journal de la Paroisse de Sainte-Marie de Libreville 1870–1907, 10–12 May 1899 entries, ACSE Microfilm T2 B3; Gabon Journal de la Paroisse de Saint-Pierre de Libreville 1884–1914, 11 May 1899 entry, ACSE Microfilm T2 B2; Monsignor Adam to Bishop of Brazzaville, 15 May 1899, ACSE boîte 4J1.7c, Correspondance Gabon-Brazzaville 1899–1946.

134. Mandat-Grancey, Au Congo, 37–38.

135. Mandat-Grancey, Au Congo, 40.

136. CGFC Lemaire to Minister of Colonies, 8 December 1900, Roi Félix Dossier, Gabon-Congo IV-16, AN FM SG.

137. The following information is taken from Monsignor Adam to Secrétaire Général Grisard, 15 May 1899, ACSE boîte 4J1.4b.

138. Monsignor Adam to Secrétaire Général Grisard, 15 May 1899.

139. Gabon Journal de Vicariat Apostolique des Deux-Guinées, 17 May 1899 entry, ACSE Microfilm T2 B1.

140. Gabon Journal de Vicariat Apostolique des Deux-Guinées, 19 May 1899 entry.

141. Raulin, Amours congolaises, 106–9.

4. Famine in the Gabon Estuary, 1914–1930

1. Bassett, The Peasant Cotton Revolution; Van Beusekom, Negotiating Development; Bogosian, "Forced Labor, Resistance, and Memory."

2. Sen, Poverty and Famines, 1.

3. Arnold, Famine, 43–46.

4. Becker, Hungry Ghosts; Conquest, The Harvest of Sorrow; de Vaal, Famine that Kills; Dejene, Environment, Famine, and Politics in Ethiopia; Gado, Une histoire des famines; Paul Greenough, Prosperity and Misery in Modern Bengal; Pankhurst, Resettlement and Famine in Ethiopia; Yang, Calamity and Reform in China.

5. For population statistics for the 1920s, see Rapport Politique, District de Kango, 1954, ANG carton 612, District de Kango Rapport Politique 1943–46.

6. Journal de la Paroisse de Sainte-Marie de Libreville 1908–1939, 20 September 1925 entry, ACSE microfilm T2 B9.

7. For a broad overview of colonial famines in Africa, see Watts, Silent Violence; Iliffe, The African Poor, 150–61; Vaughan, The Story of an African Famine.

8. Sautter, De l'Atlantique au fleuve Congo, 2:852–65; Gray, "Territoriality, Ethnicity and Colonial Rule," 325–42.

9. For a general overview of the impact of World War I on Gabon, see Loungou Mouele, "Le Gabon de 1910 à 1925"; Dubois, "Le prix d'une guerre."

10. White, Sierra Leone's Settler Women Traders, 60, 70–71; Olukoju, "Maritime Trade in Lagos," 123–24; Martin, Leisure and Society, 46.

11. Journal de Vicariat Apostolique des Deux-Guinées, April 1916 entry, ACSE microfilm T2 B1; Loungou Mouele, "Le Gabon de 1910 à 1925," 273–74; Metegue-N'nah, "Histoire de la formation du peuple Gabonais," 204. Such practices took place throughout French Equatorial Africa. See Cordell, "Extracting People from Precapitalist Production," 141–46.

12. Bishop Martrou to Bishop, 20 January 1916, ACSE boîte 4J1.4b, Correspondance Gabon 1891–1920, Lettres 1910–1920.

13. Loungou Mouele, "Le Gabon de 1910 à 1925," 320.

14. Bishop Louis Martrou to Bishop, 24 April 1916, ACSE boîte 4J1.4b, Correspondance Gabon 1891–1920, Lettres 1910–1920.

15. Chef Circ. Estuaire Bobichon to Gov. Gabon, 29 July 1916, ANG carton 911, Affaires Economiques 1916–1917.

16. Arrêté Gov. Gabon, 4 August 1914, Journal Officiel de l'Afrique Équatoriale Française (JOAEF) 1914, 417–18; Arrêté, Lt. Gov. Gabon, 11 August 1914, JOAEF 1914, 418–19; Journal de la Paroisse de Saint-Paul de Donguila 1887–1921, 14 March 1916 entry, ACSE microfilm T2 B11.

17. Lt. Gov. Gabon to Chef Circ. Estuaire, 26 July 1916, ANG carton 911, Affaires Economiques 1916–1917.

18. Dubois, "Le prix d'une guerre ," 404. Some Mpongwe still recalled the attacks nearly twenty years later. Chef de Glass Félix Adande Rapunchtombo to Chef du Départment de l'Estuaire, 29 May 1943, ANG carton 1634, Commune de Libreville Correspondance Administrative Ordinaire.

19. Julien Macé to R. Pascal, 17 November 1916, ACSE boîte 4J1.4b, Correspondance Gabon 1891–1920, Lettres 1910–1920.

20. Chef Sub. Médégue to Chef Circ. Estuaire, 23 June 1917, ANG Fonds Médouneu.

21. Chef Sub. Médegue to Chef Circ. Estuaire, 18 June 1917; Chef Sub. Médegue to Chef Sub. Ndendé, 26 September 1917, ANG Fonds Médouneu.

22. Chef Sub. Médegue to Chef Circ. Estuaire, 30 April 1918, ANG Fonds Médouneu.

23. De Waal, Famine, 65; Sunseri, Vilimani, 78–80, 93–96.

24. Chef Sub. Médegue to Chef Circ. Estuaire, 18 February, 30 April and 31 May 1918, ANG Fonds Médouneu.

25. Chef Sub. Médegue to Chef Circ. Estuaire, 18 February 1918, ANG Fonds Médouneu.

26. Georges Guibet to Lt. Gov. Gabon Thomann, 12 April 1919, ANG carton 29, Territoire du Gabon cultures vivrières, credits, vente, ravitaillement, nuisibles 1917–1920 (hereafter cited as ANG 29 Cultures).

27. Lt. Gov. Gabon Thomann to Chef Circ. Estuaire, 25 April 1919, ANG carton 29, Telegrammes Officielles 1919; Lt. Gov. Gabon to Chef Circ. Estuaire, 30 April 1919, ANG carton 221, Affaire concernant la mercuriale des prix dans les marchés du Territoire du Gabon 1918–1947.

28. Bishop Martrou to Bishop, 28 April 1917, ACSE boîte 4J1.4b, Correspondance Gabon 1891–1920, Lettres 1910–1920.

29. Rapport Annuel Colonie du Gabon 1917, 95–96, ANSOM 4(I)D14.

30. Henry Perrier to Director SME, 29 May 1917, DEFAP, fiche 2494.

31. Maire de Libreville Bobichon, "Arrêté fixant les droits de place à percevoir sur les marchés de Libreville," 1 August 1917, ANG carton 221, Affaire concernant la mercuriale des prix dans les marchés du Territoire du Gabon 1918–1947; Rapport Annuel Colonie du Gabon 1917, 11–12.

32. Rapport Annuel Colonie du Gabon 1917, 95–96.

33. Bishop Martrou to Bishop, 1 November 1918, ACSE boîte 4J1.4b, Correspondance Gabon 1891–1920, Lettres 1910–1920.

34. Bishop Martrou to Bishop, 6 May 1918, ACSE boîte 4J1.4b, Correspondance Gabon 1891–1920, Lettres 1910–1920.

35. Henry Perrier to Director SME, 12 May 1918, DEFAP, fiche 2502.

36. Chef Sub. Médégue Charbonnier to Chef Circ. Estuaire, 2, 9, and 11 July 1918, ANG Fonds Médouneu; Chef Sub. Chinchoua to Chef Circ. Estuaire, 5 July 1918, ANG 29 Cultures.

37. Chef Sub. Kango to Chef Circ. Estuaire, 12 August 1918, ANG 29 Cultures; interview, Jean Abone Ndong, Ntoum, 20 September 2000.

38. Journal de Vicariat Apostolique des Deux-Guinées, 14 September and 16 October 1918 entries, ACSE microfilm BI; ANSOM 4(I)D16, Rapport Annuel Politique Gabon 1918, 36, 50, 179.

39. "Résidence de St. Paul de Dongila," BCSE 30 (1921–22): 659; Headrick, Colonialism, Health and Illness, 178.

40. Julien Macé to Faugère, 21 April 1919, ACSE boîte 4J1.4b, Correspondance Gabon 1891–1920, Correspondance concernant la Procurs 1914–1920.

41. Lt. Gov. Gabon Marchand to Chef Circ. Estuaire, 12 March 1919, ANSOM 2D52, Ravitaillement Libreville.

42. Louis Martrou 1919, ACSE boîte 4J1.6a, Divers Gabon 1920–1949, Dossier Autorités Civils.

43. Félix Fauré to Director SME, Rapport Annuel de la Mission du Gabon, 8 September 1919, DEFAP, fiche 2515; Macé to Faugère, 21 September 1919, ACSE boîte 4J1.4b Correspondance Gabon 1891–1920 Correspondance concernant la Procure 1914–1920.

44. The following reports are in ANSOM 4(1)D19: Rapport Politique, Circonscription de l'Estuaire, 1st semester 1919; Rapports Politiques, Colonie du Gabon, 1er, 3eme et 4th semester 1919.

45. Guibet to Chefs des Subdivisions de la Circonscription de l'Estuaire-Como, 10 January 1919, and Guibet to Thomann, 12 April 1919, both in ANG 29 Cultures.

46. Guibet to Thomann, 12 April 1919.

47. Thomann to Guibet, 25 April 1919, ANG carton 29, Telegrammes Officielles 1919.

48. Chef Sub. Kango Tastevin to Chef Circ. Estuaire, 1 August 1918, ANG 29 Cultures.

49. Vecten to Chef Subdivision Kango, 12 August 1918, ANG 29 Cultures.

50. Guibet to Lt. Gov. Gabon Thomann, 20 August 1918, ANG 29 Cultures.

51. Macé to Faugère, 20 December 1919, ACSE boîte 4J1.4b, Correspondance Gabon 1891–1920, Correspondance Concernant la Procure 1914–1920.

52. "Rapport . . . guerre en 1917," 64, ANSOM 4(1)D15; "Rapport . . . guerre en 1918," Part II, 32, ANSOM 4(1)D16.

53. Chef Circ. Estuaire Georges Guibet to Gov. Gabon Marchand, 6 February 1920, ANG carton 36, Rapport sur l'attitude des indigènes en face de la hausse des prix et hausse illicte des prix de la Maison Thomas à Libreville 13 janvier–12 fevrier 1920 (hereafter cited as ANG 36 Prix); Migeod, *Across Equatorial Africa*, 14.

54. Lt. Gov. Gabon Thomann to GGFEA, March 1919, ANG 1053 SAG.

55. Migeod, *Across Equatorial Africa*, 14–15.

56. Migeod, *Across Equatorial Africa*, 14–15.

57. Marchand to Guibet, 11 January 1920, ANG 36 Prix.

58. Migeod, *Across Equatorial Africa*, 14–15.

59. Guibet to Marchand, 12 January 1920, ANG 36 Prix.

60. Guibet to Marchand, 12 January 1920.

61. Migeod, *Across Equatorial Africa*, 14.

62. Guibet to Marchand, 12 January 1920, ANG 36 Prix.

63. Marchand to Guibet, 13 January 1920.

64. Macé to Faugère, 15 January 1920, ACSE boîte 4J1.4b, Correspondance Gabon 1891–1920, Correspondance concernant la Procure 1914–1920; Marchand to GGFEA, 22 January 1920, and Guibet to Marchand, 6 February 1920, both in ANG 36 Prix.

65. Procès-Verbal, Ville de Libreville, Police Commissioner Aristride Auclair, 22 January 1920, ANG 36 Prix.

66. Police Commissioner Auclair to Guibet, 28 January 1920, ANG 36 Prix.

67. Chef Vincent Ndongo to Chef de la Circ. Estuaire, 23 Febuary 1923, ANG carton 929, Affaires Civiles 1919–1938.

68. Marchand to Guibet, 19 February 1920, ANG 36 Prix.

69. Charles Bobichon to Georges Bruel, 29 March 1920, Fonds Georges Bruel B30–63, Academie des Sciences d'Outre-Mer.

70. For general details on timber in Gabon, see Pourtier, *Le Gabon*, 2:145–88.

71. Sautter, *De l'Atlantique au fleuve Congo*, 2:1003–5; Cordell, "Extracting," 146–47.

72. Arrêté GGFEA, 26 February 1920, ANSOM 2D58, Estuaire 1925.

73. Chef Sub. Owendo Tastevin to Chef Circ. Estuaire, 1 March 1920, ANG carton 929, Affaires Civiles 1919–1938; interview, Antoine Ndong Nguéma, Nzeng Ayong, Libreville, 6 September 2000.

74. Journal de la Paroisse de Saint-Paul de Donguila 1887–1921, 20 and 26 February 1921 entries, ACSE microfilm T2 B11.

75. Journal de la Paroisse de Sainte-Marie de Libreville 1908–1939, 9 July 1921 entry, ACSE microfilm T2 B9; Rapport Politique Circonscription de l'Estuaire, January 1922, ANSOM 5D52; Lt. Gov. Marchand to Chef Circ. Estuaire, 1 February 1922, ANSOM 4(1)D22.

76. Bishop Louis Martrou to Bishop, 10 April 1921, ACSE boîte 4J1.7a, Lettres Gabon 1921–1947, Lettres 1921–1924.

77. Migeod, *Across Equatorial Africa*, 15, 22; Edward Ford to Director SME, Rapport de la Station de Baraka, July 1919–June 1920, DEFAP, fiche 2523; Journal de la Paroisse de Sainte-Marie de Libreville 1908–1939, 17 May and July 1920 entries, ACSE microfilm T2 B9; ACSE boîte 4J1.4b, Correspondance Gabon 1891–1920, Correspondance concernant la procure 1914–1920, Macé to Faugère, 21 May 1920.

78. Macé to Faugère, 15 September 1921, ACSE boîte 4J1.7a, Lettres Gabon 1921–1947, Lettres 1921–1924.

79. Lt. Gov. Gabon to Chef Circ. Estuaire Dehais, 17 May 1921, ANG carton 911, Vivres Frais 1921.

80. Ozimo Trumann to Lt. Gov. Gabon, 17 October 1921, ANG 1055 Administration Général Correspondance Diverses 1922 (hereafter cited as ANG 1055 AGCD).

81. Anguilé to Chef Circ. Estuaire, 8 October 1921, ANG 1055 AGCD.

82. Chef Sub. Owendo to Chef Circ. Estuaire, 14 October 1921, ANG carton 911, Vivres Frais 1921.

83. Chef Circ. Estuaire Moesch to Lt. Gov. Gabon, 29 December 1921, ANG carton 911, Vivres Frais 1921.

84. Henry Perrier to Director SME, 5 November 1921, DEFAP, fiche 2538.

85. Médecin-Chef Sicé, Chef du Service de la Santé Publique au Gabon to Chef Circ. Estuaire, n.d. (January 1922), ANG 1055 AGCD; Commissaire de Police, Rapport Quotidien, 5 January 1922; Commissaire de Police to Chef Circ. Estuaire, 14 April 1922.

86. Conseil d'Administration, Colonie du Gabon, 10 December 1921, ANSOM 9D9; Lt. Gov. Gabon Marchand, "Arrêté portant création de marchés destinés à la vente des produits vivrières indigènes," 10 December 1921, JOAEF 1922, 20–21.

87. Marchand, "Arrêté déterminant la nature et les quantités minima de vivres constituant la ration journalière des travailleurs dans la colonie du Gabon," 5 December 1921, JOAEF 1922, 20.

88. GGFEA to Gov. Gabon, 5 January 1922, ANSOM 3B602.

89. Commission du Ravitaillement de Libreville, Séances du 14 and 25 February 1922, ANSOM 5D52, Dossier Ravitaillement.

90. Lt. Gov. Gabon Cadier to GGFEA, 18 November 1922, ANG 1055 AGCD.

91. Chef Circ. Estuaire Moesch to Lt. Gov. Gabon, 17 April 1922, ANG 1055 AGCD.

92. Commissaire de Police to Chef Circ. Estuaire, 14 April 1922, ANG 1055 AGCD.

93. Chef Circ. Estuaire, "Note à la lettre de l'Association des Commercants, Industriels, Planteurs et Colons de Libreville," 28 February 1922, ANG carton 911, Vivres Frais.

94. Journal de la Communauté de Donguila 1922–1930, 21 January 1922 entry, Archives de la Paroisse de Donguila, Eglise Catholique du Gabon, Donguila (hereafter cited as Donguila Archives).

95. Rapport Politique, Circonscription de l'Estauire, January 1922, ANSOM 5D52; "État des Peines Disciplinaires de la Circonscription de l'Estuaire," February 1922, ANSOM 5D52, Ravitaillement Libreville.

96. "Une groupe féminine" to Lt. Gov. Gabon, 12 February 1922, AN FM, Affaires Politiques 117-3, Dossier Boisneuf 1922–1923.

97. Administrateur Adjoint Berlan, 11 April 1922, ANG 1055 AGCD.

98. "Quelque members de la race Gabonais" to Senateur Berenger, 14 February 1922, AN FM Affaires Politiques 117-3, Dossier Boisneuf 1922–1923.

99. Rapport Politique,Circonscription de l'Estuaire, January 1922, ANSOM 5D52.

100. "Une groupe féminine" and "Quelque members de la race Gabonais," ANSOM 5D52.

101. Minister of Colonies to GGFEA, 20 March 1922, ANSOM 5D52.

102. Chef Circ. Estuaire Moesch to Gov. Gabon, 24 March and 14 April 1922, ANSOM 5D52.

103. The following information is drawn from GGFEA to Minister of Colonies, 26 June 1923, ANSOM 5D2.

104. GGFEA to Minister of Colonies, 26 June 1923.

105. Jean-Baptiste N'dende to GGFEA, 9 June 1922, ANG 1055 AGCD.

106. Nkouele Nguébé and Melou Mekegne to "Grand Gouverneur du Gabon," 27 December 1921, ANG 1055 AGCD.

107. Rapport Mensuel, Circ. Como-Nkam, June 1922, ANSOM 4(1)D21.

108. Journal de la Paroisse de Sainte-Marie de Libreville 1908–1939, 16 September, 23 November, 26 December 1922 and 18 January 1923 entries, ACSE microfilm T2 B9.

109. Rapport Politique, Circ. Estuaire, September 1923, ANSOM 4(1)D25; Bishop Louis Martrou to Directeur de l'Oeuvre de la Propagation de la Foi, 21 August 1923, ACSE boîte 4J1.6a, Divers Gabon 1920–1949, Dossier Oeuvres Pontificals.

110. Bishop Louis Martrou to Bishop, 25 September 1924, ACSE boîte 4J1.7a, Lettres Gabon 1921–1947, Lettres 1921–1924.

111. Journal de la Communauté de Donguila 1922–1930, 4 October and December 1924 entries, Donguila Archives.

112. Rapport Politique, Colonie du Gabon, 4th trimester 1924, ANSOM 4(1)D28.

113. Rapport Politique, Circ. de l'Estuaire, 1st semester 1925, ANSOM 4(1)D31.

114. Since Libreville residents generally had the means to pay off their taxes, local officials could not compel them to clear roads or do manual labor. African guards with the aid of village chiefs thus rounded up rural men and women to work in the town. Chef Estuaire Vingarassamy to Lt. Gov. Gabon, 5 March 1925, ANG carton 1686, Colonie du Gabon Textes Reglementaires Relatif à l'Organisation du Regime des Prestation en A.E.F. 1925–1939; Journal de la Communuté de Donguila 1922–1930, 9 April 1925 entry, Donguila Archives.

115. Journal de la Communauté de Donguila 1922–1930, 24 June 1925 entry, Donguila Archives.

116. Chef de Sub. Kango, "États des Peines Disciplinaires," June, August, and September 1925, ANG carton 367, Affaires Concernant la Prison de Libreville et Divers Départements 1925 (hereafter cited as ANG 367 Prison).

117. "Adjucation des Jugements Rendus," Tribunal Indigène 1er Dégré, Subdivision de Chinchoua, 3rd trimester 1925, ANG 367 Prison.

118. "États des Peines Disciplinaires," Subdivision de Kango, November 1925; "États des Peines Disciplinaires," Subdivision de Libreville, November 1925; "États des Peines Disciplinaires," Subdivision de Cocobeach, December 1925, all in ANG 367 Prison.

119. Father Rémy to Bishop, 17 July 1925, ACSE boîte 4J1.7a, Lettres Gabon 1921–1947, Lettres 1925–1927.

120. Journal de la Paroisse de Sainte-Marie de Libreville 1908–1939, 17 July 1925 entry, ACSE microfilm T2 B9; Edouard Panchaud to Director SME, 18 July 1925, DEFAP, fiche 2597; Journal de la Communauté de Donguila 1922–1930, November 1925 entry, Donguila Archives.

121. Journal de la Paroisse de Sainte-Marie de Libreville 1908–1939, 20 September 1925 entry, ACSE microfilm T2 B9.

122. Journal de la Paroisse de Sainte-Marie de Libreville 1908–1939, 17 April 1926 entry, ACSE microfilm T2 B9; Bishop Louis Tardy to Bishop, 18 May 1926, ACSE boîte 4J1.7a, Lettres 1925–1927.

123. Lt. Gov. Gabon Bernard to GGFEA, 23 December 1925, ANSOM 5D58, Dossier Estuaire 1925.

124. GGFEA Antonetti, "Extrait du discours du Conseil du Gouvernement," December 1925, ANSOM 5D58, Dossier Estuaire 1925.

125. Jean-Baptiste N'dende to Lt. Gov Gabon, 15 July 1925, ANSOM 5D2.

126. President of the League of Rights of Man to GGFEA, 1 April 1926, ANSOM 5D2.

127. Laurent Antchoué to Blaise Daigne, 21 February 1926, and Blaise Daigne to Minister of Colonies, 26 April 1926, AN FM, Affaires Politiques Dossier 649-1, Laurent Antchouey.

128. Chef Circ. Estuaire Pechayrand to Lt. Gov Gabon, 10 February 1926, ANSOM 5D2.

129. GGFEA to Minister of Colonies, 2 July 1926, AN FM, Affaires Politiques Dossier 649-1.

130. GGFEA to Lt. Gov. Gabon, 5 June 1926, ANSOM 5D2.

131. Rapport du Service du Government du Gabon (Bureau des Affaires Civiles), 8 November 1924, AN FM Affaires Politiques carton 3128, Mission Texier 1924–1925.

132. Rapport (Bureau des Affaires Civiles), 8 November 1924; Rapport du Service du Gouvernement du Gabon (Situation Financière du Gabon), Response GGFEA, 13 December 1924, AN FM carton 3128, Mission Texier.

133. Response GGFEA, 13 December 1924.

134. Journal de la Communauté de Donguila 1922–1930, 1 and 12 August 1926 entries, Donguila Archives.

135. Bishop Tardy to SC Propagande, 5 November 1927, ACSE boîte 4J1.6a, Divers Gabon 1920–1949, Dossier Prospectus Status Missionis; Bishop Tardy to Oeuvre de la Sainte-Enfance, 5 November 1927, ACSE boîte 4J1.6a Divers, Gabon 1920–1949, Dossier Oeuvres Pontificals.

136. Commissaire de Police de Libreville, "Rapport quotidien," 2–3 July 1928, and Chef Circ. Estuaire Louis Bonvin to Gov. Gabon, 7 July 1928, both in ANG carton 221, Affaire concernant la mercuriale des prix dans les marchés du Territoire du Gabon 1918–1947; Edouard Penchaud to Director SME, 24 July 1928, DEFAP, fiche 2642.

137. Tardy to Oeuvre Sainte-Enfance, 5 November 1927; Director Consortium des Grands Réserves Forestiers to Dr. Daude, Chef Service Santé, Foulenzem, 4 December 1927, Director PROA (a French company) at Kango to Gov. Gabon, 26 March 1928, both in ANG carton 221, Affaire concernant la mercuriale des prix dans les marchés du Territoire du Gabon 1918–1947.

138. Journal de la Communauté de Donguila 1922–1930, 2 June 1928 entry; Journal de la Communauté de Donguila 1928–1932, 3, 7 and 27 April, 1, 9 and 20 May, 10 June and 28 October 1929 entries, Donguila Archives.

139. Rapport Politique, Circonscription de l'Estuaire, 1st trimester 1929, ANSOM 4(1)D35.

140. Géraud, "Une exploitation industrielle de la fôret équatoriale," 192–93.

141. GGFEA, "Arrêté fixant la composition de la ration des travailleurs indigènes," 30 October 1927, JOAEF 1927, 321–22; Coquery-Vidrovitch, Le Congo, 479–84.

142. Rapport Politique, Circonscription de l'Estuaire, 4th trimester 1927, ANSOM 4(1)D33; Ballard, "Development of Political Parties," 112–18.

143. Interview, Justin Ndoutoume Nkobe, Kango, 13 August 2004.

144. Interview, Frederic Meyo Mba, Libreville, Lalala à Gauche, 18 August 2004.

145. Interview, Mendame Obame, Chief of Village, Kafélé, 12 August 2004.

146. Interviews, Michel Zimbé, Lalala, Libreville, 5 January 2000; Seraphine Mba and Barthelemy Nguema Ndong, Donguila, 16 March 2000.

147. Interview, Antoine Ndong Nguéma, Nzeng Ayong, Librveille, 10 September 2000.

148. Interview, Joseph-Marie Endame, Donguila, 20 March 2000.

149. Interviews, "Crocodile" Nguema, Donguila, 25 March 2000; Michel Nzoghe Mba, Nzamalighue, 27 March 2000.

150. Interviews, Obame Mba, Lalala, Libreville, 5 February 2000; Nzong Mba and Julienne Enengba Enengbe, Nzamaligue-Donguila road, 22 March 2000.

151. Jugement du Tribunal Indigène de la Circonscription de l'Estuaire, 6 September 1926, ANSOM 5D62, Dossier Abogho Nze.

152. Jugement du Tribunal Indigène, 2 October 1926.

153. GGFEA to Lt. Gov. Gabon 23 and 24 November 1926, ANSOM 5D61, Dossier Abogho Nze.

154. Raponda Walker, Souvenirs d'un nonagénaire, 193; interviews, Michel Nzoghe Mba, Nzamaligue-Donguila road, 27 March 2000, and Joseph Nkoghe Bekale, Nzamaligue, 29 March 2000.

155. Donguila mission journal, July 1929 entry, Donguila Archives.

156. Edouard Panchaud to Directeur SME, 4 November 1928, DEFAP, fiche 2642; Father Joseph Soul, "Compte Rendu St. Paul de Donguila, 17–23 December 1928, ACSE boîte 4J1.6b Divers Gabon 1920–1949, Visites. The forthcoming work of Rachel Jean-Baptiste on Estuary marriages practices will undoubtedly clarify the issue of bridewealth.

157. Interviews, Michel Zimbé, Lalala, Libreville, 5 January 2000; Evariste Nzé Ollame, b. 1930, Fang, Cocotiers, Libreville, 19 February 2000; Justin Ndoutoume Nkobe, Kango, 12 August 2004; Frederic Meyo Mba, Lalala à Gauche, 18 August 2004.

158. De Waal, Famine, 78–80.

159. Schivelbusch, The Culture of Defeat, 34.

5. Town Life and Imported Food, 1840–1960

1. James Patten to "Boards of the United States of America," n.d. (1888), PCUSA microfilm reel 19.

2. James Patten to "Boards of the United States of America."

3. "Arrêté réglement le rationnement et la circulation des certaines merchandises et denrées," Gov. Gabon Masson, 28 June 1940, JOAEF 1940, 627–28.

4. "Arrêté réglant la vente, la conservation et la circulation du pain et de la farine," Gov. Gabon Masson, 9 July 1940, JOAEF 1940, 650; interviews, Simone Saint-Dénis, Plaine Niger, Libreville, 5 December 1999, and Charles N'no Ndong, Atong Abé, Libreville, 8 February 2000.

5. Lasserre, Libreville, 242–46.

6. Interview, Adolphe Revignet, Ozangue, Libreville, 17 February 2000.

7. Interview, Marguerite Kendé, Toulon, Libreville, 25 February 2000.

8. GGFEA Eboué to Gov. Gabon, 11 October 1941, ANG carton 981, Région de l'Estuaire, Correspondances Diverses 1941.

9. Commandant of Gabon to Minister of Colonies, 24 July 1859, ANSOM 2B22.

10. "Inventaire des Vivres au Gabon," 15 February 1849, ANSOM GGAOF 6G-6.

11. See Barret, L'Afrique occidentale, 2:24–25; Schnapper, La politique et le commerce français, 39.

12. Louet, "Établissements," Gorée et Dépencies IV-2, AN FM SG.

13. Jean-Rémy Bessieux to Aragon, 18 October 1845, ACSE boîte 211.4a, Vicariat des Deux Guinées Divers 1843–1869; Beslier, L'Apôtre du Congo, 58.

14. Contract between W. R. Browne and Tongo, Ibolo, and Mvalie at Corisco, 3 May 1869, Correspondence 1864–1870, WWP Box I.

15. Burton, Two Trips to Gorilla Land, 1:75–76; Bucher, "The Mpongwe," 73.

16. "Communauté du Gabon Rapport Annuel," 1859, ACSE boîte 211.4a, Vicariat des Deux Guinées Divers 1843–1869; Journal de la Mission 1868, 30 January and 20 April 1868 entries, and Journal de la Mission 1869, 23 February and 10 March 1869 entries, ACSE boîte 211.3b Dossier Personnel Monseigneur Le Berre, Journaux de Libreville 1861–1891; Pierre-Marie Le Berre to Archbishop, 15 September 1870, ACSE boîte 4J1.3a, Lettres 1869–1872; Raponda Walker, Souvenirs d'un nonagénaire, 27.

17. Commandant of Gabon to Commandant du Gorée, 9 October 1848, ANSOM GGAOF 6G-5; Journal de la Mission 1877–1878, 4–5 August 1877, ACSE boîte 211.3b, Dossier Personnel Monseigneur Le Berre, Journaux de Libreville 1861–1891.

18. Guennegan to Oeuvre de la Sainte Enfance, 2 February 1861, ACSE boîte 211.4a, Vicariat des Deux Guinées Divers 1843–1869; Raponda Walker, Souvenirs d'un nonagénaire, 27; Reading, Ogowe Bend, 181–82, 205; Nassau, Tales out of School, 47.

19. Kingsley, West African Studies, 88.

20. Ntoko Truman to John Lawrie, 31 July 1880, PCUSA microfilm reel 14.

21. For example, Paul Landau and T. O. Beidelman in their studies of missions in South Africa and Tanganyika make almost no reference to food in their studies of missionary attempts to shape daily social practices. See Beidelman, Colonial Evangelism, 99–152; Landau, Realm of the Word.

22. Hunt, Colonial Lexicon, 118–23.

23. Hunt, Colonial Lexicon, 118–19.

24. Milligan, Fetish Folk, 201–3; Raponda Walker, Souvenirs d'un nonagénaire, 29.

25. Nassau, Tales out of School, 35; Raponda Walker, Souvenirs d'un nonagénaire, 27. For a more detailed discussion of missionary and colonial notions of time, see Martin, Leisure and Society, 72–83.

26. Robert Nassau Diary, 23 May and 4 December 1894, 2 April 1895 entries, RNP.

27. Robert Nassau Diary, 1 July 1895 entry, RNP.

28. Bauer, Goods, Power, History, 151–57.

29. Seuhl, Gabone, 81–82.

30. Portet, En blanc sur les cartes, 59–69.

31. Barret, L'Afrique occidentale, 2:22–23.

32. Lt. Gov. Gabon to Minister of Colonies, 18 October 1889, ANSOM 2B17.

33. Robert Nassau Diary, 22 September 1898 entry, RNP.

34. Stoffel to Le Berre, 25 April 1877, ACSE boîte 4J3.1b, Letters 1877–1892, Lettres 1877–1880; Raponda Walker, Souvenirs d'un nonagénaire, 199.

35. "Communauté de Saint Pierre de Libreville," BCSE 24 (1905–10): 183.

36. "Aperçu de l'oeuvre des soeurs de la conception immaculée à Libreville," 1898, Archives des Soeurs de la Conception Immaculée de Castres, Libreville; Nassau, My Ogowe, 583–84.

37. Gauthier, Grammaire de la langue Mpongwée, xiv–xv.

38. Walker, "The Commerce of the Gaboon," 589.

39. Robert Nassau to Rev. Gillespie, 23 March 1894, PCUSA microfilm reel 21.

40. For example, see Raulin, *Amours congolaises*, 28–29; Procès-verbal du Conseil d'Administration, 29 July 1893, Gabon-Congo VII-11, AN FM SG.

41. Reading, *Ogowe Bend*, 181.

42. William Walker Diary, 21 September 1881 entry, WWP, box 3.

43. Robert Nassau Diary, 15 April 1895 entry, RNP.

44. Lydia Jones to John Laurie, 21 November 1883, PCUSA microfilm reel 18.

45. William Miller to Albert Bushnell, n.d. (1873), PCUSA microfilm reel 13.

46. For a typical example of a mixed wage in goods and money, see Journal 1886, 5 July 1886 entry, ACSE boîte 211.3b, Dossier Personnel Monseigneur Le Berre, Journaux de Libreville 1861–1891.

47. Blim, "Congo," 257–58.

48. Migeod, *Across Equatorial Africa*, 19.

49. Ntoko Truman to Dr. John Laurie, 1 June 1880, PCUSA microfilm reel 14.

50. Mrs. J. B. Cameron to John Laurie, 22 July 1880, PCUSA microfilm reel 14.

51. William Walker to Alfred Walker, 22 July 1880, Correspondence 1879–1883, WWP, box 1.

52. Ntoko Truman to John Laurie, 31 July 1880, PCUSA microfilm reel 14.

53. Joseph Reading to John Laurie, 23 October 1880, PCUSA microfilm reel 14.

54. Ntoko Truman to Dr. John Laurie, 10 October 1881, PCUSA microfilm reel 15.

55. Ntoko Truman to Dr. John Laurie, 10 October 1881.

56. Ntoko Truman to John Gillespie, 5 March 1890, PCUSA microfilm reel 19.

57. James Patton to John Gillespie, 18 December 1889, PCUSA microfilm reel 19.

58. J. Reading, B. Briar, W. Gault to Board of Foreign Missions, 25 September 1889, PCUSA microfilm reel 19.

59. William Gault to Joseph Gillespie, 19 February 1890, PCUSA microfilm reel 19.

60. Gardinier, "Schools of the American Protestant Mission."

61. Rich, "'Une Babylone Noire.'"

62. W. S. Bannerman to John Gillespie, 20 July 1892, PCUSA microfilm reel 20.

63. Commandant of Gabon to Minister of Colonies, 13 November 1882, ANSOM 2B11; Blim, "Congo," 257–58.

64. Milligan, *Fetish Folk*, 116.

65. Reade, *African Sketch Book* 1:26–27; Burton, *Two Trips to Gorilla Land*, 1:13–18.

66. Reade, *African Sketch Book*, 1:46–47.

67. Reade, *African Sketch Book*, 47.

68. Burton, *Two Trips to Gorilla Land*, 1:18.

69. Payeur-Didelot, *Trente mois au continent mystérieux*, 36.

70. A wave of beatings and assaults took place roughly from 1875 through the early 1880s. A full discussion of the brutal treatment many Kru workers received is outside the scope of this work. A good sample of the cases can be found in Commandant of Gabon to Minister of Colonies, 23 September 1876, ANSOM 2B28.

71. Commandant of Gabon to Minister of Colonies, 8 May 1876, ANSOM 2B28.

72. Barret, *L'Afrique occidentale*, 2:388.

73. Capitaine Cornut-Gentille to Commandant of Gabon, 28 October 1882, Gabon XIV-1, AN FM SG.

74. Procès-Verbal du Conseil d'Administration, 7 April 1887, Gabon-Congo VII-11, AN FM SG; Lt. de Montferrand, Captain of *Ariège*, to Minister of the Navy, 25 March 1888, Gabon XIV-1, AN FM SG.

75. Commandant of Gabon to Captain of *Loiret*, 14 August 1874; to Minister of Colonies, 13 November 1882; and to Minister of Colonies, 8 April 1884, in ANSOM 2B28, 2B11, and 2B12, respectively.

76. On the state of French Congo's finances, see Bishop of Libreville Adam to Archbishop Le Roy, 5 October 1896, ACSE boîte 4J1.4b, Correspondance Gabon 1891–1920, Lettres 1893–1900. For ration suppression, see CGFC, "Arrêté portant suppression de la ration au personnel indigene," 23 December 1896, *Bulletin Officiel Administratif du Gabon-Congo* 1897, 4–5.

77. *Bulletin mensuel de l'association des commerçants, industriels, planteurs et colons de Libreville* 1930, ANG carton 443, AEF Gabon Commerce 1923–1936.

78. Momha, "Le Gabon de 1850 à 1929," 129.

79. White, *Sierra Leone's Settler Women Traders*, 60, 70–71; Olukoju, "Maritime Trade in Lagos," 123–24; Martin, *Leisure and Society*, 46.

80. Journal de Vicariat Apostolique des Deux-Guinées, 21 December 1916 entry, ACSE microfilm T2 B1.

81. GGFEA to Lt. Gov. Gabon, 28 January 1922, ANG carton 911 Vivres Frais 1921; Coquery-Vidrovitch, *Le Congo*, 457.

82. Lt. Gov Gabon to IIA, 10 June 1929, ANG carton 823, Presidence de la République Agriculture 1929–1930, AEF Institut International d'Agriculture, Rome.

83. Julien to Macé Faugère, 30 April 1922, ACSE boîte 4J1.7a, Lettres Gabon 1921–1947, Lettres 1921–1924.

84. Rapport Politique Estuaire, March 1906, ANSOM 4(1)D3.

85. Headrick, *Colonialism, Health, and Illness*, 180–81.

86. Journal de la Paroisse de Sainte-Marie de Libreville 1908–1939, 20 September 1925 entry, ACSE microfilm T2 B9.

87. Rapport Politique, Circonscription de l'Estaurie, January 1922, ANSOM 5D52.

88. Rapport Annuel, Colonie du Gabon 1918, 179, ANSOM 4(1)D16.

89. The detail about the rebellion is taken from Commandant Militaire du Gabon to Lt. Gov. Gabon, 2 March 1923, ANG carton 675, Terr. du Gabon, Cabinet du Gouverneur Correspondance au Départ 1916, Chef Batillion Megnou.

90. Commandant Militaire du Gabon to Lt. Gov. Gabon, 2 March 1923.

91. Lt. Gov. Gabon Cadier to GGFEA, 12 March 1923, ANG carton 675.

92. Assemblée Nationale du Gabon, Journal des Débats 1959, Séance du 30 May 1959, 96, ANG.

93. Mecanicien Travaux Publics Celli to Police Commissioner of Libreville, 22 February 1922, ANG 1055 AGCD); Procès-Verbal Celli vs. Ouapa, 4 March 1921.

94. Interview, Simone Saint-Dénis, Plaine Niger, Libreville, 14 December 1999.

95. Interviews, Benoit Messany Nyanguegnona, Batavea, Libreville, 21 January 2000, and Henriette Izouré, Glass, Libreville, 1 September 2000.

96. "Rapport sur les coopératives de l'A.E.F.," 15 January 1951, 26–27, ANSOM 5D50; interview, Simone Saint-Dénis, Plaine Niger, Libreville, 14 December 1999.

97. Interview, Luc-Marc Ivanga, Montagne-Sainte, Libreville, 27 November 1999.

98. For one example, see interview, Simone Saint-Dénis, Plaine Niger, Libreville, 14 December 1999.

99. Bascou-Brescane, *Conditions de vie à Libreville*, 45.

100. A legal case involving several Fang laborers included a reference to eating a can of beef for lunch. Tribunal du premier degree de la commune de Libreville, Affaire Nzang Etogho, 28 July 1938, ANG, Registre de la Région de l'Estuaire 82. Several interviews with elderly Libreville

residents mentioned their fathers either ate or sold canned goods and rice in their stores. Interviews, Joseph-Bernard Mba Okoue, Chef de Quartier, Atong Abé, Libreville, 26 January 2000, and Benoit Nzue Essone, Nzeng Ayong, Libreville, 27 October 2000.

101. Interview, Joseph Ntoutoume Medoua, Ntoum, 23 September 2000.

102. Interview, Madame X, Louis, Libreville, 23 December 1999. The informant requested not to be identified, but the tape remains in the author's possession.

103. Lt. Jouen to President de la commission centrale du côntrole postale, Brazzaville, 15 July and 15 August 1944, ANG 897 P.R. Correspondance 1944, 1955, 1957; Augustin Berger to Madame Berger, 12 November 1944, ACSE boîte 2D5.2b3, Dossier Berger, Lettres du Père à sa famille 1937–1945.

104. Dossier Lettre du Paul Gondjout du 15 mai 1943, Nguema Pierre, Commis d'Administration, Subdivision de Libreville to Gov. du Gabon, 7 June 1943, ANSOM 5D206.

105. Gov. du Gabon Assier de Pompignan to GGFEA, 16 June 1943, ANSOM 5D206.

106. Consul General of Great Britain Bullock to GGFEA, n.d. (September 1944), and GGFEA to Gov. du Gabon, 26 September 1944, ANG carton 704, Commune de Libreville, Correspondances Diverses 1936–1946.

107. Comm. Police Port-Gentil to GGFEA, 1 December 1944, ANG carton 704.

108. "Cooperatives," November 1949, ANG carton 731, Correspondance Diverses 1950–1956.

109. "Rapport concernant l'Inspection des SIP de Kango-Njolé-Lambaréné-Woleu Ntem 15 octobre–8 novembre 1949," 24–25, ANG carton 1024, Administration Générale Correspondance au Départ 1949; Lasserre, Libreville, 184.

110. "Rapport sur les Coopératives de l'A.E.F.," 15 January 1951, 24, ANSOM 5D50.

111. Commandant Gabon to Commissaire de Division, 30 November 1871, ANSOM 2B5; Commandant of Gabon to Capt. Loiret, 9 January 1879, ANSOM 2B8; Procès-Verbal du Conseil d'Administration, 3 July 1886, Gabon-Congo VII-11, AN FM SG; Augustin Berger, "La jubilé du Frère Sidoine Stoeckler," Echo des Missions, March 1937, ACSE boîte 4J1.6b, Divers Gabon 1920–1949, Missionnaires, Prêtres et Soeurs Indigènes.

112. Augustin Berger, "La vie au Gabon," 1935, ACSE boîte 2D5.5b, Fonds Berger, Circulaires du Père Berger 1934–1950.

113. Interviews, Agathe Iwengha, Plaine Niger, Libreville, 31 January 2000, and Albert Edou, Plaine Niger, Libreville, 24 August 2000.

114. Comm. de Police de Libreville to Chef de Region de l'Estuaire, 27 January 1949, ANG carton 571, Affaires Administratives Plaintes, Enquêtes et Requêtes adressées au Chef du Territoire du Gabon 1921–1950.

115. Darlington and Darlington, African Betrayal, 335.

116. Inspecteur Zoccolat, "Politique alimentaire dans le Territoire du Gabon," 6 March 1948, AN FM Affaires Politiques Dossier 2302, Mission d'Inspection Ruffel 2302-2.

117. Inspecteur Zoccolat, "Politique alimentaire."

118. Inspecteur Mazodier, "Conditions d'existance des indigènes dans le Nord-Gabon," 20 January 1948, 4, 18, AN FM Dossier 2302, Mission d'Inspection Ruffel 2302-2.

119. Ruffel to Gov. Gabon Sadoul, 26 March 1948, 96, AN FM Dossier 2302, Mission d'Inspection Ruffel 2302-2.

120. Prats, "Le Gabon: La mise en valeur," 49.

121. Prats, "Le Gabon: La mise en valeur," 76.

122. Lasserre, Libreville, 254–55; Makongo, "L'histoire économique du Gabon," 106.

6. Food Supply in Libreville, 1930–1960

1. Bulletin mensuel de l'association des commerçants, industriels, planteurs et colons de Libreville 12, October–December 1931, ANG carton 443, A.E.F. Gabon Commerce Association des Commerçants, Industriels, Planteurs et Colons de Libreville 1923–1946.

2. Rapport Annuel, Colonie du Gabon 1931, 2, AN FM Comission Guernaut Dossier 61 B37-B38.

3. Théodore Trefon, in a recent article, contends that men who quit timber camps in the 1930s avoided farming but provides no evidence for his statement. See Trefon, "Libreville et son appétence opiniâtre de fôret," 41.

4. Interview, Edouard Soumouma, Chef de Quartier, Derrière l'Hôpital, Libreville, 18 October 2000. The Communauté Française Africaine franc was created in 1945 for use in French African colonies. Prior to this the French franc was the official currency. After 1948, one CFA franc was worth two French francs.

5. Interview, Gabriel Mabenga, Diba-Diba, Libreville, 25 February 2000.

6. Interviews, Charles N'no Ndong, Atong Abé, Libreville, 8 February 2000; Nze Ekomie, Donguila, 20 March 2000; Pierre-Celestin Evoung Ndong, Plaine Niger, Libreville, 3 September 2000; Clement Ossa Nze, Chef de Quartier, Okala, 15 September 2000; Essono, Chef de Quartier, Lalala à Droit, Libreville, 21 September 2000; Joseph Nguema Ndong, Akok, 28 October 2000.

7. Interview, Joseph Nkoghe Bekale, Nzamaligue, 29 March 2000

8. Interview, Evariste Nze Ollome, Cocotiers, Libreville, 19 February 2000.

9. Interview, Joseph Nkoghe Bekale, Nzamaligue, 29 March 2000.

10. For a discussion of resettlement see Pourtier, Le Gabon, 2:102–9.

11. Lasserre, Libreville, 155–57.

12. Chef de Subdivision de Kango Alan MacClatchy, Rapport Politique, 1st semester 1943, 31 July 1943, 5, ANG carton 612, District de Kango Rapport Politique 1943–46, 1954; Chef de Région de l'Estuaire Biscons-Ritay, Rapport Annuel, Région de l'Estuaire 1949, ANG carton 44, Rapport Politique Annuel, Territoire du Gabon 1949.

13. Depopulation is attested by a series of state reports available in the National Archives of Gabon. For some examples, see Rapport Politique, Subdivision de Chinchoua, 2nd semester 1940, and Chef Sub. Chinchoua, Rapports Politiques Chinchoua, 1st and 2nd semesters 1943, both in carton 66; and Chef District Libreville Pierre Rougeot, Rapport Politique Annuel, 1954, carton 14.

14. Chef Subdivision Medouneu, Rapport Politique Annuel 1953, ANG Fonds de Medouneu 2Dj(IV)5, Rapports Politiques 1934–1957.

15. Chef Sub. Chinchoua, Rapport Politique Chinchoua, 2nd semester 1943, ANG carton 66; Journal de la Paroisse de Donguila 1942–1946, 25 August 1943 entry, Donguila Archives; "Etat Comparatif de la Production du Caoutchouc," July 1944, ANG carton 334, Gouverneur Général Correspondance au Départ 1944.

16. Chef Subdivision Kango Alan MacClatchy, Rapport Politique, 1st semester 1943, 31 July 1943, 2, ANG carton 612, District de Kango, Rapport Politique 1943–46, 1954; interview, Félicien Ndong and Jean Ondo, km 12, Libreville, 1 March 2000.

17. Pourtier, "La crise de l'agriculture," 45–46.

18. Interview, Alice Esa Meyo and Mathias Nguema, Lalala, Libreville, 19 August 2000.

19. Interview, Jeanne Assengone Eyeghe and Marie-Therese Bella Eyeghe, Donguila, 20 March 2000.

20. Deuxième Tribunal Indigène de la Commune de Libreville, Affaire Nkoé, 3 March 1938, ANG Registres, Registre 104.

21. Premier Tribunal Indigène de la Commune de Libreville, Affaire Bologho, 21 July 1938, ANG Registres, Registre 82.

22. For a sample of studies on market women in other colonial African cities see Robertson, *Sharing the Same Bowl*, 75–97; Schmidt, *Peasants, Traders and Wives*, 55–57, 71–76, 78–81; Clark, *Onions Are My Husband; Robertson, Trouble Showed the Way*.

23. Fang and Mpongwe informants agreed on this point. Examples include the following: Interviews, Simone Saint-Dénis, Mpongwe, Plaine Niger, Libreville 5, 8, 11, and 14 December 1999; Michel Zimbé, b. 1915, Lalala, Libreville, 5 January 2000; Benoit Messany, Batavea, Libreville, 21 January 2000; Jean Ayong Mevane, Mont-Bouet, Libreville, 7 February 2000; Adolphe Revignet, Ozangue, Libreville, 17 February 2000.

24. Interview, Charles N'no Ndong, Atong Abé, Libreville, 8 February 2000.

25. Interview, Jean Kiala, Joseph Mebeke, Nkembo, Libreville, 11 October 2000.

26. Interviews, Joseph-Bernard Mba Okoue, Chef de Quartier, Atong Abé, Libreville, 26 January 2000; Henriette Izouré, Glass, 1 September 2000.

27. Interviews, Joseph-Bernard Mba Okoue, Chef de Quartier, Atong Abé, Libreville, 26 January 2000; Marie-Charlotte Nyingone, Atong Abé, 27 January 2000; Edouard Soumouma, Chef de Quartier, Derrière l'Hôpital, Libreville, 18 October 2000; Jean Ayong Mebiame, Akok, 28 October 2000.

28. Ndongo Georges to Chef Dept. Estuaire, 8 April 1935, and André Ballay to Chef Dept. Estuaire, 11 April 1935, ANG carton 929, Affaires Civiles 1919–1938; "Les habitants des races Ngouemiénés des quartiers Montagne-Sainte et Abenelang" to Prince Félix Adande, 14 January 1942, ANG carton 1634, Departement de l'Estuaire, correspondance relative aux activités du département 1942.

29. Michel Moureau, Chef de Niger to Jean Abo, "un des agitateurs des Pahouins à Niger-Glass," 11 May 1938, AN FM Affaires Politiques 653.

30. For some of the voluminous discussions on thus score, see Louis Berre to Chef Dept. Estuaire Assier de Pompignan, 1 February 1939, ANG carton 1172, Région de l'Estuaire Correspondance Arrivée et Départ 1930–1948; Andre Kringer, Georges Damas, Louis Berre and the families of Quaben, Louis, Barro and Kringer to Chef Dept. Estuaire, 1 February 1939, ANG carton 1634, Commune de Libreville, Correspondance Administrative Ordinaire.

31. Chef Reg. Estuaire Lafont to Gov. Gabon, 28 March 1946 and Ndongo Georges to Gov. Gabon, 15 April 1946, ANG carton 501, Administration Générale Correspondance Diverse 1946.

32. Comm. Police Libreville Dirand, Procès-Verbale Paul Biffo and Nganga Jean, 27 March 1946, ANG carton 501, Administration Générale Correspondance Diverse 1946.

33. Interview, Pierre Bissang et al., Gros Bosquet, Libreville, 16 October 2000.

34. La Population Fang de Libreville to Gov. Gabon, 20 October 1945, ANSOM 5D222.

35. Interview, Pierre Bissang et al., Gros Bosquet, Libreville, 16 October 2000.

36. "La Population Fang de Libreville" to Gov. Gabon, 20 October 1945; interview, Felicien Ndong and Jean Ondo, km 12, Libreville, 1 March 2000.

37. Interview, Ocloo family, Batavea, Libreville, 5 March 2000.

38. Lasserre, *Libreville*, 253–55.

39. Sec. Gen. Castex to Chef Region Estuaire, 19 September 1947, ANG carton 118, Affaires Economiques Correspondance au Départ à la Région de l'Estuaire 1947; Gov. Gabon Sadoul to Victor Paul Schummer, 11 August 1948, ANG carton 1032, Affaires Politiques et Sociales Correspondance au Départ 1948.

40. "Activités des Diverses Pêcheries de Libreville," Commissaire de Police de Libreville to Maire de la Commune de Libreville, 22 November 1957, ANG carton 988, Administration Générale Correspondances Diverses 1957–1960.

41. Subdivision de Cocobeach, Rapport Annuel 1954, ANG carton 31, Subdivision de Cocobeach, Rapports Politiques 1943–1954; Chef Reg. Estuaire Bonamy to Gov. Gabon, 27 October 1955, ANG Registre carton 13, Registre des Correspondances au Départ du Chef de Region de l'Estuaire 1955; Interview, Bertrand Alo Essone, Bambou Chine, Libreville, 1 November 2000.

42. Chef Reg. Estuaire Bonamy to Gov. Gabon, 27 October 1955.

43. During my stay in Donguila in March 2000, villagers awaited Nigerians rather than fish on their own.

44. Rapport Annuel, Colonie du Gabon, 1921, ANSOM 4(1)D19; Rapport Politique, Dept. Estuaire, 2nd trimester 1938, ANSOM 4(1)D46.

45. Service de l'Agriculture, Rapports Annuels 1958 et 1960, Rapport Annuel 1960, 9, ANG carton 762, Ministère de l'Agriculture.

46. Boserup, Conditions of Agricultural Growth.

47. For beriberi see Rapport Annuel, Colonie du Gabon 1932, "Rapport Sanitaire," 5–6, AN FM Commission Guernaut Dossier 61 B37-B38; Médecin-Chef Estuaire T. C. Jolly to Admin. Sup. du Gabon, 1 July 1935, ANG carton 136, Médecin-Chef de l'Estuaire à M. l'Administrateur Superior du Gabon Lettre 235 au Sujet de L'Epidemie du Béribéri 1 Juillet 1935.

48. GGFEA Antonetti to Gov. Gabon, 28 April 1933, ANG carton 78, Service de Santé Rapports Medical 1927–1933. The governor of Gabon praised the efforts of Estuary officials as well. See Gov. Gabon Louis Bonvin to Chef Dept. Estuaire, 14 March 1935, ANG carton 1213, Région du Gabon, Correspondance Officielle 7 Mars–16 Avril 1935.

49. Chef Reg. Estuaire Luciani to Inspecteur de la France d'Outre-Mer, 8 March 1955, ANG, Reigstre 13, Registre des Correpondances au Départ du Chef de Région de l'Estuaire 1955.

50. Bassett, The Peasant Cotton Revolution, 55–56.

51. Léon Mba to GGFEA, 2 July 1929, ANSOM 5D69, Dossier Léon Mba.

52. Journal de Voyages 1932–1933, January–February 1932 entries, Donguila Archives.

53. Interview, Veronique Ada Nkoghe and Mathieu Ndong Essono, Nzamaligue, 29 March 2000.

54. Rapport Medical, 4th semester 1948, ANG, Service de la Santé Publique, carton H172, Région Sanitaire de l'Estuaire, Rapports Annuels 1944–1945, 1952–1954.

55. On Béti chiefs and agriculture, see Guyer, "Feeding Yaoundé."

56. Procès-Verbal du Conseil des Notables du Département de l'Estuaire, 14 September 1940, ANSOM 6YI Registre des Procès-Verbals du Conseil des Notables du Département de l'Estuaire 1937–1946; Rapport Politique Annuel, Colonie du Gabon, 1942, ANSOM 4(1)D50.

57. Chef Sub. Chinchoua, Rapport Politique Chinchoua, 2nd semester 1943, ANG carton 66, Rapport Politique Subdivision de Chinchoua 2nd semester 1940; Journal de la Paroisse de Donguila 1942–1946, 25 August 1943 entry, Donguila Archives; Chef Dept. Estuaire Chevalier to Gov. Gabon, 31 July 1944, ANG carton 1172, Région de l'Estuaire Correspondance Arrivée et Depart 1930–1948.

58. Deposition Awanlele Remy, 18 September 1943, ANG carton 1172, Region de l'Estuaire Corr. 1930–1948.

59. Chef Sub. Kango Alan MacClatchy, Rapport Politique, 31 July 1943, ANG carton 612, District de Kango Rapport Politique 1943–46, 1954; Chef Travaux Publics Carayan to Gov.

Gabon, 7 August 1944, and Chief Sub. Libreville Madoc to Chef Travaux Publics, September 1944, both in ANG Travaux Publics, K10 Dossier Route Libreville-Owendo 1922–1951.

60. Lt. Jouen to President de la commission centrale du contrôle postale, 15 July 1944, ANG carton 897, Correspondance 1944, 1955, 1957.

61. Ogino Hilaire, "Compte Rendu," 21 August 1944, ANG carton 288, Confidentiel Correspondance Diverses 1938–1947.

62. Lt. Jouen to President de la commission centrale du contrôle postale, 30 September 1944, ANG carton 897.

63. Journal de la Paroisse de Donguila 1942–1946, 21 September 1944, 15 and 26 February 1945 entries, Donguila Archives; Lt. Jouen to President de la commission centrale du contrôle postale, 15 October and 30 November 1944, ANG carton 897, Correspondance 1944, 1955, 1957.

64. Journal de la Paroisse de Donguila 1942–1946, 23 April 1945 entry, Donguila Archives.

65. Superior of the Sainte Marie Mission to Police Commissioner of Libreville, 24 November 1945, ACSE boîte 2D60.1b, Fonds Pouchet Relations avec l'Administration Française, Relations avec l'Administration Française.

66. Chef Dept. Estuaire Martocq to Gov. Gabon, 13 May 1941, ANG carton 574, P.R. Affaires concernant la Police des Marchés 1937–1941; Gov. Gabon Assier de Pompignan to Chef Dept. Estuaire, 29 August 1942, and Chef Dept. Estuaire to Gov. Gabon, 21 September 1942, both in ANG carton 954, Administration Générale Affaires Politiques et Sociales 1936.

67. Procès-Verbal du Conseil des Notables du Département de l'Estuaire , 21 August 1943, ANSOM 6YI.

68. On roads and state power in Gabon, see Pourtier, Le Gabon, 2:219–28.

69. Thompson and Adloff, Emerging States, 145–47.

70. Chef Reg. Estuaire Luciani to Inspecteur de la France d'Outre-Mer, 8 March 1955, ANG Reigstre 13, Registre des Correpondances au Départ du Chef de Région de l'Estuaire 1955; Myagamory Leonard, manager of the Cooperative des Paysans Librevilleois to Ministre de l'Agriculture Pierre Yembit, 17 July 1957, ANG carton 350, Affaires concernant la Ministère de l'Agriculture, Correspondance au Depart, 1957–1960.

71. Sec.-Tres. de SIP Estuaire to Chef Dept. Estuaire, 13 January 1944, ANG carton 157, Société de Prévoyance de l'Estuaire (hereafter cited as ANG 157 SIP); Vandji, Soeurs, 140.

72. Angoue-Nzoghe, "L'appel à l'AEF," 178.

73. Chef du Service du Travaux Publics, "Construction des voies de communication 1933," n.d. (1934), ANG, Archives du Service des Travaux Publics, carton K3, Routes des Subdivisions de Libreville, Kango, Chinchoua et Cocobeach. A general discussion on road-building projects is available for the late colonial period in Pourtier, Le Gabon, 2:219–28.

74. For a small sample of forced labor and its social consequences in Central Africa, see Austen and Headrick, "Equatorial Africa under Colonical Rule," 37–38; Jean-Luc Vellut, "Mining in the Belgian Congo," in Birmingham and Martin, History of Central Africa, 2:145–48; Northrup, Beyond the Bend in the River, 126–27, 153–56, 197–201; Osuama Likaka, Rural Society and Cotton in Colonial Zaire.

75. Chef Dept. Estuaire Assier de Pompignan to Gov. Gabon, 15 December 1938, ANG carton 488, Administration Generale; Meyo-Me-Nkoghe, "La vie économique et sociale de Kango de 1900 à 1950," 77–78.

76. Thompson and Adloff, Emerging States, 146–47, 361–62.

77. Lasserre, Libreville, 136.

78. P. Pion to Lt. Gov. Gabon, 24 August 1928, ANG carton 928, Correspondance Générale, Affaires Civiles 1928–1929.

79. Procès-Verbal du Conseil des Notables du Département de l'Estuaire, 18 July 1939, ANSOM 6Y>1; Ndong Mba Francois, Edzang Pascal, Nzogo Florentin [Medouneu] to Chef Dept. Estuaire, 21 April 1944, ANG carton 157 SIP.

80. "Le Congres Pahouin," 27 February 1947, ACSE, boîte 2D60.1b, Fonds Pouchet, Relations avec l'Administration Française, Correspondance Affaires Africaines 1929–1948.

81. Thompson and Adloff, Emerging States, 168–69.

82. Chef Dept. Estuaire A. Servel to Gov. Gabon, 30 June 1937, ANG carton 986, Administration Générale, Société de Prévoyance de l'Estuaire 1939–1941; Chef Dept. Estuaire Assier de Pompignan to Gov. Gabon, 9 August 1938, and Gov. Gabon Parisot to Chef Dept. Estuaire, 15 August 1938, both in ANG carton 907, Compte Définitif de Budget de la SIP 1938.

83. Gov. Gabon Masson, 4 May 1939 (incomplete and damaged document), ANG carton 986, Administration Générale, Société de la Prévoyance de l'Estuaire 1939–1941; Inspecteur Devouton to Ministre des Colonies, 19 August 1939, AN FM Affairs Politques 649-4.

84. Gov. Gabon Yves Digo to Georges Gnambault, 3 July 1952, ANG carton 1010, Correspondance Générale, Correspondance au Départ 1952; Lasserre, Libreville, 173; Thompson and Adloff, Emerging States, 130–32.

85. Rapport de la Troisième Commission, n.d. (1950), ANG carton 1636, Conseil Réprésentatif du Gabon, Rapports des Commissions 1950; Thompson and Adloff, Emerging States, 365.

86. Conseil Réprésentatif du Gabon, Journal des Débats, Séance, 6 March 1950, 24–26, ANG.

87. Compte Définitif de Budget de la SIP 1938, President de SIP [Chef Dept. Estuaire], Compte Définitif, SIP Estuaire 1938, n.d. (September 1938), ANG carton 907.

88. "Rapport concernant l'Inspection des SIP de Kango-Njolé-Lambaréné-Woleu Ntem," 8 November 1949, 2–5, ANG carton 1024, Administration Générale, Correspondance au Départ 1949.

89. "Rapport d'Inspection Concernant la Société Indigène de Prévoyance de l'Estuaire," 5 October 1949, 3, ANG carton 1024.

90. "Rapport d'Inspection," 5 October 1949, 8–9; Chef District Libreville, Rapport Politique, January 1950, ANG carton 116, Rapports Politiques, Region de l'Estuaire 1949–1950.

91. Procès-Verbal du conseil des notables du département de l'Estuaire, 21 August 1943, ANSOM 6YI; Chef Dept. Estuaire Chevalier to Gov. Gabon, 31 July 1944, ANG carton 1172, Région de l'Estuaire, Correspondance Arrivée et Depart 1930–1948.

92. Inspecteur des Affaires Administratives Louvel to Gov. Gabon, 23 July 1944, ANG carton 1172.

93. Interviews, Antoine Ndong Nguema, Nzeng Ayong, Libreville, 6 September 2000; Edouard Soumouma, Chef de Quartier, Derrière l'Hôpital, Libreville, 18 October 2000; Jean Ayong Mebiame, Akok, 28 October 2000.

94. Journal de Voyages 1931–1932, Tournée 10 January–20 February 1930, 26–28 January 1930 entries, Donguila Archives.

95. RP Defranould to Très Révérend Père, 14 June 1934, ACSE, boîte 4J1.7a, Lettres Gabon 1921–1947, Lettres 1931–1934.

96. Chef Poste Medouneu, Rapport Politique, 2eme Semester 1936, ANG Fonds du Medouneu 2Dj(IV)5, Rapports Politiques 1934–1957.

97. Chef Dept. Woleu Ntem to Chef Sub. Medouneu, 14 December 1939, and Chef Sub. Medouneu to Chef Sub. Cocobeach, 27 December 1939, ANG carton 157 SIP.

98. Chef Sub. Cocobeach to Chef Dept. Estuaire, 13 January 1940, ANG carton 157 SIP.

99. Chef Secteur Agricole to Chef Dept. Estuaire, 16 January 1940, and Chef Sub. Mitzic to Chef Sub. Medouneu, 11 September 1940, ANG carton 157 SIP.

100. Journal de Poste de Medouneu 1941–1947, 28 June 1941 entry, ANG Registre 56; Med. Commandant Charpentier to Med. Chef du Service de la Santé au Gabon, 20 July 1941, ANG, Service de la Santé Publique, carton H10, Correspondance au Départ et à l'Arrivée du Directeur Local de la Santé Publique 1940–1941.

101. Interview, Evariste Nze Ollome, Cocotiers, Libreville, 19 February 2000

102. Interview, Benoit Nzue Essone, Nzeng Ayong, Libreville, 27 October 2000.

103. Interview, Benoit Nzue Essone, 27 October 2000.

104. Chef Sub. Medouneu to Chef Dept. Estuaire, 22 February 1943, ANG carton 157 SIP.

105. Chef Dept. Estuaire to Chef Sub. Medouneu, 10 March 1943, ANG carton 157 SIP.

106. Ndong Mba Francois, Edzang Pascal, et al. to Chef Dept. Estuaire, 21 April 1944, ANG carton 157 SIP.

107. Chef Dept. Estuaire Mercat to Chef Dept. Woleu Ntem, 10 April 1943, ANG carton 157 SIP.

108. Chef Dept. Estuaire Mercat to Gov. Gabon, 22 April 1943; Chef Dept. Estuaire Mercat to Chef Sub. Ndjole, 14 May 1943; Chef Dept. Woleu Ntem Chevalier to Chef Dept. Estuaire, 15 December 1943, all in ANG carton 157 SIP.

109. Chef Sub. Medouneu to Chef Dept. Estuaire, 5 April 1943, ANG carton 157 SIP.

110. Chef Sub. Medouneu to Chef Dept. Estuaire, 23 August 1943, and Sec. SIP Estuaire to Chef Dept. Estuaire, 13 January 1944, ANG carton 157 SIP.

111. Chef Sub. Medouneu to Chef Dept. Estuaire, 5 February 1944, ANG carton 157 SIP.

112. Chef Dept. Woleu Ntem Chevalier to Chef Dept. Estuaire, 21 January 1944, and 20 February 1944, ANG carton 157 SIP.

113. Chef Dept. Estuaire to Chef Sub. Chinchoua, 18 February 1944, and Chef Dept. Estuaire to Commandant Militaire du Gabon, 26 February 1944, ANG carton 157 SIP.

114. Sec.-Tres. SIP Estuaire to Chef Dept. Estuaire, 19 February 1944, and Chef Dept. Estuaire Chevalier to Chef Sub. Medouneu, 24 March 1944, ANG carton 157 SIP.

115. Chef Dept. Woleu Ntem, 15 December 1945 and Chef Dept. Woleu Ntem, facture SIP Woleu Ntem, 9 March 1946, ANG carton 405, Société de Prévoyance de l'Estuaire, Pieces Comptable 1941–1942, 1946. On European support see Chef Dept. Estuaire, 5 September 1944, ANG carton 157 SIP. On abandonment see Inspecteur Zoccolat, "Politique alimentaire dans le Territoire du Gabon," 6 March 1948, 7–8, AN FM Affaires Politiques Dossier 2302, Mission d'Inspection Ruffel 2302-2.

116. Thompson and Adloff, Emerging States, 366.

117. Administrators rejected sixteen out of sixteen applications sent in 1941 and 1942. See ANG carton 405, Société de Prévoyance de l'Estuaire Demandes de Prêts Agricoles 1942.

118. The rejection notice was stapled to Valentin Bibang and Jean-Baptiste Nzé to Maire de Libreville, 24 June 1941, in ANG carton 405.

119. Rapport de la Troisième Commission (Affaires Sociales), 30 August 1950, ANG carton 1636, Conseil Répresentatif du Gabon Rapports du Commissions.

120. Léon Mba to GGFEA, 7 June 1957, ANG carton 86, Correspondance au Départ Adressées au GGFEA 1957.

121. Chef Dist. Libreville Naudin to Chef Reg. Estuaire, 9 June 1959; Chef Dist. Kango Gilbert Mus to Chef Reg. Estuaire, 15 June 1959; Chef Reg. Estuaire Combes to Premier Ministre Léon Mba, 22 June 1959, all in ANG carton 988, Administration Générale Correspondances Diverses 1957–1960.

122. Philemon Payret to Pres. Rep. Gabonaise, 10 January 1959, and President Léon Mba to Blaise Paraiso, 15 December 1959, ANG carton 642, GGFEA Correspondance au Départ et à l'Arrivée 1950–1959; Dogoue to Léon Mba, 29 January 1959, ANG carton 988.

123. Dirigents du Sous-Comité du BDG de Lalala et Nkembo to Léon Mba, 27 July 1959, ANG carton 642.

124. Bernault, *Démocratie*, 314–15.

125. The move took place in 1958 or 1959. Megne M'Ellang, "Les problèmes liés à la situation et au site du marché Mont-Bouet," 3.

126. Directeur de la Station d'Elevage Fontan to President de la République Gabonaise, 21 February 1959, ANG carton 350, Affaires Concernant la Ministère de l'Agriculture 1957–1960; Cruiziot, Gaudefroy-Demombynes and Magnon, "Les Problèmes du développement rural au Gabon," République Gabonaise, Ministère de l'Agriculture, Rapport de Mission, 1961, 48. On seed for urban gardeners see Service de l'Agriculture, Rapports Annuel, 1960, 219, ANG carton 762, Ministère de l'Agriculture. On neglect see République Gabonaise, Ministère de l'Agriculture, Rapport Annuel, 1963, 59–60; Cruziot et al., "Rapport," 44–45.

127. Pourtier, "La crise de l'agriculture"; Yates, *Rentier*.

128. Wunder, *Oil Wealth*, 107–11.

129. Inspecteur Zoccolat, "Politique alimentaire dans le Territoire du Gabon," 6 March 1948, 7–8, AN FM Affairs Politiques Dossier 2302, Mission d'Inspection Ruffel 2302-2.

130. Interview, Marie-Therese Ampoué, Montaigne-Sainte, 17 July 2004.

131. Prince Adande Rapontchombo to Leon Soungani, commis BAO Port-Gentil, 26 October 1943, ANSOM 2D61. Félix himself does not seem to have supported the protest; on the contrary, he claimed Njembe members refused to accept his authority. See Félix Adende, Chef de Glass to Chef Dept. Estuaire, 25 October 1943, ANG carton 1634, Commune de Libreville, Correspondance Administrative Ordinaire 1943.

132. Félix Adende, Chef de Glass to Chef Dept. Estuaire, 25 October 1943.

133. Michel Do Marcolino to Chef Dept. Estuaire, 2 June 1942, ANG carton 1172, Région de l'Estuaire, Correspondance Arrivée et Départ 1930–1948.

134. Comm. Police Libreville Dirand to Chef Dept. Estuaire, 10 June 1942, ANG carton 1172.

135. Pierre Marie-Francois Akenda to GGFEA, 10 August 1942; Lt. Col. Blochet, Commandant Militaire du Gabon to Gov. Gabon, 22 September 1942; Chef des Services des Travaux Publics to Gov. Gabon, 3 October 1942, all in ANG carton 364, Administration Générale, Correspondance au Départ 1940–1942.

136. Gov. Gabon Assier de Pompignan to Commandant Militaire du Gabon, 21 August 1942, ANG carton 364; Commandant Militaire Gabon Driaud to Chef Dept. Estuaire, 31 May 1943, ANG carton 1634, Commune de Libreville Correspondance Administrative Ordinaire.

137. Officials took a similar position in Lambaréné in Central Gabon in the 1930s and 1940s. See Gray and Ngolet, "Lambaréné, *Okoumé* and the Transformation of Labor," 103–6.

138. Affaire Ossimba Gide, 5 August 1937; Affaire Edouard Minko, 12 August 1937; and Affaire Memba, 12 August 1937, all in ANG Registre 82, Registre du 1er Dégré du Tribunal Indigène de la Commune de Libreville 1937–1939.

139. Affaire N'Dilla, 5 August 1937, ANG Registre 82.

140. Affaire Oke Koua, 18 November 1937, ANG Registre 82.

141. Affaire Touissant Kombegnondo, 17 June 1937, ANG Registre 82.

142. Laurent Retigat to Gov. Gabon, 28 May 1938, ANG carton 602, Gouvernement Général, Secours Pécunaires aux Indigènes Nécessiteux 1942.

143. Marie Tongouni to Gov. Gabon, 6 February 1947, ANG carton 587, Conseil Répresentatif Session Ordinaire du 31 Mars 1947 et Secours aux Indigènes 1947; Assisante Sociale Boudoux, "Enquête Mepapa Henri," 20 July 1949, and Assistante Sociale Boudoux, "Enquête Nguema Isam Paul," 31 August 1949, ANG carton 268, Demandes de Secours par les Indigènes 1949; Assistante Sociale, "Enquête sociale sur la situation de N'Kiyeme Cécile," 24 March 1954, ANG carton 282, Demandes de Secours 1953–1957.

144. Gabriel Antchoué to Gov. Gabon, 8 March 1949; Comm. Police Libreville to Chef de Reg. Estuaire, 1 April 1949, both in ANG carton 268.

145. Tchitelika Nyambi to Gov. Gabon, n.d. (1949), and Comm. Police Libreville to Chef Reg. Estuaire, 25 July 1949, ANG carton 268.

146. Akota Agathe, Akébé to Gov. Gabon, 7 August 1944, and Comm. Police de Libreville to Chef Dept. Estuaire, 21 September 1944, ANG carton 474, Secours 1944–1946.

147. Ossouka Marthe to Gov. Gabon, 3 August 1944, and Comm. Police de Libreville to Chef Dept. Estuaire, 12 August 1944, ANG carton 474.

148. Helène Beyo, Oloumi, Libreville to Gov. Gabon, 3 March 1944, ANG carton 474.

149. Veuve Assengone Pauline to Chef Reg. Estuaire, 30 December 1948, ANG carton 268.

150. Interview, Essono, Chef de Quartier, Lalala à Droit, Libreville, 21 September 2000.

151. Interviews, Simone Saint-Dénis, Plaine Niger, Libreville, 11 December 1999; Adolphe Revignet, Ozangue, 17 February 2000.

152. GGFEA Eboué to Gov. Gabon, 30 April 1942, ANG carton 602, Gouvernement Général, Secours Pécunaires aux Indigènes Nécessiteux 1942.

153. GGFEA Eboué to Gov. Gabon, 30 April 1942.

154. Interviews, Jean Bongolo, Derrière l'Hôpital, Libreville, 24 November 1999; Delphine Nzoghe, Lalala, Libreville, 19 January 2000.

155. Bascou-Brescane, Conditions de vie à Libreville, 64.

156. Comm. de Police de Libreville, "Activités des Diverses Pêcheries de Libreville," 22 November 1957, ANG carton 988, Administration Générale, Correspondances Diverses 1957–1960; interview, Henriette Izouré, Glass, Libreville, 1 September 2000.

157. Interview, Annette Folqué, Plaine Niger, Libreville, 21 December 1999.

158. The neighborhood Camp des Boys at the edge of Louis was set up as a home for domestic servants of Gabonese ministers living in the ritzy neighborhood of Batterie IV in Louis. Interview, Ella Engouang Appolinaire Moren, Camp de Boys, Libreville, 2 March 2000.

159. Benoit Anghiley, "Chantier Charles Schmidt personnel," 13 April 1930, ANG carton 1172, Région de l'Estuaire Correspondance Arrivée et Départ 1930–1948.

160. Lasserre, Libreville, 281.

161. Interviews, Felicien Ndong and Jean Ondo, km 12, Libreville, 1 March 2000; Pierre-Celestin Evoung Ndong, Plaine Niger, Libreville, 3 September 2000.

162. Bascou-Brescane, Conditions de vie à Libreville, 45.

163. Lasserre, Libreville, 288–93.

164. Abbé Jean-Baptiste Adiwa, "Libreville Chronique Litteraire et Ethnographique," 1946, ACSE, boîte 2D60.5a, Fonds Pouchet Paroisses de Libreville.

165. Sessions de la Commission Permanent de l'Assemblée Territoriale du Gabon 1954, Séance 10 June 1954, 8, ANG. A few farmers threatened with little success to raise prices collectively in the following year.

166. "Note d'Information Manifestations Diverses," Police Commissioner of Libreville, 8 July 1955, ANG carton 116, Rapports Politiques Région de l'Estuaire 1949–1950.

167. Bascou-Brescane, *Conditions de vie à Libreville*, 62.

168. Lasserre, *Libreville*, 291.

169. Interviews, Joseph-Bernard Mba Okoue, Chef de Quartier, Atong Abé, Libreville, 26 January 2000; Marie-Charlotte Nyingone, Atong Abé, Libreville 27 January 2000.

170. Interview, Charles N'no Ndong, Atong Abé, Libreville, 8 February 2000.

171. Interview, Felicien Ndong and Jean Ondo, km 12, Libreville, 1 March 2000.

7. European Culinary Practices in Colonial Libreville

1. Mintz, *Tasting Food, Tasting Freedom*.

2. McNee, "Food Cultures and Food for Thought," 171.

3. For several intriguing examples of studies that probe racial differences, see Bickford-Smith, *Ethnic Pride and Racial Difference in Victorian Cape Town*; Ann Laura Stoler, "Sexual Affronts and Racial Frontiers."

4. One interesting exception to this trend is Procida, "Feeding the Imperial Appetite."

5. Peters, "National Preferences and Colonial Cuisine."

6. Ordonnateur to Commandant of Gabon, 4 April 1850, ANSOM 2B1.

7. Commandant of Gabon Brisset to Commandant de Gorée, 28 March, 25 April, and 9 October 1848, ANSOM GGAOF 6G-5.

8. "Rapport sur la situation de denrées de l'Ordannateur," 1 October 1863, ANSOM 2B31; Commandant of Gabon to Commissaire de Division, 30 November 1871, ANSOM 2B5.

9. M'Bokolo, *Noirs et blancs*, 154.

10. The ability of coastal peoples to cut Europeans off from supplies is well attested to in the literature on slavery. For some examples, see Kea, *Settlements, Trade, and Polities in the Seventeenth Century Gold Coast*; Brooks, *Landlords and Strangers*; Hawthorne, *Planting Rice and Harvesting Slaves*, 178–81.

11. Reade, *African Sketch Book*, 1:91–98.

12. Reade, *African Sketch Book*, 1:20.

13. Nordick, "Le Gabon," 158.

14. For example, several British traders tortured a cook who had supposedly stolen meat in 1876. See Commandant of Gabon Clement to M. Taylor, 3 April 1876, ANSOM 2B28.

15. Commandant of Gabon to Minister of Colonies, 10 January 1873, ANSOM 2B28.

16. Payeur-Didelot, *Trente mois au continent mystérieux*, 120.

17. Briault, *Zéro*, 65–66.

18. For a lengthy discussion of European attitudes toward African cooking, see Hansen, *Distant Companions*.

19. Commandant of Gabon to Minister of Colonies, 1 July 1886, ANSOM 2B15; Lasserre, *Libreville*, 83.

20. Beidelman, "Altruism and Domesticity," 126–27; Huber, "Dangers of Immorality," 193.

21. Mrs. J. B. Cameron to John Laurie, 22 July 1880, PCUSA microfilm reel 14.

22. "Apostolat des Soeurs," 25, Archives des Soeurs de la Conception Immaculée de Castres, Libreville.

23. Burton, *Two Trips to Gorilla Land*, 1:6.

24. "Note de la mani [sic] de M. Petit," 9 September 1895, Gabon-Congo XVII-1a, AN FM SG.

25. Nassau, "West African Native Foods," 160–62.

26. John L. Wilson, "Excursion to King William's Town," 8 July 1842, ABC 15.1, Western Africa, vol. 2, West Africa 1838–1844, ABCFM Papers; Nordick, "Le Gabon," 231-32.

27. Fourneau, *Au vieux Congo*, 132.

28. Commandant of Gabon to Minister of Colonies, 8 June 1883, ANSOM 2B11.

29. Albert Londres, *Terre d'Ébène* (Paris: Albin Michel, 1929), 222.

30. Du Chaillu, *Explorations and Adventures*, 30.

31. William Walker to Rufus Anderson, 3 January 1862, ABC 15.1, Western Africa, vol. 4, West Africa 1860–1871, ABCFM Papers.

32. Commandant Particulier to Commandant of Gabon, 30 July 1862, ANSOM 2B31.

33. For a discussion of poison beliefs in South Africa, see Bunn, "Brown Serpent of the Rocks."

34. M'Bokolo, *Noirs et blancs*, 84–85.

35. French colonial officials lagged behind their English rivals in malarial treatment. See Cohen, "Malaria and French Imperialism."

36. Robert Nassau Diary, 20 February 1891 entry, RNP.

37. Milligan, *Fetish Folk*, 52.

38. Delorme, "Lettre du 16 Janvier 1880," 279–80.

39. Nassau, *Fetichism in West Africa*, 184–85.

40. Raponda Walker and Sillans, *Plantes utiles*.

41. Polaillon and Carville, *Étude physiologique sur les effets toxiques*.

42. Nassau, *Fetishism in West Africa*, 263.

43. Barret, *L'Afrique occidentale*, 2:131.

44. Migeod, *Across Equatorial Africa*, 16.

45. This incident is taken from Nassau, *Fetichism in West Africa*, 261–62.

46. Commandant of Gabon to Minister of Colonies, 17 August 1883, ANSOM 2B11.

47. Commandant of Gabon to Minister of Colonies, 17 August 1883.

48. Ratanga-Atoz, "Résistances," 101–2.

49. Puleston, *African Drums*, 82–87. Puleston also reported Carlill's death.

50. Kingsley, *Travels in West Africa*, 655.

51. Journal de la Paroisse de Saint-Pierre de Libreville 1884–1914, 19, 21, and 22 August 1905 entries, ACSE microfilm T2 B2 Gabon.

52. Journal de la Paroisse de Sainte-Marie de Libreville 1908–1939, 31 May 1915 entry, ACSE microfilm T2 B9 Gabon.

53. "Communauté de Saint-Pierre de Liberville," BCSE 23 (1903–6): 23.

54. Blache, *Vrais noirs*, 74–75.

55. The following is taken from Dossier Affaire Fergusson, Minutes Cour Criminiel de l'AEF, 25–28 June 1922, ANSOM 5D52.

56. Geschiere, *The Modernity of Witchcraft*, 22.

57. Geschiere, *The Modernity of Witchcraft*, 212.

58. Dutch settlers in Indonesia integrated supernatural beliefs into their daily lives as well. See Gouda, *Dutch Culture Overseas*, 165–67.

59. Lt. Gov. Gabon Bernard, "Arrêté réglement le marché de Libreville et fixant les droits de place," 13 February 1928, JOAEF 1928, 279–80; Rapport Politique, Dept. de l'Estuaire, 1st trimester 1935, ANSOM 4(1)D41; Chef des Services des Travaux Publics to Gov. Gabon, 3 October 1942, ANG 364 Administration Générale Correspondance au Départ 1940–1942.

60. "Arrêtés," Chef Dept. Estuaire, 17 July 1943, 3 August 1944, and 22 September 1948, ANG carton 574, Affaires concernant la Police des Marchés 1937–1941.

61. Circonscription de l'Estuaire, Commune de Libreville, Liste des Patentes, 28 November 1930, ANG carton 613, Rapports Economiques, Terr. du Gabon 1923–1953.

62. Interview, Evariste Nze Ollome, Cocotiers, Libreville, 19 February 2000.

63. Félix Adande Rapontchombo to Gov. Gabon, 9 September 1948, ANG carton 892, Affaires Politiques et Sociales 1948–1949.

64. Conklin, Mission to Civilize, 151–211.

65. Swanson, "Sanitation Syndrome"; Curtin, "Medical Knowledge and Urban Planning"; Parnell, "Creating Racial Privilege."

66. Valdi, Le Gabon: L'homme contre la forêt, 64–67; Lasserre, Libreville, 47, 244–46.

67. Conklin, "Redefining 'Frenchness.'"

68. For details on European women's lives and social status in Brazzaville, see Martin, Leisure and Society, 189–94.

69. Rapport Politique, Circonscription de l'Estuaire, 4eme Semestre 1927, ANSOM 4(1)D33; Rapport Politique, Dept. de l'Estuaire, 1er trimestre 1936, ANSOM 4(1)D43; Inspecteur des Affaires Administratives Bartoli for Gov. Gabon Masson to GGFEA (Affaires Politiques), 31 May 1939, ANG carton 318, Correspondance Diverse 1939–1942.

70. Lasserre, Libreville, 86.

71. Boisneuf to Minister of Colonies, 5 April 1922, AN FM Affaires Politique 117-3, Dossier Boisneuf 1922–1923.

72. "Un Gabonais, Au bord Asie" to Lt. Gov. Gabon, n.d. (1921), ANG 1055 AGCD 1922.

73. Lasserre, Libreville, 273–74.

74. Brouillet, L'avion du blanc, 48–56.

75. Trautmann, Tu y reviendras, 43; Seuhl, Gabone, 81–82.

76. Delaporte, A la découverte de . . . la vie coloniale, 79–80, 104–5.

77. Scholars have considered the role of the military in introducing French consumers to canned foods but have not looked at the role of empire in shaping tastes in this area. Bruegel, "How the French Learned to Eat Canned Food."

78. Delimitation du Consortium Forestier, rapports sur les exploitations et activités, Chef Circ. Estuaire Pechayrand, "Rapport," 1 August 1925, ANG Eaux et Forêt 378.

79. Balandier, Ambiguous Africa, 152.

80. Gov. Gabon Masson to GGFEA, 30 April 1939, ANG carton 506, Affaires Concenant Echanges Commerciaux; "Arrêté," Gov. Gabon, 4 August 1947, ANG carton 574, Affaires Concernant la Police des Marchés 1937–1951; Conseil Répresentatif du Gabon, Journal des Débats 1951, Séance du 16 October 1951, 234, ANG; Makongo, "L'histoire economique du Gabon," 106.

81. Gov. Gabon Pelieu to Gérants de la Société d'Etude pour Toutes Applications du Froid SETAF, 10 December 1949, ANG carton 1178, Territoire du Gabon Correspondance à l'Arrivée et au Départ 1949.

82. Olivier Avril to Lt. Gov. Gabon, 28 May 1931; Chef Circ. Estuaire Bonvin to Gov. Gabon, 12 October 1931; Lt. Gov. Gabon Vingaramassy to Chef Circ. Estuaire, 20 October 1931, ANG carton 792, Correspondance Diverses 1934.

83. Chef Circ. Estuaire Louis Bonvin to Lt. Gov. Gabon, 1 October 1931, ANG carton 792.

84. Lt. Gov. Gabon Vingarassamy to Creput et Talon, 15 September 1931, ANG carton 2715, Estuaire du Gabon, Service de la Main d'Oeuvre, Recrutement de Manoeuvres pour la Pêche dans la Province de l'Estuaire 1931; Administrateur Superieur representant GGFEA au Gabon to Creput, 2 November 1935, ANG carton 379, Secrateriat A.C. Correspondance au Départ 1935.

85. Commissaire de Police de Port Gentil to Chef Dept. Ogooué-Maritime, n.d. (1939), and

Commissaire de Police de Libreville to Chef Dept. Estuaire, 10 October 1939, ANG carton 704, Commune de Libreville Correspondances Diverses 1936–1946.

86. Lasserre, Libreville, 3.

87. Lasserre, Libreville, 266–70.

88. Inspecteur Zoccolat, "Politique Alimentaire dans le Territoire du Gabon," 6 March 1948, 6, AN FM, Affaires Politiques Dossier 2302, Mission d'Inspection Ruffel 2302-2.

89. Lasserre, Libreville, 248.

90. Lasserre, Libreville, 270–71.

91. Howe, Theirs the Darkness, 17.

92. These ads appeared repeatedly in Agence France Presse. For example, see Agence France Presse, bulletin d'information, colonie du Gabon, 12 April 1957.

93. Lasserre, Libreville, 281.

94. Kennedy, Islands, 179–86; Martin, Leisure and Society, 187–94.

95. Tissier de Mallerais, Marcel Lefebvre, 114.

96. Trial, Okoumé, 29–30, 119.

97. Howe, Theirs the Darkness, 26–28.

98. Seuhl, Gabone.

99. Darlington and Darlington, African Betrayal, 196.

100. Darlington and Darlington, African Betrayal, 197.

101. Darlington and Darlington, African Betrayal, 96–97.

102. Darlington and Darlington, African Betrayal, 197.

103. Darlington and Darlington, African Betrayal, 197.

104. Darlington and Darlington, African Betrayal, 203.

105. Darlington and Darlington, African Betrayal, 203.

106. Darlington and Darlington, African Betrayal, 238.

107. Darlington and Darlington, African Betrayal, 246.

108. Darlington and Darlington, African Betrayal, 205–6.

109. Darlington and Darlington, African Betrayal, 205.

110. Darlington and Darlington, African Betrayal, 216, 220.

111. Lasserre, Libreville, 265–74; Martin, Leisure and Society, 194–97.

112. Brooks, Landlords and Strangers, 188–96.

Conclusion

1. Service de l'Agriculture, Rapports Annuels 1958, 1960, Rapport Annuel 1960, 9, ANG carton 762, Ministère de l'Agriculture.

2. Statistics vary, but several observers estimate that between 50 and 81 percent of the Gabonese population now lives in cities. For a general discussion of urbanization in Libreville after 1960, see Pourtier, Le Gabon, 2:253–64.

3. Interviews, Joseph-Bernard Mba Okoue, Chef de Quartier, Atong Abé, Libreville, 26 January 2000; Gabriel Mabenga, Diba-Diba, Libreville, 25 February 2000; Jean Ayong Mebiame, Akok, 28 October 2000.

4. For varying assessments of the impact of oil on Gabon, see Yates, Rentier State in Africa; Gardinier, "Petroleum Dominated Economy."

5. For an overview of state agriculture and its failures see Pourtier, "La crise de l'agriculture"; Brigette-Minette Ondoua, "Approvisionnement de la ville de Libreville," 21–24; Nsa-Ngogo, "Les conditions de vie," 355–64; Yates, Rentier State in Africa, 143–71. The situation has not improved much since the early 1980s.

6. Gardinier, "Petroleum Dominated Economy," 6–7.

7. As noted in "Current Agricultural Dilemmas in Gabon," Africa and Middle East Branch, International Economics Division, Economics and Statistics Service, U.S. Department of Agriculture, 1981, 7, 22; Pourtier, Le Gabon, 2:299–302. Despite Yugoslavian programs in the late 1970s that built roads, the situation has not improved much since 1980. See Lawson, "Gabon: Worn Out Roads and Development."

8. Yates, Rentier State in Africa, 158–60.

9. Yates, Rentier State in Africa, 214. In my stays in Libreville I did not need to ask about the high cost of living; informants complained about the situation without any prompting.

10. "Current Agricultural Dilemmas in Gabon," 14.

11. "Current Agricultural Dilemmas in Gabon," 20.

12. Yates, Rentier State in Africa, 204.

13. Deborah Bryceson has examined at length the impact of food pricing policies and transport issues in Dar Es Salaam's troubles with food shortages. See Bryceson, Liberalizing Tanzania's Food Trade; Bryceson and Jamal, Farewell to Farms. On forced resettlement see Scott, Seeing Like a State, 223–55.

14. As briefly noted in Martin, Leisure and Society, 37–39, 57–58.

15. For some examples of literature on food imports see Thaman, "Deterioration of Food Systems"; MacLeod and McGee, "The Last Frontier"; Drakakis-Smith, "Food for Thought."

16. Miller, Way of Death; Thornton, Africans and the Making of the Atlantic World.

17. Prestholdt, "On the Global Repercussions of East African Consumerism."

Bibliography

Archives

France

Archives de la Congrégation des Pères du Saint-Esprit (ACSE), Chevilly-Larue.
Archives de la Marine, Archives Nationales, Paris.
Fonds Georges Bruel. Archives des Sciences d'Outre-Mer, Paris.
Archives du Service Protestant de Mission (DEFAP), Paris.
Archives Nationales Section Outre-Mer (ANSOM), Afrique Equatoriale Française,
   Aix-en-Provence.

Gabon

Archives de la Foundation Raponda Walker, Libreville.
Archives de la Paroisse de Donguila, Eglise Catholique du Gabon, Donguila.
Archives des Soeurs de la Conception Immaculée de Castres, Libreville.
Archives Nationales du Gabon (ANG), Libreville.

United States

American Board of Commissioners for Foreign Missions (ABCFM), Letterbooks, Gabon
   Mission, 1842–71. Houghton Library, Harvard University, Cambridge,
   Massachusetts.
Robert Hammill Nassau Papers (RNP). Princeton Theological Seminary, Princeton, New
   Jersey.
Presbyterian Church of the U.S.A. (PCUSA), Letters, Gabon and Corisco Mission. Presbyterian
   Historical Society, Philadelphia, Pennsylvania.
William Walker Papers (WWP). State Historical Society of Wisconsin, Madison.

Published Sources

Akyeampong, Emmanuel. *Drink, Power, and Cultural Change: A Social History of Alcohol in Ghana,*
   c. 1800 to Recent Times. Portsmouth: Heinemann, 1996.
———. "'Wo pe tam won pe ba' (You Like Cloth but You Don't Want Children): Urbanization,
   Individualism and Gender Relations in Colonial Ghana, c. 1900–1939." In *Africa's*
   Urban Past, ed. David Anderson and Richard Rathbone, 222–34. Portsmouth:
   Heinemann, 2000.
Alford, Terry. *A Prince among Slaves.* Oxford: Oxford University Press, 1977.
Allman, Jean, ed. *Fashioning Africa: Power and the Politics of Dress.* Bloomington: Indiana
   University Press, 2005.
Allman, Jean, and Victoria Tashjian. *"I Will Not Eat Stone": A Women's History of Colonial Asante.*
   Portsmouth: Heinemann, 2000.
Alpern, Stanley. "The European Introduction of Crops into West Africa in Pre-Colonial Times."
   History in Africa 19 (1992): 13–43.
Ambouroué-Avaro, Joseph. *Un peuple Gabonais à l'aube de la colonisation.* Paris: Karthala, 1981.
Anderson, David, and Richard Rathbone, eds. *Africa's Urban Past.* Portsmouth: Heinemann, 2000.

Anderson, Eugene. *The Food of China.* New Haven CT: Yale University Press, 1988.

Angoue-Nzoghe, Jérôme. "L'appel à l'AEF: La contribution du Gabon à l'effort de guerre, 1939–1945." MA thesis, University of Rheims, 1983.

Anonymous. *Heads of Mpongwe Grammar and a Vocabulary of the Mpongwe Language.* New York: West Africa Mission, 1879.

———. "Le débat dont depend le destin de l'Afrique." *Réalités* 173 (June 1960): 39–44.

Armah, Ayi Kwei. *The Beautyful Ones are Not Yet Born.* Portsmouth: Heinemann, 1968.

Arnold, David. *Famine: Social Crisis and Historical Change.* London: Blackwell, 1988.

Assomou, Alfred. "Le mariage et la dot chez les Fang du Gabon." Ph.D. thesis, Université de Laval, 1998.

Aubame, Jean-Hilaire. *Les Béti du Gabon et d'ailleurs.* 2 vols. Paris: Karthala, 2002.

Aubry, S. "Note sur le Gabon et ses dépendances." *Revue coloniale* 13 (1854): 468–73.

Austen, Ralph, and Jonathan Derrick. *Middlemen of the Cameroons Rivers: The Duala and Their Hinterland, c. 1600–c. 1960.* Cambridge: Cambridge University Press, 1999.

Austen, Ralph, and Rita Headrick. "Equatorial Africa under Colonial Rule." In *History of Central Africa,* ed. David Birmingham and Phyllis M. Martin, vol. 2, 27–94. New York: Longman, 1983.

Avomo Ovono, Berthe Stelle. "La symbolique des aliments chez les peuples Fang, Ngwa'Myènè, Bapunu et Batéké du Gabon." BA thesis, Université Omar Bongo, 1999.

Ayingone Eki, Blandine. "Famines, epidémies et endémies au Woleu-Ntem pendant la période coloniale, 1910–1960." BA thesis, Université Omar Bongo, 1984.

Balandier, Georges. *Ambiguous Africa: Cultures in Collision.* Cleveland OH: Meridian, 1966 [1937].

———. *Sociologie actuelle de l'Afrique noire.* Paris: Presses Universitaires de France, 1955.

Ballard, John. "The Development of Political Parties in French Equatorial Africa." Ph.D. thesis, Fletcher School of Law and Diplomacy, Cambridge, 1963.

Barret, Paul. *L'Afrique occidentale: La nature et l'homme noir.* 2 vols. Paris: Challamel, 1888.

Bascou-Brescane, René. *Etude des conditions de vie à Libreville, 1961–62.* Paris: Secrétariat d'État aux affaires étrangères chargé de la coopération, 1969.

Bassett, Thomas. *The Peasant Cotton Revolution in West Africa: Cote d'Ivôire, 1880–1995.* Cambridge: Cambridge University Press, 2001.

Bates, Roberts, Valentin Mudimbe, and Jean Barr, eds. *Africa and the Disciplines: The Contributions of Research in Africa to the Social Sciences.* Chicago: University of Chicago Press, 1993.

Bauer, Arnold. *Goods, Power, History: Latin America's Material Culture.* Cambridge: Cambridge University Press, 2001.

Bauer, Arnold, and Benjamin Orlove. "Chile in the Belle Epoque: Primitive Producers, Civilized Consumers." In *The Allure of the Foreign: Imported Goods in Postcolonial Latin America,* ed. Benjamin Orlove, 113–50. Ann Arbor: University of Michigan Press, 1997.

Becker, Jasper. *Hungry Ghosts: Mao's Secret Famine.* New York: Free Press, 1996.

Behrens, Christine. *Les Kroumen de la côte occidentale d'Afrique.* Bordeaux: Centre d'études de géographie tropicale, 1974.

Beidelman, T. O. "Altruism and Domesticity: Images of Missionizing Women among the Church Missionary Society in Nineteenth-Century East Africa." In *Gendered Missions: Women and Men in Missionary Discourse and Practice,* ed. Mary Taylor Huber and Nancy Lutkeaus, 114–43. Ann Arbor: University of Michigan Press, 1999.

———. *Colonial Evangelism: A Socio-Historical Study of an East African Mission at the Grassroots.* Bloomington: Indiana University Press, 1982.

Belasco, Warren, and Philip Scranton, eds. *Food Nations: Selling Taste in Consumer Societies.* New York: Routledge, 2002.

Bennett, Albert. "Ethnographic Notes on the Fang." *Journal of the Royal Anthropological Institute of Great Britain and Ireland* 29 (1899): 66–98.

Bensaid, Georges. *Économie et nutrition: Essai à partir d'une enquête alimentaire sur deux régions du Gabon.* Libreville: Service Nationale de la Statistique, 1969.

Bernault, Florence. *Démocraties ambigües en Afrique Centrale: Congo-Brazzaville et Gabon, 1945–1965.* Paris: Karthala, 1996.

Berre, Robert. "L'Extension du pouvoir colonial français à l'interieur du Gabon (1883–1914)." Ph.D. thesis, University of Paris, 1979.

Berry, Sara. *No Condition Is Permanent: The Social Dynamics of Agrarian Change in Sub-Saharan Africa.* Madison: University of Wisconsin Press, 1993.

Beslier, G. *L'Apôtre du Congo.* Paris: Editions de la Vrai France, 1932.

Beven, E. "Du Gabon à Bata." *Bulletin de la société commerciale du Havre* 1 (1891): 193–97, 239–42.

Bhabha, Homi. "Of Mimicry and Man: The Ambivalence of Colonial Discourse." *October* 29 (1984): 125–33.

Bickford-Smith, Vivian. *Ethnic Pride and Racial Difference in Victorian Cape Town: Group Identity and Social Practice, 1875–1902.* Cambridge: Cambridge University Press, 1995.

Bigmann, Louis. *Charles N'Tchoréré.* Libreville: Lion, 1983.

Birmingham, David. "Society and Economy before AD 1400." In *History of Central Africa,* ed. David Birmingham and Phyllis M. Martin, vol. 1, 1–29. New York: Longman, 1983.

Birmingham, David, and Phyllis M. Martin. *History of Central Africa.* 3 vols. New York: Longman, 1983.

Blache, Joseph. *Vrais noirs et vrais blancs d'Afrique.* Orléans: M. Caillette, 1922.

Blier, Suzanne Preston. "Truth and Seeing: Magic, Custom, and Fetish in Art History." In *Africa and the Disciplines: The Contributions of Research in Africa to the Social Sciences,* ed. Robert Bates, Valentin Mudimbe, and Jean Barr, 139–66. Chicago: University of Chicago Press, 1993.

Blim, E. "Le Congo Français." *Bulletin de la société commerciale du Havre* (1892): 208–31, 257–71.

Bogosian, Catherine M. "Forced Labor, Resistance, and Memory in the French Soudan, 1926–1950." Ph.D. thesis, University of Pennsylvania, 2002.

Bonzo, Gertie, Norma Kitson, and Joan Wardrop. "Talking Food: A Conversation about Zimbabwe, Cooking, Eating, and Social Living." *Mots Pluriels* 15 (2000), www.arts.uwa.edu.au/MotsPluriels/MP1500jw.html#bev.

Boserup, Ester. *The Conditions of Agricultural Growth: The Economics of Agrarian Change under Population Pressure.* London: G. Allen and Unwin, 1965.

Bougerol, Christiane. "Medical Practices in the French West Indies: Master and Slave in the 17th and 18th Centuries." *History and Anthropology* 2 (1985): 125–43.

Bourdieu, Pierre. *Distinction: A Social Critique of the Judgement of Taste.* Trans. Richard Nice. Cambridge MA: Harvard University Press, 1983.

Bowdich, Edward. *Mission from Cape Coast Castle to Ashantee.* 2nd ed. London: Cass, 1966.

Brantley, Cynthia. *Feeding Families: African Realities and British Ideas of Nutrition in Early Colonial Africa.* Portsmouth: Heinemann, 2002.

Braudel, Ferdinand. *Civilization and Capitalism, 15th to 18th Century,* vol. 1. Berkeley: University of California Press, 1992.

Briault, Maurice. *Dans le forêt du Gabon.* Paris: Bernard Grasset, 1930.

―――. Récits sur le verandah. Paris: Bloud et Gay, 1939.

―――. Les sauvages d'Afrique. Paris: Payot, 1943.

―――. Une soeur missionnaire: La Soeur Saint-Charles. Paris: Téqui, 1914.

―――. Sous le zéro équatoriale. Paris: Bloud et Gay, 1927.

―――. Sur les pistes de l'AEF. Paris: Editions Alsatia, 1945.

Brooks, George. Landlords and Strangers: Ecology, Society and Trade in Western Africa, 1000–1630. Boulder CO: Westview Press, 1993.

Brouillet, Jean-Claude. L'avion du blanc. Paris: Robert Laffont, 1972.

Bruegel, Martin. "How the French Learned to Eat Canned Food," in Food Nations: Selling Taste in Consumer Societies, ed. Warren Belasco and Philip Scranton, 113–30. New York: Routledge, 2002.

Brunschwig, Henri. Brazza Explorateur, l'Ogooué, 1875–1879. Paris: Mouton, 1966.

―――. "Expeditions punitives au Gabon, 1877–1879." Cahiers d'études africaines 2 (1962): 347–62.

Bryceson, Deborah. Liberalizing Tanzania's Food Trade: Public and Private Faces of Urban Marketing Policy, 1939–1988. Portsmouth: Heinemann, 1993.

Bryceson, Deborah, and Vali Jamal. Farewell to Farms: De-Agrarianisation and Employment in Africa. Aldershot, U.K.: Ashgate, 1997.

Bucher, Henry. "John Leighton Wilson and the Mpongwe: The 'Spirit of 1776' in Mid-Nineteenth Century Africa." Journal of Presbyterian History 54 (1976): 291–315.

―――. "Liberty and Labor: The Origins of Libreville Reconsidered." Bulletin d'information de l'Afrique Noire 41 (1979): 478–96.

―――. "The Mpongwe of the Gabon Estuary: A History to 1860." Ph.D. thesis, University of Wisconsin, 1977.

―――. "Mpongwe Origins: Historiographical Perspectives." History in Africa 2 (1975): 59–89.

―――. "The Settlement of the Mpongwe Clans in the Gabon Estuary: An Historical Synthesis." Revue française d'histoire d'outre-mer 64 (1977): 149–75.

―――. "The Village of Glass and Western Intrusion: A Mpongwe Response to the American and French Presence in the Gabon Estuary 1842–1845." International Journal of African Historical Studies 3 (1973): 363–400.

Buléon, J. Sous le ciel d'Afrique: De Sainte Anne d'Auray à Sainte Anne de Fernan Vaz. Abbeville: C. Paillant, 1896.

Bundy, Colin. The Rise and Fall of the South African Peasantry. Portsmouth: Heinemann, 1979.

Bunn, David. "The Brown Serpent of the Rocks: Bushman Arrow Toxins in the Dutch and British Imagination, 1735–1780." In Transgressing Boundaries: New Directions in the Study of Culture in Africa, ed. Brenda Cooper and Andrew Steyn, 58–85. Athens: Ohio University Press, 1996.

Burke, Timothy. Lifebuoy Men, Lux Women. Durham NC: Duke University Press, 1996.

Burton, Richard. Two Trips to Gorilla Land and the Cataracts of the Congo. 2 vols. London: Sampson, Law and Searle, 1876.

Campbell, Penelope. "Presbyterian West African Mission Women Converts as Agents of Social Change." Journal of Presbyterian History 56 (1978): 121–33.

Carney, Judith. Black Rice: The African Origins of Rice Cultivation in the Americas. Cambridge MA: Harvard University Press, 2001.

Chamberlin, Christopher. "Competition and Conflict: The Development of the Bulk Export Trade in Central Gabon during the 19th Century." Ph.D. thesis, University of California at Los Angeles, 1977.

————. "The Migration of the Fang into Central Gabon during the Nineteenth Century: A New Interpretation." *International Journal of African Historical Studies* 11 (1978): 429–56.

Chanock, Martin. *Law, Custom, and Social Order: The Colonial Experience in Malawi and Zambia.* Cambridge: Cambridge University Press, 1986.

Chang, Kwang-Chih, ed. *Food in Chinese Culture: Anthropological and Historical Perspectives.* New Haven CT: Yale University Press, 1977.

Chastanet, Monique. "Les crises de subsistances dans les villages soninke du cercle de Bakel, de 1858 à 1945: Problèmes méthodologiques et perspectives de recherché." *Cahiers d'Études Africaines* 23 (1983): 5–26.

Chastanet, Monique, Françous-Xavier Fauvelle-Aymar, and Dominque Juhé-Beaulaton, eds. *Cuisine et société en Afrique: Histoire, saveurs, savoir-faire.* Paris: Karthala, 2002.

Chavannes, Charles de. *Avec Brazza.* Paris: Plon, 1935.

————. *Le Congo français.* Paris: Plon, 1937.

Cinnamon, John Manning. "The Long March of the Fang: Anthropology and History in Equatorial Africa." Ph.D. thesis, Yale University, 1998.

Clark, Gracia. *Onions Are My Husband: Survival and Accumulation by West African Market Women.* Chicago: University of Chicago Press, 1994.

Clist, Bernard. *Gabon: 100,000 ans d'histoire.* Libreville: Centre Culturel Français, 1995.

————. "Des premiers villages aux premiers européens autour de l'estuaire du Gabon: Quatre millénaires d'interactions entre l'homme et son milieu." Ph.D. thesis, Université Libre de Bruxelles, 2005.

Cohen, William. *Rulers of Empire: The French Colonial Service in Africa.* Stanford CA: Hoover Institution Press, 1971.

————. *The French Encounter with Africans.* Bloomington: Indiana University Press, 1980.

————. "Malaria and French Imperialism." *Journal of African History* 24 (1983): 23–36.

Comaroff, Jean, and John Comaroff. *Of Revolution and Revelation: Christianity, Colonialism and Consciousness in South Africa.* 2 vols. Chicago: University of Chicago Press, 1997.

Compiègne, Marquis de. *L'Afrique équatoriale: Gabonais, Pahouin, Gallois.* Paris: Plon, 1878.

Conklin, Alice. *A Mission to Civilize: The Republican Idea of Empire in France and West Africa, 1895–1930.* Stanford CA: Stanford University Press, 1997.

————. "Redefining 'Frenchness': Citizenship, Race Regeneration and Imperial Motherhood in France and West Africa 1914–1940." In *Domesticating the Empire: Race, Gender and Family Life in French and Dutch Colonialism,* ed. Julia Clancy-Smith and Frances Gouda, 68–85. Charlottesville: University of Virginia Press, 1998.

Conquest, Robert. *The Harvest of Sorrow: Soviet Collectivization and the Terror-Famine.* Oxford: Oxford University Press, 1986.

Cooper, Frederick, ed. "Conflict and Connection: Rethinking Colonial African History." *American Historical Review* 99 (1994): 1516–45.

————. *Struggle for the City: Migrant Labor, Capital, and the State in Urban Africa.* Beverly Hills CA: Sage Publications, 1983.

Cooper, Frederick, and Ann Laura Stoler. *Tensions of Empire: Colonial Cultures in a Bourgeois World.* Berkeley: University of California Press, 1997.

Coquéry-Vidrovitch, Catherine. *Brazza et la prise de possession du Gabon: La Mission de l'Ouest Africain.* Paris: Mouton, 1969.

————. *Le Congo au temps des grandes compagnies concessionaires, 1898–1930.* Paris: Mouton, 1972.

Cordell, Dennis. "Extracting People from Precapitalist Production: French Equatorial

Africa from the 1890s to the 1930s." In *African Population and Capitalism: Historical Perspectives*, ed. Dennis Cordell and Joel Gregory, 2nd ed., 137–52. Madison: University of Wisconsin Press, 1994.

Counihan, Carole. *The Anthropology of Food and Body: Gender, Meaning, and Power*. New York: Routledge, 1999.

Counihan, Carole, and Steven Kaplan, eds. *Food and Gender: Identity and Power*. Amsterdam: Harwood, 1998.

Counihan, Carole, and Penny Van Esterik, eds. *Food and Culture: A Reader*. New York: Routledge, 1997.

Cruiziot, Gaudefroy-Demombynes, and Magnon Cruiziot. "Les Problèmes du développement rural au Gabon." Rapport de Mission, République Française, 1961.

Crush, Jonathan, and Charles Ambler, eds. *Liquor and Labor in Southern Africa*. Athens: Ohio University Press, 1992.

Curtin, Philip. "Medical Knowledge and Urban Planning in Tropical Africa," *American Historical Review* 90 (1985): 594–613.

Darlington, Charles, and Alice Darlington. *African Betrayal*. New York: David McKay, 1968.

Davis, Mike. *Late Victorian Holocausts: El Niño Famines and the Making of the Third World*. New York: Verso, 2001.

De Certeau, Michel, Luce Giard, and Pierre Mayol. *The Practice of Everyday Life: Living and Cooking*. Trans. Timonthy Tomasik. Minneapolis: University of Minnesota Press, 1998.

De Dravo, Louis. "L'Exploitation forestière du Gabon, 1896–1930." MA thesis, University of Rheims, 1979.

De Vaal, Alexander. *Famine That Kills: Darfur, Sudan, 1984–1985*. New York: Oxford University Press, 1989.

Dejene, Alemneh. *Environment, Famine, and Politics in Ethiopia: A View from the Village*. Boulder CO: Lynne Rienner, 1990.

Delaporte, Maurice. *A la découverte de . . . la vie coloniale*. Paris: Editions ouvrières, 1944.

Delorme. "Lettre du 18 Août 1876." *Annales de la propagation de la foi* 49 (1877): 132–38.

———. "Lettre du 12 Juillet 1878." *Annales de la propagation de la foi* 51 (1879): 210–12.

———. "Lettre du 16 Janvier 1880." *Annales de la propagation de la foi* 52 (1880): 274–85.

Deschamps, Herbert. *Quinze ans de Gabon: Les débuts de l'établissement français, 1839–1853*. Paris: Société Française d'Outre-Mer, 1965.

Diawara, Manthia. "Toward a Regional Imaginary in Africa." In *The Cultures of Globalization*, ed. Frederic Jameson and Masao Miyoshi, 103–24. Durham NC: Duke University Press, 1998.

Diop, Ibrahim. *Eliwa Zi N'Gaba: De la contrée de N'Gabo au pays du Gabon*. Libreville: Aronogo, 1990.

Douglas, Mary. "The Deciphering of a Meal," in Douglas, *Implicit Meanings: Essays in Anthropology*, 249–75. New York: Routledge, 1975.

Drakakis-Smith, David, ed. *Economic Growth and Urbanization in the Third World*. London: Routledge, 1989.

———. "Food for Thought or Thought about Food: Urban Food Distribution Systems in the Third World," in *Cities and Development in the Third World*, ed. Robert Potter and Ademola Salau, 100–20. London: Mansell, 1990.

Du Chaillu, Paul. *Explorations and Adventures in Equatorial Africa*. New York: Harper, 1861.

Dubois, Colette. "Le prix d'une guerre: Deux colonies pendant la première guerre mondiale (Gabon, Oubangui-Chari), 1911–1923." Ph.D. thesis, University of Aix-en-Provence, 1985.

Dupré, Georges. *Un ordre et sa déstruction*. Paris: OSTROM, 1982.

Dwyer, Daisy, and Judith Bruce, eds. *A Home Divided: Women and Income in the Third World*. Stanford CA: Stanford University Press, 1988.

Elwert-Kretschmer, Karola. "Culinary Innovation, Love, and the Social Organization of Learning in a West African City." *Food and Foodways* 9, nos. 3–4 (2001): 205–33.

Engone Ndong, Callixte. "La communauté Hausa du Gabon, 1930–1990: Le commerce et la construction de son identité en région d'Oyem et sa marginalisation." Ph.D. thesis, Université de Laval, 1998.

Fabian, Johannes. *Out Of Our Minds: Reason and Madness in the Exploration of Central Africa*. Berkeley: University of California Press, 2000.

Fabre, A. *Le commerce et l'exploitation des bois au Gabon*. Paris: Société d'Éditions de Géographie, Maritime et Coloniale, 1926.

Fair, Laura Jeanne. *Pastimes and Politics: Culture, Community and Identity in Post-Abolition Zanzibar, 1890–1945*. Athens: Ohio University Press, 2001.

Falola, Toyin, and Paul Lovejoy, eds. *Pawnship in Africa: Debt Bondage in Historical Perspective*. Boulder CO: Westview, 1994.

Falola, Toyin, and Steven Salm, eds. *African Urban Spaces in Historical Perspective*. Rochester: University of Rochester Press, 2005.

Fanon, Franz. *Peaux noires et masques blancs*. Paris: Seuil, 1952.

Fay, J. Michael. "In the Land of Surfing Hippos," *National Geographic* 206, no. 2 (August 2004): 100–28.

Fehr, S. *La climatologie du Gabon*. Libreville: Institut Pédagogique National, 1983.

Fiereman, Steven. *Peasant Intellectuals: Anthropology and History in Tanzania*. Madison: University of Wisconsin Press, 1990.

Feldman-Savelsberg, Pamela. *Plundered Kitchens, Empty Wombs: Threatened Reproduction and Identity in the Cameroon Grassfields*. Ann Arbor: University of Michigan Press, 1999.

Fernandez, James. *Bwiti: An Ethnography of the Religious Imagination in Africa*. Princeton NJ: Princeton University Press, 1982.

Fleuriot de Langle, A. "Croisières à la côte d'Afrique." *Le tour du monde* 31 (1876): 241–304.

Flynn, Karen Coen. *Food, Culture, and Survival in an African City*. New York: Palgrave, 2005.

Fourneau, Alfred. *Au vieux Congo*. Paris: Comité de l'Afrique Française, 1932.

Franke, Richard. "The Effects of Colonialism and Neocolonialism on the Gastronomic Patterns of the Third World." In *Food and Evolution: Towards a Theory of Human Food Habits*, ed. Marvin Harris and Eric Ross, 455–81. Philadelphia: Temple University Press, 1987.

Friedberg, Susanne. "French Beans for the Masses: A Modern Historical Geography of Food in Burkina Faso." In *The Cultural Politics of Food and Eating: A Reader*, ed. James Watson and Melissa Caldwell, 20–41. New York: Blackwell, 2005.

Frey, Colonel. *La côte occidentale d'Afrique*. Paris: C. Marpon et E. Flammarion, 1890.

Gabon. *Mémoire du Gabon: Les trésors de la mémoire*. Geneva: SIED, 1987.

Gado, Alpha. *Une histoire des famines au Sahel: Étude des grandes crises alimentaires (XIXe–XXe siècle)*. Paris: L'Harmattan, 1993.

Gaitskell, Deborah. "Housewives, Maids or Mothers: Some Contradictions of Domesticity for Christian Women in Johannesburg, 1903–1939." *Journal of African History* 24 (1983): 241–56.

Gardinier, David. "The American Board (1842–1870) and Presbyterian Board

(1870–1892) Missions in Northern Gabon and African Responses." *Africana Journal* 17 (1998): 215–33.

———. "The American Presbyterian Mission in Gabon: Male Mpongwe Converts and Agents." *Journal of Presbyterian History* 69 (1991): 61–70.

———. "The Beginning of French Catholic Evangelization in Gabon and African Responses." *Proceedings of the French Colonial Historical Society* 2 (1978): 49–74.

———. "The Development of a Petroleum Dominated Economy in Gabon." *Essays in Economic and Business History* 17 (1999): 1–15.

———. *Historical Dictionary of Gabon.* 2nd ed. Metuchen NJ: Scarecrow Press, 1994.

———. "The Schools of the American Protestant Mission in Gabon, 1842–1870." *Revue française d'histoire d'outre-mer* 75 (1988): 168–84.

Gaulme, François. *Le pays du Cama.* Paris: Karthala, 1981.

Gauthier, Jean-Marie. *Grammaire de la langue Mpongwée.* Paris: Procure des Pères du Saint-Esprit, 1912.

———. *Étude historique sur les Mpongoués et tribus avoisinates.* Brazzaville: Mémoires de l'Institut d'Études Centrafricaines, 1950.

Géraud, Léon. *L'essor du Gabon: L'exploitation forestière des grands réseaux Français.* Paris: Société Général d'Imprimerie, 1928.

———. "Une exploitation industrielle de la fôret équatoriale (Consortium forestier des grands réseaux français)." *Revue générale des chemins de fer* 9 (March 1928): 181–97.

Geschiere, Peter. *The Modernity of Witchcraft in Africa: Politics and the Occult in Postcolonial Africa.* Charlottesville: University of Virginia Press, 1997.

Gide, André. *Voyage au Congo.* Paris: Gallimard, 1926.

Glassman, Jonathan. *Feasts and Riot: Revelry, Rebellion, and Popular Consciousness on the Swahili Coast, 1856–1888.* Portsmouth: Heinemann, 1995.

Goody, Jack. *Cooking, Cuisine and Class: A Study in Comparative Sociology.* Cambridge: Cambridge University Press, 1982.

Gouda, Frances. *Dutch Culture Overseas: Colonial Practice in the Netherlands Indies, 1900–1942.* Amsterdam: Amsterdam University Press, 1995.

Gray, Christopher. *Colonial Rule and Crisis in Equatorial Africa: Southern Gabon, c. 1850–1940.* Rochester NY: University of Rochester Press, 2002.

———. "Territoriality, Ethnicity and Colonial Rule in Southern Gabon, 1850–1960." Ph.D. thesis, Indiana University, 1995.

Gray, Christopher, and François Ngolet. "Lambaréné, *Okoumé,* and the Transformation of Labor Along the Middle Ogooué (Gabon), 1870–1945." *Journal of African History* 40 (1999): 87–107.

Greenough, Paul. *Prosperity and Misery in Modern Bengal: The Famine of 1943–1944.* Oxford: Oxford University Press, 1982.

Griffon de Bellay, M. "Le Gabon 1861–1864." *Le tour du monde* 54 (1865): 273–320.

Guyer, Jane. "Dynamic Approaches to Domestic Budgeting: Cases and Methods from Africa." In *A Home Divided: Women and Income in the Third World,* ed. Daisy Dwyer and Judith Bruce, eds., 155–72. Stanford CA: Stanford University Press, 1988.

———. "Feeding Yaoundé, Capital of Cameroon." In *Feeding African Cities,* ed. Jane Guyer, 112–53. Bloomington: Indiana University Press, 1987.

———. "The Food Economy and French Colonial Rule in Central Cameroon." *Journal of African History* 19 (1978): 577–97.

———. "Wealth in People and Self-Realization in Equatorial Africa." *Man* 28 (1993): 243–65.

———. "Wealth in People, Wealth in Things: Introduction." *Journal of African History* 36 (1995): 83–90.

Guyer, Jane, ed. *Feeding African Cities*. Bloomington: Indiana University Press, 1987.

Guyer, Jane, and Samuel M. Eno Belinga. "Wealth in People as Wealth in Knowledge: Accumulation and Composition in Equatorial Africa." *Journal of African History* 36 (1995): 91–120.

Hansen, Karen Tranberg, ed. *African Encounters with Domesticity*. New Brunswick NJ: Rutgers University Press, 1992.

———. "The Cook, His Wife, the Madam, and Their Dinner: Cooking, Gender and Class in Zambia." In *Changing Food Habits: Case Studies from Africa, South America and Europe*, ed. Carola Lentz, 73–90. Amsterdam: Harwood, 1999.

———. *Distant Companions: Servants and Employers in Zambia, 1900–1985*. Ithaca NY: Cornell University Press, 1989.

Harris, Marvin, and Eric Ross, eds. *Food and Evolution: Towards a Theory of Human Food Habits*. Philadelphia: Temple University Press, 1987.

Harms, Robert. *River of Wealth, River of Sorrow: The Central Zaire Basin in the Era of the Slave and Ivory Trade, 1500–1891*. New Haven CT: Yale University Press, 1981.

———. *The Diligent: A Voyage through the Worlds of the Slave Trade*. New York: Basic, 2002.

Hawthorne, Walter. *Planting Rice and Harvesting Slaves: Transformations along the Guinea-Bissau Coast, 1400–1900*. Portsmouth: Heinemann, 2003.

Headrick, Rita. *Colonialism, Health, and Illness in French Equatorial Africa, 1885–1935*. Atlanta GA: African Studies Association, 1994.

Hendrickson, Hildi, ed. *Clothing and Difference: Embodied Identities in Colonial and Post-Colonial Africa*. Durham NC: Duke University Press, 1996.

Hess, Karen, and Mrs. Samuel G. Stoney. *The Carolina Rice Kitchen: The African Connection*. Columbia: University of South Carolina Press, 1992.

Hladik, Claude-Marcel, Serge Bahuchet, and Igor de Garine. *Food and Nutrition in the African Rain Forest*. Paris: UNESCO/MAB, 1990.

Hodgson, Dorothy, and Sheryl McCurdy, eds. *"Wicked" Women and the Reconfiguration of Gender in the Third World*. Portsmouth: Heinemann, 2001.

Holt, Cecil, ed. *The Diary of John Holt with the Voyage of the "Maria"*. Liverpool: Henry Young and Sons, 1948.

Howe, Russell Warren. *Theirs the Darkness*. London: Herbert Jenkins, 1956.

Huber, Mary Taylor. "The Dangers of Immorality: Dignity and Disorder in Gender Relations in a Northern New Guinea Discourse." In *Gendered Missions: Women and Men in Missionary Discourse and Practice*, ed. Mary Taylor Huber and Nancy Lutkeaus, 179–206. Ann Arbor: University of Michigan Press, 1999.

Huber, Mary Taylor, and Nancy Lutkeaus, eds. *Gendered Missions: Women and Men in Missionary Discourse and Practice*, eds. Ann Arbor: University of Michigan Press, 1999.

Hunt, Nancy Rose. *A Colonial Lexicon of Birth Ritual, Medicalization, and Mobility in the Congo*. Durham NC: Duke University Press, 1999.

———. "Introduction." In *Gendered Colonialism in African History*, ed. Nancy Rose Hunt, Tessie Liu, and Jean Quataert, 1–15. Malden MA: Blackwell, 1997.

Iliffe, John. *The African Poor*. Cambridge: Cambridge University, 1987.

Isaacman, Allen, and Barbara Isaacman. *Slavery and Beyond: The Making of Men and Chikunda*

Ethnic Identities in the Unstable World of South-Central Africa, 1750–1920. Portsmouth: Heinemann, 2004.

Ivanga, François de Paul. "Contribution à l'histoire des Mpongwe des origines à 1945." BA thesis, Université Omar Bongo, 1981.

Janzen, John. *Lemba 1650–1930: A Drum of Affliction in Africa and the New World.* New York: Garland Publishing, 1982.

Janzen, John, and Steven Feierman, eds. *The Social Basis of Health and Healing in Africa.* Berkeley: University of California Press, 1992.

Jean-Baptiste, Rachel. "Une Ville Libre? Marriage, Divorce, and Sexuality in Colonial Libreville, Gabon; 1849–1960." Ph.D. thesis, Stanford University, 2005.

Jeater, Diana. *Marriage, Perversion and Power: The Construction of Moral Discourse in Southern Rhodesia, 1894–1930.* Oxford: Oxford University Press, 1993.

Jones, William. *Manioc in Africa.* Stanford CA: Stanford University Press, 1959.

Juhé-Beaulaton, Dominique. "Aliementation des hommes, des vodoun, et des ancêstres: Une histoire de cereals dans le Golfe de Guinée." In *Cuisine and société en Afrique: Histoire, saveurs, savoir-faire,* ed Monique Chastanet, François-Xavier Fauvelle-Aymar, and Dominque Juhé-Beaulaton, 53–66. Paris: Karthala, 2002.

Kankoila-Nendy, François. "Les Libérés de l'Ilisia, 1846–1853." BA thesis, University of Paris, 1978.

Kaplan. Steven. *The Bakers of Paris and the Bread Question, 1700–1775.* Durham NC: Duke University Press, 1996.

Karasch, Mary. "Manioc." In *The Cambridge World History of Food,* vol. 1, ed. Kenneth Kiple and Kriemhild Conee Ornelas, 181–87. Cambridge: Cambridge University Press, 2000.

Kea, Ray. *Settlements, Trade, and Polities in the Seventeenth Century Gold Coast.* Baltimore MD: Johns Hopkins University Press, 1982.

Kennedy, Dane. *Islands of White: Settler Society and Culture in Kenya and Southern Rhodesia, 1890–1939.* Durham NC: Duke University Press, 1987.

Kingsley, Mary. *Travels in West Africa: Congo Français, Corisco, Cameroons.* London: Macmillan, 1897.

———. *West African Studies.* New York: Macmillan, 1900.

Kiple, Kenneth, and Kriemhild Conee Ornelas, eds. *The Cambridge World History of Food.* Vol. 1. Cambridge: Cambridge University Press, 2000.

Klieman, Kairn. *"The Pygmies Were Our Compass": Bantu and Batwa in the History of West Central Africa, Early Times to c. 1900 CE.* Portsmouth: Heinemann, 2003.

Landau, Paul. *Realm of the Word: Language, Gender, and Christiantity in a Southern African Kingdom.* Portsmouth: Heinemann, 1995.

Larson, Pier. *History and Memory in the Age of Enslavement: Becoming Merina in Highland Madagascar, 1770–1822.* Portsmouth: Heinemann, 2000.

Lasserre, Guy. *Libreville: La ville et sa région.* Paris: Armand Colin, 1958.

Lawson, Antoine. "Gabon: Worn Out Roads and Development." *African News Service/Bulletin d'Information Africaine,* February 2001, www.peacelink.it/anb-bia/nr409/e04.html.

Le Berre, Pierre-Marie. "De l'esclavage au Gabon." *Bulletin de la Congrégation des Pères du Saint-Esprit* 9 (1872–74): 745–62.

———. "Lettre du 1 Mars 1873." *Annales de la propagation de la foi* 45 (1873): 219–32.

———. "Lettre du 18 Août 1876." *Annales de la propagation de la foi* 49 (1877): 432–40.

———. "Lettre du 12 Août 1881." *Annales de la propagation de la foi* 53 (1881): 407–17.

———. "Situation du Vicariat des Deux Guinées." *Annales de la propagation de la foi* 41 (1869): 100–14.

Lejeune, Léon. "Au Congo: La femme et la famille." *Le Correspondant* 198 (10 February 1900): 480–503.

———. "L'esclavage au Gabon." *Annales de la propagation de la foi* 63 (1891): 330–51.

Lessing, Doris. *The Golden Notebook*. London: Michael Joseph, 1962.

Lestrille. "Note sur le comptoir du Gabon," *Revue coloniale* 16 (1856): 424–49.

Lévi-Strauss, Claude. *The Raw and the Cooked*. Trans. John and Doreen Weightman. New York: Harper and Row, 1969.

Likaka, Osuama. *Rural Society and Cotton in Colonial Zaire*. Madison: University of Wisconsin Press, 1997.

Londres, Albert. *Terre d'Ébène*. Paris: Albin Michel, 1929.

Loungou Mouele, Théophile. "Le Gabon de 1910 à 1925: les incidences de la première guerre mondiale sur l'evolution politique, économique et sociale." Ph.D. thesis, University of Aix-en-Provence, 1984.

MacGaffey, Wyatt. *Religion and Society in Central Africa: The BaKongo of Lower Zaire*. Chicago: University of Chicago Press, 1986.

———. *Kongo Political Culture*. Bloomington: Indiana University Press, 2000.

Makongo, René. "L'histoire economique du Gabon, 1945–1960." MA thesis, Université Omar Bongo, 1983.

Mandala, Elias. "Beyond the 'Crisis' in African Food Studies," *Journal of the Historical Society* 3:3 (2003): 281–302.

———. *The End of Chidyerano: A History of Food and Daily Life in Malawi, 1860–2004*. Portsmouth: Heinemann, 2005.

Mandat-Grancey, Baron Edouard de. *Au Congo: Impressions d'un Touriste*. Paris: Plon, 1900.

Mann, Kristen. *Marrying Well: Marriage, Status and Social Change among the Educated Elite in Colonial Lagos*. Cambridge: Cambridge University Press, 1985.

Marche, Alfred. *Trois voyages dans l'Afrique occidentale*. Paris: Hachette, 1879.

Martin, Phyllis M. *The External Trade of the Loango Coast, 1576–1870*. Oxford: Oxford University Press, 1972.

———. *Leisure and Society in Colonial Brazzaville*. Cambridge: Cambridge University Press, 1995.

Martrou, Louis. "Le nomadisme chez les Fang." *Revue de géographie annuel* 3 (1909): 497–524.

———. *Dictionaire Fañ-Français*. Paris: Procure Générale, 1924.

Mary, André. *Le défi du syncrétisme: Le travail symbolique de la religion d'Eboga, Gabon*. Paris: EHESS, 1999.

Massing, Andreas. *The Economic History of the Kru (West Africa)*. Wiesbaden: Franz Steiner Verlag, 1981.

Mba-Mve, Jacques. "La politique coloniale au Gabon et l'agriculture." MA thesis, University of Aix-en-Provence, 1979.

Mbembe, Achille. *On the Postcolony*. Berkeley: University of California Press, 2001.

M'Bokolo, Elikia. *Noirs et blancs en Afrique équatoriale*. Paris: Mouton, 1981.

McCann, James. *From Poverty to Famine in Northeast Ethiopia: A Rural History, 1900–1935*. Philadelphia: University of Pennsylvania Press, 1987.

———. *Green Land, Brown Land, Black Land: An Environmental History of Africa, 1800–1999*. Portsmouth: Heinemann, 1999.

McFeely, Mary Drake. *Can She Bake a Cherry Pie? American Women and the Kitchen in the Twentieth Century*. Amherst: University of Massachusetts, 2000.

MacLeod, S., and T. G. McGee. "The Last Frontier: The Emergence of the Industrial Palate in Hong Kong," in *Economic Growth and Urbanization in the Third World*, ed. David Drakakis-Smith, 304–55. London: Routledge, 1989.

Mandala, Elias. "Beyond the 'Crisis' in African Food Studies." *Journal of the Historical Society* 3, nos. 3–4 (2003): 281–302.

McMillian, Nora. "Robert Bruce Napoleon Walker, F.R.G.S., F.A.S., F.G.S., C.M.Z.S. (1832–1901), West African Trader, Explorer and Collector of Zoological Specimens." *Archives of Natural History* 23 (1996): 125–41.

McNee, Lisa. "Food Cultures and Food for Thought: Cultivating Local Knowledges in Africa." *Pretexts: Literary and Cultural Studies* 12:2 (2003): 166–76.

Megne M'Ellang, David-Christian. "Le marché de Mont-Bouet." MA thesis, Université Omar Bongo, 1983

———. "Les problèmes liés à la situation et au site du marché Mont-Bouet." BA thesis, Université Omar Bongo, 1982.

Mekanene-Nze, Françoise. "L'evolution de l'agriculture coloniale au Gabon, 1830–1950." MA thesis, University of Rheims, 1982.

Merlet, Annie. *Le Pays des trois estuaires*. Libreville: Centre Culturel Français, 1991.

Metegue N'nah, Nicolas. "Le Gabon de 1854 à 1886: Présence français et peuples autochtones." Ph.D. thesis, University of Paris, 1974.

———. "Histoire de la formation du peuple Gabonais et de sa lutte contre la domination coloniale." Ph.D. thesis, 2 vols., University of Paris, 1994.

———. *L'Implantation coloniale au Gabon: Résistance d'un peuple (1839–1960), tome I: Les combattants de la première heure (1839–1920)*. Paris: Harmattan, 1981.

Meunier, Gilbert. "Le réseau des routes au Gabon." *Revue générale des routes* (1953): 25–48.

Meyo-Me-Nkoghe, Dieudonné. "La vie économique et sociale de Kango de 1900 à 1950." MA thesis, Université Omar Bongo, 1989.

Migeod, Frederick. *Across Equatorial Africa*. London: Heath Cranton, 1923.

Miller, Joseph. *Way of Death: Merchant Capitalism and the Angolan Slave Trade, 1730–1830*. Madison: University of Wisconsin Press, 1988.

Milligan, Robert. *The Jungle Folk of Africa*. New York: Fleming Revell, 1908.

———. *The Fetish Folk of West Africa*. New York: Fleming Revell, 1912.

Mintz, Sidney. *Sweetness and Power: The Place of Sugar in Modern History*. New York: Viking, 1985.

———. *Tasting Food, Tasting Freedom: Excursions into Eating, Culture, and the Past*. Boston: Beacon Press, 1996.

Mintz, Sidney, and Richard Price. *An Anthropological Approach to the Afro-American Past: A Caribbean Perspective*. Philadelphia: Institute for the Study of Human Issues, 1976.

Mombey, Paul. "Les Benga: Peuple du Gabon." MA thesis, Université Omar Bongo, 1988.

Momha, Roland. "Le Gabon de 1850 à 1929: Commerce colonial et société autochtone." MA thesis, Université Omar Bongo, 1986.

Morel, Gérard. *Naissance de l'église catholique au XIXe siècle sur la côte ouest de l'Afrique*. Paris: Editions du Bosquet, 1994.

Morel, Gérard, and Maria Rohrer. *Sur la route de la sainteté: Mère Cécilia*. Paris: Editions du Bosquet, 1994.

Mvé, Minko. *Gabon entre tradition et post-modernité: Dynamiques des structures d'acceuil Fang*. Paris: L'Harmattan, 2003.

Nassau, Robert. *Corisco Days: The First Thirty Years of the West Africa Mission.* Philadephia: Allen, Lane and Scott, 1892.

———. "West African Native Foods." *Journal of the American Medical Association,* 29 July 1893, 160–62.

———. *Fetichism in West Africa.* London: Duckworth and Company, 1904.

———. *Tales out of School.* Philadelphia: Allen, Lane and Scott, 1911.

———. *My Ogowe.* New York: Neale, 1914.

Ngo, Vinh Long. *Before the Revolution: The Vietnamese Peasants under the French.* Cambridge MA: Harvard University Press, 1973.

Ngolet, François. "La dispersion Ongom-Bakele en Afrique centrale: Esquisse d'anthropologie historique (origines—vers 1930)." Ph.D. thesis, Université de Montpellier, 1994.

Nguema Edzo, Michel. "L'évolution historique de Ntoum de 1905 à 1985." MA thesis, Université Omar Bongo, 1985.

———. "Ntoum de 1945 à nos jours." BA thesis, Université Omar Bongo, 1984.

Nordick, André. "Le Gabon." *Bulletin de la société de géographie de Rochefort* (1911): 124–58, 181–202.

Northrup, David. *Beyond the Bend in the River: African Labor in Eastern Zaire, 1865–1940.* Athens: Ohio University Press, 1988.

Noufflard, Charles. *Le Gabon: Ce qu'il a été, ce qu'il est, ce qu'il doit être.* Paris: Bulletin de l'Office Coloniale, 1908.

Nsa-Ngogo, Isaac. "Les conditions de vie dans les quartiers populaires à Libreville." Ph.D. thesis, University of Lyon, 1982.

Nzoghe, Anselme. "Les problèmes du travail au Gabon, 1920–1939." MA thesis, University of Aix-en-Provence, 1978.

Obiang, Paul Ngomo. "L'Agriculture traditionnelle chez les Ntumu." BA thesis, Université Omar Bongo, 1981.

Obouyou, Christian Mikassi. "Les Séké de l'Estuaire du Gabon et du bassin moyen de l'Ogooué: Structures traditionnelles et migrations." BA thesis, Université Omar Bongo, 1982.

Ogoula-M'Beye. *Galwa ou Edongo d'Antan.* Trans. Paul-Vincent Pounah. Fontenay-le-Compte: Imprimerie Loriou, n.d. (c. 1970).

Olukoju, Ayedele. "Maritime Trade in Lagos in the Aftermath of the First World War." *African Economic History* 20 (1992): 119–35.

Ondoua, Brigette-Minette. "Approvisionnement de la ville de Libreville en produits locaux de base: Example de la banane plantain." BA thesis, Université Omar Bongo, 1981.

Onwueme, I. C. *The Tropical Tuber Crops: Yams, Cassava, Sweet Potato and Cocoyams.* New York: John Wiley and Sons, 1978.

Owanga-Biye, Gervais. "Les marchés urbains du Gabon: Le cas de Libreville." Ph.D. thesis, Université de Bordeaux, 1996.

Pankhurst, Alula. *Resettlement and Famine in Ethiopia: The Villagers' Experience.* Manchester: Manchester University Press, 1992.

Parker, John. *Making the Town: Ga State and Society in Early Colonial Accra.* Portsmouth: Heinemann, 2000.

Parnell, Susan. "Creating Racial Privilege: The Origins of South African Public Health and Town Planning Legislation." *Journal of Southern African Studies* 19 (1993): 471–88.

Patterson, K. David. *The Northern Gabon Coast to 1875.* Oxford: Oxford University Press, 1975.

———. "The Vanishing Mpongwe: European Contact and Demographic Change in the Gabon River." *Journal of African History* 16 (1975): 217–38.

Payeur-Didelot. *Trente mois au continent mystérieux*. Paris: Berger-Levrault, 1899.

Péan, Pierre. *Affaires africaines*. Paris: Marabout, 1983.

Pedlar, Frederick. *The Lion and the Unicorn in Africa: A History of the Origins of the United Africa Company 1787–1931*. Portsmouth: Heinemann, 1976.

Peters, Erica. "National Preferences and Colonial Cuisine: Seeking the Familiar in French Vietnam." *Proceedings of the Annual Meeting of the Western Society for French History* 27 (2001): 150–59.

Perrault, Paul. "Banana-Manioc Farming Systems of the Tropical Forest: A Case Study in Zaire." Ph.D. thesis, Stanford University, 1979.

Petersen, Derek. *Eating Apes*. Berkeley: University of California Press, 2003.

Picard-Tortorici, Nathalie, and Michel François. *La Traite des esclaves du Gabon du XVIIIe au XIXe siècle: Essai de quantification pour le XVIIIe siècle*. Paris: EHESS, 1993.

Pilcher, Jeffrey. *¡Que vivan los tamales! Food and the Making of Mexican Identity*. Albuquerque: University of New Mexico Press, 1998.

Polaillon, Georges, and Carville. *Étude physiologique sur les effets toxiques de l'inée poison des Pahouins du Gabon*. Paris: G. Masson, 1873.

Pollock, Nancy. "The Early Development of Housekeeping and Imports in Fiji," *Pacific Studies* 12 (1989): 53–82.

———. *These Roots Remain: Food Habits in Islands of the Central and Eastern Pacific since Western Contact*. Laie HI: Institute for Polynesian Studies, 1992.

Portet, Mariette. *En blanc sur les cartes*. Versailles: Charles Cortet, 1968.

Potter, Robert, and Ademola Salau, eds. *Cities and Development in the Third World*. London: Mansell, 1990.

Pourtier, Roland. "La crise de l'agriculture dans un état minier: Le Gabon." *Etudes Rurales* 77 (1980): 39–62.

———. *Le Gabon: Espace-Histoire-Société*. 2 vols. Paris: Harmattan, 1989.

Prats, Raymond. "Le Gabon: La mise en valeur et ses problèmes." Ph.D. thesis, Université de Montpellier, 1955.

Prestholdt, Jeremy. "On the Global Repercussions of East African Consumerism." *American Historical Review* 109, no. 3 (2004): 755–81.

Preston, Jane. *Gaboon Stories*. New York: American Tract Society, 1872.

Procida, Mary. "Feeding the Imperial Appetite: Imperial Knowledge and Anglo-Indian Domesticity." *Journal of Women's History* 15, no. 2 (2003): 123–49.

"Promenades des missionnaires." *Chronique de l'institut des frères de l'instruction chrétienne de Saint-Gabriel* 87 (1927): 138–40.

Puleston, Fred. *African Drums*. New York: Farrar and Reinhart, 1930.

Purseglove, John. *Tropical Crops: Monocotyledons*. New York: Halsted Press, 1972.

Quammen, David. "The Green Abyss." *National Geographic* 199, no. 3 (March 2001): 2–37.

———. "Saving Africa's Eden." *National Geographic* 204, no. 3 (September 2003): 50–76.

Raponda Walker, André. "Le bananier plantain au Gabon." *Revue de botanique appliquée et d'agriculture tropicale* 11 (1931): 18–27.

———. *Dictionnaire Mpongwé-Français*. Paris: Classiques Africaines, 1995.

———. *Notes d'histoire du Gabon*. Libreville: Editions Raponda Walker, 1996.

———. *La mémoire du Gabon (Articles Divers)*. Libreville: Editions Raponda Walker, 1998.

———. *Souvenirs d'un nonagénaire*. Paris: Classiques Africaines, 1993.

Raponda Walker, André, and Roger Sillans. *Les Plantes utiles du Gabon*. Paris: Editions Paul Lechevalier, 1961.

———. *Rites et croyances des peuples du Gabon*. Paris: Presence Africaine, 1962.

Rapontyombo, Félix. "Lettre du 12 Octobre 1878." *Annales de la propagation de la foi* 51 (1879): 217–18.

Ratanga-Atoz, Anges. "Les résistances Gabonaises à l'imperialisme, 1870–1914." Ph.D. thesis, University of Paris, 1973.

———. "Les peuples du Gabon occidental pendant la première periode coloniale, 1839–1914." Ph.D. thesis, University de Rheims, 1996.

———. *Les peuples du Gabon occidental pendant la première periode coloniale*, tome I: *Le cadre traditionnel*. Libreville: Editions Raponda Walker, 2000.

Raulin, G. de. *Amours congolaises*. Paris: Albin Michel, 1888.

Reade, Winwood. *An African Sketch Book*. 2 vols. London: Smith, Elder and Company, 1873.

Reading, Joseph. *The Ogowe Band*. Philadelphia: Reading and Company, 1890.

———. *A Voyage along the Western Coast of Newest Africa*. 2nd ed. Freeport: Books for Library Press, 1972.

Reed, Michael. "An Ethnohistorical Study of the Political Economy of Ndjole, Gabon." Ph.D. thesis, University of Washington, 1988.

Reed, Michael, and James Barnes, eds. *Culture, Ecology, and Politics in Gabon's Rainforest*. Lewiston NY: Edwin Mellen Press, 2003.

Renwomby, Michel. "L'administration française au Gabon entre les deux guerres." MA thesis, University of Aix-en-Provence, 1979.

République Gabonaise. Ministère de l'Agriculture. J. Bidaut. *Résultats provisoires de l'enquête agricole par sondage 1960*. Libreville, 1961.

Ricard. "Notes sur le Gabon." *Revue coloniale* 14 (1855): 245–65.

Rich, Jeremy. "'Une Babylone Noire': Interracial Unions in Colonial Libreville, c. 1870–1914." *French Colonial History* 4 (2003): 145–70.

———. "Civilized Attire: Dress, Cultural Change and Status in Libreville, Gabon, ca. 1860–1914," *Cultural and Social History* 2, no. 2 (2005): 189–214.

———. "King or Knave? Félix Adende Rapontchombo and Political Survival in the Gabon Estuary." *African Studies Quarterly* 6, no. 3 (2002), URL:web.africa.ufl.edu/asq/v6/v6i3a1.htm.

———. "'I hope that the government does not forget my extraordinary services': Urban Negotiations and Welfare in Libreville (Gabon), 1937–1950," *Journal of Colonialism and Colonial History* 3, no. 3 (2002), URL:muse.jhu.edu/journals/journal_of_colonialism_and_colonial_history/v003/3.3rich.html.

———. "Leopard Men, Slaves, and Social Conflict in Colonial Libreville, c. 1860–1880." *International Journal of African Historical Studies* 34 (2001): 619–38.

———. "'We Eat Out of the Same Pot: Poison, Food and Power in Colonial Libreville, c. 1865–1921." *Mots Pluriels* 15 (September 2000), www.arts.uwa.edu.au/MotsPluriels.

———. "Where Every Language Is Heard: Senegalese and Vietnamese Migrants in Colonial Libreville, 1860–1914." In *African Urban Spaces*, ed. Toyin Falola and Steven Salm, 191–212. Rochester NY: University of Rochester Press, 2005.

Richard, Alain. *Le Gabon: Géographie active*. Libreville: Institut Pédagogique National, 1993.

Robertson, Claire. *Sharing the Same Bowl: A Socioeconomic History of Women and Class in Accra, Ghana*. Bloomington: Indiana University Press, 1984.

————. *Trouble Showed the Way: Women, Men, and Trade in the Nairobi Area, 1890–1990*. Bloomington: Indiana University Press, 1997.

Rocques, Louis. *Le pionnier du Gabon: Jean-Rémy Bessieux*. Paris: Alsatia, 1971.

Saint-Blancat. "Coutume Mpongwe." Unpublished mimeograph, 6 February 1939, Libreville.

Samba, Mampuya. *Survivance et répression de la traite négrier du Gabon au Congo*. Paris: La Bruyère, 1990.

Sautter, Giles. *De l'Atlantique au fleuve Congo*. 2 vols. Paris: Mouton, 1966.

Schivelbusch, Wolfgang. *The Culture of Defeat: On National Trauma, Mourning and Recovery*. Trans. Jefferson Chase. New York, Picador, 2001.

Schmidt, Elizabeth. *Peasants, Traders and Wives: Shona Women in the History of Zimbabwe, 1870–1939*. Portsmouth: Heinemann, 1992.

Schnapper, Bernard. *La politique et le commerce français dans le golfe du Guinée, 1838–1871*. Paris: Mouton, 1961.

Schoenbrun, David. *A Green Place, a Good Place: Agrarian Change, Gender, and Social Identity in the Great Lakes Region to the 15th Century*. Portsmouth: Heinemann, 1998.

Schroeder, Richard. "'Gone to Their Second Husbands': Marital Metaphors and Conjugal Contracts in the Gambia's Female Garden Sector." In *"Wicked" Women and the Reconfiguration of Gender in Africa*, ed. Dorothy Hodgson and Sheryl McCurdy, 85–105. Portsmouth: Heinemann, 2001.

Scott, James. *Seeing Like a State: How Certain Schemes to Improve the Human Condition Have Failed*. New Haven CT: Yale University Press, 1998.

Searing, James. *West African Slavery and Atlantic Commerce: The Senegal River Valley, 1700–1860*. Cambridge: Cambridge University Press, 1993.

Sen, Amartya. *Poverty and Famines: An Essay on Entitlement and Deprivation*. Oxford: Oxford University Press, 1980.

————. "Food Entitlements and Economic Claims." In *Hunger in History: Food Shortage, Poverty and Deprivation*, ed. Lucile Newman, 374–86. London: Basil Blackwell, 1990.

Seuhl, Antoine. *Gabone*. Paris: Baudinière, 1933.

Sharkey, Heather. *Living with Colonialism: Nationalism and Culture in the Anglo-Egyptian Sudan*. Berkeley: University of California Press, 2003.

Shaw, Rosalind. *Memories of the Slave Trade: Ritual and the Historical Imagination in Sierra Leone*. Chicago: University of Chicago Press, 2002.

Smith, Alfred Aloysius. *Trader Horn*. New York: Simon and Shuster, 1927.

Smith, Robert, and David Christian. *Bread and Salt: A Social and Economic History of Food and Drink in Russia*. Cambridge: Cambridge University Press, 1984.

Soeur Marie Germaine. *Le Christ au Gabon*. Louvain: Museum Lesianum, 1931.

Sonnet, Réné. "La pénétration française dans la région du Gabon-Como." MA thesis, University of Rheims, 1981.

Stoler, Ann Laura. "Sexual Affronts and Racial Frontiers: European Identities and the Cultural Politics of Exclusion in Colonial Southeast Asia." *Comparative Studies in Society and History* 34 (1992): 514–51.

Sundiata, Ibrahim. *From Slavery to Neoslavery: The Bight of Biafra and Fernando Po*. Madison: University of Wisconsin Press, 1996.

Sunseri, Thaddeus. *Vilimani: Labor Migration and Rural Change in Early Colonial Tanzania*. Portsmouth: Heinemann, 2002.

Super, John. *Food, Conquest, and Colonization in Sixteenth-Century America*. Albuquerque: University of New Mexico Press, 1988.

Swanson, Maynard. "The Sanitation Syndrome: Bubonic Plague and Urban Native Policy in the Cape Colony 1900–1909." Journal of African History 18 (1977): 387–410.

Swiderski, Stanislaw. La religion bouiti. 5 vols. Ottawa: Legas, 1989.

Taylor, C. Janet. "The Poison Pen." In Transgressing Boundaries: New Directions in the Study of Culture in Africa, ed. Brenda Cooper and Andrew Steyn, 86–113. Athens: Ohio University Press, 1996.

Taylor, J. G. Eating, Drinking, and Visiting in the South: An Informal History. Baton Rouge: Louisiana State University Press, 1982.

Thaman, Randolph. "Deterioration of Food Systems, Malnutrition, and Food Dependency in the Pacific Islands." Journal of Food and Nutrition 39 (1982): 109–25.

Thompson, Virginia, and Richard Adloff. The Emerging States of French Equatorial Africa. Stanford CA: Stanford University Press, 1960.

Thornton, John. The Kingdom of Kongo: Civil War and Transition, 1641–1718. Madison: University of Wisconsin Press, 1983.

———.Africans and the Making of the Atlantic World, 1450–1800. Cambridge: Cambridge University Press, 1998.

Tissier de Mallerais, Bernard. Marcel Lefebvre: Une vie. Paris: Clovis, 2002.

Tornezy, Odette. "Les travaux et les jours de la mission Sainte-Marie du Gabon (1845–1880): Agriculture et modernisation." Revue française d'histoire d'outre-mer 71 (1984): 147–90.

Touchard, F. "Note sur le Gabon." Revue maritime et coloniale (1861), 1–17.

Trautmann, René. Tu y reviendras: Roman d'aventures et des amours congolaises. Paris: Radot, 1927.

Trefon, Théodore. "Libreville et son appétence opiniâtre de fôret." Afrique Contemporaine 190 (1999): 39–54.

Trial. Georges. Okoumé. Paris: Je Sers, 1939.

Trilles, Henri. Au Gabon: Dans les rivières de Monda. Paris: Desclee, De Brouwer et Compagnie, n.d. (c. 1900).

Ugochuknwu, Françoise. "Nourriture et identification sociale au Nigeria." Mots Pluriels 15 (2000), www.arts.uwa.edu.au/MotsPluriels/MP1500fu.html.

Vail, Leroy. "The Political Economy of East-Central Africa." In History of Central Africa, ed. David Birmingham and Phyllis M. Martin, vol. 2, 200–50. New York: Longman, 1983.

Valdi, François. Le Gabon: L'homme contre la forêt. Paris: Revue Français, 1931.

Van Nguyen, Marshall. "Issues of Poverty and Poor Relief in Colonial Northern Vietnam: The Interaction between Colonial Modernism and Elite Vietnamese Thinking." Ph.D. thesis, University of British Columbia, 2002.

Van Beusekom, Monica. Negotiating Development: African Farmers and Colonial Experts at the Office du Niger, 1920–1960. Portsmouth: Heinemann, 2002.

Vandji, Marie Sidonie Oyembo. Les Soeurs de l'Immaculée Conception de Castres: 150 ans de presence missionnaire au Gabon. Libreville: CERGEP, 1999.

Vansina, Jan. Paths in the Rainforest. Madison: University of Wisconsin Press, 1990.

Vaughan, Megan. Curing Their Ills: Colonial Power and African Illness. Stanford CA: Stanford University Press, 1991.

———. The Story of an African Famine: Gender and Famine in Twentieth-Century Malawi. Cambridge: Cambridge University Press, 1987.

Vaughan, Megan, and Henrietta Moore. Cutting Down Trees: Gender, Nutrition, and Agricultural Change in the Northern Province of Zambia, 1890–1990. Portsmouth: Heinemann, 1994.

Verschave, François-Xavier. Noir silence: Qui arrêtera la Françafrique? Paris: Arènes, 2000.

Von Oppen, Achim. «Cassava, 'The Lazy Man's Food'? Indigenous Agricultural Innovation and Dietary Change in Northwestern Zambia, ca. 1650–1970.» In *Changing Food Habits*, ed. Carola Lentz, 73–90. Amsterdam: Harwood Academic Press, 1999.

Walker, Robert Bruce Napoleon. "The Commerce of the Gaboon: Its History and Future Prospects." *Journal of the Society of Arts* 24 (1876): 585–97.

Walker, William. "Letter of May 14, 1857." *Missionary Herald* 53 (1857): 347.

——. "Letter of May 13, 1858." *Missionary Herald* 54 (1858): 311–12.

——. "Letter of October 9, 1863." *Missionary Herald* 60 (1863): 39.

Watson, Jamees, and Melissa Caldwell, eds. *The Cultural Politics of Food and Eating: A Reader.* New York: Blackwell, 2005.

Watts, Michael. *Silent Violence: Food, Famine, and Peasantry in Northern Nigeria.* Berkeley: University of California Press, 1983.

Weiss, Brad. *The Making and Unmaking of the Haya Lived World.* Chicago: University of Chicago Press, 1997.

White, E. Frances. *Sierra Leone's Settler Women Traders: Women on the Afro-European Frontier.* Ann Arbor: University of Michigan Press, 1987.

White, Luise. *The Comforts of Home.* Chicago: University of Chicago Press, 1990.

——. *Speaking With Vampires: Rumor and History in Colonial Africa.* Berkeley: University of California Press, 2000.

——. "'They Could Make Their Victims Dull': Genders and Genres, Fantasies and Cures in Colonial Southern Uganda." *American Historical Review* 100 (1995): 1379–1402.

Wilson, John Lieghton. "Mr. Wilson's Description of the Gaboon." *Missionary Herald* 39 (1843): 229–40.

——. *Western Africa: Its History, Condition and Prospects.* New York: Harper and Company, 1856.

Wright, Deborah. *Aren't I a Woman? Female Slaves in the Plantation South.* 2nd ed. New York: W. W. Norton, 1999.

Wright, Donald. *The World and a Very Small Place in Africa.* Armonk NY: M. E. Sharpe, 1997.

Wright, Marcia. *Strategies of Slaves and Women: Life-stories from East/Central Africa.* London: James Currey, 1993.

Wunder, Sven. *Oil Wealth and the Fate of the Forest: A Comparative Study of Eight Tropical Countries.* New York: Routledge, 2003.

Wylie, Diana. *Starving on a Full Stomach: Hunger and the Triumph of Cultural Racism in South Africa.* Charlottesville: University of Virginia Press, 2001.

Wyse, Akintola. *The Krio of Sierra Leone: An Interpretive History.* London: C. Hurst, 1991.

Yang, Dali. *Calamity and Reform in China: State, Rural Society, and Institutional Change since the Great Leap Famine.* Stanford CA: Stanford University Press, 1996.

Yates, Douglas. *The Rentier State in Africa: Oil Rent Dependency and Neocolonialism in the Republic of Gabon.* Trenton NJ: Africa World Press, 1996.

Zinoman, Peter. *The Colonial Bastille: A History of Imprisonment in Vietnam, 1862–1940.* Berkeley: University of California Press, 2001.

Index

Index note: page references in italics indicate a figure or table on the designated page.

Abdijan, 148
Adam, Bishop, 61
Ada Nkoghe, Veronique, 112
Adende, Félix, as clan leader, 121, 131, 137, 156n71
Adiwa, Jean-Baptiste, 125
Africa: cannibalism in, 88; colonial historiography of, xii, xiii, 9, 56, 148; forms of poverty and hunger in, 34–35; impact of Atlantic commerce on, 148; "Scramble for Africa" in, 56
Agakaza clan, in Gabon Estuary, 5, 6, 8, 9, 29, 36, 154n22
Agence France Press, 140
agriculture: gender roles in, 27–30, 43, 109–10, 183n22; influences of plantation slavery on, 27–29; social status in, 27, 28–30; Société de Prévoyance Indigène (SIP) program for, 115–16
Akele: communities of, 14; fishing by, 54; food production and trade by, 26, 33, 54
Akenda, Pierre-Marie, 121
Akok, *xx*, 116, 145
alcohol: imported, xiv, 60, 170n128; Mpongwe use of, 10, 11
Algeria: hunger in, 85; independence of, ix
American Board of Commissioners for Foreign Missions (ABCFM), 10
amours congolaises, 12
Anghiley, Benoit, 124
Angola: European trade in, 6; workers from, 58
angoma, 53
Anongo-Ambani, village of, 6
Antchoué, Gabriel, 122
Antchouey, Laurence, 79
Antonetti, Governor-General, 76, 79
Armah, Ayi Kwei, xi
Asiga clan, in Gabon Estuary, 5, 7, 8, 11, 22, 29
Assengone, Pauline, 123
atanga fruit, 25, 54

Atong Abé, neighborhood of, 15, 110, 145
Aubame, Jean-Hilaire, 19, 100, 119
Ayémé, *xx*

banana leaves, versatile uses of, 25
bananas: cultivation of, 24–25; introduction of, 24–25; in Libreville markets, 77; in Mpongwe diet, 24–25; supernatural meanings associated with, 25
Bantu-speaking peoples: in Central Africa, 4; migration to Libreville, 42; root crops cultivated by, 5
Baraka: French military camp at, 100; Protestant mission at, 7, 53, 90, 91–95
Barret, Paul, 133
Bassett, Thomas, 112
Bastille Day, 48
Batavea, neighborhood of, 57
Bay of Mondah, *xx*
beans, cultivation of, 25
beef, as luxury item, 88, 104, 139
béki, 31
Belgian Congo, 99
Bella Eyeghe, Marie-Therese, 109
Benga: fishing specialties of, 26, 54; food production and trade by, 26, 33, 54
Bennett, Albert, 55
Berenger, Senator, 75
beriberi, 97, 99–100, 111
Bernard, Governor, 78, 79
Berre, Louis, 110
Berry, Sara, xv
Bessieux, Jean-Rémy, 30
Béti, agricultural practices of, 113
big men (*aga*): leadership of, 5–6; trade strategies and rivalries of, 10, 14; wealth of, 42
Bilogho, 109
bilop, 17
Biye, Ahinto, 109
Bloc Démocratique Gabonais (BDG), 19, 119
Bobichon, Charles, 68, 72
Boisneuf, Senator, 137
Bongo, Albert-Bernard, x
Bongo, Omar, rule of, ix, x, xvi, 120, 145

Boppell, Sadie, 52
Boserup, Esther, 111
Bouet-Willaumez, Edouard, 8, 9
Bourdieu, Pierre, xvii
bovine sleeping sickness, 87, 178n11
Braudel, Ferdinand, xvii
Brazzaville, 20, 116, 148
bread, supply of, 57–58, 102, 104
breadfruit, 50
Briault, Maurice, 29, 34, 39, 54, 130
bridewealth: of Fang, 14, 156n88;
    manipulation of, 17, 55, 83, 177n156;
    of Mpongwe, 14
Brooks, George, 143
Brouillet, Jean-Claude, 19
Burton, Richard, 29, 38, 51, 96, 131
bush fruits, 82
bush meat, in Gabonese markets, xvi, xix, 26,
    119, 138–39
Bushnell, Albert, 92
bwiti, 17, 25, 82

Cadier, as Lt. Governor and Governor, 74,
    76, 100
cafets, 127
Cameroon: agricultural practices in, 113;
    colonial war with Gabon, 15–16, 66–67;
    Fang migration from, 51; food resources
    from, 113, 146; trade in, 6, 136
canned foods, 102, 138, 181n100, 192n77
cannibalism, 88
Cape Esterias, xx, 26
Cape Santa Clara, xx
Catholic Church, missions in Gabon, 10, 41
cayenne pepper, 25
Charbonnier, Administrator, 76, 77
Chikunda slave soldiers, 29
Chinchoua, 109
Cinnamon, John, 17
clan chiefs, 10, 61, 62
Clément, Commandant, 39, 40
Cocobeach, xx, 111
Como River, xx, 3, 52, 54, 55, 81
Compagnie Française de l'Afrique
    Occidentale, 136
conjunctional poverty, 34
Consortium des Grands Réseaux Français,
    16, 72–73
cores, in world-systems theory, 148

Corisco Bay, xx
corn, cultivation of, 52
"culture of defeat," 83

Dahomey: trade in, 136; workers/laborers
    from, 57, 58, 111
Daigne, Blaise, 58, 79
Dakar: French superiors in, 11, 48;
    metropolitan growth of, 18
Damas, Georges, 103
Dar Es Salaam, food supply in, 147, 194n13
Darfur: famine in, 65; wild animal
    populations in, 67
Darlington, Alice, 141–43
Davis, Mike, xiv
de Brazza, Pierre Savorgnan, 13, 50, 56
De Certeau, Michel, xi–xii
Deemin, Joseph, 124
de Gaulle, Charles, ix, 123
de Mandat-Grancey, Edouard, 61
Dénis, as clan leader, 8, 30
de Pompignan, Assier, 103
Derrière l'Hôpital, neighborhood of, 57
Dika, trade by, 49
diseases/illnesses: beriberi, 97, 99–100, 111;
    bovine sleeping sickness, 87, 178n11;
    dysentery, 33, 100; influenza, 16, 69, 84;
    malaria, 132; sleeping sickness in, 16;
    smallpox, 33
Donguila, xx, 74, 80
Duala, 148
Du Chaillu, Paul, 30, 51, 131–32
dye wood, trade in, 9, 12
dysentery, 33, 100

Eating Apes (Peterson), xii
Eboué, Félix, 103, 123
ekorge, 53
elephants, damage to Estuary crops by, 26,
    31, 33, 53, 67, 68, 109, 119
Elf Oil, x, 145
Elizia, 11, 47
Elwert-Kretschmer, Karola, xiv
Endame Ndong, Felicien, 82–83, 113
Esa Meyo, Alice, 109
esen, 53
Essissis clan, 5
Essono, 123
Ethiopia, famine in, 65, 85

famine: in Africa, xiv, 33, 34, 36, 64–85, 98;
associated with war, 33; in China, 65; as
crisis of exchange, 65; cultural impact of,
83–84; deaths related to, 65–66; ecological factors contributing to, 65; in Gabon
Estuary, xviii, 64–85; in Libreville, 33, 34,
36, 42, 72–75, 98; refugees associated with,
67, 69; social conflict associated with,
68–72; in Soviet Ukraine, 65; in Third
World, xiii; in West Africa, 65
Fang: clans of, 13, 14–15; "Congrès Pahouin"
platform of, 115; disputes and violence
between clans of, 51–52, 55–56; eating
taboos of, 31; famine in Estuary communities of, 80–84; females escaping
villages of, 17, 157n106; fish supplied by,
52, 53, 54, 70; food production and trade
by, xviii, 2, 45, 46, 52–54, 62, 70, 167n58;
gender bias in roles of, 14, 52; impact of
World War I on, 17, 64, 157n104; manioc in
diet of, 2; migration into Gabon Estuary,
13–14, 50–56; populations in Libreville,
17, 18, 101–2, 109; social organization of,
52; violence against women among, 17,
55–56, 157n106, 168n85; women's roles in,
17, 52–53, 54–56, 83, 157n106, 167n78
Fanon, Franz, xi
farigna, 24
Fay, Michael, xii
Ferguson, Andrew, 135–36
Fischer, Madame, 131
fish: in Gabon Estuary diet, 26; supplied to
Libreville, 70, 108, 121
fishing: workers/specialists in, 18, 51, 52, 53,
54, 111
Flynn, Karen Coen, xiv
food consumption: in African history, xiii,
20–21, 105–6; colonial influences on, xii,
xix, 149; cultural changes related to, xiv,
xv, 152n22; economic changes associated
with, xv; government and social controls
of, xix, 148–49; indigenous superstitions
related to, 25, 31, 32, 132–36; influences
of servitude and slavery, 27–35, 42; paradigm of want and, xiv; replacement of culinary styles in, xiii, 105–6; role of imported foods in Libreville, 86–106; self-worth
related to rations, 92; social expression
through, xiv, xviii, 153n33
Fougamou, 106

Foulenzem, 4
France: and agricultural policies for
Gabonese colony, xvi–xvii, xix, 115–16;
and colonial rule of Gabon, ix, xvi–xvii,
xix, 8–21, 48; Fourth Republic of, 19; Free
French in, 87; Vichy government in, 87
Franco-Prussian War, 12, 50
Franke, Richard, xiii
Free French, 87
French Congo, 13, 15, 59, 60, 98
French Equatorial Africa: federation of, 15,
59, 64; funding of, 20, 123; on human
rights, 76; policies of food production, 73
Friedberg, Susan, xiv

Gabon: agricultural strategies of, x, xviii–xix,
112–20, 146, 147; bush meat in markets of,
xvi, xix, 26, 119, 138–39; colonial war with
Cameroon, 66–67; ecological changes in,
146; European trade in, 6–8; famine in,
16, 33, 34, 36, 42, 64–85, 98; French agricultural policies of, 112–15; French citizenship in, 102–3; French language in,
x; impact of World War I on, 15–18; independence of, ix, xviii; movement of rural
populations in, 108, 109; oil reserves and
industry in, x, 1, 105, 145, 147; railroad
systems in, 146; recruitment of farm labor
in, 48–52; slave trade in, xi, 6–8, 35–41;
timber industry in, xi, xviii, 16, 17–18, 19,
52; transportation problems in, 106, 113,
114–15, 146, 186n74; wild animal populations during World War I in, 67–68
Gabon Estuary, xx; agricultural practices in,
xvii, 112–16, 149; archaeological findings
in, 4; clan conflicts and short-term wars
in, 46; colonial food supply systems in,
23–27, 74–77; economic impact of World
War I on, 17, 64; educational opportunities in, 145; environment and topography of, xvii, 3–6; famine in, 33, 34, 42, 47,
64–85, 99; Fang populations in, 13–15,
23, 50–56; fishing in, 111, 184n43; French
control of, 8–21; manioc cultivation of,
24; place names of, 6, 154n30; population
density in, 148; road construction in, 20,
114, 115; SIP program in, 115–16; soil composition of, 3; timber industry in, 64;
toxic/poisonous plants in, 31
Gabriel, Mabenga, 108

Galwa, communities of, 5
Gardinier, David, 146
Gault, William, 95
Germany, colonial control of Cameroon, 15–16, 66–67
Geschiere, Peter, 136
Ghana, xiii, 111
Giard, Luce, xii
Glass: bistros and gourmet dining in, 127, 143; European trade in historic village of, 6; fetish practices in, 60, 71, 134; as Libreville neighborhood, 121; markets and shopping areas in, 73, 103; Mpongwe families in, 111
Gold Coast, 58, 103, 111
Goody, Jack, xiii
Gorée, French superiors in, 11, 48
Goungoué Creek, 3
Gray, Christopher, 6
Great Depression, xviii, 17, 18, 83, 111, 112
Great Leap Forward, 85
Guibet, Georges, 68, 69, 71, 72, 79
Guinea, ix
Guyer, Jane, xiii
Guyon, Governor, 67

Ham Nghi, 56
Hatton and Cookson, 9, 130, 134, 135, 136
Hausa, traders in Gabon, 18, 136
Haut Ogooué, 78
Hawthorne, Walter, 27
Holt, John, 19
Holy Ghost Fathers, 10
Howe, Russell Warren, 140
human rights, rhetoric of, 16, 72, 77
Hunt, Nancy Rose, 88

Igombiné Creek, 3
Ikoi Creek, xx
Iliffe, John, 34
imported food: as currency, 86; Libreville dependency on, x, xv–xix, 86–106, 149, 151n5
India, hunger in, 85
indigènat code, 15, 59
Indochina, 99
influenza, 16, 69, 84
inyemba, 31, 32
Issembé, Jean-Rémy, 80, 124
ivanga, 121

Ivanga, Luc-Marc, 101
ivory, trade in, 9, 12, 30, 33, 50, 52, 54, 136
Ivory Coast, 99

Jean-Baptiste, Rachel, 2, 38
Joseph, Nkoghe Bekale, 109
Justin, Ndoutoume Nkobe, 81

Kafélé, xx
Kango: as district in Estuary, xx, 65, 77, 78, 81, 116; missions in, 52, 55, 69; populations in, 109
Kaplan, Steven, xvi
Kingsley, Mary, 45, 57, 88, 135
King William, as clan leader, 8
kinship, 35, 39, 40–41
kisini, 30
Klieman, Kairn, 3, 4
Kougouleu, xx
Kringer, village of, 6
Kru: "chop" preferences of, 96–97; as workers/laborers in Libreville, 48, 58, 91, 96–97, 132, 165n20, 170–71n70

Lagos, 18, 20, 148
Lalala, neighborhood of, xii, 15, 109, 123, 139
Lambaréné, 4, 5, 114
Larson, Pier, 27
Lasserre, Guy, 109, 115, 125, 137, 140
Lawlin, Captain, 132
League of the Rights of Man (LRM), 16, 65, 70, 75, 76, 77, 79, 137
Le Berre, Pierre-Marie, 41, 50
Lefebvre, Marcel, 140
lemons, 25
leopard man murders, 13, 62
Lessing, Doris, xiii
Lewis, Ovendo, 95
Liberia, Kru workers from, 48, 58, 165n20
Libreville, xx; affluent communities in, 147; archaeological findings in, 4; bread supply for, 57–58; bush meat in markets of, xvi, xix; Cité de la Démocratie in, 145; collapse of clan leadership in, 36; colonial control of food sales, 59–63, 74–77; contemporary food supply issues of, 107–26; cost of living in, x, xix, 125, 151n4; culinary practices in, xvii–xviii, xix, 98, 105–6, 127–44; decline of domestic slaves in, 12–13, 45–63; dependence on imported

foods in, xv–xix, 86–106, 146, 149; eating habits in, 2–21; employment opportunities in, 36; environment and topography of, 3–6; European populations in, 139–41; famine in, 33, 34, 36, 42, 72–75, 98; Fang populations in, 18, 101–2, 109; fetish practices in, 60, 71; fishing workers in, 18, 111; food boycotts in, 59–63, 70–72; food consumption practices in, xvii–xviii, 108, 121; food entitlement behaviors in, xv, xviii, 59–63, 70–72; food ration system in, 90–98, 102–3; food supply systems for, 45–63, 104–26, 149; French colonial control of, 9–21; French cuisine in, 1–2; impact of World War I on, 15–18, 66–85; indigènat code in, 15, 59; isolation of, 20, 98–99, 106, 108, 114, 139; late colonial years of, 18–20; local markets in, xii, xvi, xix, 110; migrant populations in, xviii, 2, 13, 107, 108, 111, 145, 146, 156n82, 169n109; neighborhoods of, 39, 57, 60, 71, 109, 110, 123, 139; as political seat of power, 19–20; population growth of, 107–26, 145–49, 150; post-colonial food supply of, 120–26; racial divisions in, 137–41; resettlement of slaves in, 35; road systems to and from, 3, 13, 46, 146; schools in, 14–15, 30; smallpox epidemic in, 33; social status and access to food, 120–26; soil composition of, 3; town life in, 86–106; Vietnamese populations in, 56–57, 168n91; West African populations in, 56–59; white women in, 137–38, 141–43
Loango, workers/laborers from, 24, 58, 135, 158n10
Loubet, as Medouneu subdivision chief, 117, 118
Louis, village of, 6, 39, 110, 127, 143, 189n158
Louise, Mère, 131

Mabenga, Gabriel, 18
Macé, Julien, 67, 99
Mafoungou, Guillaume, 135–36
malaria, 132
malnutrition, in Third World, xiii
Mandala, Elias, xii, xiv–xv, 21
manioc: blight of, 68; cultivation of, 22, 23–24, 53; in Gabonese meals, xiii, 2; in Libreville markets, 77, 114; as "manioc congo," 2; preparation of, 24, 158n8; sales

of, x, 4; South American origins of, 3–24; versatility of, 24
manioc flour, 34
Marchand, Governor, 69, 71, 74, 76
Marthe, Oussaka, 123
Martinique, 35
Martrou, Louis, 66, 67, 68, 73, 77
Masson, Georges, 19, 86–87
Mba, Léon: chieftaincy of, 17, 65, 83, 112; death of, x; as first president of Gabon, ix, xvi, 19, 103, 119, 120, 142, 145
Mba, Pauline, 142, 145–46
Mba Nkoghe, Valerie, 110
Mbembe, Achille, xv, xvi
Mbé River, 3
mbur, 53
McNee, Lisa, 128
Médegue, subdivision of, 77
Medouneu, agricultural products of, 106, 109, 116–17, 121, 146
Mercat, Roland, 117
métis, 102
mevung, 14
mfini, 53
Michel, Zimbé, 53
Migeod, Frederick, 92
Mikiel, as French sailor, 129, 130
Miller, William, 92, 96
Milligan, Robert, 38, 132
Mindoube, neighborhood of, 110
Mintz, Sidney, 128
missions/missionaries: Catholic, 37, 41; on civilized Africans, 88–96; domestic slaves of, 92, 179n46; famines in the area of, 36–37; farming practices of, 49–50; food consumption by, 86–96; food supply systems of, 49–50, 86–96, 178n21; "knife-and-fork" doctrine of, 88, 178n21; moral influences over Libreville, 10, 14, 15, 61; on Mpongwe social order, 10; opinions on Mpongwe social and labor practices, xviii, 10, 39; Protestant, 37; role in freedom of slaves, 41; on rumors of poisoning, 132–36; schools and education by, 10–11, 37, 50; views on local eating habits, 90, 91; visits to Fang communities, 83–84; work in Gabon Estuary, 22
Miss Kate, 58
Mitzic, 117
Moesch, Administrator, 74, 75, 76

Mondah Bay, 54, 111
Mont-Bouet, neighborhood of, 110, 119, 145
Monts de Cristal, 3
Morris, Loembe, 70, 71
Mouheha, Charles, 76
Mpongwe: ancestors of, 4, 5; communities
  in Gabon Estuary, 2, 4–5; contact with
  Europeans, 5, 6–8; domestic slaves of, 23,
  27–42; eating habits and styles of, xv, 30,
  42, 106, 123–25, 149; economic impact of
  World War I on, 64; on equal treatment
  and salaries, 90; farming practices of, 23,
  27–42; fish in diet of, 26; food supply
  system in colonial Gabon, 22–24, 26;
  foreign dress and tastes adopted by, 29,
  30, 42, 88; French culinary practices by,
  106; marriage practices of, 38–39; mas-
  culine roles in, 29, 43; master and slave
  relationships in, 43; as Omyene-speaking peoples, 4; political organization and
  clans of, 5; roles of women in, 11–12, 14,
  18–19, 28–30, 38, 109, 123, 124, 183n22;
  in slave trade, 42, 43, 164n168; status
  and position in Libreville, 41–42, 46, 62;
  supernatural meaning associated with
  foods, 25, 31, 32; territorial mobility of, 6;
  trade strategies/alliances of, 2, 5–6,
  7–8, 9, 10–11, 19, 22, 27, 34, 35, 43, 46, 52,
  62, 124, 147; treaties signed with France,
  9; wealth and status in, 7, 155n46, 41–42;
  women's rights in, 60, 75, 88–89
M'Pyra bridge, fetish placed in, 60, 71
mvut fruit, 25

Nairobi, 20
Napoleonic Wars, 8
Nassau, Robert: as Protestant missionary in
  Gabon, 28, 32, 36, 39, 41, 54, 88–89, 90,
  91, 95–96; on rumors of poisonings, 132,
  133, 134
National Geographic, xii
Ndar, Marie, 38
N'dende, Jean-Baptiste, 15, 70, 71, 79
Ndong, Eyeghe, 82
Ndongo, Georges, 110
Ndongo, Vincent, 72
Nguema, Paul, 103
Nigeria, 111
njembe, 14, 121, 132, 134
Nk'Azuwa, village of, 6

Nkembo, neighborhood of, 18, 49, 109, 145
Nkok, xx
Nkoltang, xx
Nkomi, communities of, 5
N'no Ndong, Charles, 110, 125
Nomba, village of, 70
Nordick, André, 130
n'tchivo, 140
ntchwe-mbezo, 31
N'Toko, as clan chief, 9
Ntoum, xx, 115, 116
nyembwe, 25, 140
Nzamaligue, village of, 112
Nze, Abogho, 82
Nzebi clan, 18
Nzeme Creek, 3
Nzeng Ayong, neighborhood of, 110
Nze Ollome, Evariste, 109
Nzue Essone, Benoit, 117

Obame, Ange, 116
Obello, Fang town of, 76
Ocloo, Michael, 111, 114
odika, 25, 159n29
Ogden, Phoebe, 131
Ogooué River, 4, 5, 24, 51, 68, 90, 114
oil: Gabonese resources and industry of, x, 1,
  105, 145, 147; impact on local economies,
  145, 146, 147
Okala, xx
okra, in Gabonese diet, 25
okumé trees, 4, 16, 64
Olumi, village of, 6
omowétchi, 36, 60, 71, 72, 170n130
ompindi, 28, 41
Omyene-speaking peoples: communities of,
  5, 153n15; Mpongwe as, 4; on sorcerers
  and poison, 31, 32
onions, 116
oral traditions: on Estuary place names, 6;
  stories of famine in, 81–82
oranges, 22, 25
Orungu: communities of, 5, 34; fish supplied
  by, 50, 51
Ouapa, as servant, 100–101
Owendo, xx
Oyem, 118
Ozangué, neighborhood of, 110

palm nuts, in Gabonese diet, 25

papaya, 25, 69
Parti Démocratique Gabonais, 103
Patton, James, 94
Peace Corps, 143
Pechayrand, as Estuary head, 79
Pecqueur, as retail merchant, 131
Pélisson, Ray, 104
Perrier, Henry, 68
Peterson, Derek, xii; Eating Apes, xii
pineapples, 116
plantains: cultivation of, 24–25, 52, 54, 146; in Gabonese meals, xiii, 24–25; supplies of, x, 69
Plantes utiles du Gabon (Walker and Sillans), 31
Point-Denis, xx
Pointe-Noire, 104
poison/poisoning: indigent knowledge of, 31–33; rumors in Gabon of, 131–36
polygamy, 55, 61
Pongara Point, xx
Popular Front, 102
Port-Gentil, 20, 118
potatoes, 116, 117–18, 121
Pourtier, Roland, 6, 30, 120
poverty: features of, 66; forms of, 34–35
Prestholdt, Jeremy, 148
Preston, Jane, 28, 29
pygmy peoples, in Gabon Estuary, 5

Quaben, village of, 6, 10, 35

Rapontchombo, Félix Adende: beef imports by, 88; as clan leader, 8–9, 10, 11, 12, 22, 61, 121, 131, 137, 156n71; dinner parties by, 22–23; slaves owned by, 22, 23, 36
Reade, Winwood, 96, 130
Reading, Joseph, 91, 94
Réalités, ix
Re-Dowé, as clan chief, 9, 10, 110
Remboué River, xx, 3
Retigat, Laurence, 122
rice: cultivation of, 2, 27, 48, 146; imported during Gabon famine, 99, 100, 105
Rio Muni, xx, 4, 26, 33
R'Ogouarouwé, as clan chief, 9
rubber, trade in, 9, 12, 45, 52, 54, 109, 113, 136

Sahel, famine in, 65
Saint-Charles, Soeur, 131
Saint-Dénis, Simone, 101

Sainte Marie mission, 41, 53, 57, 59, 61
São Tomé: manioc trade in, 24; as Portuguese settlement, 7, 8; runaway slaves from, 58; slave trade on, 50
sardines, 26, 73, 78, 102, 114, 124
Sarraut, Albert, 16
Schivelbusch, Wolfgang, 83
Séké (Sékiani): communities of, 7, 14; fish supplied by, 51, 54; food production and trade by, 26, 33, 49, 51, 54; ritual specialists in, 36, 72; wars with Mpongwe, 33
Sen, Amartya, xiv, 65
Senegal: as French port of call, 8; laborers/workers from, 48, 58
Shaw, Rosalind, 28
Shell Oil, 145
Sibang, village of, 73, 115, 116, 121
Sierra Leone: British settlements in, 11, 47; divination in, 27–28; workers/laborers from, 58
Sillans, Roger, 31; Plantes utiles du Gabon, 31
Sisters of the Immaculate Conception, 10, 131
Slave Coast, 27
slaves/slavery: accused of poisonings, 32–33, 131–36, 161n91; Atlantic African trade in, 6–7, 9, 148; capital punishment of, 35–36, 40; culinary influences of, 27–35; as domestics in Libreville, 11, 12; former slaves owning slaves, 41; French restriction of, 35, 40; gradual independence in Gabon of, 44; illicit trade of, 9, 155n55; master-slave relationships in, 34, 35–41, 43–44, 130; purchased by Mpongwe women, 38; role in Gabonese food supply system, xvi, xvii, 22, 23; wealth and exchange of goods for, 7
sleeping sickness, 16
smallpox, 33
Société de Prévoyance Indigène (SIP), 115
Soumouma, Edouard, 108
Spanish influenza, 69
squash, cultivation of, 25, 52, 53
structural poverty and famine, 34
Sudan, famine in, 85
sugar cane, cultivation of, 116
sweet potatoes, cultivation of, 52

Tanzania: food supplies in, 147; forced resettlements in, 147; wild animal populations in, 67

Tardy, Louis, 80
taro, cultivation of, 25
Tastevin, Louis, 70, 73, 79–80, 82
Tati, as Vili cook, 135
taxes, 54, 55, 68, 78, 113, 175n114
Tchibanga, 118
Téké, 142
textiles, as currency, 49
Thomann, Governor, 68, 69
timber: decline in industry of, 108; famine in
    worker camps of, 66, 73, 74; food supplies
    to worker camps in, 77, 80, 84, 99–100;
    Gabonese industry of, xi, xviii, 4, 16,
    17–18, 19, 45, 52, 64, 108, 182nn3–4; of
    okumé trees, 4, 16, 64, 73
tobacco, as currency, 49, 54, 92
Togo, 111, 136
Touré, Samoré, 13
Touré, Sekou, ix
Trans-Gabonais railroad, 146
Trial, Georges, 140
Truman, Ntoko, 86, 93–94
Trumann, Ozimo, 73
Tsini Creek, 3

Union Sociale et Démocratique Gabonaise
    (USDG), 19

Vane, François de Paul, 101
Vansina, Jan, 4
Vecten, letters of protest by, 69–70
Vietnam: French colonial rule of, 56–57,
    168n91; French culinary practices in, 128;

hunger in, 85; workers/laborers from,
    56–57, 168n91
Vili, as workers/laborers, 122, 125, 135

Walker, André Raponda, 4, 31, 60; Plantes
    utiles du Gabon, 31
Walker, R. B. N., 60
Walker, William, as Protestant missionary in
    Gabon, 7, 23, 31, 32, 33, 36, 93, 96
Watts, Michael, xiv
West Africa: famine in, 65; workers/laborers
    from, 56–59
White, Richard, 8
Whydah, port of, 27
wild pigs, 53, 67
Wilson, John L., 7, 10, 22–23, 132
witchcraft, 31, 32, 136
Woermann company, 9, 133–34
Woleu Ntem: agricultural products from, 114;
    road construction in, 146; SIP program
    in, 117, 118
World War I: economic impact on Gabon,
    15–18, 64, 66–85; forced recruitment
    during, 66, 68
World War II, economic growth in Gabon
    during, 19
Wunder, Sven, 120
Wylie, Diana, xvi, 26

yams, cultivation of, 5, 25, 52
Yaoundé, xiii, 113
Yates, Douglas, 120, 147

In the France Overseas series

The French Navy and the Seven Years' War
Jonathan R. Dull

French Colonialism Unmasked
The Vichy Years in French West Africa
Ruth Ginio

Making the Voyageur World
Travelers and Traders in the North American Fur Trade
Carolyn Podruchny

A Workman Is Worthy of His Meat
Food and Colonialism in Gabon
Jeremy Rich

Silence Is Death
The Life and Work of Tahar Djaout
Julija Šukys

Beyond Papillon
The French Overseas Penal Colonies, 1854–1952
Stephen A. Toth

Madah-Sartre
The Kidnapping, Trial, and Conver(sat/s)ion of Jean-Paul Sartre and Simone de Beauvoir
Written and translated by Alek Baylee Toumi
With an introduction by James D. Le Sueur